"As Thomas Merton demonstrates in 'No Man Is an Island,' the integrated life of the spirit 'puts us in the fullest possible contact with reality.' The layman, consequently, should find Father Merton's chapters of vital personal significance . . . it may well serve as a primer for the general reader interested in learning life's meaning and living accordingly."
Saturday Review

". . . unity of meaning, intense, burning, heroically reaching for the purest sincerity, characterizes this book of flame in which, with deeper tones and from profounder levels of the contemplative life, Thomas Merton returns to thoughts which are of absolute importance for the spiritual life of man . . . a major work of spirituality, one which puts the true challenge of life in its most inspiring and provocative terms."
America

"The gift of Thomas Merton is that as he progresses to theological ripeness he has not laid his lute away. No strange arpeggio comes from it in his expository writing but simple, rich tones. The point is of no small importance."
Rev. Gerald S. Sloyan in *Worship*

"In 'No Man Is an Island,' Thomas Merton has written an important book. Its subject is love of God, love of self, love of one another."
Our Sunday Visitor

"Each individual will find spiritual help here."
Boston *Herald*

"The book will interest Catholic and non-Catholic alike, and even its most casual reader will be swiftly aware that he is far from being an island aloof in the vast, turbulent sea of human life, but is intimately caught up with every other man in the all-embracing Mystical Body of Christ."
Books on Trial

No Man Is An Island

by Thomas Merton

IMAGE BOOKS

A DIVISION OF DOUBLEDAY & COMPANY, INC.

GARDEN CITY, NEW YORK

Image Books Edition: 1967
by special arrangement with Harcourt,
Brace & World, Inc.
Image Books Edition published September 1967

DILECTISSIMIS FRATRIBUS
SCHOLASTICIS ET NEO-SACERDOTIBUS
IN ABBATIA B.V.M. de GETHSEMANI
AUCTOR, QUI ET MAGISTER SPIRITUS,
PERAMANTER
D.D.

Contents

Author's Note

Leaving system to others, and renouncing the attempt to lay down universal principles which have been exposed by better men elsewhere,* I only desire in this book to share with the reader my own reflections on certain aspects of the spiritual life. I consider that the spiritual life is the life of man's real self, the life of that interior self whose flame is so often allowed to be smothered under the ashes of anxiety and futile concern. The spiritual life is oriented toward God, rather than toward the immediate satisfaction of the material needs of life, but it is not, for all that, a life of unreality or a life of dreams. On the contrary, without a life of the spirit, our whole existence becomes unsubstantial and illusory. The life of the spirit, by integrating us in the real order established by God, puts us in the fullest possible contact with reality—not as we imagine it, but as it really is. It does so by making us aware of our own real selves, and placing them in the presence of God.

This book is, then, a sequel to a previous volume called *Seeds of Contemplation*. But instead of going on from where that book left off, it goes back to cover some of the ground that was taken for granted before the earlier volume began. This book is intended to be simpler, more fundamental, and more detailed. It treats of some of the basic verities on which the spiritual life depends. It is

* For example, *The Love of God* by Dom Aelred Graham, O.S.B., New York, 1939; *Transformation in Christ* by Dietrich von Hildebrand, New York, 1948; *The Theology of the Spiritual Life* by J. de Guibert, S.J., New York, 1953.

dedicated to the scholastics studying for the priesthood at the Abbey of Gethsemani, who will perhaps recognize in it some notions they have received in spiritual direction.

Fr. M. Louis, o.c.s.o.

Abbey of Gethsemani
January, 1955

Prologue

NO MAN IS AN ISLAND

No matter how ruined man and his world may seem to be, and no matter how terrible man's despair may become, as long as he continues to be a man his very humanity continues to tell him that life has a meaning. That, indeed, is one reason why man tends to rebel against himself. If he could without effort see what the meaning of life is, and if he could fulfill his ultimate purpose without trouble, he would never question the fact that life is well worth living. Or if he saw at once that life had no purpose and no meaning, the question would never arise. In either case, man would not be capable of finding himself so much of a problem.

Our life, as individual persons and as members of a perplexed and struggling race, provokes us with the evidence that it must have meaning. Part of the meaning still escapes us. Yet our purpose in life is to discover this meaning, and live according to it. We have, therefore, something to live for. The process of living, of growing up, and becoming a person, is precisely the gradually increasing awareness of what that something is. This is a difficult task, for many reasons.

First of all, although men have a common destiny, each individual also has to work out his own personal salvation for himself in fear and trembling. We can help one another to find out the meaning of life, no doubt. But in the last analysis the individual person is responsible for living his own life and for "finding himself." If he persists in shifting this responsibility to somebody else, he fails to find out the meaning of his own existence. You cannot tell me who I am, and I cannot tell you who you are. If you do not know your own identity, who is going to identify you? Others can give you a name or a number, but they can never tell you who you really are. That is something you yourself can only discover from within.

That brings us to a second problem. Although in the end we alone are capable of experiencing who we are, we are instinctively gifted in watching how others experience themselves. We learn to live by living together with others, and by living like them—a process which has disadvantages as well as blessings.

The greatest of disadvantages is that we are too prone to welcome everybody else's wrong solution to the problems of life. There is a natural laziness that moves us to accept the easiest solutions—the ones that have common currency among our friends. That is why an optimistic view of life is not necessarily always a virtuous thing. In a time like ours, only the coarse grained still have enough resistance to preserve their fair-weather principles unclouded by anxiety. Such optimism may be comfortable: but is it safe? In a world where every lie has currency, is not anxiety the more real and the more human reaction?

Now anxiety is the mark of spiritual insecurity. It is the fruit of unanswered questions. But questions cannot go unanswered unless they first be asked. And there is a far worse anxiety, a far worse insecurity, which comes from being afraid to ask the right questions—because they might turn out to have no answer. One of the moral diseases we communicate to one another in society comes from huddling together in the pale light of an insufficient answer to a question we are afraid to ask.

But there are other diseases also. There is the laziness that pretends to dignify itself by the name of despair, and that teaches us to ignore both the question and the answer. And there is the despair which dresses itself up as science or philosophy and amuses itself with clever answers to clever questions—none of which have anything to do with the problems of life. Finally there is the worst and most insidious despair, which can mask as mysticism or prophecy, and which intones a prophetic answer to a prophetic question. That, I think, is likely to be a monk's professional hazard, so I purify myself of it at the beginning, like Amos who complained, "I am not a prophet, nor am I the son of a prophet, but I am a herdsman, plucking wild figs" (Amos, 7:14).

The prophetic illusion—which is quite common in our time—is at the opposite extreme from the gregarious illusion, which is more common still in every time. The false prophet will accept any answer, provided that it is his own, provided it is *not* the answer of the herd. The sheep mentality, on the other hand, accepts any answer that circulates in its own flock, provided only that it is *not* the answer of a prophet who has not been dead for at least five hundred years.

If I know anything of intellectual honesty, and I am not so certain that I do, it seems to me that the honest position lies somewhere in between. Therefore the meditations in this book are intended to be at the same time traditional, and modern, and my own. I do not intend to divorce myself at any point from Catholic tradition. But neither do I intend to accept points of that tradition blindly, and without understanding, and without making them really my own. For it seems to me that the first responsibility of a man of faith is to make his faith really part of his own life, not by rationalizing it but by living it.

After all, these meditations are musings upon questions that are, to me, relatively or even absolutely important. They do not always pretend to be final answers to final questions, nor do they even claim to face those questions in the most fundamental possible terms. But at least I can hope they are thoughts that I have honestly thought out for myself and that, for better or for worse, mean something in my own life and in the lives of those I live with. They point, therefore, toward what seems to me to be the meaning of life. They do not aim to include everything that life can possibly mean, nor do they take in a broad general view of all that matters. They are simply observations of a few things that seem to me to matter. If there is a thread of unity running through them all, I should say it was the following idea:

What every man looks for in life is his own salvation and the salvation of the men he lives with. By salvation I mean first of all the full discovery of who he himself really is. Then I mean something of the fulfillment of his own God-given powers, in the love of others and of God. I mean also the discovery that he cannot find himself in himself alone, but that he must find himself in and through others. Ultimately, these propositions are summed up in two lines of the Gospel: "If any man would save his life, he must lose it," and, "Love one another as I have loved you." It is also contained in another saying from St. Paul: "We are all members one of another."

The salvation I speak of is not merely a subjective, psychological thing—a self-realization in the order of nature. It is an objective and mystical reality—the finding of ourselves in Christ, in the Spirit, or, if you prefer, in the supernatural order. This includes and sublimates and perfects the natural self-realization which it to some extent presupposes, and usually effects, and always transcends. Therefore this discovery of ourselves is always a losing of ourselves—a death and a resurrection. "Your life is hidden with Christ in God." The discovery of ourselves in God, and of God in ourselves, by a charity that also finds all other men in God with ourselves is, therefore, not the discovery of ourselves but of Christ. First of all, it is the realization that "I live now not I but Christ liveth in me," and secondly it is the penetration of that tremendous mystery which St. Paul sketched out boldly—and darkly—in his great Epistles: the mystery of the recapitulation, the summing up of all in Christ. It is to see the world in Christ, its beginning and its end. To see all things coming forth from God in the *Logos* Who becomes incarnate and descends into the lowest depths of His own creation and gathers all to Himself in order to restore it finally to the Father at the end of time. To find "ourselves" then is to find not only our poor, limited, perplexed souls, but to find the power of God that raised Christ from the dead and "built us together in Him unto a habitation of God in the Spirit" (Ephesians 2:22).

This discovery of Christ is never genuine if it is nothing but a flight from ourselves. On the contrary, it cannot be an escape. It must be a fulfillment. I cannot discover God in myself and myself in Him unless I have the courage to face myself exactly as I am, with all my limitations, and to accept others as they are, with all *their* limitations. The religious answer is not religious if it is not fully real. Evasion is the answer of superstition.

This matter of "salvation" is, when seen intuitively, a very simple thing. But when we analyze it, it turns into a complex tangle of paradoxes. We become ourselves by dying to ourselves. We gain only what we give up, and if we give up everything we gain everything. We cannot find ourselves within ourselves, but only in others, yet at the same time before we can go out to others we must first find ourselves. We must forget ourselves in order to become truly conscious of who we are. The best way to love ourselves is to love others, yet we cannot love others unless we love ourselves since it is written, "Thou shalt love thy neighbor as thyself." But if we love ourselves in the wrong way, we become incapable of loving anybody else. And indeed when we love ourselves wrongly we hate ourselves; if we hate ourselves we cannot help hating others. Yet there is a sense in which we must hate others and leave them in order to find God. Jesus said: "If any man come to me and hate not his father and his mother . . . yea and his own life also, he cannot be my disciple" (Luke 14:26). As for this "finding" of God, we cannot even look for Him unless we have already found Him, and we cannot find Him unless he has first found us. We cannot begin to seek Him without a special gift of His grace, yet if we wait for grace to move us, before beginning to seek Him, we will probably never begin.

The only effective answer to the problem of salvation must therefore reach out to embrace both extremes of a contradiction at the same time. Hence that answer must be supernatural. That is why all the answers that are not supernatural are imperfect: for they only embrace one of the contradictory terms, and they can always be denied by the other.

Take the antithesis between love of self and love of another. As long as there is question of material things, the two loves are opposed. The more goods I keep for my own enjoyment, the less there are for others. My pleasures and comforts are, in a certain sense, taken from someone else. And when my pleasures and comforts are inordinate, they are not only taken from another, but they are stolen. I must learn to deprive myself of good things in order to give them to others who have a greater need of them than I. And so I must in a certain sense "hate" myself in order to love others.

Now there is a spiritual selfishness which even poisons the good act of giving to another. Spiritual goods are greater than the material, and it is possible for me to love selfishly in the very act of depriving myself of material things for the benefit of another. If my gift is intended to bind him to me, to put him under an obligation, to exercise a kind of hidden moral tyranny over his soul, then in loving him I am really loving myself. And this is a greater and more insidious selfishness, since it traffics not in flesh and blood but in other persons' souls.

Natural asceticism presents various insufficient answers to this problem. Each answer contains a hidden temptation. The first is temptation to the hedonism of Eros: we deny ourselves just enough to share with one another the pleasures of life. We admit a certain selfishness, and feel that in doing so we are being realistic. Our self-denial is, then, just sufficient to provide us with a healthy increase in our mutual satisfactions. In a bourgeois world, Eros knows how to mask as Christian charity.

Next comes the temptation to destroy ourselves for love of the other. The only value is love of the other. Self-sacrifice is an absolute value in itself. And the desire of the other is also absolute in itself. No matter what the lover desires, we will give up our life or even our soul to please him. This is the asceticism of Eros, which makes it a point of honor to follow the beloved even into hell. For what greater sacrifice could man offer on the altar of love than the sacrifice of his own immortal soul? Heroism in this sacrifice is measured precisely by madness: it is all the greater when it is offered for a more trivial motive.

Yet another temptation goes to the other extreme. With Sartre, it says: *"L'enfer, c'est les autres!"* ("Other people—that's hell!"). In that case, love itself becomes the great temptation and the great sin. Because it is an inescapable sin, it is also hell. But this too is only a disguised form of Eros—Eros in solitude. It is the love that is mortally wounded by its own incapacity to love another, and flies from others in order not to have to give itself to them. Even in its solitude this Eros is most tortured by its inescapable need of another, not for the other's sake but for its own fulfillment!

All these three answers are insufficient. The third says we must love only ourselves. The second says we must love only another. The first says that in loving another we simply seek the most effective way to love ourselves. The true answer, which is supernatural, tells us that we must love ourselves in order to be able to love others, that we must find ourselves by giving ourselves to them. The words of Christ are clear: "Thou shalt love thy neighbor as thyself."

This is not merely a helpful suggestion, it is the fundamental law of human existence. It forms part of the first and greatest commandment, and flows from the obligation to love God with all our heart and soul and strength. This double commandment, giving us two aspects of the same love, obliges us to another asceticism, which is not the answer of Eros, but the answer of Agapé.

Whatever may be said in the following pages rests upon this foundation. Man is divided against himself and against God by his own selfishness, which divides him against his brother. This division cannot be healed by a love that places itself only on one side of the rift. Love must reach over to both sides and draw them together. We cannot love ourselves unless we love others, and we cannot love others unless we love ourselves. But a selfish love of ourselves makes us incapable of loving others. The difficulty of this commandment lies in the paradox that it would have us love ourselves unselfishly, because even our love of ourselves is something we owe to others.

This truth never becomes clear as long as we assume that each one of us, individually, is the center of the universe. We do not exist for ourselves alone, and it is only when we are fully convinced of this fact that we begin to love ourselves properly and thus also love others. What do I mean by loving ourselves properly? I mean, first of all, desiring to live, accepting life as a very great gift and a great good, not because of what it gives us, but because of what it enables us to give to others. The modern world is beginning to discover, more and more, that the quality and vitality of a man's life depend on his own secret will to go on living. There is a dark force for destruction within us, which someone has called the "death instinct." It is a terribly powerful thing, this force generated by our own frustrated self-love battling with itself. It is the power of a self-love that has turned into self-hatred and which, in adoring itself, adores the monster by which it is consumed.

It is therefore of supreme importance that we consent to live not for ourselves but for others. When we do this we will be able first of all to face and accept our own limitations. As long as we secretly adore ourselves, our own deficiencies will remain to torture us with an apparent defilement. But if we live for others, we will gradually discover that no one expects us to be "as gods." We will see that we are human, like everyone else, that we all have weaknesses and deficiencies, and that these limitations of ours play a most important part in all our lives. It is because of them that we need others and others need us. We are not all weak in the same spots, and so we supplement and complete one another, each one making up in himself for the lack in another.

Only when we see ourselves in our true human context, as members of a race which is intended to be one organism and "one body," will we begin to understand the positive importance not only of the successes but of the failures and accidents in our lives. My successes are not my own. The way to them was prepared by others. The fruit of my labors is not my own: for I am preparing the way for the achievements of another. Nor are my failures my own. They may spring from the failure of another, but they are also compensated for by another's achievement. Therefore the meaning of my life is not to be looked for merely in the sum total of my own achievements. It is seen only in the complete integration of my achievements and failures with the achievements and failures of my own generation, and society, and time. It is seen, above all, in my integration in the mystery of Christ. That was what the poet John Donne realized during a serious illness when he heard the death knell tolling for another. "The Church is Catholic, universal," he said, "so are all her actions, all that she does belongs to all. . . . Who bends not his ear to any bell which upon any occasion rings? but who can remove it from that bell which is passing a piece of himself out of this world?"

Every other man is a piece of myself, for I am a part and a member of mankind. Every Christian is part of my own body, because we are members of Christ. What I do is also done for them and with them and by them. What they do is done in me and by me and for me. But each one of us remains responsible for his own share in the life

16

of the whole body. Charity cannot be what it is supposed to be as long as I do not see that my life represents my own allotment in the life of a whole supernatural organism to which I belong. Only when this truth is absolutely central do other doctrines fit into their proper context. Solitude, humility, self-denial, action and contemplation, the sacraments, the monastic life, the family, war and peace—none of these makes sense except in relation to the central reality which is God's love living and acting in those whom He has incorporated in His Christ. Nothing at all makes sense, unless we admit, with John Donne, that: "No man is an island, entire of itself; every man is a piece of the continent, a part of the main."

1. Love can be kept only by being given away

1. A happiness that is sought for ourselves alone can never be found: for a happiness that is diminished by being shared is not big enough to make us happy.

There is a false and momentary happiness in self-satisfaction, but it always leads to sorrow because it narrows and deadens our spirit. True happiness is found in unselfish love, a love which increases in proportion as it is shared. There is no end to the sharing of love, and, therefore, the potential happiness of such love is without limit. Infinite sharing is the law of God's inner life. He has made the sharing of ourselves the law of our own being, so that it is in loving others that we best love ourselves. In disinterested activity we best fulfill our own capacities to act and to be.

Yet there can never be happiness in compulsion. It is not enough for love to be shared: it must be shared freely. That is to say it must be given, not merely taken. Unselfish love that is poured out upon a selfish object does not bring perfect happiness: not because love requires a return or a reward for loving, but because it rests in the happiness of the beloved. And if the one loved receives love selfishly, the lover is not satisfied. He sees that his love has failed to make the beloved happy. It has not awakened his capacity for unselfish love.

Hence the paradox that unselfish love cannot rest perfectly except in a love that is perfectly reciprocated: because it knows that the only true peace is found in selfless love. Selfless love consents to be loved selflessly for the sake of the beloved. In so doing, it perfects itself.

The gift of love is the gift of the power and the capacity to love, and, therefore, to give love with full effect is also to receive it. So, love can only be kept by being given away, and it can only be given perfectly when it is also received.

2. Love not only prefers the good of another to my own, but it does not even compare the two. It has only one good: that of the beloved, which is, at the same time, my own. Love shares the good with another not by dividing it with him, but by identifying itself with him so that his good becomes my own. The same good is enjoyed in its wholeness by two in one spirit, not halved and shared by two souls. Where love is really disinterested, the lover does not even stop to inquire whether he can safely appropriate for himself some part of the good which he wills for his friend. Love seeks its whole good in the good of the beloved, and to divide that good would be to diminish love. Such a division would not only weaken the action of love, but in doing so would also diminish its joy. For love does not seek a joy that follows from its effect: its joy is in the effect itself, which is the good of the beloved. Consequently, if my love be pure I do not even have to seek for myself the satisfaction of loving. Love seeks one thing only: the good of the one loved. It leaves all the other secondary effects to take care of themselves. Love, therefore, is its own reward.

3. To love another is to will what is really good for him. Such love must be based on truth. A love that sees no distinction between good and evil, but loves blindly merely for the sake of loving, is hatred, rather than love. To love blindly is to love selfishly, because the goal of such love is not the real advantage of the beloved but only the exercise of love in our own souls. Such love cannot seem to be love unless it pretends to seek the good of the one loved. But since it actually cares nothing for the truth, and never considers that it may go astray, it proves itself to be selfish. It does not seek the true advantage of the beloved or even our own. It is not interested in the truth,

but only in itself. It proclaims itself content with an apparent good: which is the exercise of love for its own sake, without any consideration of the good or bad effects of loving.

When such love exists on the level of bodily passion it is easily recognized for what it is. It is selfish, and, therefore, it is not love. Those whose love does not transcend the desires of their bodies, generally do not even bother to deceive themselves with good motives. They follow their passions. Since they do not deceive themselves, they are more honest, as well as more miserable, than those who pretend to love on a spiritual plane without realizing that their "unselfishness" is only a deception.

4. Charity is neither weak nor blind. It is essentially prudent, just, temperate, and strong. Unless all the other virtues blend together in charity, our love is not genuine. No one who really wants to love another will consent to love him falsely. If we are going to love others at all, we must make up our minds to love them well. Otherwise our love is a delusion.

The first step to unselfish love is the recognition that our love may be deluded. We must first of all purify our love by renouncing the pleasure of loving as an end in itself. As long as pleasure is our end, we will be dishonest with ourselves and with those we love. We will not seek their good, but our own pleasure.

5. It is clear, then, that to love others well we must first love the truth. And since love is a matter of practical and concrete human relations, the truth we must love when we love our brothers is not mere abstract speculation: it is the moral truth that is to be embodied and given life in our own destiny and theirs. This truth is more than the cold perception of an obligation, flowing from moral precepts. The truth we must love in loving our brothers is the concrete destiny and sanctity that are willed for them by the love of God. One who really loves another is not merely moved by the desire to see him contented and healthy and prosperous in this world. Love cannot be satisfied with anything so incomplete. If I am to love my brother, I must somehow enter deep into the mystery of God's love for him. I must be moved not only by human

sympathy but by that divine sympathy which is revealed to us in Jesus and which enriches our own lives by the outpouring of the Holy Spirit in our hearts.

The truth I love in loving my brother cannot be something merely philosophical and abstract. It must be at the same time supernatural and concrete, practical and alive. And I mean these words in no metaphorical sense. The truth I must love in my brother is God Himself, living in him. I must seek the life of the Spirit of God breathing in him. And I can only discern and follow that mysterious life by the action of the same Holy Spirit living and acting in the depths of my own heart.

6. Charity makes me seek far more than the satisfaction of my own desires, even though they be aimed at another's good. It must also make me an instrument of God's Providence in their lives. I must become convinced and penetrated by the realization that without my love for them they may perhaps not achieve the things God has willed for them. My will must be the instrument of God's will in helping them create their destiny. My love must be to them the "sacrament" of the mysterious and infinitely selfless love God has for them. My love must be for them the minister not of my own spirit but of the Holy Spirit. The words I speak to them must be no other than the words of Christ Who deigns to reveal Himself to them in me.

Such a conception of charity is, above all, proper to a priest. It is an aspect of the grace of Orders. It is, so to speak, inseparable from the priesthood, and a priest cannot be at peace with himself or with God unless he is trying to love others with a love that is not merely his but God's own love. Only this charity which is as strong and as sure as the Spirit of God Himself can save us from the lamentable error of pouring out on others a love that leads them into error and urges them to seek happiness where it can never be found.

7. In order to love others with perfect charity I must be true to them, to myself, and to God.

The true interests of a person are at once perfectly his own and common to the whole Kingdom of God. That is because these interests are all centered in God's designs for his soul. The destiny of each one of us is intended, by the Lord, to enter into the destiny of His entire Kingdom. And the more perfectly we are ourselves the more we are able to contribute to the good of the whole Church of God. For each person is perfected by the virtues of a child of God, and these virtues show themselves differently in everyone, since they come to light in the lives of each one of the saints under a different set of providential circumstances.

If we love one another truly, our love will be graced with a clear-sighted prudence which sees and respects the designs of God upon each separate soul. Our love for one another must be rooted in a deep devotion to Divine Providence, a devotion that abandons our own limited plans into the hands of God and seeks only to enter into the invisible work that builds His Kingdom. Only a love that senses the designs of Providence can unite itself perfectly to God's providential action upon souls. Faithful submission to God's secret working in the world will fill our love with piety, that is to say with supernatural awe and respect. This respect, this piety, gives our love the character of worship, without which our charity can never be quite complete. For love must not only *seek* the truth in the lives of those around us; it must *find* it there. But when we find the truth that shapes our lives we have found more than an idea. We have found a Person. We have come upon the actions of One Who is still hidden, but Whose work proclaims Him holy and worthy to be adored. And in Him we also find ourselves.

8. A selfish love seldom respects the rights of the beloved to be an autonomous person. Far from respecting the true being of another and granting his personality room to grow and expand in its own original way, this love seeks to keep him in subjection to ourselves. It insists that he conform himself to us, and it works in every possible way to make him do so. A selfish love withers and dies unless it is sustained by the attention of the beloved. When we love thus, our friends exist only in order that we may love them. In loving them we seek to make pets of them, to keep them tame. Such love fears nothing more than the escape of the beloved. It requires his subjection because that is necessary for the nourishment of our own affections.

23

Selfish love often appears to be unselfish, because it is willing to make any concession to the beloved in order to keep him prisoner. But it is supreme selfishness to buy what is best in a person, his liberty, his integrity, his own autonomous dignity as a person, at the price of far lesser goods. Such selfishness is all the more abominable when it takes a complacent pleasure in its concessions, deluded that they are all acts of selfless charity.

A love, therefore, that is selfless, that honestly seeks the truth, does not make unlimited concessions to the beloved.

May God preserve me from the love of a friend who will never dare to rebuke me. May He preserve me from the friend who seeks to do nothing but change and correct me. But may He preserve me still more from one whose love is only satisfied by being rebuked.

If I love my brothers according to the truth, my love for them will be true not only to them but to myself.

I cannot be true to them if I am not true to myself.

"The Lord trieth the just and the wicked, but he that loveth iniquity hateth his own soul" (Psalm 10:6).

"Iniquity" is inequality, injustice, which seeks more for myself than my rights allow and which gives others less than they should receive. To love myself more than others is to be untrue to myself as well as to them. The more I seek to take advantage of others the less of a person will I myself be, for the anxiety to possess what I should not have narrows and diminishes my own soul.

Therefore the man who loves himself too much is incapable of loving anyone effectively, including himself. How then can he hope to love another?

"An unjust man allureth his friend and leadeth him into a way that is not good" (Proverbs 16:29).

9. Charity must teach us that friendship is a holy thing, and that it is neither charitable nor holy to base our friendship on falsehood. We can be, in some sense, friends to all men because there is no man on earth with whom we do not have something in common. But it would be false to treat too many men as intimate friends. It is not possible to be intimate with more than very few, because there are only very few in the world with whom we have practically everything in common.

Love, then, must be true to the ones we love and to

ourselves, and also to its own laws. I cannot be true to myself if I pretend to have more in common than I actually have with someone whom I may like for a selfish and unworthy reason.

There is, however, one universal basis for friendship with all men: we are all loved by God, and I should desire them all to love Him with all their power. But the fact remains that I cannot, on this earth, enter deeply into the mystery of their love for Him and of His love for them.

Great priests, saints like the Curé d'Ars, who have seen into the hidden depths of thousands of souls, have, nevertheless, remained men with few intimate friends. No one is more lonely than a priest who has a vast ministry. He is isolated in a terrible desert by the secrets of his fellow men.

10. When all this has been said, the truth remains that our destiny is to love one another as Christ has loved us. Jesus had very few close friends when He was on earth, and yet He loved and loves all men and is, to every soul born into the world, that soul's most intimate friend. The lives of all the men we meet and know are woven into our own destiny, together with the lives of many we shall never know on earth. But certain ones, very few, are our close friends. Because we have more in common with them, we are able to love them with a special selfless perfection, since we have more to share. They are inseparable from our own destiny, and, therefore, our love for them is especially holy: it is a manifestation of God in our lives.

11. Perfect charity gives supreme praise to the liberty of God. It recognizes His power to give Himself to those who love Him purely without violating the purity of their love. More than that: selfless charity, by receiving from God the gift of Himself, becomes able, by that fact alone, to love with perfect purity. For God Himself creates the purity and the love of those who love Him and one another with perfect charity.

His charity must not be represented as hunger. It is the banquet of the Kingdom of Heaven, to which many were invited by the great King. Many could not come to the banquet because they desired something beyond it, something for themselves—a farm, a wife, a yoke of oxen. They did not know that if they had sought first the banquet and the Kingdom they would have received everything else besides.

Charity is not hungry. It is the *juge convivium*—the perpetual banquet where there is no satiety, a feast in which we are nourished by serving others rather than by feeding ourselves. It is a banquet of prudence also, in which we know how to give to each other his just measure.

"And the Lord said: Who, thinkest thou, is the faithful and wise steward, whom his lord setteth over his family, to give them their measure of wheat in due season? Blessed is that servant, whom when his lord shall come, shall find him so doing" (Luke 12:43–44).

But to feed others with charity is to feed them with the Bread of Life, Who is Christ, and to teach them also to love with a love that knows no hunger.

"I am the Bread of Life: he who comes to Me shall not hunger, and he who believes in Me shall never thirst" (John 6:35).

2. Sentences on hope

1. We are not perfectly free until we live in pure hope. For when our hope is pure, it no longer trusts exclusively in human and visible means, nor rests in any visible end. He who hopes in God trusts God, Whom he never sees, to bring him to the possession of things that are beyond imagination.

When we do not desire the things of this world for their own sake, we become able to see them as they are. We see at once their goodness and their purpose, and we become able to appreciate them as we never have before. As soon as we are free of them, they begin to please us. As soon as we cease to rely on them alone, they are able to serve us. Since we depend neither on the pleasure nor on the assistance we get from them, they offer us both pleasure and assistance, at the command of God. For Jesus has said: "Seek first the kingdom of God, and His justice and all these things [that is all that you need for your life on earth] will be given to you besides" (Matthew 6:33).

Supernatural hope is the virtue that strips us of all things in order to give us possession of all things. We do not hope for what we have. Therefore, to live in hope is to live in poverty, having nothing. And yet, if we abandon ourselves to economy of Divine Providence, we have everything we hope for. By faith we know God without seeing Him. By hope we possess God without feeling His presence. If we hope in God, by hope we already possess Him, since hope is a confidence which He creates in our souls

27

as secret evidence that He has taken possession of us. So the soul that hopes in God already belongs to Him, and to belong to Him is the same as to possess Him, since He gives Himself completely to those who give themselves to Him. The only thing faith and hope do not give us is the clear vision of Him Whom we possess. We are united to Him in darkness, because we have to hope. *Spes quae videtur non est spes.**

Hope deprives us of everything that is not God, in order that all things may serve their true purpose as means to bring us to God.

Hope is proportionate to detachment. It brings our souls into the state of the most perfect detachment. In doing so, it restores all values by setting them in their right order. Hope empties our hands in order that we may work with them. It shows us that we have something to work for, and teaches us how to work for it.

Without hope, our faith gives us only an acquaintance with God. Without love and hope, faith only knows Him as a stranger. For hope casts us into the arms of His mercy and of His providence. If we hope in Him, we will not only come to know that He is merciful but we will experience His mercy in our own lives.

2. If, instead of trusting in God, I trust only in my own intelligence, my own strength, and my own prudence, the means that God has given to me to find my way to Him will all fail me. Nothing created is of any ultimate use without hope. To place your trust in visible things is to live in despair.

And yet, if I hope in God, I must also make a confident use of the natural aids which, with grace, enable me to come to Him. If He is good, and if my intelligence is His gift, then I must show my trust in His goodness by making use of my intelligence. I must let faith elevate, heal, and transform the light of my mind. If He is merciful, and if my freedom is a gift of His mercy, I must show my trust in His mercy by making use of my free will. I must let hope and charity purify and strengthen my human

* "For we are saved by hope. But hope that is seen, is not hope. For what a man seeth, why doth he hope for?" (Romans 8:24).

liberty and raise me to the glorious autonomy of a son of God.

Some who think they trust in God actually sin against hope because they do not use the will and the judgment He has given them. Of what use is it for me to hope in grace if I dare not make the act of will that corresponds with grace? How do I profit by abandoning myself passively to His will if I lack the strength of will to obey His commands? Therefore, if I trust in God's grace I must also show confidence in the natural powers He has given me, not because they are my powers but because they are His gift. If I believe in God's grace, I must also take account of my own free will, without which His grace would be poured out upon my soul to no purpose. If I believe that He can love me, I must also believe that I can love Him. If I do not believe I can love Him, then I do not believe Him Who gave us the first commandment: "Thou shalt love the Lord thy God with thy whole heart and thy whole mind and all thy strength, and thy neighbor as thyself."

3. We can either love God because we hope for something from Him, or we can hope in Him knowing that He loves us. Sometimes we begin with the first kind of hope and grow into the second. In that case, hope and charity work together as close partners, and both rest in God. Then every act of hope may open the door to contemplation, for such hope is its own fulfillment.

Better than hoping for anything from the Lord, besides His love, let us place all our hope in His love itself. This hope is as sure as God Himself. It can never be confounded. It is more than a promise of its own fulfillment. It is an effect of the very love it hopes for. It seeks charity because it has already found charity. It seeks God knowing that it has already been found by Him. It travels to Heaven realizing obscurely that it has already arrived.

4. All desires but one can fail. The only desire that is infallibly fulfilled is the desire to be loved by God. We cannot desire this efficaciously without at the same time desiring to love Him, and the desire to love Him is a desire that cannot fail. Merely by desiring to love Him, we are beginning to do that which we desire. Freedom is

perfect when no other love can impede our desire to love God.

But if we love God for something less than Himself, we cherish a desire that can fail us. We run the risk of hating Him if we do not get what we hope for.

It is lawful to love all things and to seek them, once they become means to the love of God. There is nothing we cannot ask of Him if we desire it in order that He may be more loved by ourselves or by other men.

5. It would be a sin to place any limit upon our hope in God. We must love Him without measure. All sin is rooted in the failure of love. All sin is a withdrawal of love from God, in order to love something else. Sin sets boundaries to our hope, and locks our love in prison. If we place our last end in something limited, we have withdrawn our hearts entirely from the service of the living God. If we continue to love Him as our end, but place our hope in something else together with Him, our love and our hope are not what they should be, for no man can serve two masters.

6. Hope is the living heart of asceticism. It teaches us to deny ourselves and leave the world not because either we or the world are evil, but because unless a supernatural hope raises us above the things of time we are in no condition to make a perfect use either of our own or of the world's true goodness. But we possess ourselves and all things in hope, for in hope we have them not as they are in themselves but as they are in Christ: full of promise. All things are at once good and imperfect. The goodness bears witness to the goodness of God. But the imperfection of all things reminds us to leave them in order to live in hope. They are themselves insufficient. We must go beyond them to Him in Whom they have their true being.

We leave the good things of this world not because they are not good, but because they are only good for us insofar as they form part of a promise. They, in turn, depend on our hope and on our detachment for the fulfillment of their own destiny. If we misuse them, we ruin ourselves together with them. If we use them as children of God's promises, we bring them, together with ourselves, to God.

"For the expectation of the creature waiteth for the revelation of the sons of God. . . . Because the creature also itself shall be delivered from the servitude of corruption into the liberty of the glory of the children of God" (Romans 8:19–21).

Upon our hope, therefore, depends the liberty of the whole universe. Because our hope is the pledge of a new heaven and a new earth, in which all things will be what they were meant to be. They will rise, together with us, in Christ. The beasts and the trees will one day share with us a new creation and we will see them as God sees them and know that they are very good.

Meanwhile, if we embrace them for themselves, we discover both them and ourselves as evil. This is the fruit of the tree of the knowledge of good and evil—disgust with the things we have misused and hatred of ourselves for misusing them.

But the goodness of creation enters into the framework of holy hope. All created things proclaim God's fidelity to His promises, and urge us, for our sake and for their own, to deny ourselves and to live in hope and to look for the judgment and the general resurrection.

An asceticism that is not entirely suspended from this divine promise is something less than Christian.

7. The devil believes in God but he has no God. The Lord is not *his* God. To be at enmity with life is to have nothing to live for. To live forever without life is everlasting death: but it is a living and wakeful death without the consolation of forgetfulness. Now the very essence of this death is the absence of hope. The damned have confirmed themselves in the belief that they cannot hope in God. We sometimes think of the damned as men who think of only themselves as good, since all sin flows from pride that refuses to love. But the pride of those who live as if they believed they were better than anyone else is rooted in a secret failure to believe in their own goodness. If I can see clear enough to realize that I am good because God has willed me to be good, I will at the same time be able to see more clearly the goodness of other men and of God. And I will be more aware of my own

failings. I cannot be humble unless I first know that I am good, and know that what is good in me is not my own, and know how easy it is for me to substitute an evil of my own choice for the good that is God's gift to me.

8. Those who abandon everything in order to seek God know well that He is the God of the poor. It is the same thing to say that He is the God of the poor and that He is a jealous God—to say that He is a jealous God and a God of infinite mercy. There are not two Gods, one jealous, Whom we must fear, and one merciful, in Whom we must place our hope. Our hope does not consist in pitting one of these gods against the other, bribing one to pacify the other. The Lord of all justice is jealous of His prerogative as the Father of mercy, and the supreme expression of His justice is to forgive those whom no one else would ever have forgiven.

That is why He is, above all, the God of those who can hope where there is no hope. The penitent thief who died with Christ was able to see God where the doctors of the law had just proved impossible Jesus's claim to divinity.

9. Only the man who has had to face despair is really convinced that he needs mercy. Those who do not want mercy never seek it. It is better to find God on the threshold of despair than to risk our lives in a complacency that has never felt the need of forgiveness. A life that is without problems may literally be more hopeless than one that always verges on despair.

10. One of the greatest speculative problems in theology is resolved in practical Christian living by the virtue of hope. The mystery of free will and grace, of predestination and co-operation with God is resolved in hope which effectively co-ordinates the two in their right relation to one another. The one who hopes in God does not *know* that he is predestined to Heaven. But if he perseveres in his hope and continually makes the acts of will inspired by divine grace he will be among the predestined: for that is the object of his hope and "hope confoundeth not" (Romans 5:5). Each act of hope is his own free act, yet it is also a gift of God. And the very essence of hope is

freely to expect all the graces necessary for salvation as free gifts from God. The free will that resolves to hope in His gifts recognizes, by that very fact, that its own act of hope is also His gift: and yet it also sees that if it did not will to hope, it would not let itself be moved by Him. Hope is the wedding of two freedoms, human and divine, in the acceptance of a love that is at once a promise and the beginning of fulfillment.

11. The faith that tells me God wills all men to be saved must be completed by the hope that God wills *me* to be saved, and by the love that responds to His desire and seals my hope with conviction. Thus hope offers the substance of all theology to the individual soul. By hope all the truths that are presented to the whole world in an abstract and impersonal way become for me a matter of personal and intimate conviction. What I believe by faith, what I understand by the habit of theology, I possess and make my own by hope. Hope is the gateway to contemplation, because contemplation is an experience of divine things and we cannot experience what we do not in some way possess. By hope we lay hands on the substance of what we believe and by hope we possess the substance of the promise of God's love.

Jesus is the theology of the Father, revealed to us. Faith tells me that this theology is accessible to all men. Hope tells me that He loves me enough to give Himself to me. If I do not hope in His love for me, I will never really know Christ. I hear of Him by faith. But I do not achieve the contact that knows Him, and thereby knows the Father in Him, until my faith in Him is completed by hope and charity: hope that grasps His love for me and charity that pays Him the return of love I owe.

12. Hope seeks not only God in Himself, not only the means to reach Him, but it seeks, finally and beyond all else, God's glory revealed in ourselves. This will be the final manifestation of His infinite mercy, and this is what we pray for when we say "Thy Kingdom come."

3. Conscience, freedom, and prayer

1. To consider persons and events and situations only in the light of their effect upon myself is to live on the doorstep of hell. Selfishness is doomed to frustration, centered as it is upon a lie. To live exclusively for myself, I must make all things bend themselves to my will as if I were a god. But this is impossible. Is there any more cogent indication of my creaturehood than the insufficiency of my own will? For I cannot make the universe obey me. I cannot make other people conform to my own whims and fancies. I cannot make even my own body obey me. When I give it pleasure, it deceives my expectation and makes me suffer pain. When I give myself what I conceive to be freedom, I deceive myself and find that I am the prisoner of my own blindness and selfishness and insufficiency.

It is true, the freedom of my will is a great thing. But this freedom is not absolute self-sufficiency. If the essence of freedom were merely the act of choice, then the mere fact of making choices would perfect our freedom. But there are two difficulties here. First of all, our choices must really be free—that is to say they must perfect us in our own being. They must perfect us in our relation to other free beings. We must make the choices that enable us to fulfill the deepest capacities of our real selves. From this flows the second difficulty: we too easily assume that we *are* our real selves, and that our choices are really the ones we want to make when, in fact, our acts of free choice are (though morally imputable, no doubt) largely dictated by psychological compulsions, flowing from our inordinate ideas of our own importance. Our choices are too often dictated by our false selves.

Hence I do not find in myself the power to be happy merely by doing what I like. On the contrary, if I do nothing except what pleases my own fancy I will be miserable almost all the time. This would never be so if my will had not been created to use its own freedom in the love of others.

My free will consolidates and perfects its own autonomy by freely co-ordinating its action with the will of another. There is something in the very nature of my freedom that inclines me to love, to do good, to dedicate myself to others. I have an instinct that tells me that I am less free when I am living for myself alone. The reason for this is that I cannot be completely independent. Since I am not self-sufficient I depend on someone else for my fulfillment. My freedom is not fully free when left to itself. It becomes so when it is brought into the right relation with the freedom of another.

At the same time, my instinct to be independent is by no means evil. My freedom is not perfected by subjection to a tyrant. Subjection is not an end in itself. It is right that my nature should rebel against subjection. Why should my will have been created free, if I were never to use my freedom?

If my will is meant to perfect its freedom in serving another will, that does not mean it will find its perfection in serving *every* other will. In fact, there is only one will in whose service I can find perfection and freedom. To give my freedom blindly to a being equal to or inferior to myself is to degrade myself and throw away my freedom. I can only become perfectly free by serving the will of God. If I do, in fact, obey other men and serve them it is not for their sake alone that I will do so, but because their will is the sacrament of the will of God. Obedience to man has no meaning unless it is primarily obedience to God. From this flow many consequences. Where there is no faith in God there can be no real order; therefore, where there is no faith obedience is without any sense. It can only be imposed on others as a matter of expediency. If there is no God, no government is logical except tyranny. And in actual fact, states that reject the idea of God tend either to tyranny or to open disorder. In either case, the end is disorder, because tyranny is itself a disorder.

If I did not believe in God I think I would be bound in conscience to become an anarchist. Yet, if I did not believe in God, I wonder if I could have the consolation of being bound in conscience to do anything.

2. Conscience is the soul of freedom, its eyes, its energy, its life. Without conscience, freedom never knows what to do with itself. And a rational being who does not know what to do with himself finds the tedium of life unbearable. He is literally bored to death. Just as love does not find its fulfillment merely in loving blindly, so freedom wastes away when it merely "acts freely" without any purpose. An act without purpose lacks something of the perfection of freedom, because freedom is more than a matter of aimless choice. It is not enough to affirm my liberty by choosing "something." I must use and develop my freedom by choosing something *good*.

I cannot make good choices unless I develop a mature and prudent conscience that gives me an accurate account of my motives, my intentions, and my moral acts. The word to be stressed here is *mature*. An infant, not having a conscience, is guided in its "decisions" by the attitude of somebody else. The immature conscience is one that bases its judgments partly, or even entirely, on the way other people seem to be disposed toward its decisions. The good is what is admired or accepted by the people it lives with. The evil is what irritates or upsets them. Even when the immature conscience is not entirely dominated by people outside itself, it nevertheless acts only as a representative of some other conscience. The immature conscience is not its own master. It is merely the delegate of the conscience of another person, or of a group, or of a party, or of a social class, or of a nation, or of a race. Therefore, it does not make real moral decisions of its own, it simply parrots the decisions of others. It does not make judgments of its own, it merely "conforms" to the party line. It does not really have motives or intentions of its own. Or if it does, it wrecks them by twisting and rationalizing them to fit the intentions of another. That is not moral freedom. It makes true love impossible. For if I am to love truly and freely, I must be able to give something that is truly my own to another. If my heart does not first belong to me, how can I give it to another? It is not mine to give!

3. Free will is not given to us merely as a firework to be shot off into the air. There are some men who seem to think their acts are freer in proportion as they are without purpose, as if a rational purpose imposed some kind of limitation upon us. That is like saying that one is richer if he throws money out the window than if he spends it.

Since money is what it is, I do not deny that you may be worthy of all praise if you light your cigarettes with it. That would show you had a deep, pure sense of the ontological value of the dollar. Nevertheless, if that is all you can think of doing with money you will not long enjoy the advantages that it can still obtain.

It may be true that a rich man can better afford to throw money out the window than a poor man: but neither the spending nor the waste of money is what makes a man rich. He is rich by virtue of what he has, and his riches are valuable to him for what he can do with them.

As for freedom, according to this analogy, it grows no greater by being wasted, or spent, but it is given to us as a talent to be traded with until the coming of Christ. In this trading we part with what is ours only to recover it with interest. We do not destroy it or throw it away. We dedicate it to some purpose, and this dedication makes us freer than we were before. Because we are freer, we are happier. We not only have more than we had but we become more than we were. This having and being come to us in a deepening of our union with the will of God. Our will is strengthened in obedience to the demands of objective reality. Our conscience is enlightened and it looks out upon a vastly widened horizon. We are able to see far nobler possibilities for the exercise of our freedom because we have grown in charity, and because we are enriched in divine grace we find in ourselves the power to attain ends that had been beyond us before.

All these fruits are meant to be gathered by our freedom when we do the will of God. It is for this that we account ourselves happy when we know His will and do it, and realize that the greatest unhappiness is to have no sense of His purposes or His designs either for ourselves or for the rest of the world. "I walked at large," says the Psalmist, "because I have sought after thy commandments" (Psalm 118:45). "I have been delighted in the way of thy testimonies as in all riches. . . . Unless thy law had been my meditation, I had then perhaps perished in my abjection . . ." (Psalm 118:14, 92). "We are happy, O Israel, because the things that are pleasing to God are made known to us" (Baruch 4:4).

4. Our free acts must not only have a purpose, they must have the right purpose. And we must have a conscience that teaches us how to choose the right purposes. Conscience is the light by which we interpret the will of God in our own lives.

This light is twofold. First, there is the psychological conscience, which is better called consciousness. It reports to us the actions we perform. It is aware of them, and through them it is aware of itself. Second, there is our moral conscience, which tells us not only *that* we act, and *how* we act, but *how well* we act. It judges the value of our acts. The psychological and moral consciences are both faculties of the intelligence. They are two kinds of awareness of ourselves telling us what we really are.

Man is distinguished from the rest of creation by his intelligence and his freedom. He matures in his manhood by growing in wisdom and by gaining a more prudent and effective command of his own moral activity. Character and maturity are therefore measured by the clarity and discretion of our moral conscience. Conscience is the summary of the whole man, although a man is much more than an animated conscience. Conscience is the indication of hidden things, of imperceptible acts and tendencies that are much more important than itself. It is the mirror of a man's depths. The reality of a person is a deep and hidden thing, buried not only in the invisible recesses of man's own metaphysical secrecy but in the secrecy of God Himself.

Conscience is the face of the soul. Its changing expressions manifest more precisely the moral action of the soul than the changes of man's countenance manifest the emotions within him. Even the outward face of man is only a reflection of his conscience. True, only a very little of what is in a man's soul ever shines out in his face: but the little that is there is enough to speak eloquently of the conscience within.

5. One of the most important functions of the life of prayer is to deepen and strengthen and develop our moral conscience. The growth of our psychological conscience, although secondary, is not without importance also. The psychological conscience has its place in our prayer, but prayer is not the place for its proper development.

When we look inward and examine our psychological conscience our vision ends in ourselves. We become aware of our feelings, our inward activity, our thoughts, our judgments, and our desires. It is not healthy to be too constantly aware of all these things. Perpetual self-examination gives an overanxious attention to movements that should remain instinctive and unobserved. When we attend too much to ourselves, our activity becomes cramped and stumbling. We get so much in our own way that we soon paralyze ourselves completely and become unable to act like normal human beings.

It is best, therefore, to let the psychological conscience alone when we are at prayer. The less we tinker with it the better. The reason why so many religious people believe they cannot meditate is that they think meditation consists in having religious emotions, thoughts, or affections of which one is, oneself, acutely aware. As soon as they start to meditate, they begin to look into the psychological conscience to find out if they are experiencing anything worthwhile. They find little or nothing. They either strain themselves to produce some interior experience, or else they give up in disgust.

6. The psychological conscience is most useful to us when it is allowed to act instinctively and without too much deliberate reflection on our own part. We should be able to see *through* our consciousness without seeing it at all. When the consciousness acts properly it is very valuable in prayer because it lends tone and quality to the action of the moral conscience, which is actually central in prayer.

At times the psychological conscience quickly gets paralyzed under the stress of futile introspection. But there is another spiritual activity that develops and liberates its hidden powers of action: the perception of beauty. I do not mean by this that we must expect our consciousness to respond to beauty as an effete and esoteric thing. We ought to be alive enough to reality to see beauty all around us. Beauty is simply reality itself, perceived in a special way that gives it a resplendent value of its own. Everything that is, is beautiful insofar as it is real—though the associations which they may have acquired for men may not always make things beautiful to us. Snakes are beautiful, but not to us.

One of the most important—and most neglected—elements in the beginnings of the interior life is the ability to respond to reality, to see the value and the beauty in ordinary things, to come alive to the splendor that is all around us in the creatures of God. We do not see these things because we have withdrawn from them. In a way we have to. In modern life our senses are so constantly bombarded with stimulation from every side that unless we developed a kind of protective insensibility we would go crazy trying to respond to *all* the advertisements at the same time!

The first step in the interior life, nowadays, is not, as some might imagine, learning *not* to see and taste and hear and feel things. On the contrary, what we must do is begin by unlearning our wrong ways of seeing, tasting, feeling, and so forth, and acquire a few of the right ones.

For asceticism is not merely a matter of renouncing television, cigarettes, and gin. Before we can begin to be ascetics, we first have to learn to see life as if it were something more than a hypnotizing telecast. And we must be able to taste something besides tobacco and alcohol: we must perhaps even be able to taste these luxuries themselves as if they too were good.

How can our conscience tell us whether or not we are renouncing things unless it first of all tells us that we know how to use them properly? For renunciation is not an end in itself: it helps us to use things better. It helps us to give them away. If reality revolts us, if we merely turn away from it in disgust, to whom shall we sacrifice it? How shall we consecrate it? How shall we make of it a gift to God and to men?

In an aesthetic experience, in the creation or the contemplation of a work of art, the psychological conscience is able to attain some of its highest and most perfect fulfillments. Art enables us to find ourselves and lose ourselves at the same time. The mind that responds to the intellectual and spiritual values that lie hidden in a poem, a painting, or a piece of music, discovers a spiritual vitality that lifts it above itself, takes it out of itself, and makes it present to itself on a level of being that it did not know it could ever achieve.

7. The soul that picks and pries at itself in the isolation of its own dull self-analysis arrives at a self-consciousness that is a torment and a disfigurement of our whole personality. But the spirit that finds itself above itself in the intensity and cleanness of its reaction to a work of art is "self-conscious" in a way that is productive as well as sublime. Such a one finds in himself totally new capacities for thought and vision and moral action. Without a moment of self-analysis he has discovered himself in discovering his capacity to respond to a value that lifts him above his normal level. His very response makes him better and different. He is conscious of a new life and new powers, and it is not strange that he should proceed to develop them.

It is important, in the life of prayer, to be able to respond to such flashes of aesthetic intuition. Art and prayer have never been conceived by the Church as enemies, and where the Church has been austere it has only been because she meant to insist on the essential difference between art and entertainment. The austerity, gravity, sobriety, and strength of Gregorian chant, of twelfth-century Cistercian architecture, of Carolingian minuscule script, have much to say about the life of prayer, and they have had much to do, in the past, with forming the prayer and the religious consciousness of saints. They have always done so in proportion as they have freed souls from concentration upon themselves, as well as from mere speculation about technical values in the arts and in asceticism. One can be at the same time a technical expert in chant and a man of prayer, but the moments of prayer and of technical criticism do not usually coincide.

If the Church has emphasized the function of art in her public prayer, it has been because she knew that a true and valid aesthetic formation was necessary for the wholeness of Christian living and worship. The liturgy and the chant and Church art are all supposed to form and spiritualize man's consciousness, to give him a tone and a maturity without which his prayer cannot normally be either very deep or very wide or very pure.

There is only one reason why this is completely true: art is not an end in itself. It introduces the soul into a higher spiritual order, which it expresses and in some sense explains. Music and art and poetry attune the soul to God because they induce a kind of contact with the Creator and Ruler of the Universe. The genius of the artist finds its way by the affinity of creative sympathy, or conaturality, into the living law that rules the universe. This law is nothing but the secret gravitation that draws all things to God as to their center. Since all true art lays bare the action of this same law in the depths of our own nature, it makes us alive to the tremendous mystery of being, in which we ourselves, together with all other living and existing things, come forth from the depths of God and return again to Him. An art that does not produce something of this is not worthy of its name.

8. Before passing from the psychological conscience to the moral conscience, let us look at the subconscious mind. Too many religious people ignore the subconscious altogether. They either blithely suppose that it plays no part in their lives, or else they assume that it is simply an old attic that is not worth visiting, full of the rubbish from which we make our dreams.

It would be a great mistake to turn the interior life into a psychological experiment and make our prayer the object of psychoanalysis. If it is true and valid prayer, it needs no such analysis. But note that I have said *if*: for if it is not true prayer, it might very well benefit from analysis. The disheartening prevalence of false mysticism, the deadening grip that false asceticism sometimes gets on religious souls, and the common substitution of sentimentality for true religious feeling—all these things seem to warrant a little investigation of the subconscious substrate of what passes for "religion." However, that is by no means the province of the present book.

Only a few statements need be made here.

The subconscious mind plays a very important part in the interior life, even though it remains behind the scenes.

Just as a good play depends on the scene, the lighting, and all the rest, so too our interior life owes much of its character to the setting and lighting and background and atmosphere which are provided, without any deliberate action of our own, by our subconscious mind.

In fact, it sometimes happens that the whole tone and atmosphere of a person's life of prayer—a certain emphasis on solitude or on sacrifice or on asceticism or on apostolic radiation—is provided by elements in the subconscious mind. For the subconscious mind is a storehouse of images and symbols, I might almost say of "experiences" which provides us with more than half the material of what we actually experience as "life." Without our knowing it, we see reality through glasses colored by the subconscious memory of previous experiences.

It is, therefore, important that our subconscious mind should enable us to live as our true selves. Indeed, it often happens that a man's true self is literally buried in the subconscious, and never has a chance to express itself except in symbolic protest against the tyranny of a malformed conscience that insists on remaining immature.

I do not say that we should try, without training or experience, to explore our own subconscious depths. But we ought at least to admit that they exist, and that they are important, and we ought to have the humility to admit we do not know all about ourselves, that we are not experts at running our own lives. We ought to stop taking our conscious plans and decisions with such infinite seriousness. It may well be that we are *not* the martyrs or the mystics or the apostles or the leaders or the lovers of God that we imagine ourselves to be. Our subconscious mind may be trying to tell us this in many ways—and we have trained ourselves, with the most egregious self-righteousness to turn a deaf ear.

9. The psychological conscience is secondary in the life of the spirit. Although it can seize upon an occasional reflection of ultimate reality, the psychological conscience cannot remain for long in union with a realm that is beyond our consciousness. But moral conscience can.

The moral conscience translates the general laws of being into the less general moral law, and, what is most important, it not only interprets the moral law to fit the circumstances of our own lives, but apprehends concretely, at every moment, that which is far more than any abstract norm of conduct. The moral conscience, by showing us the way of obedience to the inspirations of actual grace, *grasps and possesses at each moment of time the living law that is the will and love of God for ourselves.*

The distinction between the general abstract formulation of moral law, and the living, personal, concrete manifestation of God's will in our own lives is one of the most fundamental truths of Christianity, for it is the distinction between the letter, which kills, and the spirit, which gives life. Jesus, Who came not to destroy the law but in order that every jot and tittle of the law should be fulfilled (Matthew 5:17–18), also taught that in order for the law to be fulfilled the doctors of the law would have to be confounded.

The justice of the scribes, who perfectly understood the letter of the law, was not sufficient to gain anyone admittance to the Kingdom of Heaven. It was necessary for the law to be fulfilled in spirit and in truth. It was necessary that men should be perfect in the law, not by the exterior observance of precepts but by the interior transformation of their whole being into sons of God. Then they would be children of their Father in Heaven, perfect as He is perfect (Matthew 5:45, 48). They would no longer keep the law with a formalistic perfection that defeated the whole purpose of the law, but they would realize that the sabbath was made for man, not man for the sabbath. They would cease to make void the law of God for the human traditions of ritualists and lawyers who could not understand Jesus when He taught that man must be born of the Holy Ghost in order to enter the Kingdom of God.*

In Christ we die to the letter of the law so that our conscience can no longer see things in the dead light of formalism and exterior observance. Our hearts refuse the

---

* "Unless a man be born again of water and the Holy Ghost, he cannot enter the kingdom of God. That which is born of flesh is flesh, and that which is born of the Spirit is spirit. . . . Nicodemus answered and said: 'How can these things be done?' Jesus answered and said to him: 'Art thou a doctor in Israel and knowest not these things?' " (John 3:5, 6, 9–10).

dry husks of literal abstraction and hunger for the living bread and the eternal waters of the spirit which spring up to life everlasting.

"Therefore my brethren you are become dead to the Law by the body of Christ. . . . We are loosed from the law of death, wherein we were detained, so that we should serve in newness of spirit and not in the oldness of the letter" (Romans 7:4, 6). The law of life in the New Testament of Christ's grace is not merely a written document. It is the fulfillment, by charity, of God's designs in the consciences of those who answer the impulsions of His grace. The new law is not merely an exterior code of conduct but an interior life, the life of Jesus Himself, living by His spirit in those who remain united to Him by charity. The new law is expressed not only in the demands made upon us by divine and ecclesiastical precepts but above all by the exigencies of the Holy Spirit Himself, alive and active in the depths of our souls, constantly urging us to yield our wills to the gravitational pull of charity, drawing us, through self-sacrifice, to the fulfillment of God's will in our own lives.

St. Paul knew that his own inspired writings were as nothing compared to the "writing" of Christ in the hearts of those who heard him. "You are the epistle of Christ," he told the Corinthians, "ministered by us and written not with ink, but with the Spirit of the living God. . . . [Who] hath made us fit ministers of the New Testament not in the letter but in the spirit. For the letter killeth, but the spirit quickeneth" (II Corinthians 3:3, 6).

10. The whole function of the life of prayer is, then, to enlighten and strengthen our conscience so that it not only knows and perceives the outward, written precepts of the moral and divine laws, but above all lives God's law in concrete reality by perfect and continual union with His will. The conscience that is united to the Holy Spirit by faith, hope, and selfless charity becomes a mirror of God's own interior law which is His charity. It becomes perfectly free. It becomes its own law because it is completely subject to the will of God and to His Spirit. In the perfection of its obedience it "tastes and sees that the Lord is sweet," and knows the meaning of St. Paul's

statement that the "law is not made for the just man" (I Timothy 1:9).

11. We do not have to create a conscience for ourselves. We are born with one, and no matter how much we may ignore it, we cannot silence its insistent demand that we do good and avoid evil. No matter how much we may deny our freedom and our moral responsibility, our intellectual soul cries out for a morality and a spiritual freedom without which it knows it cannot be happy. The first duty of every man is to seek the enlightenment and discipline without which his conscience cannot solve the problems of life. And one of the first duties of society to the men who compose it is to enable them to receive the spiritual formation they need in order to live by the light of a prudent and mature conscience. I say "spiritual" and not merely "religious," for religious formation is sometimes no more than an outward formality, and therefore it is not really religious, nor is it a "formation" of the soul.

12. As a man is, so he prays. We make ourselves what we are by the way we address God. The man who never prays is one who has tried to run away from himself because he has run away from God. But unreal though he be, he is more real than the man who prays to God with a false and lying heart.

The sinner who is afraid to pray to God, who tries to deny God in his heart, is, perhaps, closer to confessing God than the sinner who stands before God, proud of his sin because he thinks it is a virtue. The former is more honest than he thinks, for he acknowledges the truth of his own state, confesses that he and God are not at peace with one another. The latter is not only a liar himself, but tries to make God a liar also, by calling upon Him to approve of his own lie. Such was the Pharisee in the parable, the holy man who practiced many virtues, but who lied before God because he thought his piety made him better than other men. He despised sinners, and worshiped a false god who despised them like himself.

13. Prayer is inspired by God in the depth of our own nothingness. It is the movement of trust, of gratitude, of

adoration, or of sorrow that places us before God, seeing both Him and ourselves in the light of His infinite truth, and moves us to ask Him for the mercy, the spiritual strength, the material help that we all need. The man whose prayer is so pure that he never asks God for anything does not know who God is, and does not know who he is himself: for he does not know his own need of God.

All true prayer somehow confesses our absolute dependence on the Lord of life and death. It is, therefore, a deep and vital contact with Him Whom we know not only as Lord but as Father. It is when we pray truly that we really *are*. Our being is brought to a high perfection by this, which is one of its most perfect activities. When we cease to pray, we tend to fall back into nothingness. True, we continue to exist. But since the main reason for our existence is the knowledge and love of God, when our conscious contact with Him is severed we sleep or we die. Of course, we cannot always, or even often, remain clearly conscious of Him. Spiritual wakefulness demands only the habitual awareness of Him which surrounds all our actions in a spiritual atmosphere without formally striking our attention except at certain moments of keener preception. But if God leaves us so completely that we are no longer disposed to think of Him with love, then we are spiritually dead.

Most of the world is either asleep or dead. The religious people are, for the most part, asleep. The irreligious are dead. Those who are asleep are divided into two classes, like the Virgins in the parable, waiting for the Bridegroom's coming. The wise have oil in their lamps. That is to say they are detached from themselves and from the cares of the world, and they are full of charity. They are indeed waiting for the Bridegroom, and they desire nothing else but His coming, even though they may fall asleep while waiting for Him to appear. But the others are not only asleep: they are full of other dreams and other desires. Their lamps are empty because they have burned themselves out in the wisdom of the flesh and in their own vanity. When He comes, it is too late for them to buy oil. They light their lamps only after He has gone. So they fall asleep again, with useless lamps, and when they wake up they trim them to investigate, once again, the matters of a dying world.

14. There are many levels of attention in prayer.

First of all, there is purely exterior attention. We "say prayers" with our lips, but our hearts are not following what we say although we think we would like to mean what we are saying. If we do not cultivate something better than this, we will seldom really pray. If we are quite content to pray without paying attention to our prayer or to God, it shows we have not much idea of who God is, and that we do not really appreciate the grace and the privilege of being able to speak to Him in prayer. For prayer is a gift of God, a gift which is by no means given to all men. Perhaps it is given to few because so few desire it, and of those who have received it so few have received it with gratitude.

At other times, we think of God in prayer but our thoughts of Him are not concerned with prayer. They are thoughts about Him that do not establish any contact with Him. So, while we pray, we are speculating about God and about the spiritual life, or composing sermons, or drawing up theological arguments. These thoughts are all right in their place, but if we take prayer seriously we will not call them prayer. For such thoughts cannot satisfy the soul that desires to find God in prayer. On the contrary, they leave it with a feeling of emptiness and dissatisfaction. At the same time, when one is really a man of prayer, speculative thoughts about God in the time of study or of intellectual work can often lead into prayer and give place to it; but only on condition that prayer is more to him than speculation.

Again, in prayer we are distracted by our practical difficulties, the problems of our state of life, the duties we have to face. It is not possible to avoid such distractions all the time, but if we know what prayer means, and know Who God is, we will be able to turn these thoughts themselves into motives of prayer. But we will not be satisfied with such prayer as this. It is good, indeed, to turn distractions into material for petition, but it is better not to be distracted, or at least not to be drawn away from God by our distractions.

Then there is the prayer that is well used: words or

thoughts serve their purpose and lead our minds and hearts to God, and in our prayer we receive light to apply these thoughts to our own problems and difficulties, to those of our friends, or to those of the Church. But sometimes this prayer, which is, of course, valid, leaves our hearts unsatisfied because it is more concerned with our problems, with our friends, and ourselves, than it is with God. However, if we are humble men, we will be grateful for ever so little light in our prayer, and will not complain too much, for it is a great thing to receive even a little light from so great a God.

There is a better way of prayer, a greater gift from God, in which we pass through our prayer to Him, and love Him. We taste the goodness of His infinite mercy. We know that we are indeed His sons, although we know our unworthiness to be called the sons of God. We know His infinite mercy in Jesus, and we know the meaning of the fact that we, who are sinners, indeed have a Savior. And we learn what it is to know the Father in this Savior, Jesus, His Son. We enter thus into a great mystery which cannot be explained, but only experienced. But in this prayer we still remain conscious of ourselves, we can reflect upon ourselves, and realize that we are the subjects of this great experience of love, as well as the objects of God's love.

In the beginning this reflexive quality in our prayer does not disturb us. But as we mature in the spiritual life it begins to be a source of unrest and dissatisfaction. We are ashamed to be so much aware of ourselves in our prayer. We wish we were not in the way. We wish our love for God were no longer spoiled and clouded by any return upon ourselves. We wish we were no longer aware that we rejoiced in His love, for we fear that our rejoicing might end in selfishness and self-complacency. And although we are grateful for the consolation and the light of His love, we wish we ourselves could disappear and see only Jesus. These two moments of prayer are like the two phases of the Apostles' vision of the Transfigured Christ on Mount Tabor. At first Peter, James, and John were delighted with the vision of Jesus, Moses, and Elias. They thought it would be a fine thing to build three tabernacles and stay there on the mountain forever. But they were overshadowed by a cloud, and a voice came out of the cloud striking them with fear, and when they re-gained their vision they saw no one but Jesus alone.

So too there is another stage in our prayer, when con-solation gives place to fear. It is a place of darkness and anguish and of conversion: for here a great change takes place in our spirit. All our love for God appears to us to have been full of imperfection, as indeed it has. We begin to doubt that we have ever loved Him. With shame and sorrow we find that our love was full of complacency, and that although we thought ourselves modest, we over-flowed with conceit. We were too sure of ourselves, not afraid of illusion, not afraid to be recognized by other men as men of prayer. Now we see things in a different light, for we are in the cloud, and the voice of the Father fills our hearts with unrest and fear, telling us that we must no longer see ourselves: and yet, to our terror, Jesus does not appear to us and all that we see is—ourselves. Then what we find in our souls becomes terrible to us. Instead of complacently calling ourselves sinners (and secretly believing ourselves just) we begin to find that the sins of our past life were really sins, and really *our* sins—and we have not regretted them! And that since the time when we were grave sinners, we have still sinned without realizing it, because we were too sure we were the friends of God, and we have taken His graces lightly, or taken them to ourselves, and turned them to our own selfish profit, and used them for our own vanity, and even ex-ploited them to lift ourselves above other men, so that in many ways we have turned the love of God into selfishness and have reveled in His gifts without thanking Him or using them for His glory.

Then we begin to see that it is just and right that we be abandoned by God, and left to face many and great temptations. Nor do we complain of these temptations, for we are forced to recognize that they are only the ex-pression of the forces that were always hiding behind the façade of our supposed virtues. Dark things come out of the depths of our souls, and we have to consider them and recognize them for our own, and then repudiate them, lest we be saddled with them for eternity. Yet they return, and we cannot escape them. They plague us in our prayer. And while we face them, and cannot get rid of them, we realize more clearly than ever before our great need for

God, and the tremendous debt we owe His honor, and we try to pray to Him and it seems that we cannot pray. Then begins a spiritual revaluation of all that is in us. We begin to ask ourselves what is and is not *real* in our ideals!

This is the time when we really learn to pray in earnest. For now we are no longer proud enough to expect great lights and consolations in our prayer. We are satisfied with the driest crust of supernatural food, glad to get anything at all, surprised that God should even pay the slightest attention. And if we cannot pray (which is a source of concern) yet we know more than ever before how much we desire to pray. If we could be consoled at all, this would be our only consolation.

The man who can face such dryness and abandonment for a long time, with great patience, and ask nothing more of God but to do His holy will and never offend Him, finally enters into pure prayer. Here the soul goes to God in prayer without any longer adverting either to itself or to its prayer. It speaks to Him without knowing what it is saying because God Himself has distracted the mind from its words and thoughts. It reaches Him without thoughts because, before it can think of Him, He is already present in the depths of the spirit, moving it to love Him in a way it cannot explain or understand. Time no longer means anything in such prayer, which is carried on in instants of its own, instants that can last a second or an hour without our being able to distinguish one from another. For this prayer belongs less to time than to eternity.

This deep interior prayer comes to us of its own accord, that is, by the secret movement of the Spirit of God, at all times and in all places, whether we be praying or not. It can come at work, in the middle of our daily business, at a meal, on a silent road, or in a busy thoroughfare, as well as at Mass, or in Church, or when we recite the psalms in choir. However, such prayer draws us naturally to interior and even exterior solitude. It does not depend on exterior conditions, but it has effected such an interior isolation and solitariness in our own souls that we naturally tend to seek silence and solitude for our bodies as well as for our souls. And it is good for the soul to be in solitude for a great part of the time. But if it should seek solitude for its own comfort and consolation, it will have to endure more darkness and more anguish and more trial. Pure prayer only takes possession of our hearts for good when we no longer desire any special light or grace or consolation for ourselves, and pray without any thought of our own satisfaction.

Finally, the purest prayer is something on which it is impossible to reflect until after it is over. And when the grace has gone we no longer seek to reflect on it, because we realize that it belongs to another order of things, and that it will be in some sense debased by our reflecting on it. Such prayer desires no witness, even the witness of our own souls. It seeks to keep itself entirely hidden in God. The experience remains in our spirit like a wound, like a scar that will not heal. But we do not reflect upon it. This living wound may become a source of knowledge, if we are to instruct others in the ways of prayer; or else it may become a bar and an obstacle to knowledge, a seal of silence set upon the soul, closing the way to words and thoughts, so that we can say nothing of it to other men. For the way is left open to God alone. This is like the door spoken of by Ezechiel, which shall remain closed because the King is enthroned within.

4. Pure intention

1. If God were merely another contingent being like myself, then to do His will would seem to be just as futile as doing my own. Our happiness consists in doing the will of God. But the essence of this happiness does not lie merely in an agreement of wills. It consists in a union with God. And the union of wills which makes us happy in God must ultimately be something deeper than an agreement.

2. First of all, let us not all be too glib in our statements about the will of God. God's will is a profound and holy mystery, and the fact that we live our everyday lives engulfed in this mystery should not lead us to underestimate its holiness. We dwell in the will of God as in a sanctuary. His will is the cloud of darkness that surrounds His immediate presence. It is the mystery in which His divine life and our created life become "one spirit," since, as St. Paul says, "Those who are joined to the Lord are one spirit" (I Corinthians 6:17).

There are religious men who have become so familiar with the concept of God's will that their familiarity has bred an apparent contempt. It has made them forget that God's will is more than a concept. It is a terrible and transcendent reality, a secret power which is given to us, from moment to moment, to be the life of our life and the soul of our own soul's life. It is the living flame of God's own Spirit, in Whom our own soul's flame can play, if it wills, like a mysterious angel. God's will is not an abstraction, not a machine, not an esoteric system. It

53

is a living concrete reality in the lives of men, and our souls are created to burn as flames within His flame. The will of the Lord is not a static center drawing our souls blindly toward itself. It is a creative power, working everywhere, giving life and being and direction to all things, and above all forming and creating, in the midst of an old creation, a whole new world which is called the Kingdom of God. What we call the "will of God" is the movement of His love and wisdom, ordering and governing all free and necessary agents, moving movers and causing causes, driving drivers and ruling those who rule, so that even those who resist Him carry out His will without realizing that they are doing so. In all His acts God orders all things, whether good or evil, for the good of those who know Him and seek Him and who strive to bring their own freedom under obedience to His divine purpose. All that is done by the will of God in secret is done for His glory and for the good of those whom He has chosen to share in His glory.

3. Shall I be content to do God's will for my own advantage?

It is better to do His will with a weak, but deliberate co-operation than to do His will unconsciously, unwillingly, and in spite of myself. But let me not confine my idea of perfection to the selfish obedience that does God's will merely for the sake of my own profit. True happiness is not found in any other reward than that of being united with God. If I seek some other reward besides God Himself, I may get my reward but I cannot be happy.

The secret of pure intention is not to be sought in the renunciation of all advantage for ourselves. Our intentions are pure when we identify our advantage with God's glory, and see that our happiness consists in doing His will because His will is right and good. In order to make our intentions pure, we do not give up all idea of seeking our own good, we simply seek it where it can really be found: in a good that is beyond and above ourselves. Pure intention identifies our own happiness with the common good of all those who are loved by God. It seeks its joy in God's own will to do good to all men in order that He may be glorified in them.

And, therefore, a pure intention is actually the most

efficacious way of seeking our own advantage and our own happiness.

4. An impure intention is one that yields to the will of God while retaining a preference for my own will. It divides my will from His will. It gives me a choice between two advantages: one in doing His will and one in doing my own. An impure intention is imprudent, because it weighs truth in the balance against illusion; it chooses between a real and an apparent good as if they were equal.

A pure intention sees that the will of God is always good. An impure intention, without doubting in theory that God wills what is universally best, practically doubts that He can always will what is best for me in willing what is best for all. And so the man whose intention is not pure is compelled by his own weakness and imprudence to pass judgment on the will of God before he obeys it. He is not free to do the will of God with perfect generosity. He diminishes his love and his obedience by making an adjustment between God's will and his own, and so the will of God comes to have, for him, a variety of values: richer when it is more pleasing to him, poorer when it offers less immediate satisfaction, valueless when it demands a sacrifice of his own selfish interests.

5. Only a pure intention can be clear-sighted and prudent. The man of impure intentions is hesitant and blind. Since he is always caught between two conflicting wills, he cannot make simple and clear-cut decisions. He has twice as much to think about as the man who seeks only the will of God, since he has to worry about his own will and God's will at the same time. He cannot be really happy, because happiness is impossible without interior freedom, and we do not have interior freedom to do what we please without anxiety, unless we take pleasure in nothing but the will of God.

6. The man of impure intentions may not clearly realize that he is deceiving himself. Blinded by his own selfishness, he cannot even see that he is blinded. The hesitation that divides him between God's will and his own is by no means clear. It does not involve a practical choice between two clearly seen alternatives. It plunges him into

a confusion of doubtful choices, a welter of possibilities. If he had enough interior peace to listen to his own conscience, he would hear it telling him that he does not really know what he is doing. He realizes obscurely that if he knew himself better he would be less likely to deceive himself. He knows that he is blindly following his own selfish ideas, under cover of motives he has not taken time to examine. But he does not really want to examine them, because if he did so he might find out that his will and the will of God were directly opposed to one another. He might discover that there was no alternative for him but to do the will of God, which he does not really want to do.

7. Sanctity does not consist merely in *doing* the will of God. It consists in *willing* the will of God. For sanctity is union with God, and not all those who carry out His will are united with His will. Even those who commit sin contribute, by the effects of their sin, to the fulfillment of the will of God. But because they sin they formally will what God does not will. And a man can also sin by failing to will what God wills him to do. In either case, he may do what God wills while himself willing the opposite.

It is not always necessary to find out what God wills in order to do it. A man can live like a tree or an animal, doing the divine will all his life and never knowing anything about it. But if we are to will what He wills we must begin to know something of what He wills. We must at least desire to know what He wills.

If the Lord has given me intelligence, it is because He wills me to see something of His intentions for me, in order that I may enter into His plans with a free and intelligent co-operation. And so I cannot merely shut my eyes and will "whatever He wills" without ever looking up to see what He is doing.

It is true that we do not always know what the will of God for us really is. Perhaps we know it far less often than we imagine. That does not mean that we must not seek to know it. He wills that we obey in everything that we know to be commanded by Him, that we do nothing that He has forbidden, that we will all that He wills us to will and reject all that He wills us to reject. After that we must solve all our doubts by testing them with His known will, and by doing what is uncertain only in the light of what is certainly His will.

8. How can I find out what is the will of God for me?

Before the Lord wills me to do anything, He first of all wills me to *be*. What I do must depend on what I am. Therefore, my being itself contains in its own specific nature a whole code of laws, ways of behaving, that are willed for me by the God Who has willed me to be.

My rational nature as a free and intelligent being postulates that I guide my actions not by blind instinct but by reason and free choice. But if God has willed me to be a man, and if the response of my manhood to His divine command is an act of will, my fundamental homage to the creative will of God is the will, on my own part, to be the man He wants me to be.

A man is only perfectly a man when he consents to live as a son of God. The consent to live as a son implies the consciousness of a divine inheritance: "If we are sons, heirs also and joint heirs with Christ" (Romans 8:17).

It is the will of God that we live not only as rational beings, but as "new men" regenerated by the Holy Spirit in Christ. It is His will that we reach out for our inheritance, that we answer His call to be His sons. We are born men without our own consent, but the consent to be sons of God has to be elicited by our own free will. We are obliged to learn what this consent consists of, and we find that it is an act of faith in Christ, by which we receive into our hearts the Spirit of God. The Holy Spirit is the One Who makes us sons of God, justifying our souls by His presence and His charity, granting us the power to live and act as sons of God. "For the Spirit Himself giveth testimony to our spirit that we are the sons of God" (Romans 8:16).

Now the divine inheritance which God the Father gives to us in the Spirit of His love is simply the life of His incarnate Word in our souls. If we would live like sons of God, we must reproduce in our own lives the life and the charity of His only begotten Son. We must, therefore, live by the commandments and the counsels and by the Spirit of Jesus. And in order to do this we must search the Scriptures and understand the Gospels, in order to find out what Jesus is like and what His commandments are.

Besides that, we have to seek Him where He is to be found living among us on earth: in the Kingdom He came to establish, which is His Church. We must listen to His voice not only in the Scriptures but in the authority which, as we read in the Scriptures, He constituted over us to rule and sanctify and teach us by His own light, and His own holiness and His own power. It was to the Apostles and to their successors that Jesus said: "The Paraclete, the Holy Ghost whom the Father will send in my name, He will teach you all things and bring all things to your mind whatsoever I shall have said to you" (John 14:26).

We receive the Holy Spirit through the Church and her sacraments. The Church, herself guided and enlivened and formed by the Spirit of Jesus, forms Christ in our souls, and gives us His life in giving us His Holy Spirit, that we may know Him as she knows Him and that we may be united to Him as she is, in the bonds of perfect charity and in the wisdom of contemplation.

If we have His Spirit in our hearts, we will be urged by the charity of Christ to live in charity and self-sacrifice like Jesus, Who said: "Whosoever doth not carry his Cross and come after me cannot be my disciple" (Luke 14:26).

9. The Spirit of God makes Himself known in our hearts by awakening in us the recognition of God's love for us in His Son Jesus Christ, and by showing us how to keep His commandments. "By this hath the charity of God appeared towards us, because God hath sent His only begotten Son into the world, that we may live by Him. . . . By this is the Spirit of God known: Every spirit which confesseth that Jesus Christ is come in the flesh, is of God. . . . By this we know the spirit of truth and the spirit of error. . . . Everyone that loveth is born of God. He that loveth not, knoweth not God, for God is charity" (I John 4).

Above all, the Holy Spirit teaches us to live, not according to the flesh but according to divine charity. "If you live by the flesh you shall die, but if by the spirit you mortify the deeds of the flesh, you shall live" (Romans 8:13). "Now the works of the flesh are manifest which are fornication, uncleanness, immodesty, luxury, idolatry,

58

witchcrafts, enmities, contentions, emulations, wraths, quarrels, dissensions, sects, envies, murders, drunkenness, revellings and such like. Of which I foretell you as I have foretold to you that they who do such things shall not obtain the Kingdom of God" (Galatians 5:19–21).

If we have the Spirit of God in our hearts, we will live by His law of charity, inclined always to peace rather than dissension, to humility rather than arrogance, to obedience rather than rebellion, to purity and temperance, to simplicity and quietness and calm, to strength, generosity, and wisdom, to prudence and all-embracing justice, and we will love others more than ourselves, for it is the commandment of Jesus that we should love one another as He has loved us (John 15:12).

None of these things can be done without prayer, and we must turn to prayer first of all, not only to discover God's will but above all to gain the grace to carry it out with all the strength of our desire.

10. The will of God, which the Spirit of God Himself teaches us in the secrecy of our inmost being, must always remain as much of a mystery as God Himself. Our desire to know His will implies rather a desire to recognize certain signs of the mystery of His will, than to penetrate the mystery in itself. If we do not remember this distinction we no longer revere the holiness and the mystery of God's will in itself. We judge the invisible reality of His will by the visible and sometimes contemptible signs which show us where His will is found.

When we speak of God's will, we are usually speaking only of some recognizable sign of His will. The signpost that points to a distant city is not the city itself, and sometimes the signs that point to a great place are in themselves insignificant and contemptible. But we must follow the direction of the signpost if we are to get to the end of our journey.

Everything that exists and everything that happens bears witness to the will of God. It is one thing to see a sign and another thing to interpret that sign correctly. However, our first duty is to recognize signs for what they are. If we do not even regard them as indications of anything beyond themselves, we will not try to interpret them.

Of all the things and all the happenings that proclaim God's will to the world, only very few are capable of being interpreted by men. And of these few, fewer still find a capable interpreter. So that the mystery of God's will is made doubly mysterious by the signs that veil it from our eyes. To know anything at all of God's will we have to participate, in some manner, in the vision of the prophets: men who were always alive to the divine light concealed in the opacity of things and events, and who sometimes saw glimpses of that light where other men saw nothing but ordinary happenings.

And yet if we are too anxious to pry into the mystery that surrounds us we will lose the prophet's reverence and exchange it for the impertinence of soothsayers. We must be silent in the presence of signs whose meaning is closed to us. Otherwise we will begin incontinently to place our own superstitious interpretation upon everything —the number of steps to a doorway, a card pulled out of the pack, the shadow of a ladder, the flight of birds. God's will is not so cheap a mystery that it can be unlocked by any key like these!

Nevertheless, there are some signs that everyone must know. They must be easily read and seen, and they are indeed very simple. But they come sparingly, few in number; they show us clearly enough the road ahead but not for more than a few paces. When we have taken those few paces, what will happen? We must learn to be poor in our dependence on these clear signs, to take them as they come, not to demand more of them than we need, not to make more of them than they really tell.

If I am to know the will of God, I must have the right attitude toward life. I must first of all know what life is, and to know the purpose of my existence.

It is all very well to declare that I exist in order to save my soul and give glory to God by doing so. And it is all very well to say that in order to do this I obey certain commandments and keep certain counsels. Yet knowing this much, and indeed knowing all moral theology and ethics and canon law, I might still go through life conforming myself to certain indications of God's will without ever fully giving myself to God. For that, in the last analysis, is the real meaning of His will. He does not need our sacrifices, He asks for our *selves*. And if He prescribes certain acts of obedience, it is not because obedience is the beginning and the end of everything. It is only the beginning. Charity, divine union; transformation in Christ: these are the end.

So let me clearly realize first of all that what God wants of me is myself. That means to say that His will for me points to one thing: the realization, the discovery, and the fulfillment of my self, my true self, in Christ. And that is why the will of God so often manifests itself in demands that I sacrifice myself. Why? Because in order to find my true self in Christ, I must go beyond the limits of my own narrow egoism. In order to save my life, I must lose it. For my life in God is and can only be a life of unselfish charity.

When Jesus said "He that would save his life will lose it, and he that would lose his life for my sake shall find it" He was teaching us the great truth that God's will for us is, before all else, that we should find ourselves, find our true life, or, as the Vulgate text has it, find our *souls*. God's will for us is not only that we should be the persons He means us to be, but that we should share in His work of creation and *help Him to make us* into the persons He means us to be. Always, and in all things, God's will for me is that I should shape my own destiny, work out my own salvation, forge my own eternal happiness, in the way He has planned it for me. And since no man is an island, since we all depend on one another, I cannot work out God's will in my own life unless I also consciously help other men to work out His will in theirs. His will, then, is our sanctification, our transformation in Christ, our deeper and fuller integration with other men. And this integration results not in the absorption and disappearance of our own personality, but in its affirmation and its perfection.

Everything that God wills in my life is directed to this double end: my perfection as part of a universal whole, and my perfection in myself as an individual person, made in God's image and likeness. The most important part of man's education is the formation of a conscience that is capable of seeing God's will in this correct light, and guiding the response of his own will in strong, prudent and loving decisions. So to live is true wisdom.

This view of life as a growth in God, as a transformation in Christ, and as a supernatural self-realization in the mystical body of Christ is the only one that really helps us to recognize and interpret the will of God correctly. Without this view of life, we will not even be able to see the most obvious manifestations of the divine will—the manifestations that are made clear to us in the ordinary circumstances of our everyday life. For in the course of each day the duties of our state, the claims made on us by those around us, the demands on our energy, our patience, and our time, all make known to us the will of God and show us the way to realize ourselves in Him by losing ourselves in charity. But the pharisee who splits hairs and rationalizes his way out of these chances for self-dedication, although he may theorize and dogmatize about the will of God, never fully does that will for he never really abandons himself to the influence of divine charity.

Of such men God spoke through the prophet Isaias, saying: "For they seek me from day to day, and desire to know my ways as a nation that hath done justice and hath not forsaken the judgement of their God; they ask of me judgements of justice: they are willing to approach to God. Why have we fasted, and thou hast not regarded: have we humbled our souls and thou hast not taken notice? Behold in the day of your fast your own will is found, and you exact of all your debtors" (Isaias 58:2–3).

11. Wherever we have some sign of God's will, we are obliged to conform to what the sign tells us. We should do so with a pure intention, obeying God's will because it is good in itself as well as good for us. It takes more than an occasional act of faith to have such pure intentions. It takes a whole life of faith, a total consecration to hidden values. It takes sustained moral courage and heroic confidence in the help of divine grace. But above all it takes the humility and spiritual poverty to travel in darkness and uncertainty, where so often we have no light and see no sign at all.

12. If sanctity consists in willing the will of God, as well as in doing it, perfect sanctity consists in willing the will of God perfectly. But absolute perfection is not possible,

in this matter, to any man on earth. In order to will perfectly what God wills, we would have to know as perfectly as He does what He wills. Our perfection will consist in explicitly willing whatever of God's will is certain to us, implicitly willing all that we do not know, and doing all this with the motive that is best and most perfect for us.

It is not enough to do the will of God because His will is unavoidable. Nor is it enough to will what He wills because we have to. We have to will His will because we love it. Yet it would be a false idea of perfection for an imperfect person suddenly to try to act with a perfection he does not possess. It is not the will of God that we should obey Him while at the same time telling Him lies about our interior dispositions. If our dispositions are bad, let us ask Him to make them better, but let us not tell Him that they are really very good. Still less is it enough to say, "Thy will be done" and then do the opposite. It is better to be like the son in the parable, who said, "I will not" (Matthew 21:28), but afterward went to work in the vineyard, than to be like the other one who said, "I go, sir," and then did not obey.

13. If, in trying to do the will of God, we always seek the highest abstract standard of perfection, we show that there is still much we need to learn about the will of God. For God does not demand that every man attain to what is theoretically highest and best. It is better to be a good street sweeper than a bad writer, better to be a good bartender than a bad doctor, and the repentant thief who died with Jesus on Calvary was far more perfect than the holy ones who had Him nailed to the cross. And yet, abstractly speaking, what is more holy than the priesthood and less holy than the state of a criminal? The dying thief had, perhaps, disobeyed the will of God in many things: but in the most important event of his life He listened and obeyed. The Pharisees had kept the law to the letter and had spent their lives in the pursuit of a most scrupulous perfection. But they were so intent upon perfection as an abstraction that when God manifested His will and His perfection in a concrete and definite way they had no choice but to reject it.

14. Let me then wish to do God's will because it is His

will. Let me not seek to measure His will by some abstract standard of perfection outside Himself. His will is measured by the infinite reality of His love and wisdom, with which it is identified. I do not have to ask if His will be wise, once I know it is His.

If I do His will as a free act of homage and adoration paid to a wisdom that I cannot see, His will itself becomes the life and substance and reality of my worship. But if I do His will as a perfunctory adjustment of my own will to the unavoidable, my worship is hollow and without heart.

15. The perfect love of God's will is a union so close that God Himself both utters and fulfills His will at the same instant in the depths of my own soul. Pure intention, in this highest sense, is a secret and spiritual word of God which not only commands my will to act, or solicits my co-operation, but fulfills what He says in me. The action is at once perfectly mine and perfectly His. But its substance comes entirely from Him. In me, it is entirely received: only to be offered back to Him in the silent ovation of His own inexpressible love. Such words, such "intentions," which at once seek and find what they seek and give it back to God, resound with power and authority through all my faculties, so that my entire being is transformed into an expression and a fulfillment of what they say. This is what Jesus meant when he said that it was His "food" to do the will of the Father Who sent Him. The will of God, accomplished as it is uttered, identifying us at once with Him Who speaks and with what He says in us, makes our entire being a perfect reflection of Him Who desires to see His will done in our hearts. The thing willed is not important, only He Who wills it, for He cannot will anything that is against His will, that is to say, against His wisdom and His perfection.

Once we have heard the voice of the Almighty fulfilling His own command by speaking it in our hearts, we realize that our contemplation can never again be a mere looking or a mere seeking: it must also be a doing and a fulfillment. We hunger for the transforming words of God, words spoken to our spirit in secret and containing our whole destiny in themselves. We come to live by nothing but this voice. Our contemplation is rooted in the mystery of Divine Providence, and in its actuality. Providence can no longer be for us a philosophical abstraction. It is no longer a supernatural agency to provide us with food and clothing at the right time. Providence itself becomes our food and our clothing. God's mysterious decisions are themselves our life.

16. This fact tends to resolve the antinomy between action and contemplation. "Action" is no longer a matter of resigning ourselves to works that seem alien to our life in God: for the Lord Himself places us exactly where He wants us to be and He Himself works in us. "Contemplation" is no longer merely the brief, satisfying interlude of reward in which our works are relieved by recollection and peace. Action and contemplation now grow together into one life and one unity. They become two aspects of the same thing. Action is charity looking outward to other men, and contemplation is charity drawn inward to its own divine source. Action is the stream, and contemplation is the spring. The spring remains more important than the stream, for the only thing that really matters is for love to spring up inexhaustibly from the infinite abyss of Christ and of God.

It is for us to take care that these living waters well up in our own hearts. God will make it His own concern to guide our action, if we live in Him, and He will turn the stream into whatever channels He wills. "As the divisions of the waters, so the heart of the king is in the hand of the Lord: whithersoever He will, He shall turn it" (Proverbs 21:1).

17. When action and contemplation dwell together, filling our whole life because we are moved in all things by the Spirit of God, then we are spiritually mature. Our intentions are habitually pure. Johannes Tauler somewhere makes a distinction between two degrees of pure intention, one of which he calls *right* intention, and the other *simple* intention. They may serve to explain the union of action and contemplation in one harmonious whole.

When we have a *right* intention, our intention is pure. We seek to do God's will with a supernatural motive. We mean to please Him. But in doing so we still consider the work and ourselves apart from God and outside Him.

Our intention is directed chiefly upon the work to be done. When the work is done, we rest in its accomplishment, and hope for a reward from God.

But when we have a *simple* intention, we are less occupied with the thing to be done. We do all that we do not only for God but so to speak *in* Him. We are more aware of Him who works in us than of ourselves or of our work. Yet this does not mean that we are not fully conscious of what we do, or that realities lose their distinctness in a kind of sweet metaphysical blur. It may happen that one who works with this "simple" intention is more perfectly alive to the exigencies of his work and does the work far better than the worker of "right" intention who has no such perspective. The man of right intentions makes a juridical offering of his work to God and then plunges himself into the work, hoping for the best. For all his right intention he may well become completely dizzy in a maze of practical details.

A right intention demands that we work with enough detachment to keep ourselves *above* the work to be done. But it does not altogether prevent us from gradually sinking into it over our ears. When this happens, we have to pull ourselves out, leave the work aside, and try to recover our balance and our right intention in an interval of prayer.

The man of simple intention, because he is essentially a contemplative, works always in an atmosphere of prayer. I do not say merely that he works in an atmosphere of peace. Anyone who works sanely at a job he likes can do as much as that. But the man of simple intention works in an atmosphere of prayer: that is to say he is recollected. His spiritual reserves are not all poured out into his work, but stored where they belong, in the depths of his being, with his God. He is detached from his work and from its results. Only a man who works purely for God can at the same time do a very good job and leave the results of the job to God alone. If our intention is less than simple, we may do a very good job, but in doing so we will become involved in the hope of results that will satisfy ourselves. If our intention is less than right we will be concerned neither for the job nor for its results, because we have not bothered to take a personal interest in either of them.

A simple intention rests in God while accomplishing

all things. It takes account of particular ends in order to achieve them for Him: but it does not rest in them. Since a simple intention does not need to rest in any particular end, it has already reached the end as soon as the work is begun. For the end of a simple intention is to work in God and with Him—to sink deep roots into the soil of His will and to grow there in whatever weather He may bring.

A right intention is what we might call a "transient" intention: it is proper to the active life which is always moving on to something else. Our right intention passes from one particular end to another, from work to work, from day to day, from possibility to possibility. It reaches ahead into many plans. The works planned and done are all for the glory of God: but they stand ahead of us as milestones along a road with an invisible end. And God is always there at the end. He is always "future," even though He may be present. The spiritual life of a man of right intention is always more or less provisional. It is more possible than actual, for he always lives as if he had to finish just one more job before he could relax and look for a little contemplation.

Nevertheless, even in contemplative monasteries a "right" intention is more common than a really simple intention. Contemplatives, too, can live in a world where things to be done obscure the vision of Him for Whom they are done. It makes no difference if these things to be done are within ourselves. Perhaps the confusion is only made more difficult by the fact that our right intention has nothing tangible to take hold of, and reaches out all day long for merits, sacrifices, degrees of virtue and of prayer. In fact, without a simple intention, a life of prayer tends to be not only difficult but even incomprehensible. For the aim of the contemplative life is not merely to enable a man to say prayers and make sacrifices with a right intention: it is to teach him to live in God.

18. Simple intention is a rare gift of God. Rare because it is poor. Poverty is a gift that few religious people really relish. They want their religion to make them at least spiritually rich, and if they renounce all things in this world, they want to lay hands not only on life everlasting

67

but, above all, on the "hundredfold" promised to us even before we die.

Actually, that hundredfold is found in the beatitudes, the first of which is poverty.

Our intention cannot be completely simple unless it is completely poor. It seeks and desires nothing but the supreme poverty of having nothing but God. True, anyone with a grain of faith realizes that to have God and nothing else besides is to have everything in Him. But between the thought of such poverty and its actualization in our lives lies the desert of emptiness through which we must travel in order to find Him.

With a right intention, you quietly face the risk of losing the fruit of your work. With a simple intention you renounce the fruit before you even begin. You no longer even expect it. Only at this price can your work also become a prayer.

19. A simple intention is a perpetual death in Christ. It keeps our life hidden with Christ in God. It seeks its treasure nowhere except in heaven. It prefers what cannot be touched, counted, weighed, tasted, or seen. But it makes our inner being open out, at every moment, into the abyss of divine peace in which our life and actions have their roots.

A right intention aims only at right action.

But even in the midst of action, a simple intention, renouncing all things but God alone, seeks Him alone. The secret of simple intention is that it is content to seek God and does not insist on finding Him right away, knowing that in seeking Him it has already found Him. Right intention knows this too, but not by experience, and therefore it obscurely feels that seeking God is still not enough.

Simple intention is a divine medicine, a balm that soothes the powers of our soul wounded by inordinate self-expression. It heals our actions in their secret infirmity. It draws our strength to the hidden summit of our being, and bathes our spirit in the infinite mercy of God. It wounds our souls in order to heal them in Christ, for a simple intention manifests the presence and action of Christ in our hearts. It makes us His perfect instruments, and transforms us into His likeness, filling our whole lives

68

with His gentleness and His strength and His purity and His prayer and His silence.

Whatever is offered to God with a right intention is acceptable to Him.

Whatever is offered to God with a simple intention is not only accepted by Him by reason of our good will, but is pleasing to Him in itself. It is a good and perfect work, performed entirely by His love. It draws its perfection not from our poor efforts alone but from His mercy which has made them rich. In giving the Lord the works of a right intention I can be sure that I am giving Him what is not bad. But in offering Him the works of a simple intention I am giving Him what is best. And beyond all that I can give Him or do for Him, I rest and take my joy in His glory.

5. The word of the Cross

1. The word of the Cross is foolishness, says St. Paul, to them that perish (I Corinthians 1:18). Yet among those to whom the Cross was folly and scandal were ascetics and religious men who had evolved a philosophy of suffering and who cultivated self-denial.

There is, therefore, much more in the word of the Cross than the acceptance of suffering or the practice of self-denial. The Cross is something positive. It is more than a death. The word of the Cross is foolishness to them that perish—but to them that are saved "it is the power of God" (I Corinthians 1:18).

2. The Christian must not only accept suffering: he must make it holy. Nothing so easily becomes unholy as suffering.

Merely accepted, suffering does nothing for our souls except, perhaps, to harden them. Endurance alone is no consecration. True asceticism is not a mere cult of fortitude. We can deny ourselves rigorously for the wrong reason and end up by pleasing ourselves mightily with our self-denial.

Suffering is consecrated to God by faith—not by faith in suffering, but by faith in God. To accept suffering stoically, to receive the burden of fatal, unavoidable, and incomprehensible necessity and to bear it strongly, is no consecration.

Some men believe in the power and the value of suffering. But their belief is an illusion. Suffering has no power and no value of its own.

It is valuable only as a test of faith. What if our faith fails in the test? Is it good to suffer, then? What if we enter into suffering with a strong faith in suffering, and then discover that suffering destroys us?

To believe in suffering is pride: but to suffer, believing in God, is humility. For pride may tell us that we are strong enough to suffer, that suffering is good for us because we are good. Humility tells us that suffering is an evil which we must always expect to find in our lives because of the evil that is in ourselves. But faith also knows that the mercy of God is given to those who seek Him in suffering, and that by His grace we can overcome evil with good. Suffering, then, becomes good by accident, by the good that it enables us to receive more abundantly from the mercy of God. It does not make us good by itself, but it enables us to make ourselves better than we are. Thus, what we consecrate to God in suffering is not our suffering but our *selves*.

3. Only the sufferings of Christ are valuable in the sight of God, Who hates evil, and to Him they are valuable chiefly as a sign. The death of Jesus on the Cross has an infinite meaning and value not because it is a death, but because it is the death of the Son of God. The Cross of Christ says nothing of the power of suffering or of death. It speaks only of the power of Him Who overcame both suffering and death by rising from the grave.

The wounds that evil stamped upon the flesh of Christ are to be worshiped as holy not because they are wounds, but because they are *His* wounds. Nor would we worship them if He had merely died of them, without rising again. For Jesus is not merely someone who once loved men enough to die for them. He is a man whose human nature subsists in God, so that He is a divine person. His love for us is the infinite love of God, which is stronger than all evil and cannot be touched by death.

Suffering, therefore, can only be consecrated to God by one who believes that Jesus is not dead. And it is of the very essence of Christianity to face suffering and death not because they are good, not because they have meaning, but because the Resurrection of Jesus has robbed them of their meaning.

4. The saint is not one who accepts suffering because he likes it, and confesses this preference before God and men in order to win a great reward. He is one who may well hate suffering as much as anybody else, but who so loves Christ, Whom he does not see, that he will allow His love to be proved by any suffering. And he does this not because he thinks it is an achievement, but because the charity of Christ in his heart demands that it be done.

The saint is one so attuned to the spirit and heart of Christ that he is compelled to answer the demands of love by a love that matches that of Christ. This is for him a need so deep and so personal and so exacting that it becomes his whole destiny. The more he answers the secret action of Christ's love in his own heart, the more he comes to know that love's inexorable demands.

But the life of the Christian soul must always be a thing whole and simple and complete and incommunicable. The saints may seem to desire suffering in a universal and abstract way. Actually, the only sufferings anyone can validly desire are those precise, particular trials that are demanded of us in the designs of Divine Providence for our own lives.

Some men have been picked out to bear witness to Christ's love in lives overwhelmed by suffering. These have proclaimed that suffering was their vocation. But that should not lead us to believe that in order to be a saint one must go out for suffering in the same way that a college athlete goes out for football. No two men have to suffer exactly the same trials in exactly the same way. No one man is ever called to suffer merely for the sake of suffering.

What, after all, is more personal than suffering? The awful futility of our attempts to convey the reality of our sufferings to other people, and the tragic inadequacy of human sympathy, both prove how incommunicable a thing suffering really is.

When a man suffers, he is most alone. Therefore, it is in suffering that we are most tested as persons. How can we face the awful interior questioning? What shall we answer when we come to be examined by pain? Without God, we are no longer persons. We lose our manhood and our dignity. We become dumb animals under pain, happy if we can behave at least like quiet animals and die without too much commotion.

5. When suffering comes to put the question: "Who are you?" we must be able to answer distinctly, and give our own name. By that I mean we must express the very depths of what we are, what we have desired to be, what we have become. All these things are sifted out of us by pain, and they are too often found to be in contradiction with one another. But if we have lived as Christians, our name and our work and our personality will fit the pattern stamped in our souls by the sacramental character we wear. We get a name in baptism. That is because the depths of our soul are stamped, by that holy sacrament, with a supernatural identification which will eternally tell us who we were meant to be. Our baptism, which drowns us in the death of Christ, summons upon us all the sufferings of our life: their mission is to help us work out the pattern of our identity received in the sacrament.

If, therefore, we desire to be what we are meant to be, and if we become what we are supposed to become, the interrogation of suffering will call forth from us both our own name and the name of Jesus. And we will find that we have begun to work out our destiny which is to be at once ourselves and Christ.

6. Suffering, and the consecration it demands, cannot be understood perfectly outside the context of baptism. For baptism, in giving us our identity, gives us a divine vocation to find ourselves in Christ. It gives us our identity in Christ. But both the grace and character of baptism give our soul a spiritual conformity to Christ *in His sufferings*. For baptism is the application to our souls of the Passion of Christ.

Baptism engrafts us into the mystical vine which is the body of Christ, and makes us live in His life and ripen like grapes on the trellis of His Cross. It brings us into the communion of the saints whose life flows from the Passion of Jesus. But every sacrament of union is also a sacrament of separation. In making us members of one another, baptism also more clearly distinguishes us, not only from those who do not live in Christ, but also and even especially from one another. For it gives us our personal, incommunicable vocation to reproduce in our own lives the life and sufferings and charity of Christ in a way unknown to anyone else who has ever lived under the sun.

7. Suffering can only be perfectly consecrated to God, then, if it is seen as a fruit of baptism. It makes some sense only when it is plunged in the waters of the sacrament. Only these waters give it power to wash and purify. Only baptism sets out clearly *who* it is that must be formed and perfected by tribulation.

Suffering, therefore, must make sense to us not as a vague universal necessity, but as something demanded by our own personal destiny. When I see my trials not as the collision of my life with a blind machine called fate, but as the sacramental gift of Christ's love, given to me by God the Father along with my identity and my very name, then I can consecrate them and myself with them to God. For then I realize that my suffering is not my own. It is the Passion of Christ, stretching out its tendrils into my life in order to bear rich clusters of grapes, making my soul dizzy with the wine of Christ's love, and pouring that wine as strong as fire upon the whole world.

8. Useless and hateful in itself, suffering without faith is a curse.

A society whose whole idea is to eliminate suffering and bring all its members the greatest amount of comfort and pleasure is doomed to be destroyed. It does not understand that all evil is not necessarily to be avoided. Nor is suffering the only evil, as our world thinks.

If we consider suffering to be the greatest evil and pleasure the greatest good, we will live continually submerged in the only great evil that we ought to avoid without compromise: which is sin. Sometimes it is absolutely necessary to face suffering, which is a lesser evil, in order to avoid or to overcome the greatest evil, sin.

What is the difference between physical evil—suffering —and moral evil—sin? Physical evil has no power to penetrate beneath the surface of our being. It can touch our flesh, our mind, our sensibility. It cannot harm our spirit without the work of that other evil which is sin. If we suffer courageously, quietly, unselfishly, peacefully, the things that wreck our outer being only perfect us within,

74

and make us, as we have seen, more truly ourselves because they enable us to fulfill our destiny in Christ. They are sent for this purpose, and when they come we should receive them with gratitude and joy.

Sin strikes at the very depth of our personality. It destroys the one reality on which our true character, identity, and happiness depend: our fundamental orientation to God. We are created to will what God wills, to know what He knows, to love what He loves. Sin is the will to do what God does not will, to know what He does not know, to love what He does not love. Therefore every sin is a sin against truth, a sin against obedience, and against love. But in all these three things sin proves itself to be a supreme injustice not only against God but, above all, against ourselves.

For what is the good of knowing what God does not know? To know what He does not know is to know what is not. And why love what He does not love? Is there any purpose in loving nothing: for He loves everything that is. And our destiny is to love all things that He loves, just as He loves them. The will to love what is not is at the same time a refusal to love what is. And why should we destroy ourselves by willing what God does not will? To will against His will is to turn our will against ourselves. Our deepest spiritual need is for whatever thing God wills for us. To will something else is to deprive ourselves of life itself. So, when we sin, our spirit dies of starvation.

Physical evil is only to be regarded as a real evil insofar as it tends to foment sin in our souls. That is why a Christian must seek in every way possible to relieve the sufferings of others, and even take certain necessary steps to alleviate some sufferings of his own: because they are occasions of sin. It is true that we can also have compassion for others merely because suffering is an evil in its own right. This compassion is also good. But it does not really become charity unless it sees Christ in the one suffering and has mercy on him with the mercy of Christ. Jesus had pity on the multitudes not only because they were sheep without a shepherd, but also simply because they had no bread. Yet He did not feed them with miraculous loaves and fishes without thought for their place in His Father's Kingdom. Bodily works of mercy look beyond the flesh and into the spirit, and when they are integrally

Christian they not only alleviate suffering but they bring grace: that is, they strike at sin.

9. Suffering is wasted if we suffer entirely alone. Those who do not know Christ, suffer alone. Their suffering is no communion. The awful solitude of suffering is not meant to seek communion in vain. But all communion is denied to it except that which unites our spirit with God in the Passion of Jesus Christ.

What can human sympathy offer us in the loneliness of death? Flowers are an indecency in a death without God. They only serve to cover the body. The thing that has died has become a thing to be decorated and rejected. May its hopeless loneliness be forgotten and not remind us of our own!

How sad a thing is human love that ends with death: sadder when it pitiably tries to reach out to some futile communication with the dead. The poor little rice cakes at a pagan tomb! Sad, too, is the love that has no communion with those we love when they suffer. How miserable it is to have to stand in mute sorrow with nothing to say to those we love, when they are in great pain. It is a terrible confession that our love is not big enough to surmount suffering. Therefore we are desperately compelled to fight off suffering as long as we can, lest it come in the way and block off our love forever.

But a love that ends with either suffering or death is not worth the trouble it gives us. And if it must dread death and all suffering, it will inevitably bring us little joy and very much sorrow.

The Name and the Cross and the Blood of Jesus have changed all this. In His Passion, in the sacraments which bring His Passion into our lives, the helplessness of human love is transformed into a divine power which raises us above all evil. It has conquered everything. Such love knows no separation. It fears suffering no more than young crops fear the spring rain.

But the strength of such love, and such communion, is not found merely in a doctrine. The Christian has more than a philosophy of suffering. Sometimes, indeed, he may have no philosophy at all. His faith may be so inarticulate as to seem absurd. Nevertheless, he knows the peace of one who has conquered everything. Why is this? Because

Christianity is Christ living in us, and Christ has conquered everything. Furthermore, He has united us to one another in Himself. We all live together in the power of His death which overcame death. We neither suffer alone nor conquer alone nor go off into eternity alone. In Him we are inseparable: therefore, we are free to be fruitfully alone whenever we please, because wherever we go, whatever we suffer, whatever happens to us, we are united with those we love in Him because we are united with Him.

His love is so much stronger than death that the death of a Christian is a kind of triumph. And although we rightly sorrow at the sensible separation from those we love (since we are also meant to love their human presence), yet we rejoice in their death because it proves to us the strength of our mutual love. The conviction in our hearts, the unshakeable hope of communion with our dead in Christ, is always telling us that they live and that He lives and that we live. This is our great inheritance, which can only be increased by suffering well taken: this terrific grip of the divine life on our own souls, this grip of clean love that holds us so fast that it keeps us eternally free. This love, this life, this presence, is the witness that the spirit of Christ lives in us, and that we belong to Him, and that the Father has given us to Him, and no man shall snatch us out of His hand.

10. Heroism alone is useless, unless it be born of God. The fortitude given us in the charity of Christ is not complicated by pride. First of all, divine strength is not usually given us until we are fully aware of our own weakness and know that the strength we receive is indeed received: and that it is a gift. Then, the fortitude that comes to us from God is His own strength, which is beyond comparison. And pride is born of comparison.

11. To know the Cross is not merely to know our own sufferings. For the Cross is the sign of salvation, and no man is saved by his own sufferings. To know the Cross is to know that we are saved by the sufferings of Christ; more, it is to know the love of Christ Who underwent suffering and death in order to save us. It is, then, to know Christ. For to know His love is not merely to know the story of His love, but to experience in our spirit that

77

we are loved by Him, and that in His love the Father manifests His own love for us, through His Spirit poured forth into our hearts. To know all this is to understand something of the Cross, that is: to know Christ. This explains the connection between suffering and contemplation. For contemplation is simply the penetration, by divine wisdom, into the mystery of God's love, in the Passion and Resurrection of Jesus Christ.

12. The holy were not holy because they were rejected by men, but because they were acceptable to God. Saints are not made saints merely by suffering.

The Lord did not create suffering. Pain and death came into the world with the fall of man. But after man had chosen suffering in preference to the joys of union with God, the Lord turned suffering itself into a way by which man could come to the perfect knowledge of God.

13. The effect of suffering upon us depends on what we love.

If we love ourselves selfishly, suffering is merely hateful. It has to be avoided at all costs. It brings out all the evil that is in us, so that the man who loves only himself will commit any sin and inflict any evil on others merely in order to avoid suffering himself.

Worse, if a man loves himself and learns that suffering is unavoidable, he may even come to take a perverse pleasure in suffering itself, showing that he loves and hates himself at the same time.

In any case, if we love ourselves, suffering inexorably brings out selfishness, and then, after making known what we are, drives us to make ourselves even worse than we are.

If we love others and suffer for them, even without a supernatural love for other men in God, suffering can give us a certain nobility and goodness. It brings out something fine in the nature of man, and gives glory to God Who made man greater than suffering. But in the end a natural unselfishness cannot prevent suffering from destroying us along with all we love.

If we love God and love others in Him, we will be glad to let suffering destroy anything in us that God is pleased to let it destroy, because we know that all it destroys is unimportant. We will prefer to let the accidental trash of life be consumed by suffering in order that His glory may come out clean in everything we do.

If we love God, suffering does not matter. Christ in us, His love, His Passion in us: that is what we care about. Pain does not cease to be pain, but we can be glad of it because it enables Christ to suffer in us and give glory to His Father by being greater, in our hearts, than suffering would ever be.

14. We have said that suffering has value in our lives only when it is consecrated to God. But consecration is a priestly act. Our sufferings then must be consecrated to God by His Church. She alone has power to drown our anguish in the Blood of Christ, for she alone possesses the infinite riches of His Passion and delegates men to exercise His priestly power. She alone has the seven sacraments by which the weakness and poverty of fallen man are transfigured in the death and Resurrection of Jesus.

It would not be enough for the Church to console us in our suffering, and her sacred rites are by no means meant to bring us only comfort.

The wisdom of the Church does, indeed, reach into the remotest corners of our human sensibility, for the Church is supremely human. But she is also divine. She anoints the souls of men with the Holy Spirit, stamping upon them a sacramental character which identifies them with the Crucified Christ, so that they can both suffer with His strength and compassionate the sufferings of others with His mercy.

Baptism makes all men share in the priesthood of Christ by sealing them with the sign of His death, which is our life. It gives them power to offer their sufferings, their good works, their acts of virtue, their courageous faith, their charitable mercy, their life itself to God, not as gifts of their own but as the sufferings, virtues, and merits of Jesus.

But baptism demands to be completed by the Eucharist. The Church has placed this most perfect sacrifice in the hands of her anointed priests, in whom Christ gathers the sufferings and sorrows and good works and joys of mankind to His heart and offers them all to the Father in the renewed sacrifice of His own body and blood.

15. When is suffering useless? When it only turns us in upon ourselves, when it only makes us sorry for ourselves, when it changes love into hatred, when it reduces all things to fear. Useless suffering cannot be consecrated to God because its fruitlessness is rooted in sin. Sin and useless suffering increase together. They encourage one another's growth, and the more suffering leads to sin, the more sin robs suffering of its capacity for fruitful consecration.

But the grace of Christ is constantly working miracles to turn useless suffering into something fruitful after all. How? By suddenly stanching the wound of sin. As soon as our life stops bleeding out of us in sin, suffering begins to have creative possibilities. But until we turn our wills to God, suffering leads nowhere, except to our own destruction.

16. The great duty of the religious soul is to suffer in silence. Too many men think they can become holy by talking about their trials. The awful fuss we sometimes make over the little unavoidable tribulations of life robs them of their fruitfulness. It turns them into occasions for self-pity or self-display, and consequently makes them useless.

Be careful of talking about what you suffer, for fear that you may sin. Job's friends sinned by the pious sententiousness of their explanation of suffering: and they sinned in giving Job a superficial explanation. Sometimes no explanation is sufficient to account for suffering. The only decent thing is silence—and the sacraments. The Church is very humble and very reserved in her treatment of suffering. She is never sanctimonious or patronizing. She is never sentimental. She knows what suffering is.

17. In order to face suffering in peace:

Suffer without imposing on others a theory of suffering, without weaving a new philosophy of life from your own material pain, without proclaiming yourself a martyr, without counting out the price of your courage, without disdaining sympathy and without seeking too much of it.

We must be sincere in our sufferings as in anything else. We must recognize at once our weakness and our pain, but we do not need to advertise them. It is well to realize that we are perhaps unable to suffer in grand style, but we must still accept our weakness with a kind of heroism. It is always difficult to suffer fruitfully and well, and the difficulty is all the greater when we have no human resources to help us. It is well, also, not to tempt God in our sufferings, not to extend ourselves, by pride, into an area where we cannot endure.

We must face the fact that it is much harder to stand the long monotony of slight suffering than a passing onslaught of intense pain. In either case what is hard is our own poverty, and the spectacle of our own selves reduced more and more to nothing, wasting away in our own estimation and in that of our friends.

We must be willing to accept also the bitter truth that, in the end, we may have to become a burden to those who love us. But it is necessary that we face this also. The full acceptance of our abjection and uselessness is the virtue that can make us and others rich in the grace of God. It takes heroic charity and humility to let others sustain us when we are absolutely incapable of sustaining ourselves.

We cannot suffer well unless we see Christ everywhere —both in suffering and in the charity of those who come to the aid of our affliction.

18. In order to give glory to God and overcome suffering with the charity of Christ:

Suffer without reflection, without hate, suffer with no hope of revenge or compensation, suffer without being impatient for the end of suffering.

Neither the beginning of suffering is important nor its ending. Neither the source of suffering is important nor its explanation, provided it be God's will. But we know that He does not will useless, that is to say sinful, suffering. Therefore in order to give Him glory we must be quiet and humble and poor in all that we suffer, so as not to add to our sufferings the burden of a useless and exaggerated sensibility.

In order to suffer without dwelling on our own affliction, we must think about a greater affliction, and turn to Christ on the Cross. In order to suffer without hate we must drive out bitterness from our heart by loving Jesus. In order to suffer without hope of compensation, we should find all our peace in the conviction of our union with Jesus. These things are not a matter of ascetic technique but of simple faith: they mean nothing without prayer, without desire, without the acceptance of God's will.

In the end, we must seek more than a passive acceptance of whatever comes to us from Him, we must desire and seek in all things the positive fulfillment of His will. We must suffer with gratitude, glad of a chance to do His will. And we must find, in this fulfillment, a communion with Jesus, Who said: "With desire have I desired to eat this Pasch with you before I suffer" (Luke 22:15).

6. Asceticism and sacrifice

1. If my soul silences my flesh by an act of violence, my flesh will take revenge on the soul, secretly infecting it with a spirit of revenge. Bitterness and bad temper are the flowers of an asceticism that has punished only the body. For the spirit is above the flesh, but not completely independent of the flesh. It reaps in itself what it sows in its own flesh. If the spirit is weak with the flesh, it will find in the flesh the image and accusation of its own weakness. But if the spirit is violent with the flesh it will suffer, from the flesh, the rebound of its own violence. The false ascetic begins by being cruel to everybody because he is cruel to himself. But he ends by being cruel to everybody but himself.

2. There is only one true asceticism: that which is guided not by our own spirit but by the Spirit of God. The spirit of man must first subject itself to grace and then it can bring the flesh in subjection both to grace and to itself. "If by the Spirit you mortify the deeds of the flesh, you shall live" (Romans 8:13).

But grace is charitable, merciful, kind, does not seek its own interests. Grace inspires us with no desire except to do the will of God, no matter what His will may be, no matter whether it be pleasing or unpleasant to our own nature.

Those, then, who put their passions to death not with the poison of their own ambition but with the clean blade of the will of God will live in the silence of true interior peace, for their lives are hidden with Christ in God. Such is the meek "violence" of those who take Heaven by storm.

3. The spiritual life is not a mere negation of matter. When the New Testament speaks of "the flesh" as our enemy, it takes the flesh in a special sense. When Christ said: "The flesh profiteth nothing" (John 6:64), he was speaking of flesh without spirit, flesh living for its own ends, not only in sensual but even in spiritual things.

It is one thing to live *in* the flesh, and quite another to live *according to* the flesh. In the second case, one acquires that "prudence of the flesh which is opposed to God" because it makes the flesh an end in itself. But as long as we are on this earth our vocation demands that we live spiritually while still "in the flesh."

Our whole being, both body and soul, is to be spiritualized and elevated by grace. The Word Who was made flesh and dwelt among us, Who gave us His flesh to be our spiritual food, Who sits at the right hand of God in a body full of divine glory, and Who will one day raise our bodies also from the dead, did not mean us to despise the body or take it lightly when He told us to deny ourselves. We must indeed control the flesh, we must "chastise it and bring it into subjection," but this chastisement is as much for the body's benefit as for the soul's. For the good of the body is not found in the body alone but in the good of the whole person.

4. The spiritual man, who lives as a son of God, seeks the principle of his life above the flesh and above human nature itself. "As many as received Him, He gave them the power to become the sons of God, to them that believe in His name. Who are born not of blood, nor of the will of the flesh, nor of the will of man, but of God" (John 1:12–13). God Himself, then, is the source of the spiritual life. But He communicates His life and His Spirit to men, made of body and soul. It is not His plan to lure the soul out of the body, but to sanctify the two together, divinizing the whole man so that the Christian can say: "I live, now not I but Christ liveth in me. And that I live now in the flesh, I live in the faith of the Son of God Who loved me" (Galatians 2:20). "That the justification of the law might be fulfilled in us who walk not according to

the flesh but according to the spirit . . . You are not in the flesh but in the Spirit if so be that the Spirit of God dwell in you" (Romans 8:4, 9).

5. We cannot become saints merely by trying to run away from material things. To have a spiritual life is to have a life that is spiritual in all its wholeness—a life in which the actions of the body are holy because of the soul, and the soul is holy because of God dwelling and acting in it. When we live such a life, the actions of our body are directed to God by God Himself and give Him glory, and at the same time they help to sanctify the soul.

The saint, therefore, is sanctified not only by fasting when he should fast but also by eating when he should eat. He is not only sanctified by his prayers in the darkness of the night, but by the sleep that he takes in obedience to God, Who made us what we are. Not only His solitude contributes to his union with God, but also his supernatural love for his friends and his relatives and those with whom he lives and works.

God, in the same infinite act of will, wills the good of all beings and the good of each individual thing: for all lesser goods coincide in the one perfect good which is His love for them. Consequently it is clear that some men will become saints by a celibate life, but many more will become saints as married men, since it is necessary that there be more married men than celibates in the world. How then can we imagine that the cloister is the only place in which men can become saints? Now the life of the body seems to receive less consideration in the cloister than it does in secular life. But it is clear that married life, for its success, presupposes the capacity for a deeply human love which ought to be spiritual and physical at the same time. The existence of a sacrament of matrimony shows that the Church neither considers the body evil nor repugnant, but that the "flesh" spiritualized by prayer and the Holy Ghost, yet remaining completely physical, can come to play an important part in our sanctification.

6. It gives great glory to God for a person to live in this world using and appreciating the good things of life without care, without anxiety, and without inordinate passion. In order to know and love God through His gifts, we have

to use them as if we used them not (I Corinthians 7:31)
—and yet we have to *use* them. For to use things as if we used them not means to use them without selfishness, without fear, without afterthought, and with perfect gratitude and confidence and love of God. All inordinate concern over the material side of life was reproved by Christ when He said: "What one of you, by taking thought, can add to his stature one cubit?" (Matthew 6:27). But we cannot use created things without anxiety unless we are detached from them. At the same time, we become detached from them by using them sparingly—and yet without anxiety.

The tremulous scrupulosity of those who are obsessed with pleasures they love and fear narrows their souls and makes it impossible for them to get away from their own flesh. They have tried to become spiritual by worrying about the flesh, and as a result they are haunted by it. They have ended in the flesh because they began in it, and the fruit of their anxious asceticism is that they "use things not," but do so as if they used them. In their very self-denial they defile themselves with what they pretend to avoid. They do not have the pleasure they seek, but they taste the bitter discouragement, the feeling of guilt which they would like to escape. This is not the way of the spirit. For when our intention is directed to God, our very use of material things sanctifies both them and us, provided we use them without selfishness and without presumption, glad to receive them from Him Who loves us and Whose love is all we desire.

7. Our self-denial is sterile and absurd if we practice it for the wrong reasons or, worse still, without any valid reason at all. Therefore, although it is true that we must deny ourselves in order to come to a true knowledge of God, we must also have some knowledge of God and of our relationship with Him in order to deny ourselves intelligently.

In order to be intelligent, our self-denial must first of all be humble. Otherwise it is a contradiction in terms. If we deny ourselves in order to think ourselves better than other men our self-denial is only self-gratification.

But our renunciation must be more than intelligent and humble. It must also be supernatural. It must be ordered not merely to our own moral perfection or to the good of the society we live in, but to God. Nothing comes to God but what comes from God, and our self-denial cannot be supernatural unless it be guided by the grace of the Holy Spirit. The light of His grace teaches us the distinction between what is good and evil in ourselves, what is from God and what is from ourselves, what is acceptable to God and what merely flatters our own self-esteem. But the Holy Spirit also teaches us the difference between asceticism and sacrifice, and shows us that for a Christian asceticism is not enough.

Asceticism is content systematically to mortify and control our nature. Sacrifice does something more: it offers our nature and all its faculties to God. A self-denial that is truly supernatural must aspire to offer God what we have renounced ourselves. The perfection of Christian renunciation is the total offering of ourselves to God in union with the sacrifice of Christ.

The meaning of this sacrifice of ourselves is that we renounce the dominion of our own acts and of our own life and of our own death into the hands of God so that we do all things not for ourselves or according to our own will and our own desires, but for God, and according to His will.

The spirit of Christian sacrifice is well described in these lines of St. Paul: "None of us liveth to himself, and no man dieth to himself. For whether we live, we live unto the Lord, and whether we die we die unto the Lord. Therefore whether we live or die, we are in the Lord. For to this end Christ died and rose again; that He might be the Lord of the dead and of the living" (Romans 14:7–9).

To offer this sacrifice perfectly we must practice asceticism, without which we cannot gain enough control over our hearts and their passions to reach such a degree of indifference to life and death. But here again, the Holy Spirit teaches us that indifference is not enough. We must indeed become indifferent to the things we have renounced: but this indifference should be the effect of love for God, in whose honor we renounce them. More than an effect, it is really only an aspect of that love.

Because we love God alone, beyond and above all things, and because our love shows us that He infinitely exceeds the goodness of them all, we become indifferent to all that is not God. But at the same time our love enables us to find, in God Himself, the goodness and the reality of all the things we have renounced for His sake. We then see Him Whom we love in the very things we have renounced, and find them again in Him. Although the grace of the Holy Spirit teaches us to use created things "as if we used them not"—that is to say, with detachment and indifference, it does not make us indifferent to the value of the things in themselves. On the contrary, it is only when we are detached from created things that we can begin to value them as we really should. It is only when we are "indifferent" to them that we can really begin to love them. The indifference of which I speak must, therefore, be an indifference not to things themselves but to their effects in our own lives.

The man who loves himself more than God, loves things and persons for the good he himself can get out of them. His selfish love tends to destroy them, to consume them, to absorb them into his own being. His love of them is only one aspect of his own selfishness. It is only a kind of prejudice in his own favor. Such a man is by no means indifferent to the impact of things, persons, and events on his own life. But he is really detached from the good of things and persons themselves, considered quite apart from any good of his own. With respect to the good he gets out of them, he is neither detached nor unconcerned. But with respect to their own good he is completely indifferent.

The man who loves God more than himself is also able to love persons and things for the good that they possess in God. That is the same as saying he loves the glory they give to God: for that glory is the reflection of God in the goodness He has given to His creatures. Such a man is indifferent to the impact of things in his own life. He considers things only in relation to God's glory and God's will. As far as his own temporal advantage and satisfaction go, he is detached and unconcerned. But he is no more indifferent to the value of things in themselves than he is indifferent to God. He loves them in the same act with which he loves God. That is: he loves them in the act by which he has renounced them. And in that love by renouncing them he has regained them on a higher level.

8. To say that Christian renunciation must be ordered to God is to say that it must bear fruit in a deep life of prayer and then in works of active charity. Christian renunciation is not a matter of technical self-denial, beginning and ending within the narrow limits of our own soul. It is the first movement of a liberty which escapes the boundaries of all that is finite and natural and contingent, enters into a contact of charity with the infinite goodness of God, and then goes forth from God to reach all that He loves.

Christian self-denial is only the beginning of a divine fulfillment. It is inseparable from the inward conversion of our whole being from ourselves to God. It is the denial of our unfulfillment, the renunciation of our own poverty, that we may be able to plunge freely into the plenitude and the riches of God and of His creation without looking back upon our own nothingness.

Self-denial delivers us from the passions and from selfishness. It delivers us from a superstitious attachment to our own ego as if it were a god. It delivers us from the "flesh" in the technical New Testament sense, but it does not deliver us from the body. It is no escape from matter or from the senses, nor is it meant to be. It is the first step toward a transformation of our entire being in which, according to the plan of God, even our bodies will live in the light of His divine glory and be transformed in Him together with our souls.

9. Nothing that we consider evil can be offered to God in sacrifice. Therefore, to renounce life in disgust is no sacrifice. We give Him the best we have, in order to declare that He is infinitely better. We give Him all that we prize, in order to assure Him that He is more to us than our "all." One of the chief tasks of Christian asceticism is to make our life and our body valuable enough to be offered to God in sacrifice.

Our asceticism is not supposed to make us weary of a life that is vile. It is not supposed to make our bodies, which are good, appear to us to be evil. It is not supposed to make us odious to ourselves. An asceticism that makes all pleasure seem gross and disgusting and all the activities of the flesh abominable is a perversion of the nature which

God made good and which even sin has not succeeded in rendering totally vile.

The real purpose of asceticism is to disclose the difference between the evil use of created things, which is sin, and their good use, which is virtue. It is true that our self-denial teaches us to realize that sin, which appears to be good from a certain point of view, is really evil. But self-denial should not make us forget the essential distinction between sin, which is a negation, and pleasure, which is a positive good. In fact, it should make that distinction clearly known. True asceticism shows us that there is no necessary connection between sin and pleasure: that there can be sins that seek no pleasure, and other sins that find none.

Pleasure, which is good, has more to do with virtue than it has with sin. The virtue that is sufficiently resolute to pay the price of self-denial will eventually taste greater pleasure in the things it has renounced than could ever be enjoyed by the sinner who clings to those same things as desperately as if they were his god.

We must, therefore, gain possession of ourselves, by asceticism, in order that we may be able to give ourselves to God. No inspiration of the Spirit of God will ever move us to cast off the body as if it were evil, or to destroy its faculties as if they were the implacable enemies of God and could never be educated to obey His grace. He Who made our flesh and gave it to our spirit as its servant and companion, will not be pleased by a sacrifice in which the flesh is murdered by the spirit and returned to Him in ruin.

Yet someone will say that many of the saints did, in fact, walk into God's Heaven upon the ruins of their body. If they did so, and if they were really saints, it was not because their flesh was destroyed by their own spirit but because the love of God, which possessed them, led them into a situation in which the renunciation of health or of life itself was necessary for the sake of some greater good. The sacrifice was both justified and holy. They did not consider their own flesh evil, and destroy it for being so. They knew that it was good and that it came from God, but they knew that charity itself is a greater good than life, and that man has no greater love than that he lay down his life for his friend. It was for the sake of love, for the sake of other men, or for God's truth, that they sacrificed their bodies. For no man can become a saint merely by hating himself. Sanctity is the exact opposite of suicide.

10. There is no such thing as a sacrifice of ourselves that is merely self-destruction. We sacrifice ourselves to God by the spiritualization of our whole being through obedience to His grace. The only sacrifice He accepts is the purity of our love. Any renunciation that helps us to love God more is good and useful. A renunciation that may be noble in itself is useless for us if God does not will us to make it.

In order to spiritualize our lives and make them pleasing to God, we must become quiet. The peace of a soul that is detached from all things and from itself is the sign that our sacrifice is truly acceptable to God.

Bodily agitation agitates the soul. But we cannot tranquilize our spirit by forcing a violent immobility upon the flesh and its five senses. The body must be governed in such a way that it works peacefully, so that its action does not disturb the soul.

Peace of soul does not, therefore, depend on physical inactivity. On the contrary, there are some people who are perfectly capable of tasting true spiritual peace in an active life but who would go crazy if they had to keep themselves still in absolute solitude and silence for any length of time.

It is for each one to find out for himself the kind of work and environment in which he can best lead a spiritual life. If it is possible to find such conditions, and if he is able to take advantage of them, he should do so. But what a hopeless thing the spiritual life would be if it could only be lived under ideal conditions! Such conditions have never been within the reach of most men, and were never more inaccessible than in our modern world. Everything in modern city life is calculated to keep man from entering into himself and thinking about spiritual things. Even with the best of intentions a spiritual man finds himself exhausted and deadened and debased by the constant noise of machines and loudspeakers, the dead air and the glaring lights of offices and shops, the everlasting suggestions of advertising and propaganda. The whole mechanism of modern life is geared for a flight from God and from the spirit into the wilderness of neurosis. Even our monasteries are not free from the smell and clatter of our world.

Bodily agitation, then, is an enemy to the spirit. And by agitation I do not necessarily mean exercise or movement. There is all the difference in the world between agitation and work.

Work occupies the body and the mind and is necessary for the health of the spirit. Work can help us to pray and be recollected if we work properly. Agitation, however, destroys the spiritual usefulness of work and even tends to frustrate its physical and social purpose. Agitation is the useless and ill-directed action of the body. It expresses the inner confusion of a soul without peace. Work brings peace to the soul that has a semblance of order and spiritual understanding. It helps the soul to focus upon its spiritual aims and to achieve them. But the whole reason for agitation is to hide the soul from itself, to camouflage its interior conflicts and their purposelessness, and to induce a false feeling that "we are getting somewhere." Agitation—a condition of spirit that is quite normal in the world of business—is the fruit of tension in a spirit that is turning dizzily from one stimulus to another and trying to react to fifteen different appeals at the same time. Under the surface of agitation, and furnishing it with its monstrous and inexhaustible drive, is the force of fear or elemental greed for money, or pleasure, or power. The more complex a man's passions, the more complex his agitation. All this is the death of the interior life. Occasional churchgoing and the recitation of hasty prayers have no power to cleanse this purulent wound.

No matter what our aims may be, no matter how spiritual, no matter how intent we think we are upon the glory of God and His Kingdom, greed and passion enter into our work and turn it into agitation as soon as our intention ceases to be pure. And who can swear that his intentions are pure, even down to the subconscious depths of his will, where ancient selfish motives move comfortably like forgotten sea monsters in waters where they are never seen!

In order to defend ourselves against agitation, we must be detached not only from the immediate results of our work—and this detachment is difficult and rare—but from the whole complex of aims that govern our earthly lives.

We have to be detached from health and security, from pleasures and possessions, from people and places and conditions and things. We have to be indifferent to life itself, in the Gospel sense, living like the lilies of the field, seeking first the Kingdom of Heaven and trusting that all our material needs will be taken care of into the bargain. How many of us can say, with any assurance, that we have even begun to live like this?

Lacking this detachment, we are subject to a thousand fears corresponding to our thousand anxious desires. Everything we love is uncertain: when we are seeking it, we fear we may not get it. When we have obtained it, we fear even more that it may be lost. Every threat to our security turns our work into agitation. Even a word, even the imagined thought we place in the mind of another, suspecting him of suspecting us—these are enough to turn our day into a millrace of confusion and anxiety and haste and who knows what other worse things besides!

We must, first of all, gain a supernatural perspective, see all things in the light of faith, and then we will begin the long, arduous labor of getting rid of all our irrational fears and desires. Only a relatively spiritual man is able even to begin this work with enough delicacy to avoid becoming agitated in his very asceticism!

11. It is just as easy to become attached to an ascetic technique as to anything else under the sun. But that does not mean we must renounce all thought of being systematic in our self-denial. Let us only be careful to remember that systems are not ends in themselves. They are means to an end. Their proximate end is to bring peace and calm to a detached spirit, to liberate the spirit from its passions, so that we can respond more readily to reason and to divine grace. The ultimate end of all techniques, when they are used in the Christian context, is charity and union with God.

Discipline is not effective unless it is systematic, for the lack of system usually betrays a lack of purpose. Good habits are only developed by repeated acts, and we cannot discipline ourselves to do the same thing over again with any degree of intelligence unless we go about it systematically. It is necessary, above all in the beginning of our spiritual life, to do certain things at fixed times: fasting on certain days, prayer and meditation at definite hours of the day, regular examinations of conscience, regularity in frequenting the sacraments, systematic application to our duties of state, particular attention to virtues which are most necessary for us.

To desire a spiritual life is, thus, to desire discipline. Otherwise our desire is an illusion. It is true that discipline is supposed to bring us, eventually, to spiritual liberty. Therefore our asceticism should make us spiritually flexible, not rigid, for rigidity and liberty never agree. But our discipline must, nevertheless, have a certain element of severity about it. Otherwise it will never set us free from the passions. If we are not strict with ourselves, our own flesh will soon deceive us. If we do not command ourselves severely to pray and do penance at certain definite times, and make up our mind to keep our resolutions in spite of notable inconvenience and difficulty, we will quickly be deluded by our own excuses and let ourselves be led away by weakness and caprice.

12. It is very helpful to have a spiritual director who will guide our efforts in self-discipline, and although direction is not absolutely necessary, in theory, for a sound spiritual life, there are, nevertheless, in practice many men who will never get anywhere without it. Besides the valuable instruction a good director can give us, we also need his encouragement and his corrections. It is much easier to persevere in our penance, meditation, and prayer if we have someone to remind us of the resolutions we have begun to forget. Spiritual direction will protect us, in some measure, against our own instability. The function of the director is to orientate our discipline toward spiritual freedom. It takes a good director to do this, and good directors are rare.

13. Asceticism is utterly useless if it turns us into freaks. The cornerstone of all asceticism is humility, and Christian humility is first of all a matter of supernatural common sense. It teaches us to take ourselves as we are, instead of pretending (as pride would have us imagine) that we are something better than we are. If we really know ourselves we quietly take our proper place in the order designed by God. And so supernatural humility adds much to our human dignity by integrating us in the society of other men and placing us in our right relation to them

and to God. Pride makes us artificial, and humility makes us real.

St. Paul teaches (II Thessalonians 3) that Christian humility and asceticism should normally help us to lead quite ordinary lives, peacefully earning our bread and working from day to day in a world that will pass away. Work and a supernatural acceptance of ordinary life are seen by the Apostle as a protection against the restless agitation of false mysticism. The Christian has rejected all the values of the world. He does not set his heart on temporal security and happiness. But it does not follow that he cannot continue to live in the world, or be happy in time. He works and lives in simplicity, with more joy and greater security than other men, because he does not look for any special fulfillment in this life. He avoids the futile agitation that surrounds the pursuit of purely temporal ends. He lives in peace amid the vanity of transient things. Nor does he merely despise their vanity: for behind the shadow he sees the substance, and creatures speak to him of joy in their Creator. It is supreme humility to see that ordinary life, embraced with perfect faith, can be more saintly and more supernatural than a spectacular ascetical career. Such humility dares to be ordinary, and that is something beyond the reach of spiritual pride. Pride always longs to be unusual. Humility not so. Humility finds all its peace in hope, knowing that Christ must come again to elevate and transfigure ordinary things and fill them with His glory.

14. God is more glorified by a man who uses the good things of this life in simplicity and with gratitude than by the nervous asceticism of someone who is agitated about every detail of his self-denial. The former uses good things and thinks of God. The latter is afraid of good things, and consequently cannot use them properly. He is terrified of the pleasure God has put in things, and in his terror thinks only of himself. He imagines God has placed all the good things of the world before him like a bait in a trap. He worries at all times about his own "perfection." His struggle for perfection becomes a kind of battle of wits with the Creator Who made all things good. The very goodness of creatures becomes a threat to the purity of this virtuous one, who would like to abstain from everything. But he cannot. He is human, like the rest of

men, and must make use like them of food and drink and sleep. Like them he must see the sky, and love, in spite of himself, the light of the sun! Every feeling of pleasure fills him with a sense of guilt. It has besmirched his own adored perfection. Strange that people like this should enter monasteries, which have no other reason for existing than the love of God!

15. All nature is meant to make us think of paradise. Woods, fields, valleys, hills, the rivers and the sea, the clouds traveling across the sky, light and darkness, sun and stars, remind us that the world was first created as a paradise for the first Adam, and that in spite of his sin and ours, it will once again become a pardise when we are all risen from death in the second Adam. Heaven is even now mirrored in created things. All God's creatures invite us to forget our vain cares and enter into our own hearts, which God Himself has made to be His paradise and our own. If we have God dwelling within us, making our souls His paradise, then the world around us can also become for us what it was meant to be for Adam—his paradise. But if we seek paradise outside ourselves, we cannot have paradise in our hearts. If we have no peace within ourselves, we have no peace with what is all around us. Only the man who is free from attachment finds that creatures have become his friends. As long as he is attached to them, they speak to him only of his own desires. Or they remind him of his sins. When he is selfish, they serve his selfishness. When he is pure, they speak to him of God.

16. If we are not grateful to God, we cannot taste the joy of finding Him in His creation. To be ungrateful is to admit that we do not know Him, and that we love His creatures not for His sake but for our own. Unless we are grateful for our own existence, we do not know who we are, and we have not yet discovered what it really means to be and to live. No matter how high an estimate we may have of our own goodness, that estimate is too low unless we realize that all we have comes to us from God.

The only value of our life is that it is a gift of God.

Gratitude shows reverence to God in the way it makes use of His gifts.

7. Being and doing

1. We are warmed by fire, not by the smoke of the fire. We are carried over the sea by a ship, not by the wake of a ship. So too, what we are is to be sought in the invisible depths of our own being, not in our outward reflection in our own acts. We must find our real selves not in the froth stirred up by the impact of our being upon the beings around us, but in our own soul which is the principle of all our acts.

But my soul is hidden and invisible. I cannot see it directly, for it is hidden even from myself. Nor can I see my own eyes. They are too close to me for me to see them. They are not meant to see themselves. I know I have eyes when I see other things with them.

I can see my eyes in a mirror. My soul can also reflect itself in the mirror of its own activity. But what is seen in the mirror is only the reflection of who I am, not my true being. The mirror of words and actions only partly manifests my being.

The words and acts that proceed from myself and are accomplished outside myself are dead things compared with the hidden life from which they spring. These acts are transient and superficial. They are quickly gone, even though their effects may persist for a little while. But the soul itself remains. Much depends on how the soul sees itself in the mirror of its own activity.

2. My soul does not find itself unless it acts. Therefore it must act. Stagnation and inactivity bring spiritual death. But my soul must not project itself entirely into the out-

ward effects of its activity. I do not need to *see* myself, I merely need to *be* myself. I must think and act like a living being, but I must not plunge my whole self into what I think and do, or seek always to find myself in the work I have done. The soul that projects itself entirely into activity, and seeks itself outside itself in the work of its own will is like a madman who sleeps on the sidewalk in front of his house instead of living inside where it is quiet and warm. The soul that throws itself outdoors in order to find itself in the effects of its own work is like a fire that has no desire to burn but seeks only to go up in smoke.

The reason why men are so anxious to see themselves, instead of being content to be themselves, is that they do not really believe in their own existence. And they do not fully believe that they exist because they do not believe in God. This is equally true of those who say they believe in God (without actually putting their faith into practice) and of those who do not even pretend to have any faith.

In either case, the loss of faith has involved at the same time a complete loss of all sense of reality. Being means nothing to those who hate and fear what they themselves are. Therefore they cannot have peace in their own reality (which reflects the reality of God). They must struggle to escape their true being, and verify a false existence by constantly viewing what they themselves do. They have to keep looking in the mirror for reassurance. What do they expect to see? Not themselves! They are hoping for some sign that they have become the god they hope to become by means of their own frantic activity—invulnerable, all powerful, infinitely wise, unbearably beautiful, unable to die!

When a man constantly looks and looks at himself in the mirror of his own acts, his spiritual double vision splits him into two people. And if he strains his eyes hard enough, he forgets which one is real. In fact, reality is no longer found either in himself or in his shadow. The substance has gone out of itself into the shadow, and he has become two shadows instead of one real person.

Then the battle begins. Whereas one shadow was meant to praise the other, now one shadow accuses the other. The activity that was meant to exalt him, reproaches and condemns him. It is never real enough. Never active enough. The less he is able to *be* the more he has to *do*. He becomes his own slave driver—a shadow whipping a shadow to death, because it cannot produce reality, infinitely substantial reality, out of his own nonentity.

Then comes fear. The shadow becomes afraid of the shadow. He who "is not" becomes terrified at the things he cannot do. Whereas for a while he had illusions of infinite power, miraculous sanctity (which he was able to guess at in the mirror of his virtuous actions), now it has all changed. Tidal waves of nonentity, of powerlessness, of hopelessness surge up within him at every action he attempts.

Then the shadow judges and hates the shadow who is not a god, and who can do absolutely nothing.

Self-contemplation leads to the most terrible despair: the despair of a god that hates himself to death. This is the ultimate perversion of man who was made in the image and likeness of the true God, who was made to love eternally and perfectly an infinite good—a good (note this well) which he was to find *dwelling within himself!*

In order to find God in ourselves, we must stop looking at ourselves, stop checking and verifying ourselves in the mirror of our own futility, and be content to *be* in Him and to do whatever He wills, according to our limitations, judging our acts not in the light of our own illusions, but in the light of His reality which is all around us in the things and people we live with.

3. All men seek peace first of all with themselves. That is necessary, because we do not naturally find rest even in our own being. We have to learn to commune with ourselves before we can communicate with other men and with God. A man who is not at peace with himself necessarily projects his interior fighting into the society of those he lives with, and spreads a contagion of conflict all around him. Even when he tries to do good to others his efforts are hopeless, since he does not know how to do good to himself. In moments of wildest idealism he may take it into his head to make other people happy: and in doing so he will overwhelm them with his own unhappiness. He seeks to find himself somehow in the work of making others happy. Therefore he throws himself into the work.

As a result he gets out of the work all that he put into it: his own confusion, his own disintegration, his own unhappiness.

It is useless to try to make peace with ourselves by being pleased with everything we have done. In order to settle down in the quiet of our own being we must learn to be detached from the results of our own activity. We must withdraw ourselves, to some extent, from effects that are beyond our control and be content with the good will and the work that are the quiet expression of our inner life. We must be content to live without watching ourselves live, to work without expecting an immediate reward, to love without an instantaneous satisfaction, and to exist without any special recognition.

It is only when we are detached from ourselves that we can be at peace with ourselves. We cannot find happiness in our work if we are always extending ourselves beyond ourselves and beyond the sphere of our work in order to find ourselves greater than we are.

Our Christian destiny is, in fact, a great one: but we cannot achieve greatness unless we lose all interest in being great. For our own idea of greatness is illusory, and if we pay too much attention to it we will be lured out of the peace and stability of the being God gave us, and seek to live in a myth we have created for ourselves. It is, therefore, a very great thing to be little, which is to say: to be ourselves. And when we are truly ourselves we lose most of the futile self-consciousness that keeps us constantly comparing ourselves with others in order to see how big we are.

4. The fact that our being necessarily demands to be expressed in action should not lead us to believe that as soon as we stop acting we cease to exist. We do not live merely in order to "do something"—no matter what. Activity is just one of the normal expressions of life, and the life it expresses is all the more perfect when it sustains itself with an ordered economy of action. This order demands a wise alternation of activity and rest. We do not live more fully merely by doing more, seeing more, tasting more, and experiencing more than we ever have before. On the contrary, some of us need to discover that we will not begin to live more fully until we have the courage to

do and see and taste and experience much less than usual.

A tourist may go through a museum with a Baedeker, looking conscientiously at everything important, and come out less alive than when he went in. He has looked at everything and seen nothing. He has done a great deal and it has only made him tired. If he had stopped for a moment to look at one picture he really liked and forgotten about all the others, he might console himself with the thought that he had not completely wasted his time. He would have discovered something not only outside himself but in himself. He would have become aware of a new level of being in himself and his life would have been increased by a new capacity for being and for doing.

Our being is not to be enriched merely by activity or experience as such. Everything depends on the *quality* of our acts and our experiences. A multitude of badly performed actions and of experiences only half-lived exhausts and depletes our being. By doing things badly we make ourselves less real. This growing unreality cannot help but make us unhappy and fill us with a sense of guilt. But the purity of our conscience has a natural proportion with the depth of our being and the quality of our acts: and when our activity is habitually disordered, our malformed conscience can think of nothing better to tell us than to multiply the *quantity* of our acts, without perfecting their quality. And so we go from bad to worse, exhaust ourselves, empty our whole life of all content, and fall into despair.

There are times, then, when in order to keep ourselves in existence at all we simply have to sit back for a while and do nothing. And for a man who has let himself be drawn completely out of himself by his activity, nothing is more difficult than to sit still and rest, doing nothing at all. The very act of resting is the hardest and most courageous act he can perform: and often it is quite beyond his power.

We must first recover the possession of our own being before we can act wisely or taste any experience in its human reality. As long as we are not in our own possession, all our activity is futile. If we let all our wine run out of the barrel and down the street, how will our thirst be quenched?

5. The value of our activity depends almost entirely on the humility to accept ourselves as we are. The reason why we do things so badly is that we are not content to do what we can.

We insist on doing what is not asked of us, because we want to taste the success that belongs to somebody else.

We never discover what it is like to make a success of our own work, because we do not want to undertake any work that is merely proportionate to our powers.

Who is willing to be satisfied with a job that expresses all his limitations? He will accept such work only as a "means of livelihood" while he waits to discover his "true vocation." The world is full of unsuccessful businessmen who still secretly believe they were meant to be artists or writers or actors in the movies.

6. The fruitfulness of our life depends in large measure on our ability to doubt our own words and to question the value of our own work. The man who completely trusts his own estimate of himself is doomed to sterility. All he asks of any act he performs is that it be *his* act. If it is performed by him, it must be good. All words spoken by him must be infallible. The car he has just bought is the best for its price, for no other reason than that he is the one who has bought it. He seeks no other fruit than this, and therefore he generally gets no other.

If we believe ourselves in part, we may be right about ourselves. If we are completely taken in by our own disguise, we cannot help being wrong.

7. The measure of our being is not to be sought in the violence of our experiences. Turbulence of spirit is a sign of spiritual weakness. When delights spring out of our depths like leopards we have nothing to be proud of: our soul's life is in danger. For when we are strong we are always much greater than the things that happen to us, and the soul of a man who has found himself is like a deep sea in which there may be many fish: but they never come up out of the sea, and not one of them is big enough to trouble its placid surface. His "being" is far greater than anything he feels or does.

8. The deep secrecy of my own being is often hidden

from me by my own estimate of what I am. My idea of what I am is falsified by my admiration for what I do. And my illusions about myself are bred by contagion from the illusions of other men. We all seek to imitate one another's imagined greatness.

If I do not know who I am, it is because I think I am the sort of person everyone around me wants to be. Perhaps I have never asked myself whether I really wanted to become what everybody else seems to want to become. Perhaps if I only realized that I do not admire what everyone seems to admire, I would really begin to live after all. I would be liberated from the painful duty of saying what I really do not think and of acting in a way that betrays God's truth and the integrity of my own soul.

Why do we have to spend our lives striving to be something that we would never want to be, if we only knew what we wanted? Why do we waste our time doing things which, if we only stopped to think about them, are just the opposite of what we were made for?

We cannot be ourselves unless we know ourselves. But self-knowledge is impossible when thoughtless and automatic activity keeps our souls in confusion. In order to know ourselves it is not necessary to cease all activity in order to think about ourselves. That would be useless, and would probably do most of us a great deal of harm. But we have to cut down our activity to the point where we can think calmly and reasonably about our actions. We cannot begin to know ourselves until we can see the real reasons why we do the things we do, and we cannot be ourselves until our actions correspond to our intentions, and our intentions are appropriate to our own situation. But that is enough. It is not necessary that we succeed in everything. A man can be perfect and still reap no fruit from his work, and it may happen that a man who is able to accomplish very little is much more of a person than another who seems to accomplish very much.

9. A man who fails well is greater than one who succeeds badly.

One who is content with what he has, and who accepts the fact that he inevitably misses very much in life, is far better off than one who has much more but who worries about all he may be missing. For we cannot make the best of what we are, if our hearts are always divided between what we are and what we are not.

The lower our estimate of ourselves and the lower our expectations, the greater chance we have of using what we have. If we do not know how poor we are we will never be able to appreciate what we actually have. But, above all, we must learn our own weakness in order to awaken to a new order of action and of being—and experience God Himself accomplishing in us the things we find impossible.

We cannot be happy if we expect to live all the time at the highest peak of intensity. Happiness is not a matter of intensity but of balance and order and rhythm and harmony.

Music is pleasing not only because of the sound but because of the silence that is in it: without the alternation of sound and silence there would be no rhythm. If we strive to be happy by filling all the silences of life with sound, productive by turning all life's leisure into work, and real by turning all our being into doing, we will only succeed in producing a hell on earth.

If we have no silence, God is not heard in our music. If we have no rest, God does not bless our work. If we twist our lives out of shape in order to fill every corner of them with action and experience, God will silently withdraw from our hearts and leave us empty.

Let us, therefore, learn to pass from one imperfect activity to another without worrying too much about what we are missing. It is true that we make many mistakes. But the biggest of them all is to be surprised at them: as if we had some hope of never making any.

Mistakes are part of our life, and not the least important part. If we are humble, and if we believe in the Providence of God, we will see that our mistakes are not merely a necessary evil, something we must lament and count as lost: they enter into the very structure of our existence. It is by making mistakes that we gain experience, not only for ourselves but for others. And though our experience prevents neither ourselves nor others from making the same mistake many times, the repeated experience still has a positive value.

10. We cannot avoid missing the point of almost everything we do. But what of it? Life is not a matter of getting

something out of everything. Life itself is imperfect. All created beings begin to die as soon as they begin to live, and no one expects any one of them to become absolutely perfect, still less to stay that way. Each individual thing is only a sketch of the specific perfection planned for its kind. Why should we ask it to be anything more?

If we are too anxious to find absolute perfection in created things we cease to look for perfection where alone it can be found: in God. The secret of the imperfection of all things, of their inconstancy, their fragility, their falling into nothingness, is that they are only a shadowy expression of the one Being from Whom they receive their being. If they were absolutely perfect and changeless in themselves, they would fail in their vocation, which is to give glory to God by their contingency.

It was the desire to "be as gods"—changelessly perfect in their own being—that led Adam and Eve to taste the fruit of the forbidden tree. What could be duller than an immutable man and an unchanging woman, eternally the same! As long as we are on earth our vocation is precisely to be imperfect, incomplete, insufficient in ourselves, changing, hapless, destitute, and weak, hastening toward the grave. But the power of God and His eternity and His peace and His completeness and His glory must somehow find their way into our lives, secretly, while we are here, in order that we may be found in Him eternally as He has meant us to be. And in Him, in our eternity, there will be no change in the sense of corruption, but there will be unending variety, newness of life, progression in His infinite depth. There, rest and action will not alternate, they will be one. Everything will be at once empty and full. But only if we have discovered how to combine emptiness and fullness, good will and indifferent results, mistakes and successes, work and rest, suffering and joy, in such a way that all things work together for our good and for the glory of God.

The relative perfection which we must attain to in this life if we are to live as sons of God is not the twenty-four-hour-a-day production of perfect acts of virtue, but a life from which practically all the obstacles to God's love have been removed or overcome.

One of the chief obstacles to this perfection of selfless charity is the selfish anxiety to get the most out of everything, to be a brilliant success in our own eyes and in the eyes of other men. We can only get rid of this anxiety by being content to miss something in almost everything we do. We cannot master everything, taste everything, understand everything, drain every experience to its last dregs. But if we have the courage to let almost everything else go, we will probably be able to retain the one thing necessary for us—whatever it may be. If we are too eager to have everything, we will almost certainly miss even the one thing we need.

Happiness consists in finding out precisely what the "one thing necessary" may be, in our lives, and in gladly relinquishing all the rest. For then, by a divine paradox, we find that everything else is given us together with the one thing we needed.

8. Vocation

1. Each one of us has some kind of vocation. We are all called by God to share in His life and in His Kingdom. Each one of us is called to a special place in the Kingdom. If we find that place we will be happy. If we do not find it, we can never be completely happy. For each one of us, there is only one thing necessary: to fulfill our own destiny, according to God's will, to be what God wants us to be.

We must not imagine that we only discover this destiny by a game of hide-and-seek with Divine Providence. Our vocation is not a sphinx's riddle, which we must solve in one guess or else perish. Some people find, in the end, that they have made many wrong guesses and that their paradoxical vocation is to go through life guessing wrong. It takes them a long time to find out that they are happier that way.

In any case, our destiny is the work of two wills, not one. It is not an immutable fate, forced upon us without any choice of our own, by a divinity without heart.

Our vocation is not a supernatural lottery but the interaction of two freedoms, and, therefore, of two loves. It is hopeless to try to settle the problem of vocation outside the context of friendship and of love. We speak of Providence: that is a philosophical term. The Bible speaks of our Father in Heaven. Providence is, consequently, more than an institution, it is a person. More than a benevolent stranger, He is our Father. And even the term Father is too loose a metaphor to contain all the depths of the mystery: for He loves us more than we love ourselves, as if we were Himself. He loves us moreover with our own wills, with our own decisions. How can we understand the mystery of our union with God Who is closer to us than we are to ourselves? It is His very closeness that makes it difficult for us to think of Him. He Who is infinitely above us, infinitely different from ourselves, infinitely "other" from us, nevertheless dwells in our souls, watches over every movement of our life with as much love as if we were His own self. His love is at work bringing good out of all our mistakes and defeating even our sins.

In planning the course of our lives, we must remember the importance and the dignity of our own freedom. A man who fears to settle his future by a good act of his own free choice does not understand the love of God. For our freedom is a gift God has given us in order that He may be able to love us more perfectly, and be loved by us more perfectly in return.

2. Love is perfect in proportion to its freedom. It is free in proportion to its purity. We act most freely when we act purely in response to the love of God. But the purest love of God is not servile, not blind, not limited by fear. Pure charity is fully aware of the power of its own freedom. Perfectly confident of being loved by God, the soul that loves Him dares to make a choice of its own, knowing that its own choice will be acceptable to love.

At the same time pure love is prudent. It is enlightened with a clear-sighted discretion. Trained in freedom, it knows how to avoid the selfishness that frustrates its action. It sees obstacles and avoids or overcomes them. It is keenly sensitive to the smallest signs of God's will and good pleasure in the circumstances of its own life, and its freedom is conditioned by the knowledge of all these. Therefore, in choosing what will please God, it takes account of all the slightest indications of His will. Yet if we add all these indications together, they seldom suffice to give us absolute certitude that God wills one thing to the exclusion of every other. He Who loves us means by this to leave us room for our own freedom, so that we may dare to choose for ourselves, with no other certainty than that His love will be pleased by our intention to please Him.

3. Every man has a vocation to *be* someone: but he must understand clearly that in order to fulfill this vocation he can only be one person: himself.

Yet we have said that baptism gives us a sacramental character, defining our vocation in a very particular way since it tells us we must become ourselves in Christ. We must achieve our identity in Him, with whom we are already sacramentally identified by water and the Holy Spirit.

What does this mean? We must be ourselves by being Christ. For a man, to be is to live. A man only lives as a man when he knows truth and loves what he knows and acts according to what he loves. In this way he *becomes* the truth that he loves. So we "become" Christ by knowledge and by love.

Now there is no fulfillment of man's true vocation in the order of nature. Man was made for more truth than he can see with his own unaided intelligence, and for more love than his will alone can achieve and for a higher moral activity than human prudence ever planned.

The prudence of the flesh is opposed to the will of God. The works of the flesh will bury us in hell. If we know and love and act only according to the flesh, that is to say, according to the impulses of our own nature, the things we do will rapidly corrupt and destroy our whole spiritual being.

In order to be what we are meant to be, we must know Christ, and love Him, and do what He did. Our destiny is in our own hands since God has placed it there, and given us His grace to do the impossible. It remains for us to take up courageously and without hesitation the work He has given us, which is the task of living our own life as Christ would live it in us.

It takes intrepid courage to live according to the truth, and there is something of martyrdom in every truly Christian life, if we take martyrdom in its original sense as a "testimony" to the truth, sealed in our own sufferings and in our blood.

4. Being and doing become one, in our life, when our

life and being themselves are a "martyrdom" for the truth. In this way we identify ourselves with Christ, Who said: "For this was I born, and for this came I into the world; that I should give testimony to the truth" (John 18:36). Our vocation is precisely this: to bear witness to the truth of Christ by laying down our lives at His bidding. Therefore, He added to the words we have just quoted: "Everyone that is of the truth, heareth my voice." And in another place He said: "I know my sheep, and they know me" (John 10:14).

This testimony need not take the special form of a political and public death in defense of Christian truth or virtue. But we cannot avoid the "death" of our own will, of our own natural tendencies, of the inordinate passions of our flesh and of our whole selfish "being," in order to submit ourselves to what our own conscience tells us to be the truth and the will of God and the inspiration of the Spirit of Christ.

5. Therefore asceticism is unavoidable in Christian life. We cannot escape the obligation to deny ourselves. This obligation is made inevitable by the fact that the truth cannot live in us unless we freely and by our own volition recognize and cast out the falsity of sin from our own souls.

This is the one job that we alone can do, and we must have the courage to do it if we wish to live as we were meant to live, and find our true being in God. No one else can turn our minds to the truth, renounce error for us, convert our wills from selfishness to charity and from sin to God. The example and the prayers of others may help us to find our way in this work. But we alone can do it.

It is true that God is the One Who produces in our hearts both our good desires and their effect, "for it is God who worketh in you both to will and to accomplish, according to His good will" (Philippians 2:13). Nevertheless, if we do not ourselves freely desire and manfully carry out His will, His grace will be without effect: since the effect of grace is to make us freely do His will.

Consequently, the truth of God lives in our souls more by the power of superior moral courage than by the light of an eminent intelligence. Indeed, spiritual intelligence itself depends on the fortitude and patience with which we sacrifice ourselves for the truth, as it is communicated to our lives concretely in the providential will of God.

6. The importance of courageous sacrifice, in accomplishing our work of finding and witnessing to the truth, cannot be overemphasized. It is all-important. We cannot possess the truth fully until it has entered into the very substance of our life by good habits and by a certain perfection of moral activity. And we cannot act so without a terrible struggle against temptation, a struggle that divides our whole being against itself with conflicting loyalties. The greatest temptations are not those that solicit our consent to obvious sin, but those that offer us great evils masking as the greatest goods.

These apparent goods must be *sacrificed precisely as goods* before we can tell accurately whether they are good or evil. What is more, the things we are called upon to sacrifice may indeed remain perfectly good in themselves. That does not mean that our sacrifice of them is vain, or that we can take them back as soon as we have seen they are not evil. No: the fulfillment of every individual vocation demands not only the renouncement of what is evil in itself, but also *of all the precise goods that are not willed for us by God.*

It takes exceptional courage and integrity to make such a sacrifice. We cannot do it unless we are really seeking to do the will of God for His sake alone. The man who is content to keep from disobeying God, and to satisfy his own desires wherever there is nothing to prevent him from doing so, may indeed lead a life that is not evil: but his life will remain a sad confusion of truth and falsity and he will never have the spiritual vision to tell one clearly from the other. He will never fully live up to his vocation.

7. Our Father in Heaven has called us each one to the place in which He can best satisfy His infinite desire to do us good. His inscrutable choice of the office or the state of life or particular function to which we are called is not to be judged by the intrinsic merit of those offices and states but only by the hidden love of God. My vocation is the one I love, not because I think it is the best vocation in the Church, but because it is the one God has

willed for me. If I had any evidence that He willed something else for me, I would turn to that on the instant. Meanwhile, my vocation is at once my will and His. I did not enter it blindly. He chose it for me when His inscrutable knowledge of my choice moved me to choose it for myself. I know this well enough when I reflect on the days when no choice could be made. I was unable to choose until His time had come. Since the choice has been made, there have been no signs in favor of changing it, and the presumption is that there will be no change. That does not mean there *cannot* be a change.

8. If we are called to the place in which God wills to do us the most good, it means we are called where we can best leave ourselves and find Him. The mercy of God demands to be known and recognized and set apart from everything else and praised and adored in joy. Every vocation is, therefore, at once a vocation to sacrifice and to joy. It is a call to the knowledge of God, to the recognition of God as our Father, to joy in the understanding of His mercy. Our individual vocation is our opportunity to find that one place in which we can most perfectly receive the benefits of divine mercy, and know God's love for us, and reply to His love with our whole being.

That does not mean that our individual vocation selects for us a situation in which God will become visible to the eyes of our human nature and accessible to the feelings of our heart of flesh. On the contrary, if we are called where we will find Him we must go where flesh and blood will lose Him, for flesh and blood cannot possess the Kingdom of God (I Corinthians 15:50). God sometimes gives Himself to us where He seems to be taken away.

9. If I am called to the solitary life it does not necessarily mean that I will suffer more acutely in solitude than anywhere else: but that I will suffer more effectively. And for the rest, I will find there a greater joy because I shall know God in my sacrifice. In order to do this, I will not be too much aware of myself or of my sacrifice.

And there I will be most free to praise Him, even though my praise may be lowly and inarticulate and unworthy and poor. It will be most free, most mine, most Christ's. It will be the praise He seeks from me.

One who is not called to solitude will lose sight of God when he is alone and become troubled and turn upon himself in anxiety and in the end will become imprisoned in himself, unable to thank God or praise Him or do anything at all. He will have to look for Him somewhere else.

We know when we are following our vocation when our soul is set free from preoccupation with itself and is able to seek God and even to find Him, even though it may not appear to find Him. Gratitude and confidence and freedom from ourselves: these are signs that we have found our vocation and are living up to it even though everything else may seem to have gone wrong. They give us peace in any suffering. They teach us to laugh at despair. And we may have to.

10. There is something in the depths of our being that hungers for wholeness and finality. Because we are made for eternal life, we are made for an act that gathers up all the powers and capacities of our being and offers them simultaneously and forever to God. The blind spiritual instinct that tells us obscurely that our own lives have a particular importance and purpose, and which urges us to find out our vocation, seeks in so doing to bring us to a decision that will dedicate our lives irrevocably to their true purpose. The man who loses this sense of his own personal destiny, and who renounces all hope of having any kind of vocation in life has either lost all hope of happiness or else has entered upon some mysterious vocation that God alone can understand.

Most human vocations tend to define their purpose not only by placing the one called in a definite relation to God, but also by giving him a set place among his fellow men. The vocation of each one of us is fixed just as much by the need others have for us as by our own need for other men and for God. Yet when I speak here of a need, I do not mean to exclude the untrammeled exercise of spiritual freedom. If I am called to the priesthood, it may be because the Church has need of priests and, therefore, that she has need of me. And it may also happen that my own peace and spiritual balance and the happiness of my whole life may ultimately depend on my becoming a priest. But the Church is not determined to accept me as a priest simply because she needs priests, nor am I forced to become a priest by the pressure of my own spiritual condition.

The freedom that is exercised in the choice of priestly vocations is a mystery hidden in God, a mystery that reaches out of the obscurity of God's Providence to select, sometimes, unlikely men to be "other Christs" and sometimes to reject those who are, in the eyes of men, best fitted for such a vocation.

11. What is the function of a priest in the world? To teach other men? To advise them? To console them? To pray for them? These things enter into his life, but they can be done by anyone. Every man in the world is called to teach and to advise and to console some other man, and we are all bound to pray for one another that we may be saved. These actions require no special priesthood, other than our baptismal participation in the priesthood of Christ, and they can be exercised even without this. Nor is the priest's distinctive vocation simply that he must be a man of God. The monk is a man of God and he does not have to be a priest.

The priest is called to be another Christ in a far more particular and intimate sense than the ordinary Christian or the monk. He must keep alive in the world the sacramental presence and action of the Risen Savior. He is a visible human instrument of the Christ Who reigns in Heaven, Who teaches and sanctifies and governs the Church through His anointed priests. The words of the priest are not to be merely his own words or his own doctrine. They should always be the doctrine of the One Who sent him. The action of the priest upon souls should come from something more than his own poor human power to advise and to console. Human though his acts may be, poor and deficient in themselves, they must be supported by the sacramental action of Jesus Christ and vivified by the hidden working of the Divine Spirit.

The priest is just as much sanctified by the actions he performs in the course of his sacred ministry as are those souls for whom he performs them. The Mass is, indeed, normally more fruitful for the priest who celebrates it than for any of those who assist at it. Indeed, one might say that the priest's holiness should be as great as the cumulative holiness of all those to whom he administers the sacraments. In any case, his vocation is to keep alive in the world the sanctity and the sanctifying power of the One High Priest, Jesus Christ.

This explains at once the beauty and the terror of the priestly vocation. A man, weak as other men, imperfect as they are, perhaps less well endowed than many of those to whom he is sent, perhaps even less inclined to be virtuous than some of them, finds himself caught, without possibility of escape, between the infinite mercy of Christ and the almost infinite dreadfulness of man's sin. He cannot help but feel in the depths of his heart something of Christ's compassion for sinners, something of the eternal Father's hatred of sin, something of the inexpressible love that drives the Spirit of God to consume sin in the fires of sacrifice. At the same time he may feel in himself all the conflicts of human weakness and irresolution and dread, the anguish of uncertainty and helplessness and fear, the inescapable lure of passion. All that he hates in himself becomes more hateful to him, by reason of his close union with Christ. But also by reason of his very vocation he is forced to face resolutely the reality of sin in himself and in others. He is bound by his vocation to fight this enemy. He cannot avoid the battle. And it is a battle that he alone can never win. He is forced to let Christ Himself fight the enemy in him. He must do battle on the ground chosen not by himself but by Christ. That ground is the hill of Calvary and the Cross. For, to speak plainly, the priest makes no sense at all in the world except to perpetuate in it the sacrifice of the Cross, and to die with Christ on the Cross for the love of those whom God would have him save.

12. Then there is the monastic vocation.

If the priest can be in some sense defined by other men's need of his sanctifying action in the world, this is less obviously true of the monk. For although it is true that the presence of every holy man in the world exercises a sanctifying effect, the monk does not exist precisely in order that others may be holy.

That is why it would be a mistake to assume that the

essence of the monastic vocation is public prayer. The monk does, indeed, pray for other men and for the whole Church. But that is not the sole or even the main reason for his existence. Still less does the monk justify his existence by teaching, by writing, by the study of Scripture or of Gregorian chant, or by farming and raising cattle. There are plenty of cows in the world without monks to raise them.

It is true that the monastic vocation bears witness to the infinite transcendence of God, because it proclaims to the whole world that God has a right to call some men apart in order that they may live for Him alone. But in entering the monastery the monk should think of something more than this. Indeed, it would not be good for him to be too conscious of the fact that his sacrifice may still have some meaning to other men. If he dwells too long on the fact that the world remembers him, his very consciousness will re-establish the ties that he is supposed to have cut beyond recovery. For the essence of the monastic vocation is precisely this leaving of the world and all its desires and ambitions and concerns in order to live not only for God, but by Him and in Him, not for a few years but forever.

The one thing that most truly makes a monk what he is, is this irrevocable break with the world and all that is in it, in order to seek God in solitude.

The world itself is even quicker to realize this fact than the monk who allows the purity of his vocation to be tarnished by concessions to the secular spirit. The first ones to condemn the monastery that has become infected with worldliness are those who, in the world, are themselves least monastic, for even those who have abandoned their religion often retain a high and exacting idea of religious perfection. St. Benedict saw that it was a matter of primary importance for the monk to "become a stranger to the ways of this world"—*a saeculi actibus se facere alienum*. But in establishing this principle, the Father of Western Monasticism was not simply thinking of public edification. He was thinking of the most urgent need of the monk's own soul.

13. The grace that calls a man to the monastery demands more than a physical change of environment. There is

no genuine monastic vocation that does not imply, at the same time, a complete interior conversion. This conversion can never be effected merely by a change of clothing or by the adoption of a stricter rule of life.

The habit does not make the monk, and neither do observances. The essential characteristic of a monastic vocation is that it draws the monk into solitude, to a life of self-renunciation and of prayer, in order to seek God alone. Where these features are not found, the vocation may, indeed, be a religious one, but it is not, properly speaking, monastic. It is a pity that monasteries of the ancient monastic Orders sometimes offer their subjects a life in which these elements are realized only in theory and not in fact.

Where the essentials of the monastic life are maintained, it matters little what accidental variations may be added to it. A monastic community can be physically and spiritually isolated from the world, can offer its monks a true life of prayer, and can at the same time maintain a school or some parishes without serious danger to the monastic spirit as it is interpreted by some branches of the Benedictine family. In the same way, the monastic life need not be disturbed by the presence of a small and well-ordered industry, carried on by the monks for their own support. But if the spirit of solitude and prayer, and the exclusive love of God alone are not found in a monastery, it makes no difference how strict the rule may be, how inviolate the enclosure, how zealous the exterior zeal for liturgical functions: the men who live there are not really monks. The interior change, the *metanoia*, the turning to God which constitutes the very essence of the monastic calling, has not taken place in their souls.

14. The interior "conversion" that makes a monk will usually show itself outwardly in certain ways: obedience, humility, silence, detachment, modesty. All of these can be summed up in the one word: *peace*.

The monastery is a house of God: therefore, a sanctuary of peace. True, this peace is bought at a price. It is not the tranquillity of a rich man's country home. It is the peace of poor men who are supernaturally content with their poverty, not because it delivers them from the worries and responsibilities of the world, nor yet because it helps them to lead a life that is essentially healthier and better balanced than the life of the world: but because it inexplicably puts them in possession of the God of all peace.

The peace of the monastic life is not to be accounted for by a natural and human explanation. Enter a monastery and see the life close at hand. You will find that what looks so perfect from the windows of the guest house is in reality full of the seams and cracks of human imperfection. The tempo of community life is not invariably serene. The order of the day can sometimes become unbalanced, surcharged, distracting as well as exhausting. Usages and observances are sometimes twisted into ridiculous formalities. There are moments when everything in the monastery seems to conspire to make peace and prayer impossible. These things inevitably ripple the surface of life in the best of communities. Their function is to remind us that the peace of the monks depends, ultimately, on something deep and hidden in their own souls. Monastic regularity is certainly most important in preserving peace. If regularity were to be lost forever, peace could not last long. But even where the life goes on according to rule, the rule alone is not sufficient to explain the peace of those who live by it. We must look deeper into the mystery of faith by which, in the secret recesses of their souls, the monks remain in possession of God no matter what may happen to disturb the surface of their lives.

The monastic life burns before the invisible God like a lamp before a tabernacle. The wick of the lamp is faith, the flame is charity, and the oil, by which the flame is fed, is self-sacrifice.

15. The monastic Orders are, of all religious Orders, the ones with the most ancient and the most monumental traditions. To be called to the monastic life is to be called to a way of sanctity that is rooted in the wisdom of the distant past, and yet is living and young, with something peculiarly new and original to say to the men of our own time. One cannot become a monk in the fullest sense of the word unless one's soul is attuned to the transforming and life-giving effect of the monastic tradition. And if this is true everywhere, it is especially true in America—a coun-

try in which men are not used to ancient traditions, and are not often ready to understand them.

What is the monastic tradition? It is the whole monastic way of life as it has been practiced and handed down from generation to generation since the times of the first monks, the Fathers of the Egyptian desert, who in their turn felt that they were simply putting into practice the poverty and charity of the Apostles and first disciples of Christ. The monastic tradition is, therefore, a body of customs and attitudes and beliefs which sum up the whole wisdom of the monastic way of life. It tells the monk how to be a monk in the simplest and most effective way—the way in which monks have always been monks. But at the same time it tells him how to be a monk in the peculiar circumstances of his own time and place and culture.

Monastic tradition tells us for example what place prayer, reading, and work have in our lives. It shows us that hospitality is an important aspect of the monastic vocation. It teaches us that we must be men of penance and self-discipline, yet at the same time it teaches us the proper measure and discretion to be followed in all these things. It shows us clearly the relative unimportance of exterior observance when it is compared with the interior spirit and the real essentials of the monastic life. In a word, it sets everything in order in the monastic life.

Where the sense of monastic tradition is lacking, monks immediately begin to lead unbalanced lives. They are unable to learn true discretion. They cannot acquire a sense of proportion. They forget what they are supposed to be. They are not able to settle down and live at peace in the monastery. They cannot get along with their superiors or their brethren. Why do all these things happen? Because the monks who have never learned how to be real monks are driving themselves crazy trying to live the monastic life with the spirit and the methods appropriate to some other kind of life. Only a true sense of monastic tradition can preserve sanity and peace in monasteries. But this sense is not acquired automatically, especially in a monastery that has little or no sense of tradition. It must be learned. And it cannot be learned without direct contact with the channels of life through which it comes. That is why St. Benedict urged his own monks to read Cassian, St. Basil, and the Desert Fathers. But the reading of ancient monastic books is only one of these channels, and by no means the most important. The only way to become a monk is to live among real monks, and to learn the life from their example.

16. In this matter of monastic tradition, we must carefully distinguish between tradition and convention. In many monasteries there is very little living tradition, and yet the monks think themselves to be traditional. Why? Because they cling to an elaborate set of *conventions*. Convention and tradition may seem on the surface to be much the same thing. But this superficial resemblance only makes conventionalism all the more harmful. In actual fact, conventions are the death of real tradition as they are of all real life. They are parasites which attach themselves to the living organism of tradition and devour all its reality, turning it into a hollow formality.

Tradition is living and active, but convention is passive and dead. Tradition does not form us automatically: we have to work to understand it. Convention is accepted passively, as a matter of routine. Therefore convention easily becomes an evasion of reality. It offers us only pretended ways of solving the problems of living—a system of gestures and formalities. Tradition really teaches us to live and shows us how to take full responsibility for our own lives. Thus tradition is often flatly opposed to what is ordinary, to what is mere routine. But convention, which is a mere repetition of familiar routines, follows the line of least resistance. One goes through an act, without trying to understand the meaning of it all, merely because everyone else does the same. Tradition, which is always old, is at the same time ever new because it is always reviving—born again in each new generation, to be lived and applied in a new and particular way. Convention is simply the ossification of social customs. The activities of conventional people are merely excuses for *not* acting in a more integrally human way. Tradition nourishes the life of the spirit; convention merely disguises its interior decay.

Finally, tradition is creative. Always original, it always opens out new horizons for an old journey. Convention, on the other hand, is completely unoriginal. It is slavish imitation. It is closed in upon itself and leads to complete sterility.

Tradition teaches us how to love, because it develops and expands our powers, and shows us how to give ourselves to the world in which we live, in return for all that we have received from it. Convention breeds nothing but anxiety and fear. It cuts us off from the sources of all inspiration. It ruins our productivity. It locks us up within a prison of frustrated effort. It is, in the end, only the mask for futility and for despair. Nothing could be better than for a monk to live and grow up in his monastic tradition, and nothing could be more fatal than for him to spend his life tangled in a web of monastic conventions.

What has been said here of the monastic Orders applies even more strongly to some other forms of religious life in which tradition is less strong and convention can more easily hold sway.

17. We would be better able to understand the beauty of the religious vocation if we remembered that marriage too is a vocation. The religious life is a special way of sanctity, reserved for comparatively few. The ordinary way to holiness and to the fullness of Christian life is marriage. Most men and women will become saints in the married state. And yet so many Christians who are not called to religious life or to the priesthood say of themselves: "I have no vocation!" What a mistake! They have a wonderful vocation, all the more wonderful because of its relative freedom and lack of formality. For the "society" which is the family lives beautifully by its own spontaneous inner laws. It has no need of codified rule and custom. Love is its rule, and all its customs are the living expression of deep and sincere affection. In a certain sense, the vocation to the married state is more desirable than any other, because of the fact that this spontaneity, this spirit of freedom and union in charity is so easily accessible, for the ordinary man, in family life. The formalism and artificiality which creep into religious communities are with difficulty admitted into the circle of a family where powerful human values triumphantly resist the incursions of falsity.

Married people, then, instead of lamenting their supposed "lack of vocation," should highly value the vocation they have actually received. They should thank God for the fact that this vocation, with all its responsibilities and hardships, is a safe and sure way to become holy without being warped or shriveled up by pious conventionalism. The married man and the mother of a Christian family, if they are faithful to their obligations, will fulfill a mission that is as great as it is consoling: that of bringing into the world and forming young souls capable of happiness and love, souls capable of sanctification and transformation in Christ. Living in close union with God the Creator and source of life, they will understand better than others the mystery of His infinite fecundity, in which it is their privilege to share. Raising children in difficult social circumstances, they will enter perhaps more deeply into the mystery of divine Providence than others who, by their vow of poverty, ought ideally to be more directly dependent on God than they, but who in fact are never made to feel the anguish of insecurity.

18. All vocations are intended by God to manifest His love in the world. For each special calling gives a man some particular place in the Mystery of Christ, gives him something to do for the salvation of all mankind. The difference between the various vocations lies in the different ways in which each one enables men to discover God's love, appreciate it, respond to it, and share it with other men. Each vocation has for its aim the propagation of divine life in the world.

In marriage, God's love is made known and shared under the sacramentalized veils of human affection. The vocation to marriage is a vocation to a supernatural union which sanctifies and propagates human life and extends the Kingdom of God in the world by bringing forth children who will be members of the Mystical Christ. All that is most human and instinctive, all that is best in man's natural affections is here consecrated to God and becomes a sign of divine love and an occasion of divine grace.

In married life, divine love is more fully incarnate than in the other vocations. For that reason it is easier to apprehend, easier to appreciate. But its extension, being less spiritual, is less wide. The sphere of action of the father and mother's love extends only to their own children and to their relatives and to a circle of friends and associates.

In order to extend the effectiveness of divine charity, the other vocations progressively spiritualize our human lives and actions in order to spread them over a wider and wider area. So, in the active religious life or in the secular priesthood the physical expression of human love is sacrificed, family life is given up, and the potentialities of love thus set free are extended to a whole parish or to a hospital or a school. In the active life instinctive human affections are consecrated to God more fully than in family life, and in a less incarnate fashion. But it is nevertheless still easy to see and appreciate the action of God's love in the corporal works of mercy—care of the sick and the poor, as well as in the tender care of homeless children, of the aged, and so on. Here too the labors and difficulties and sacrifices of the life bring with them a corresponding protection of human values in the soul of the one "called." In dealing with other people, one retains one's sense of relatedness and integration.

In the contemplative life the problems and difficulties are more interior and also much greater. Here divine love is less incarnate. We must apprehend it and respond to it in a still more spiritual way. Fidelity is much more difficult. The human affections do not receive much of their normal gratification in a life of silence and solitude. The almost total lack of self-expression, the frequent inability to "do things for" other people in a visible and tangible way can sometimes be a torture and lead to great frustration. That is why the purely contemplative vocation is not for the immature. One has to be very strong and very solid to live in solitude.

Fortunately, the monastic life is not so purely contemplative that it does not provide for a certain amount of activity and self-expression. Living and working together in the monastic community, the monks normally preserve their sense of relatedness and do not lose their humanity. On the contrary, if they are faithful to the spirit of their rule, they will find human affection deepened and spiritualized into a profound union of charity which is no longer dependent on personal moods and fancies. And then they will come to realize something of their mission to embrace the whole world in a spiritual affection that is not limited in time or in space.

19. The higher one ascends in the scale of vocations the more careful the selection of the candidates must be. Nor-

mally, in the married life, selection takes care of itself: the will of God can be incarnate in a decision based on natural attraction. In the active life attraction and aptitude normally go together, and the one "called" can be accepted on the basis of his ability to do the required work in peace and with spiritual joy.

Normally, more than half the people who present themselves for admission to contemplative monasteries have no vocation. "Attraction" to the contemplative life is a much less serious criterion of vocation than attraction to the active life. The stricter and more solitary a contemplative Order may be, the greater will be the gap between "attraction" and "aptitude." That is especially true in a time like ours, in which men cannot find the normal amount of silence and solitude that human nature requires for its sound functioning. There are perhaps very many nuns and brothers in active Orders who have perfectly good active vocations, but who are so overworked and so starved for a normal life of prayer that they imagine they need to become Trappists or Carthusians. In some cases the solution may indeed be a transit to an enclosed Order, but more often all that is required is a proper adjustment in their own religious institute. The problem of such adjustments is too big even to be mentioned here.

The higher a man ascends in the scale of vocations the more he must be able to spiritualize and extend his affections. To live alone with God, he must really be able to live *alone*. You cannot live alone if you cannot stand loneliness. And you cannot stand loneliness if your desire for "solitude" is built on frustrated need for human affection. To put it in plain language, it is hopeless to try to live your life in a cloister if you are going to eat your heart out thinking that nobody loves you. You have to be able to disregard that whole issue, and simply love the whole world in God, embracing all your brethren in that same pure love, without seeking signs of affection from them and without caring whether or not you ever get any. If you think this is very easy, I assure you that you are mistaken.

20. To say that the enclosed, contemplative life is harder than the active life is not to say that the contemplative works harder, or that he has greater responsibilities and

obligations to meet. The contemplative life is in many respects easier than the active life. But it is not easier to live it *well*.

It is relatively easy to "get by" in a contemplative monastery, to keep the rules, to be at the right place at the right time, and to go through all the motions. Admittedly the routine is laborious and tiresome, but you can get used to it. What is hard is not the business of putting forth physical effort, but the work of *really leading an interior life of prayer* underneath all the externals.

The mere fact that *everything* in a contemplative monastery is supposed to be geared for a life of prayer is precisely what makes it difficult, for those who do not have true vocations, to live fruitfully in the cloister. It is not too hard for them to lead lives of prayer when there is more working than praying in the daily round of duties. In a life where all is prayer, those who do not have a special contemplative vocation often end up by praying less than they would actually do in the active life.

21. Attraction to a certain kind of life and the ability to lead that life are not yet sufficient to establish that one has a vocation. Indeed, the element of attraction, which may be important in many cases, is not always in evidence. A man can be called to the priesthood and still have a sensible repugnance for some of the aspects of his vocation. A Trappist vocation does not necessarily exclude a shrinking from the austerity of Trappist life. The one thing that really decides a vocation is *the ability to make a firm decision* to embrace a certain state of life and *to act on that decision*.

If a person can never make up his mind, never firmly resolve to do what is demanded in order to follow a vocation, one can say that in all probability he has not received the vocation. The vocation may have been offered him: but that is something no one can decide with certainty. Whether or not he is resisting grace, the fact seems to be that he is "not called." But a calm and definite decision that is not deterred by obstacles and not broken by opposition is a good sign that God has given His grace to answer His call, and that he has corresponded to it.

In deciding a vocation one normally consults a spiritual director. His function is to give advice, encouragement, suggestions, and help. He may in certain cases forbid a person to carry out the idea of becoming a priest or a religious. But if he judges that a person can prudently follow a vocation, it remains for that person himself to make the final decision. No one, not even a director or confessor, not even an ecclesiastical superior, can decide for him. He must decide himself, since his own decision is the expression of his vocation. If he then applies for admission to a seminary or monastery, and if his application is accepted, he can say that he probably "has a vocation."

22. These thoughts on vocation are evidently incomplete. But there is one gap that needs to be filled in order to avoid confusion. We have spoken of the active and contemplative lives without, so far, referring to the vocation which St. Thomas rates higher than any other: the apostolic life in which the fruits of contemplation are shared with others.

Instead of speaking of this vocation in theory, let us rather look at its perfect embodiment in one of its greatest saints: Francis of Assisi. The stigmatization of St. Francis was a divine sign of the fact that he was, of all saints, the most Christlike. He had succeeded better than any other in the work of reproducing in his life the simplicity and the poverty and the love of God and of men which marked the life of Jesus. More than that, he was an Apostle who incarnated the whole spirit and message of the Gospels most perfectly. Merely to know St. Francis is to understand the Gospel, and to follow him in his true, integral spirit, is to live the Gospel in all its fullness. The genius of his sancitity made him able to communicate to the world the teachings of Christ not in this or that aspect, not in fragments expanded by thought and analysis, but in all the wholeness of its existential simplicity. St. Francis was, as all saints must try to be, simply "another Christ."

His life did not merely reproduce this or that mystery of the life of Christ. He did not merely live the humble virtues of the divine infancy and of the hidden life at Nazareth. He was not merely tempted with Christ in the desert or weary with Him in the travels of His apostolate. He did not only work miracles like Jesus. He was not only crucified with Him. All these mysteries were united in the life of Francis, and we find them all in him, now singly and now together. The risen Christ lived again perfectly in this saint who was completely possessed and transformed by the Spirit of divine charity.

St. Thomas's phrase *contemplata aliis tradere* (to share with others the fruits of contemplation) is not properly understood unless we have in mind the image of a St. Francis walking the roads of medieval Italy, overflowing with the joy of a message that could only be communicated to him directly by the Spirit of God. The wisdom and the salvation preached by Francis were not only the overflow of the highest kind of contemplative life, but they were quite simply the expression of the fullness of the Christian Spirit—that is to say of the Holy Spirit of God.

No man can be an apostle of Christ unless he is filled with the Holy Ghost. And no man can be filled with the Holy Ghost unless he does what is normally expected of a man who follows Christ to the limit. He must leave all things, in order to recover them all in Him.

The remarkable thing about St. Francis is that in his sacrifice of everything he had also sacrificed all the "vocations" in a limited sense of the word. After having been edified for centuries by all the various branches of the Franciscan religious family, we are surprised to think that St. Francis started out on the roads of Umbria without the slightest idea that he had a "Franciscan vocation." And in fact he did not. He had thrown all vocations to the winds together with his clothes and other possessions. He did not think of himself as an apostle, but as a tramp. He certainly did not look upon himself as a monk: if he had wanted to be a monk, he would have found plenty of monasteries to enter. He evidently did not go around conscious of the fact that he was a "contemplative." Nor was he worried by comparisons between the active and contemplative lives. Yet he led both at the same time, and with the highest perfection. No good work was alien to him—no work of mercy, whether corporal or spiritual, that did not have a place in his beautiful life! His freedom embraced everything.

Francis could have been ordained priest. He refused out of humility (for that too would have been a "vocation" and he was beyond vocations). Yet he had in fact the perfection and quintessence of the apostolic spirit of sacrifice and charity which are necessary in the life of every priest. It takes a moment of reflection to reconcile oneself to the thought that St. Francis never said Mass—a fact which is hardly believable to one who is penetrated with his spirit.

If there was any recognized vocation in his time that Francis might have associated with his own life, it was the vocation of hermit. The hermits were the only members of any set class of religious persons that he consistently imitated. He frequently went off into the mountains to pray and live alone. But he never thought that he had a "vocation" to do nothing else but that. He stayed alone as long as the Spirit held him in solitude, and then let himself be led back into the towns and villages by the same Spirit.

If he had thought about it, he might have recognized that his vocation was essentially "prophetic." He was like another Elias or Eliseus, taught by the Spirit in solitude, but brought by God to the cities of men with a message to tell them.

All the many facets of the vocation of a St. Francis show us that we are beyond the level of ordinary "states of life." But it is for that very reason that, whenever we speak of the "mixed life" or the "Apostolic vocation" we would do well to think of it in terms of a Francis or of an Elias. The "mixed life" is too easily reduced to its lowest common denominator, and at that level it is nothing more than a form of the active life. As such, it suffers by comparison with the contemplative life. Why? Because the dignity of the apostolic life, in the teaching of St. Thomas, flows not from the element of action that is in it but from the element of contemplation. A life of preaching without contemplation is nothing but an "active life," and though it may be very holy and meritorious, it cannot lay claim to the dignity ascribed by St. Thomas to the life which "shares with others the fruits of contemplation."

But in proportion as the mendicant friar approaches the ideal of his founder, in proportion as he *lives* the poverty and charity of Francis or Dominic, and plunges into the loving knowledge of God which is granted only to little ones, in proportion as he abandons himself to the Holy Spirit, he will far outstrip the contemplative perfection of those whose contemplation is given them for themselves alone.

9. The measure of charity

1. In the economy of divine charity we have only as much as we give. But we are called upon to give as much as we have, and more: as much as we are. So the measure of our love is theoretically without limit. The more we desire to give ourselves in charity, the more charity we will have to give. And the more we give the more truly we shall be. For the Lord endows us with a being proportionate to the giving for which we are destined.

Charity is the life and the riches of His Kingdom, and those are greatest in it who are least: that is, who have kept nothing for themselves, retaining nothing but their desire to give.

He who tries to retain what he is and what he has, and keep it for himself, buries his talent. When the Lord comes in judgment, this servant is found to have no more than he had at the beginning. But those who have made themselves less, by giving away what they had, shall be found both to be and to have more than they had. And to him who has most shall be given that which the unprofitable servant kept for himself.

"And he said to them that stood by: Take the pound away from him and give it to him that hath ten pounds. And they said to him: 'Lord, he hath ten pounds!' But I say to you, that to every one that hath shall be given, and he shall abound: and from him that hath not, even that which he hath shall be taken away" (Luke 19:24–26).

2. If I love my brother with a perfect love, I will want him to be free from every love but the love of God. Of

129

all loves, charity alone is not possessive, because charity alone does not desire to be possessed. Charity seeks the greatest good of the one loved: and there is no greater good than charity. All other goods are contained in it. Charity is without fear: having given all that it has, it has nothing left to lose. It brings true peace, since it is in perfect concord with all that is good, and fears no evil.

Charity alone is perfectly free, always doing what it pleases: since it wills nothing except to love and cannot be prevented from loving. Without charity, knowledge is fruitless. Love alone can teach us to penetrate the hidden goodness of the things we know. Knowledge without love never enters into the inner secrets of being. Only love can truly know God as He is, for God is love.

Short of perfection, charity still feels fear: for it fears that it is not yet perfect. It is not yet perfectly free, since there is something left that it cannot do. It is still not at rest, for it is not yet perfectly given. It is still in the dark: for since it has not completely abandoned itself to God, it does not yet know Him. So it is still uncertain about finding Him in the things it knows.

No mere effort of ours can make our love perfect. The peace, certitude, liberty, fearlessness of pure love, are gifts of God. Love that is not yet perfect must learn perfection by waiting upon His good pleasure, and bearing its own imperfection until the time is ripe for complete self-surrender. We cannot give unless there be someone to receive what we are giving. The gift of our charity is not perfect until God is ready to accept it. He makes us wait for the time of our whole-giving, so that by giving ourselves many times and in many ways in part, we may have more to surrender in the end.

3. We tend to identify ourselves with those we love. We try to enter into their own souls and become what they are, thinking as they think, feeling as they feel, and experiencing what they experience.

But there is no true intimacy between souls who do not know how to respect one another's solitude. I cannot be united in love with a person whose very personality my love tends to obscure, to absorb, and to destroy. Nor can I awaken true love in a person who is invited, by my love, to be drowned in the act of drowning me with love.

If we know God, our identification of ourselves with those we love will be patterned on our union with God, and subordinate to it. Thus our love will begin with the knowledge of its own limitations and rise to the awareness of its greatness. For in ourselves we will always remain separate and remote from one another, but in God we can be one with those we love.

We cannot find them in God without first perfectly finding ourselves in Him. Therefore we will take care not to lose ourselves in looking for them outside Him. For love is not found in the void that exists between our being and the being of the one we love. There is an illusion of unity between us when our thoughts, our words, or our emotions draw us out of ourselves and suspend us together for a moment over the void. But when this moment has ended, we must return into ourselves or fall into the void. There is no true love except in God, Who is the source both of our own being and of the being we love.

4. Charity is a love that fortifies the ones we love in the secrecy of their own being, their own integrity, their own contemplation of God, their own free charity for all who exist in Him.

Such love leads to God because it comes from Him. It leads to a union between souls that is as intimate as their own union with Him. The closer we are to God, the closer we are to those who are close to Him. We can come to understand others only by loving Him Who understands them from within the depths of their own being. Otherwise we know them only by the surmises that are formed within the mirror of our own soul.

If we are angry, we will think them always angry. If we are afraid, we will think them alternately cowardly or cruel. If we are carnal, we will find our own carnality conveniently reflected in everyone who attracts us. And it is true that the instinct of connaturality may discover these things when the other person has not yet realized them to be there. So it is that we can attract others to us and draw the evil out of them by the force of our own passions. But in doing this we do not come to know them as they are: we only deform them so that we may know them as they are not. In doing so we bring an even greater deformity upon our own souls.

God knows us from within ourselves, not as objects, not as strangers, not as intimates, but as our own selves. His knowledge of us is the pure light of which our own self-knowledge is only a dim reflection. He knows us in Himself, not merely as images of something outside Him, but as "selves" in which His own self is expressed. He finds Himself more perfectly in us than we find ourselves.

He alone holds the secret of a charity by which we can love others not only as we love ourselves, but as He loves them. The beginning of this love is the will to let those we love be perfectly themselves, the resolution not to twist them to fit our own image. If in loving them we do not love what they are, but only their potential likeness to ourselves, then we do not love them: we only love the reflection of ourselves we find in them. Can this be charity?

5. Do not ask me to love my brother merely in the name of an abstraction—"society," the "human race," the "common good." Do not tell me that I ought to love him because we are both "social animals." These things are so much less than the good that is in us that they are not worthy to be invoked as motives of human love. You might as well ask me to love my mother because she speaks English.

We need abstractions, perhaps, in order to *understand* our relations with one another. But I may understand the principles of ethics and still hate other men. If I do not love other men, I will never discover the meaning of the "common good." Love is, itself, the common good.

There are plenty of men who will give up their interests for the sake of "society," but cannot stand any of the people they live with. As long as we regard other men as obstacles to our own happiness we are the enemies of society and we have only a very small capacity for sharing in the common good.

6. We are obliged to love one another. We are not strictly bound to "like" one another. Love governs the will: "liking" is a matter of sense and sensibility. Nevertheless, if we really love others it will not be too hard to like them also.

If we wait for some people to become agreeable or attractive before we begin to love them, we will never begin.

If we are content to give them a cold impersonal "charity" that is merely a matter of obligation, we will not trouble to try to understand them or to sympathize with them at all. And in that case we will not really love them, because love implies an efficacious will not only to do good to others exteriorly but also to find some good in them to which we can respond.

7. Some people never reveal any of the good that is hidden in them until we give them some of the good, that is to say, some of the charity, that is in ourselves.

We are so much the children of God that by loving others we can make them good and lovable, in spite of themselves.

We are obliged to become perfect as our heavenly Father is perfect (Matthew 5:48). That means that we do not regard the evil in others, but give them something of our own good in order to bring out the good He has buried in them.

A Christian does not restrain his desire for revenge merely in order that he himself may be good, but in order that his enemy may be made good also. Charity knows its own happiness, and seeks to see it shared by everyone.

Charity, in order to be perfect, needs an equal. It cannot be content to love others as inferiors, but raises them to its own level. For unless it can share everything with the beloved, charity is not at rest. So it cannot find contentment merely in its own perfection. It demands the perfection of all.

8. There is a difference between loving men in God and loving God in men. The two loves are the same: they are charity, which has God for its object and which, by either act, attains directly to Him.

Yet there is a significant difference in emphasis, a difference of "focus" which gives these two acts a different character.

A life in which we love God in men is necessarily an active life. But the contemplative loves men in God.

When we love God in men, we seek to discover Him over and over in one individual after another. When we love men in God, we do not seek them. We find them without seeking them in Him Whom we have found. The first kind of love is active and restless. It belongs more to time and to space than the other, which already participates in the changeless peace of eternity.

All charity grows in the same way: by increasing its intensity. Yet the love of God in men also extends itself in every direction to find new soil for its roots. The love of men in God grows only in depth: it plunges deeper and deeper into God, and by that very fact enlarges its capacity to love men.

When we love God in other men, our charity seeks to make His life grow in them. It surrounds that growth with anxious care. Our love develops more and more in our own soul while we watch its maturing in the souls of others.

But when we love men in God, we seek God and find Him with our whole being, and the growth of our love is simply the constant renewal of this supernatural encounter—an ever greater fullness of knowledge and of immersion in Him. The more we are plunged in Him, the better we can recognize Him wherever He is to be found: and the readier we are to see Him in other men.

To say that our contemplative charity finds our brothers in God, rather than seeing God in our brothers, is to say that it does not watch anxiously over His growth in their souls, and grow with them: but that it grows by itself in Him and, as a consequence, finds that others are also growing along with it.

If I love other men in God I can find them without turning away from Him. If I seek God in other men I find Him without turning away from them. In either case, when charity is fully mature, the brother whom I love is not too much of a distraction from the God in Whom my love for him terminates.

9. Jesus did not come to seek God in men. He drew men to Himself by dying for them on the Cross, in order that He might be God in them. All charity comes to a focus in Christ, because charity is His life in us. He draws us to Himself, unites us to one another in His Holy Spirit, and raises us up with Himself to union with the Father.

Philosophy, which is abstract, speaks of "society" and the "common good." Theology, which is supremely concrete, speaks of the Mystical Body of Christ and of the Holy Ghost. It makes a great difference whether you look at life from the point of view of philosophy or from that of theology.

The common good never protests when it is violated. But the Holy Ghost speaks for Himself, argues, protests, urges, and insists. The common good does not move our wills. But "the charity of Christ is poured forth in our hearts by the Holy Ghost Who is given to us" (Romans 5:5). The common good is too vague and too tame to put our passions to death within us: it can do nothing to defend itself against them! But the Holy Ghost promulgates in our hearts a law of love and self-denial which kills our selfishness and raises us up as new men in Christ: "For if by the Spirit you mortify the deeds of the flesh, you shall live!" (Romans 8:13).

The common good gives us no strength, teaches nothing either about life or about God. It passively waits for our homage and makes no murmur if it receive none. But "the Spirit also helpeth our infirmity. For we know not what we should pray for as we ought, but the Spirit Himself asketh for us" (Romans 8:26). And the Father strengthens us by His Spirit "with might unto the inward man, so that Christ may dwell by faith in our hearts, and that we may be rooted and founded in charity" (Ephesians 3:16).

The common good can offer us nothing except a kind of universal compromise in which the interests of countless human beings like ourselves will appear to be realized without too much conflict. The common good extends our horizons, no doubt, but only in order to give us a kind of Siberian landscape to contemplate: it is a vast, abstract steppe without any particular features, flat, low, mournful, under a cold gray sky. No wonder that men find the "common good" so uninteresting that they will build any selfish structure that serves to break its monotony!

10. The Holy Spirit not only widens our horizons. He lifts us into an entirely different world—a supernatural order, where, as the "Spirit of Promise" He makes known to us the things that are hidden for us in God. "We have received not the Spirit of this world, but the Spirit that is of God: that we may know the things that are given us from God . . . as it is written: Eye hath not seen, nor ear heard, nor hath it entered into the heart of man,

what things God hath prepared for them that love Him. But to us God hath revealed them by His Spirit. For the Spirit searcheth all things: yea, the deep things of God" (I Corinthians 2:9–12).

The things that are revealed to us by the Holy Spirit are the true common good: they are the infinite good which is God Himself, and the good of all His creatures in Him. Hence the Holy Spirit is not merely a leveler of individual interests, an arbiter, a judge who decrees some great universal compromise. God is the highest good not only of the collectivity but also and more particularly of each person in it. That is why in Scriptural language there is such constant use of the analogy of Father and Son. "Whosoever are led by the Spirit of God, they are the sons of God" (Romans 8:14). "Behold what manner of charity the Father hath bestowed upon us, that we should be called and should be the sons of God" (I John 3:1). Those who tend to stress the Christian collectivity so much that they make it a kind of totalitarian state of the spirit obscure the great truth of Christian personalism which is absolutely fundamental in our idea of the Mystical Body of Christ.

If the relation of our souls with God are the relations of sons to a father, that already brings out quite clearly that we are not mere units in a collectivity—employees in a factory, subjects in a state, soldiers in an army. We are sons, with rights of our own, rights that are the object of a most special care on the part of our Father. And the greatest of these rights is that which makes us His sons, and entitles us to a particular and special love of our own as sons, as individuals, as persons.

But our sonship before God is not a mere metaphor, or a legal fiction. It is a supernatural reality. This reality is the work of the Holy Ghost who not only confers upon us certain rights in the eyes of God, but even heightens and perfects our personality to the point of identifying us, each individually, with the only-begotten Son of God, Christ, the Incarnate Word. Consequently each Christian is not only a person in his own right, but his own personality is elevated by identification with the one Person Who is the object of all the Father's love: the Word of God. Each one of us becomes completely himself when, in the Spirit of God, he is transformed in Christ. "But we all, beholding the glory of the Lord with open face, are transformed into the same image from glory to glory, as by the Spirit of the Lord" (II Corinthians 3:18).

11. If I say that the Holy Spirit is the "common good" of the Church, it is because He is also the "common good" of the Father and the Son. He is the bond between Them and He is given to us in order that we may love the Father in the Son and be loved by Him as He loves His own Son.

The Holy Spirit makes us other Christs by doing in us the work He does in the soul of Christ: He comes to us as the love of the Father and the Son for us. He awakens in us love for the Father in the Son, by drawing us to Jesus. "By this is the spirit of God known. Every spirit which confesseth that Jesus Christ is come in the flesh is of God" (I John 4:2).

The Holy Spirit has, therefore, for His chief function to draw us into the mystery of the incarnation and of our redemption by the Word made flesh. He not only makes us understand something of God's love as it is manifested to us in Christ, but He also makes us live by that love and experience its action in our hearts. When we do so, the Spirit lets us know that this life and action are the life and action of Christ in us. And so the charity that is poured forth in our hearts by the Holy Spirit brings us into an intimate, experiential communion with Christ. It is only by the Holy Spirit that we truly know and love Jesus and come through Him to the knowledge and love of the Father.

That is why St. Paul calls the Holy Spirit the "Spirit of Christ" and says: "You are not in the flesh but in the spirit, if so be that the Spirit of God dwell in you. Now if any man have not the Spirit of Christ, he is none of His" (Romans 8:9).

The Spirit of Christ, the Holy Spirit, is the life of the Mystical Body of Christ, His Church. Just as the soul is the vital principle on which the unity and action of a physical organism depend, so the Holy Spirit is the principle of life, unity, and action which draws the souls of men together to live as one in the "Whole Christ." But the Holy Spirit does not act independently of Jesus's own will. On the contrary: poured out upon Christ without measure, the Holy Spirit is given to each one of us "according to the measure of the giving of Christ" (Ephesians 4:7). Each one of us has in his heart the charity that Christ confers upon him, according to his merits, and the Spirit dwells in us in obedience to the will of Christ, the Head and Sanctifier of the Mystical Body.

It is by the Holy Spirit that we love those who are united to us in Christ. The more plentifully we have received of the Spirit of Christ, the more perfectly we are able to love them: and the more we love them the more we receive of the Spirit. It is clear, however, that since we love them by the Spirit Who is given to us by Jesus, it is Jesus Himself Who loves them in us.

The measure of charity is, therefore, in itself infinite, because charity is the gift of a Divine and Infinite Person. But the actual measure of charity in our souls is the "measure" that we have received from Christ. The question next to be answered, then, is: How much can we receive?

12. First of all, in order to receive anything at all of the Holy Spirit and of His love, we must first be baptized: that is to say that we must enter either sacramentally or by martyrdom or at least by a most perfect desire into the Mystery of the Passion and Resurrection of Christ. We must yield our souls to the action of His love, without which we cannot be elevated above our own natural level to participate in the things of God.

No mere ascetic technique, no symbolic and purely human religious rite can bring us within the sacramental orbit of the love of Christ. He Himself must cast out the spirit of evil from our soul by the "finger of God" which is the Holy Spirit. Jesus Himself must baptize us with the Holy Spirit and with fire in order to make us "new creatures." St. John the Baptist said of the Savior: "I indeed baptize you with water unto penance, but he that shall come after me is mightier than I, whose shoes I am not worthy to bear: He shall baptize you in the Holy Ghost and fire" (Matthew 3:11). And Jesus Himself made it clear that this baptism of the Holy Spirit was to be identified with the sacramental baptism given by His Church: for it is He Who acts in the person of the baptizing priest, and works invisibly within the soul of the catechumen, washing it with His Holy Spirit at the same time as the priest performs the sacramental ablution—the outward sign of the interior grace conferred upon the soul by Christ Himself. "And Jesus said: amen I say to thee, unless a man be born again of water and the Holy Ghost he cannot enter into the Kingdom of God" (John 3:5).

It is necessary that a man be redeemed and set apart from "the world" before he can receive the Holy Spirit, because "the world" in the New Testament is the collective name for all those subjected to the desire of temporal and carnal things as ends in themselves. The world in this sense is ruled by selfishness and illusion, and the "prince of this world" is also the "father of lies." But the Paraclete Whom Jesus obtains for us from the Father and sends to dwell in our hearts forever "is the Spirit of Truth whom the world cannot receive, because it seeth Him not nor knowest Him: but you shall know Him because He shall abide with you and be in you" (John 14:17).

13. Once we have the Spirit dwelling in our hearts, the measure of the giving of Christ corresponds to our own desire. For in teaching us of the indwelling of His Spirit of charity, Jesus always reminds us to ask, in order that we may receive. The Holy Spirit is the most perfect gift of the Father to men, and yet He is the one gift which the Father gives most easily. There are many lesser things that, if we ask for them, may still have to be refused us. But the Holy Spirit will never be refused. "If then you being evil know how to give good gifts to your children, how much more will your Father in heaven give the good Spirit to them that ask Him?" (Luke 11:13).

14. The first thing we must do when we recognize the presence of God's grace in our hearts is to desire more charity. The desire for love is itself a beginning of love, and from the moment we desire more we already have more: and our desire is itself the pledge of even more to come. This is because an efficacious desire to love God makes us turn away from everything that is opposed to His will.

It is by desiring to grow in love that we receive the Holy Spirit, and the thirst for more charity is the effect of this more abundant reception.

The desire for charity is more than a blind hunger of the soul (although in certain circumstances it is very blind and very much of a hunger). It is clear-sighted in the sense that the intelligence enlightened by the Holy Spirit turns to the Father and asks for an increase of love in the name of the Son. That is to say that the desire for charity in a mature Christian soul is a lucid, deep, peaceful, active, and supremely fruitful knowledge of the Holy Trinity.

This charity knows the Holy and Most Blessed Trinity of three Persons in one God, not by straining to keep in view three distinct "units" at once, which would be as difficult as it is false, but by seeking the Son, hidden in the Father, by the love of the Holy Spirit. There is only one love which draws us into one God. But this love is, as God Himself is, triune. For charity unites us to the three Divine Persons from which it comes—the Father is its inexhaustible source, the Son the hearth of its splendid brightness, and the Holy Spirit the power of its eternal unity.

All this Jesus has taught us in very concrete terms. "I go to the Father, and whatsoever you shall ask the Father in my name, that will I do, that the Father may be glorified in the Son. . . . If you love me, keep my commandments, and I will ask the Father and He will give you another Paraclete, that He may abide with you forever" (John 14:13–16).

This last text gives us another way in which the measure of our love is increased: by obedience. Love does the will of the beloved. In obeying the Holy Spirit we receive a great increase of His charity in our hearts. For charity is the divine life which makes us sons of God. The more we obey the Spirit, the more we are moved and live as sons of God, and the greater our capacity for being enlightened and strengthened by His inspirations. "For whosoever are led by the Spirit of God, they are the Sons of God" (I Romans 8:14). The Vulgate has *"aguntur"* for "led" in this sentence, suggesting that the soul that obeys the interior movement of the Holy Spirit is driven and impelled by charity to act as a son of God. The "charity of Christ presseth us," says St. Paul, in another place (II Corinthians 5:14). For the Holy Ghost speaks with a strong and almost unbearable insistence in the souls He would drive to increase their love.

This gives us the secret of the measure of charity. It is not merely our own desire but the desire of Christ in His Spirit that drives us to grow in love. Those who seldom or never feel in their hearts the desire for the love of God and other men, and who do not thirst for the pure waters of desire which are poured out in us by the strong, living God, are usually those who have drunk from other rivers or have dug for themselves broken cisterns.

It is not that the Holy Spirit does not wish to move them with His love: but they have no relish for the interior and spiritual movement of a pure and selfless charity. The world cannot receive the Spirit of God because it cannot know Him, and it cannot know Him because it does not know how to taste and see that the Lord is full of delights for the soul of the man who obeys Him.

If we have no taste for the things of God, we can at least desire to have that taste, and if we ask for it, it will be given us. But at the same time we must deny ourselves the taste for other things which kill the desire for God.

And so that brings us to another element that determines the measure of our love for God: self-denial. We receive as much of the charity of Christ as we are willing to deny ourselves of any other love. The one who has most in the realm of the spirit is the one who loves least in the order of the flesh. I say the one who loves least, not the one who eats least or drinks least or sleeps least: and a good married man may have more love for God than a second-rate monk. But the test, in any event, is detachment of the will and the desire to renounce oneself completely in order to obey God. In brief, then, the measure of our charity is the measure of our desire: that in turn is measured by God's own desires, and we let Him have His desires in us when we deny ourselves our own.

15. Even though the divine life that is given to us in Christ, by the Holy Spirit, is essentially the same life that we shall lead in Heaven, the possession of that life can never give us perfect rest on earth. A Christian is essentially an exile in this world in which he has no lasting city. The very presence of the Holy Spirit in his heart makes him discontent with worldly and material values.

He cannot place his trust in the things of this life. His treasure is somewhere else, and where his treasure is, his heart is also.

16. We are saved by hope for that which we do not see and we wait for it with patience.

The Holy Spirit is the One Who fills our heart with this hope and this patience. If we did not have Him speaking constantly to the depths of our conscience, we could not go on believing in what the world has always held to be mad. The trials that seem to defy our hope and ruin the very foundations of all patience are meant, by the Spirit of God, to make our hope more and more perfect, basing it entirely in God, removing every visible support that can be found in this world. For a hope that rests on temporal power or temporal happiness is not theological. It is merely human, and has no supernatural strength to give us.

But the hope of Christians is not merely focused on Heaven. Heaven itself is only the prelude to the final consummation revealed by Christ. The doctrine of the general resurrection teaches us that the glory of God's love is to be in a certain sense the common good of all things, not only of the souls of those who are saved in Christ but also of their bodies and of the whole material universe.

St. Paul tells us that the whole world and all the creatures in it, having fallen with man and having become, like man, subject to vanity and corruption, also unconsciously await re-establishment and fulfillment in the glory of the general resurrection. "For the expectation of the creature waiteth for the revelation of the sons of God. . . . Because the creature also itself shall be delivered from the servitude of corruption, into the liberty of the glory of the children of God" (Romans 8:19–21).

Now in the context of Pauline theology, this means only one thing: that the world and those in it redeemed by Christ must share in the Resurrection of Jesus from the dead. The Resurrection of Christ is, therefore, the heart of the Christian faith. Without it, the death of Jesus on the Cross is no more than the tragedy of an honest man—the death of a Jewish Socrates. Without the Resurrection, the teaching of Jesus is simply a collection of incoherent fragments with a vague moral reference: the Gospels lose most of their meaning.

The teaching and the miracles of Christ were not meant simply to draw the attention of men to a doctrine and a set of practices. They were meant to focus our attention upon God Himself revealed in the Person of Jesus Christ. Once again, theology is essentially concrete. Far from being a synthesis of abstract truths, our theology is centered in the Person of Jesus Himself, the Word of God, the Way, the Truth, and the Life. To understand this theology we must receive the Holy Spirit, who reminds us of all that Christ has said and done, and who introduces us into the abyss of the "deep things of God." The perfection of this theology is eternal life, which is "to know the one true God and Jesus Christ Whom He has sent" (John 17:3).

Without the Resurrection, there is no sharing in the divine life. The death of Jesus on the Cross expiated our sins, but it was only after He had risen that He breathed upon His disciples, giving them the Holy Ghost with the power to forgive sin, to baptize, to teach and preach to all nations and to renew His life-giving sacrifice.

If Christ is not risen from the dead then it is futile to say that He lives in His Church and in the souls of all Christians. For when we say that Christ lives in us, we do not mean that He is present in our minds as a model of perfection or as a noble memory or as a brilliant example: we mean that by His Spirit He Himself becomes the principle of new life and new actions which are truly and literally His life and His actions as well as our own. It is no metaphor for the Christian to say with St. Paul: "I live, now not I, but Christ liveth in me" (Galatians 2:20).

But in the mind of St. Paul the Resurrection of Christ demands our resurrection also, and the two are so inseparable that "if there be no Resurrection of the dead, then Christ is not risen again" (I Corinthians 15:13). It is clear then that the general resurrection is so fundamental a doctrine in the Christian faith that no man who does not accept it can truly call himself a Christian. For St. Paul adds: "If Christ be not risen again, then is our preaching vain and your faith is also vain" (I Corinthians 15:17).

If our whole faith rests on the Resurrection of Jesus, if the Holy Ghost comes to us only from the Risen Christ, and if the whole of God's creation looks to the general resurrection in which it will share in the glory of the sons of God, then for a Christian the "common good" is really centered in the Resurrection of Christ from the dead. Anyone who wants to penetrate into the heart of Christianity and to draw forth from it the rivers of living water that give joy to the City of God (Psalm 45:5) he must enter into this mystery. And the Mystery of the Resurrection is simply the completion of the Mystery of the Cross. We cannot enter into this mystery without the help of the Holy Spirit. But if we do, then "the Spirit of Him that raised up Jesus from the dead shall quicken also your mortal bodies, because of His Spirit that dwelleth in you" (Romans 8:11). "For this corruptible body must put on incorruption, and this mortal must put on immortality. And when this mortal hath put on immortality, then shall come to pass that saying that is written: 'Death is swallowed up in victory'" (I Corinthians 15:53–54).

17. In summary, then, the measure of our charity is theoretically infinite, because it depends on God's charity toward us, and this is infinite. In concrete reality, God has shown His charity for us in the Person of Christ. We live in Christ by His Spirit, and we at last become perfect in charity when we share perfectly in the mystery of the Resurrection in which Christ made us participate in His divine Sonship.

We will be perfect Christians when we have risen from the dead.

10. Sincerity

1. We make ourselves real by telling the truth. Man can hardly forget that he needs to know the truth, for the instinct to know is too strong in us to be destroyed. But he can forget how badly he also needs to tell the truth. We cannot know truth unless we ourselves are conformed to it.

We must be true inside, true to ourselves, before we can know a truth that is outside us. But we make ourselves true inside by manifesting the truth as we see it.

2. If men still admire sincerity today, they admire it, perhaps, not for the sake of the truth that it protects, but simply because it is an attractive quality for a person to have. They like to be sincere not because they love the truth, but because, if they are thought to be sincere, people will love them. And perhaps they carry this sincerity to the point of injustice—being too frank about others and themselves, using the truth to fight the truth, and turning it to an instrument of ridicule in order to make others less loved. The "truth" that makes another man seem cheap hides another truth that we should never forget, and which would make him remain always worthy of honor in our sight. To destroy truth with truth under the pretext of being sincere is a very insincere way of telling a lie.

3. We are too much like Pilate. We are always asking, "What is truth?" and then crucifying the truth that stands before our eyes.

But since we have asked the question, let us answer it.

If I ask, "What is truth?" I either expect an answer or I do not. Pilate did not. Yet his belief that the question did not require an answer was itself his answer. He thought the question could not be answered. In other words, he thought it was true to say that the question, "What is truth?" had no satisfactory answer. If, in thinking that, he thought there was no truth, he clearly disproved his own proposition by his very thought of it. So, even in his denial, Pilate confessed his need for the truth. No man can avoid doing the same in one way or another, because our need for truth is inescapable.

What, then, is truth?

Truth, in things, is their reality. In our minds, it is the conformity of our knowledge with the things known. In our words, it is the conformity of our words to what we think. In our conduct, it is the conformity of our acts to what we are supposed to be.

4. It is curious that our whole world is consumed with the desire to know what things are, and actually does find out a tremendous amount about their physical constitution, and verifies its findings—and still does not know whether or not there is such a thing as truth!

Objective truth is a reality that is found both within and outside ourselves, to which our minds can be conformed. We must know this truth, and we must manifest it by our words and acts.

We are not required to manifest everything we know, for there are some things we are obliged to keep hidden from men. But there are other things that we must make known, even though others may already know them.

We owe a definite homage to the reality around us, and we are obliged, at certain times, to say what things are and to give them their right names and to lay open our thought about them to the men we live with.

The fact that men are constantly talking shows that they need the truth, and that they depend on their mutual witness in order to get the truth formed and confirmed in their own minds.

But the fact that men spend so much time talking about nothing or telling each other the lies that they have heard from one another or wasting their time in scandal and detraction and calumny and scurrility and ridicule shows that our minds are deformed with a kind of contempt for reality. Instead of conforming ourselves to what is, we twist everything around, in our words and thoughts, to fit our own deformity.

The seat of this deformity is in the will. Although we still may speak the truth, we are more and more losing our desire to live according to the truth. Our wills are not true, because they refuse to accept the laws of our own being: they fail to work along the lines demanded by our own reality. Our wills are plunged in false values, and they have dragged our minds along with them, and our restless tongues bear constant witness to the disorganization inside our souls—"the tongue no man can tame, an unquiet evil, full of deadly poison. By it we bless God and the Father, and we curse men who are made in the likeness of God. . . . Doth a fountain send forth out of the same hole sweet and bitter water?" (James 3:8–11).

5. Truthfulness, sincerity, and fidelity are close kindred. Sincerity is fidelity to the truth. Fidelity is an effective truthfulness in our promises and resolutions. An inviolate truthfulness makes us faithful to ourselves and to God and to the reality around us: and, therefore, it makes us perfectly sincere.

Sincerity in the fullest sense must be more than a temperamental disposition to be frank. It is a simplicity of spirit which is preserved by the *will* to be true. It implies an obligation to manifest the truth and to defend it. And this in turn recognizes that we are free to respect the truth or not to respect it, and that the truth is to some extent at our own mercy. But this is a terrible responsibility, since in defiling the truth we defile our own souls.

Truth is the life of our intelligence. The mind does not fully live unless it thinks straight. And if the mind does not see what it is doing, how can the will make good use of its freedom? But since our freedom is, in fact, immersed in a supernatural order, and tends to a supernatural end that it cannot even know by natural means, the full life of the soul must be a light and strength which are infused into it supernaturally by God. This is the life of sanctifying grace, together with the infused virtues of faith, hope, charity, and all the rest.

Sincerity in the fullest sense is a divine gift, a clarity

of spirit that comes only with grace. Unless we are made "new men," created according to God "in justice and the holiness of truth," we cannot avoid some of the lying and double-dealing which have become instinctive in our natures, corrupted, as St. Paul says, "according to the desire of error" (Ephesians 4:22).

One of the effects of original sin is an instinctive prejudice in favor of our own selfish desires. We see things as they are not, because we see them centered on ourselves. Fear, anxiety, greed, ambition, and our hopeless need for pleasure all distort the image of reality that is reflected in our minds. Grace does not completely correct this distortion all at once: but it gives us a means of recognizing and allowing for it. And it tells us what we must do to correct it. Sincerity must be bought at a price: the humility to recognize our innumerable errors, and fidelity in tirelessly setting them right.

The sincere man, therefore, is one who has the grace to know that he may be instinctively insincere, and that even his natural sincerity may become a camouflage for irresponsibility and moral cowardice: as if it were enough to recognize the truth, and do nothing about it!

6. How is it that our comfortable society has lost its sense of the value of truthfulness? Life has become so easy that we think we can get along without telling the truth. A liar no longer needs to feel that his lies may involve him in starvation. If living were a little more precarious, and if a person who could not be trusted found it more difficult to get along with other men, we would not deceive ourselves and one another so carelessly.

But the whole world has learned to deride veracity or to ignore it. Half the civilized world makes a living by telling lies. Advertising, propaganda, and all the other forms of publicity that have taken the place of truth have taught men to take it for granted that they can tell other people whatever they like provided that it sounds plausible and evokes some kind of shallow emotional response.

Americans have always felt that they were protected against the advertising business by their own sophistication. If we only knew how naïve our sophistication really is! It protects us against nothing. We love the things we pretend to laugh at. We would rather buy a bad toothpaste that is well advertised than a good one that is not advertised at all. Most Americans wouldn't be seen dead in a car their neighbors had never heard of.

Sincerity becomes impossible in a world that is ruled by a falsity that it thinks it is clever enough to detect. Propaganda is constantly held up to contempt, but in contemning it we come to love it after all. In the end we will not be able to get along without it.

This duplicity is one of the great characteristics of a state of sin, in which a person is held captive by the love for what he knows he ought to hate.

7. Your idea of me is fabricated with materials you have borrowed from other people and from yourself. What you think of me depends on what you think of yourself. Perhaps you create your idea of me out of material that you would like to eliminate from your own idea of yourself. Perhaps your idea of me is a reflection of what other people think of you. Or perhaps what you think of me is simply what you think I think of you.

8. How difficult it is for us to be sincere with one another, when we do not know either ourselves or one another! Sincerity is impossible without humility and supernatural love. I cannot be candid with other men unless I understand myself and unless I am prepared to do everything possible in order to understand them.

But my understanding of them is always clouded by the reflection of myself which I cannot help seeing in them.

It takes more courage than we imagine to be perfectly simple with other men. Our frankness is often spoiled by a hidden barbarity, born of fear.

False sincerity has much to say, because it is afraid. True candor can afford to be silent. It does not need to face an anticipated attack. Anything it may have to defend can be defended with perfect simplicity.

The arguments of religious men are so often insincere, and their insincerity is proportionate to their anger. Why do we get angry about what we believe? Because we do not really believe it. Or else what we pretend to be defending as the "truth" is really our own self-esteem. A man of sincerity is less interested in defending the truth

149

than in stating it clearly, for he thinks that if the truth be clearly seen it can very well take care of itself.

9. Fear is perhaps the greatest enemy of candor. How many men fear to follow their conscience because they would rather conform to the opinion of other men than to the truth they know in their hearts! How can I be sincere if I am constantly changing my mind to conform with the shadow of what I think others expect of me? Others have no right to demand that I be anything else than what I ought to be in the sight of God. No greater thing could possibly be asked of a man than this! This one just expectation, which I am bound to fulfill, is precisely the one they usually do not expect me to fulfill. They want me to be what I am in their sight: that is, an extension of themselves. They do not realize that if I am fully myself, my life will become the completion and the fulfillment of their own, but that if I merely live as their shadow, I will serve only to remind them of their own unfulfillment.

If I allow myself to degenerate into the being I am imagined to be by other men, God will have to say to me, "I know you not!"

10. The delicate sincerity of grace is never safe in a soul given to human violence. Passion always troubles the clear depths of sincerity, except when it is perfectly in order. And passion is almost never perfectly in order, even in the souls of the saints.

But the clean waters of a lake are not made dirty by the wind that ruffles their surface. Sincerity can suffer something of the violence of passion without too much harm, as long as the violence is suffered and not accepted.

Violence is fatal to sincerity when we yield it our consent, and it is completely fatal when we find peace in passion rather than in tranquillity and calm.

Spiritual violence is most dangerous when it is most spiritual—that is, when it is least felt in the emotions. It seizes the depths of the will without any surface upheaval and carries the whole soul into captivity without a struggle. The emotions may remain at peace, may even taste a delight of their own in this base rapture. But the deep peace of the soul is destroyed, because the image of truth has been shattered by rebellion. Such is the violence, for example, of unresisted pride.

There is only one kind of violence that captures the Kingdom of Heaven. It is the seeming violence of grace, which is really order and peace. It establishes peace in the soul's depth even in the midst of passion. It is called "violent" by reason of the energy with which it resists passion and sets order in the house of the soul. This violence is the voice and the power of God Himself, speaking in our soul. It is the authority of the God of peace, speaking within us, in the sanctuary, in His holy place.

The God of peace is never glorified by human violence.

11. The truth makes us saints, for Jesus prayed that we might be "sanctified in truth." But we also read that "knowledge puffeth up"—*scientia inflat.*

How is it that knowledge can make us proud?

There is no truth in pride. If our knowledge is true, then it ought to make us humble. If humble, holy.

As soon as truth is in the intellect, the mind is "sanctified" by it. But if the whole soul is to be sanctified, the will must be purified by this same truth which is in the intelligence. Even though our minds may see the truth, our wills remain free to "change the truth of God into a lie" (Romans 1:25).

There is a way of knowing the truth that makes us true to ourselves and God, and, therefore, makes us more real and holier. But there is another way of receiving the truth that makes us untrue, unholy. The difference between these two lies in the action of our will.

If my will acts as the servant of the truth, consecrating my whole soul to what the intelligence has seen, then I will be sanctified by the truth. I will be sincere. "My whole body will be lightsome" (Matthew 6:22).

But if my will takes possession of truth as its master, as if the truth were my servant, as if it belonged to me by right of conquest, then I will take it for granted that I can do with it whatever I please. This is the root of all falsity.

The saint must see the truth as something to serve, not as something to own and manipulate according to his own good pleasure.

12. In the end, the problem of sincerity is a problem of love. A sincere man is not so much one who sees the truth and manifests it as he sees it, but one who loves the truth with a pure love. But truth is more than an abstraction. It lives and is embodied in men and things that are real. And the secret of sincerity is, therefore, not to be sought in a philosophical love for abstract truth but in a love for real people and real things—a love for God apprehended in the reality around us.

It is difficult to express in words how important this notion is. The whole problem of our time is not lack of knowledge but lack of love. If men only loved one another they would have no difficulty in trusting one another and in sharing the truth with one another. If we all had charity we would easily find God. "For charity is of God, and everyone that loveth is born of God, and knoweth God" (I John 4:7).

If men do not love, it is because they have learned in their earliest childhood that they themselves are not loved, and the duplicity and cynicism of our time belongs to a generation that has been conscious, since its cradle, that it was not wanted by its parents.

The Church understands human love far better and more profoundly than modern man, who thinks he knows all about it. The Church knows well that to frustrate the creative purpose of human generation is to confess a love that is insincere. It is insincere because it is less than human, even less than animal. Love that seeks only to enjoy and not to create is not even a shadow of love. It has no power. The psychological impotence of our enraged generation must be traced to the overwhelming accusation of insincerity which every man and woman has to confront, in the depths of his own soul, when he seeks to love merely for his own pleasure. A love that fears to have children for any motive whatever is a love that fears love. It is divided against itself. It is a lie and contradiction. The very nature of love demands that its own creative fulfillment should be sought *in spite of every obstacle*. Love, even human love, is stronger than death. Therefore, it is even more obvious that true love is stronger than poverty or hunger or anguish. And yet the men of our time do not love with enough courage to risk even discomfort or inconvenience.

Is it surprising that the Church should completely disregard all the economic arguments of those who think money and comfort are more important than love? The life of the Church is itself the highest form of love, and in this highest love all lesser loves are protected and enshrined by a divine sanction. It is inevitable that in a day when men are emptying human love of all its force and content, the Church should remain its last defender. But it is surely ironical that even the physical pleasure of human love should be more effectively protected by the wise doctrine of the Church than by the sophisms of those whose only apparent end is pleasure. Here, too, the Church knows what she is talking about when she reminds us that man is made of body and soul, and that the body fulfills its functions properly only when it is completely subjected to the soul and when the soul is subjected to grace, that is, to divine love. In the doctrine of the Church, the virtue of temperance is meant not to crush or divert the human instinct for pleasure, but to make reasonable pleasure serve its own end: to bring man to perfection and happiness in union with God. And, thus, the Church is bound by her own inflexible logic to leave man all the ordinate fullness of the pleasures that are necessary for the well-being of the person and of the community. She never considers pleasure merely as a "necessary evil" which has to be tolerated. It is a good that can contribute to man's sanctification: but it is a good that fallen man finds it extremely difficult to put to proper use. Hence the stringency of her laws. But let us not forget the purpose of those laws, which is to guarantee not only the rights of God but also the rights of man himself: and even the legitimate rights of man's own physical body.

Once again, do not accuse me of exaggeration in tracing the problem of sincerity to its roots in human love. The selfishness of an age that has devoted itself to the mere cult of pleasure has tainted the whole human race with an error that makes all our acts more or less lies against God. An age like ours cannot be sincere.

13. Our ability to be sincere with ourselves, with God, and with other men is really proportionate to our capacity for sincere love. And the sincerity of our love depends in large measure upon our capacity to believe ourselves

loved. Most of the moral and mental and even religious complexities of our time go back to our desperate fear that we are not and can never be really loved by anyone.

When we consider that most men want to be loved as if they were gods, it is hardly surprising that they should despair of receiving the love they think they deserve. Even the biggest of fools must be dimly aware that he is not worthy of adoration, and no matter what he may believe about his right to be adored, he will not be long in finding out that he can never fool anyone enough to make her adore him. And yet our idea of ourselves is so fantastically unreal that we rebel against this lack of "love" as though we were the victims of an injustice. Our whole life is then constructed on a basis of duplicity. We assume that others are receiving the kind of appreciation we want for ourselves, and we proceed on the assumption that since we are not lovable as we are, we must become lovable under false pretenses, as if we were something better than we are.

The real reason why so few men believe in God is that they have ceased to believe that even a God can love them. But their despair is, perhaps, more respectable than the insincerity of those who think they can trick God into loving them for something they are not. This kind of duplicity is, after all, fairly common among so-called "believers," who consciously cling to the hope that God Himself, placated by prayer, will support their egotism and their insincerity, and help them to achieve their own selfish ends. Their worship is of little value to themselves and does no honor to God. They not only consider Him a potential rival (and, therefore, place themselves on a basis of equality with Him), but they think He is base enough to make a deal with them, and this is a great blasphemy.

14. If we are to love sincerely, and with simplicity, we must first of all overcome the fear of not being loved. And this cannot be done by forcing ourselves to believe in some illusion, saying that we are loved when we are not. We must somehow strip ourselves of our greatest illusions about ourselves, frankly recognize in how many ways we are unlovable, descend into the depths of our being until we come to the basic reality that is in us, and learn to see that we are lovable after all, in spite of everything!

This is a difficult job. It can only really be done by a lifetime of genuine humility. But sooner or later we must distinguish between what we are not and what we are. We must accept the fact that we are not what we would like to be. We must cast off our false, exterior self like the cheap and showy garment that it is. We must find our real self, in all its elemental poverty but also in its very great and very simple dignity: created to be a child of God, and capable of loving with something of God's own sincerity and His unselfishness.

Both the poverty and the nobility of our inmost being consists in the fact that it is a *capacity* for love. It can be loved by God, and when it is loved by Him, it can respond to His love by imitation—it can turn to Him with gratitude and adoration and sorrow; it can turn to its neighbor with compassion and mercy and generosity.

The first step in this sincerity is the recognition that although we are worth little or nothing in ourselves, we are potentially worth very much, because we can hope to be loved by God. He does not love us because we are good, but we become good when and because He loves us. If we receive this love in all simplicity, the sincerity of our love for others will more or less take care of itself. Centered entirely upon the immense liberality that we experience in God's love for us, we will never fear that His love could fail us. Strong in the confidence that we are loved by Him, we will not worry too much about the uncertainty of being loved by other men. I do not mean that we will be indifferent to their love for us: since we wish them to love in us the God Who loves them in us. But we will never have to be anxious about their love, which in any case we do not expect to see too clearly in this life.

15. The whole question of sincerity, then, is basically a question of love and fear. The man who is selfish, narrow, who loves little and fears much that he will not be loved, can never be deeply sincere, even though he may sometimes have a character that seems to be frank on the surface. In his depths he will always be involved in duplicity. He will deceive himself in his best and most serious intentions. Nothing he says or feels about love, whether human or divine, can safely be believed, until his love be purged at least of its basest and most unreasonable fears.

But the man who is not afraid to admit everything that he sees to be wrong with himself, and yet recognizes that he may be the object of God's love precisely because of his shortcomings, can begin to be sincere. His sincerity is based on confidence, not in his illusions about himself, but in the endless, unfailing mercy of God.

16. Sincerity is, perhaps, the most vitally important quality of true prayer. It is the only valid test of our faith, our hope, and our love of God. No matter how deep our meditations, nor how severe our penances, how grand our liturgy, how pure our chant, how noble our thoughts about the mysteries of God; they are all useless if we do not really mean what we say. What is the good of bringing down upon ourselves the curses uttered by the ancient prophets and taken up again by Christ Himself: "Hypocrites, well hath Isaias prophesied of you, saying: 'This people honoreth me with their lips, but their heart is far from me'" (Matthew 15:7–8) (cf. Isaias 29:13).

Since the monk is a man of prayer and a man of God, his most important obligation is sincerity. Everywhere in St. Benedict's Rule we are reminded of this. Those who are not true monks "lie to God by their tonsure," he says (*Rule*, chapter I). The first thing to be sought in a candidate for the monastic life is sincerity in seeking God—*si vere Deum quaerit*. One of the instruments of good works, by which the monk becomes a saint, is to "utter truth from his heart and from his lips," and another is that he should not desire to be called a saint without being one, but become a saint in all truth. In order that the truth of his virtue might be more certain, he must desire to manifest it in deeds rather than words. But above all in his prayer, his thoughts must agree with what he sings: (*mens concordet voci*). Like Jesus Himself, St. Benedict prefers that prayer should be short and pure, rather than that the monk should multiply empty words or meditations without meaning.

The most important thing in prayer is that we present ourselves as we are before God as He is. This cannot be done without a generous effort of recollection and self-searching. But if we are sincere, our prayer will never be fruitless. Our sincerity itself establishes an instant contact with the God of all truth.

11. Mercy

1. How close God is to us when we come to recognize and to accept our abjection and to cast our care entirely upon Him! Against all human expectation He sustains us when we need to be sustained, helping us to do what seemed impossible. We learn to know Him, now, not in the "presence" that is found in abstract consideration—a presence in which we dress Him in our own finery—but in the emptiness of a hope that may come close to despair. For perfect hope is achieved on the brink of despair when, instead of falling over the edge, we find ourselves walking on the air. Hope is always just about to turn into despair, but never does so, for at the moment of supreme crisis God's power is suddenly made perfect in our infirmity. So we learn to expect His mercy most calmly when all is most dangerous, to seek Him quietly in the face of peril, certain that He cannot fail us though we may be upbraided by the just and rejected by those who claim to hold the evidence of His love.

2. *Cum vero infirmor, tunc potens sum.* "When I am weak, then I am strong" (II Corinthians 12:10).

Our weakness has opened Heaven to us, because it has brought the mercy of God down to us and won us His love. Our unhappiness is the seed of all our joy. Even sin has played an unwilling part in saving sinners, for the infinite mercy of God cannot be prevented from drawing the greatest good out of the greatest evil. Sin was destroyed in the midst of the sin of those who thought they could destroy Christ. Sin can never do anything good. It cannot even destroy itself, which would indeed be a great good. But the love of Christ for us, and the mercy of God, destroyed sin by taking upon itself the burden of all our sins and by paying the price that was due to them. So the Church sings that Christ died on the tree of the Cross that life might arise from the same stem from which death had first grown: *ut unde mors oriebatur, inde vita resurgeret*.

The Christian concept of mercy is, therefore, the key to the transformation of a whole universe in which sin still seems to reign. For the Christian does not escape evil, nor is he dispensed from suffering, nor is he withdrawn from the influence and from the effects of sin: nor is he himself impeccable. He too, unfortunately, can sin. He has not been completely delivered from evil. Yet his vocation is to deliver the whole world from evil and to transform it in God: by prayer, by penance, by charity, and, above all, by mercy. God, Who is all-holy, not only has had mercy on us, but He has given His mercy into the hands of potential sinners in order that they may be able to choose between good and evil, and may overcome evil with good, and may earn His mercy for their own souls by having mercy on others.

God has left sin in the world in order that there may be forgiveness: not only the secret forgiveness by which He Himself cleanses our souls, but the manifest forgiveness by which we have mercy on one another and so give expression to the fact that He is living, by His mercy, in our own hearts.

3. "Blessed are they that mourn." Can this be true? Is there any greater wretchedness than to taste the dregs of our own insufficiency and misery and hopelessness, and to know that we are certainly worth nothing at all? Yet it is blessed to be reduced to these depths if, in them, we can find God. Until we have reached the bottom of the abyss, there is still something for us to choose between all and nothing. There is still something in between. We can still evade the decision. When we are reduced to our last extreme, there is no further evasion. The choice is a terrible one. It is made in the heart of darkness, but with an intuition that is unbearable by its angelic clarity: when

we who have been destroyed and seem to be in hell miraculously choose God!

4. Only the lost are saved. Only the sinner is justified. Only the dead can rise from the dead, and Jesus said, "I came to seek and to save that which was lost" (Luke 9:10).

5. Some men are only virtuous enough to forget that they are sinners without being wretched enough to remember how much they need the mercy of God.

It is possible that some who have led bad lives on earth may be higher in Heaven than those who appeared to be good in this life. What is the value of a virtuous life, if it be a life without love and without mercy? Love is the gift of God's mercy to human sorrow, not the reward of human self-sufficiency. Great sorrow for great evil is a tremendous gift of love, and takes us out of ourselves in ecstasy at the mercy of God: "Because she has loved much, much has been forgiven."

Yet the best thing of all is the love of the Virgin Mother of God, who never offended Him, but who received from Him the greatest mercy of all: that of knowing her own nothingness in the midst of the greatest perfection, and of being the poorest of all the saints because she was the richest.

Her charity corresponded perfectly to her humility. She who was lowest in her own eyes saw without tremor that she was highest in God's eyes. She was glad of this because He was glad of it, and for no other reason.

Thus, she who was weakest became most powerful and overthrew the pride of all the strongest angels who had fallen because they wanted their power to be their own, as if it had come from themselves and belonged to no other. She, on the other hand, had no power of her own, but she had received the greatest mercy, had been the most loved and was, therefore, the most worthy of love and the most capable of loving God in return. By the power of what she did not have, she has received power over us all, and we belong to her by the right of God's mercy: in whose distribution she is sovereign, by her prayers.

6. In the holiness of God, all extremes meet—infinite mercy and justice, infinite love and endless hatred of sin, infinite power and limitless condescension to the weakness of His creatures. His holiness is the cumulation of all His other attributes, His being in its infinite transcendency, His otherness and utter difference from every other being.

Yet the supreme manifestation of God's holiness is the death of Christ on the Cross. Here, too, all extremes meet. And here man, who has run away from God and buried himself in corruption and in death in order not to see the holiness of His face, finds himself confronted, in death itself, with the Redeemer Who is his life.

We must adore and acknowledge God's holiness by desiring Him to have mercy on us, and this is the beginning of all justice. To desire Him to be merciful to us is to acknowledge Him as God. To seek His pity when we deserve no pity is to ask Him to be just with a justice so holy that it knows no evil and shows mercy to everyone who does not fly from Him in despair.

Perfect hope in the mercy of God is the prerogative of those who have come closest to His sanctity. And because they are closest to holiness they seem to themselves to be farthest away from it: for the contrast and the opposition between holiness and themselves is felt to be unbearable. Under such circumstances it seems like presumption to hope at all, yet hope is an imperative necessity in their souls, because they are seized and possessed by the inexorable holiness of God. Therefore, while they see that it is seemingly impossible for their sins to be condoned, they are overwhelmed by the gratuitous actuality of their forgiveness. Such forgiveness could not come from anyone but God.

7. The power that manifests itself in our weakness is the power that was the strength of Christ's weakness—the love of the Father, Who raised Him from the dead. Jesus went down into the dust of death in order that the power of His Resurrection might be manifest in our own lives. This power is seen, not in our natural gifts, not in talents or human wisdom or in man's strength. It is made evident only in the contest between what *appears* in us—what is human and our own—and by what does not appear: the secret power of grace.

8. "Blessed are the merciful, for they shall obtain mercy" (Matthew 5:7).

We can have the mercy of God whenever we want it, by being merciful to others: for it is God's mercy that acts on them, through us, when He leads us to treat them as He is treating us. His mercy sanctifies our own poverty by the compassion that we feel for their poverty, as if it were our own. And this is a created reflection of His own divine compassion, in our own souls. Therefore, it destroys our sins, in the very act by which we overlook and forgive the sins of other men.

Such compassion is not learned without suffering. It is not to be found in a complacent life, in which we platonically forgive the sins of others without any sense that we ourselves are involved in a world of sin. If we want to know God, we must learn to understand the weaknesses and sins and imperfections of other men as if they were our own. We must feel their poverty as Christ experienced our own.

9. We can only get to Heaven by dying for other people on the cross. And one does not die on a cross by his own unaided efforts. He needs the help of an executioner. We have to die, as Christ died, for those whose sins are to us more bitter than death—most bitter because they are just like our own. We have to die for those whose sins kill us, and who are killed, in spite of our good intentions, by many sins of our own.

If my compassion is true, if it be a deep compassion of the heart and not a legal affair, or a mercy learned from a book and practiced on others like a pious exercise, then my compassion for others is God's mercy for me. My patience with them is His patience with me. My love for them is His love for me.

10. When the Lord hears my prayer for mercy (a prayer which is itself inspired by the action of His mercy), then He makes His mercy present and visible in me by moving me to have mercy on others as He has had mercy on me. This is the way in which God's mercy fulfills His divine justice: mercy and justice seem to us to differ, but in the works of God they are both expressions of His love.

His justice is the love that gives to each one of His

creatures the gifts that His mercy has previously decreed. And His mercy is His love, doing justice to its own exigencies, and renewing the gift which we had failed to accept.

11. The mercy of God does not suspend the laws of cause and effect. When God forgives me a sin, He destroys the guilt of sin but the effects and the punishment of sin remain. Yet it is precisely in punishing sin that God's mercy most evidently identifies itself with His justice. Every sin is a violation of the love of God, and the justice of God makes it impossible for this violation to be perfectly repaired by anything but love. Now love is itself the greatest gift of God to men. Charity is our own highest perfection and the source of all our joy. This charity is the free gift of His mercy. Filling us with divine charity and calling us to love Him as He has first loved us and to love other men as He has loved us all, God's mercy makes it possible for us to give full satisfaction to His justice. The justice of God can, therefore, best be satisfied by the effects of His own mercy.

Those who refuse His mercy satisfy His justice in another way. Without His mercy, they cannot love Him. Without love for Him they cannot be "justified" or "made just." That is to say: they cannot conform to Him Who is love. Those who have not received His mercy are in a state of injustice with regard to Him. It is their own injustice that is condemned by His justice. And in what does their injustice consist? In the refusal of His mercy. We come, then, in the end, to this basic paradox: that we owe it to God to receive from Him the mercy that is offered to us in Christ, and that to refuse this mercy is the summation of our "injustice." Clearly, then, only the mercy of God can make us just, in this supernatural sense, since the primary demand of God's justice upon us is that we receive His mercy.

12. Do you want to know God? Then learn to understand the weaknesses and imperfections of other men. But how can you understand the weaknesses of others unless you understand your own? And how can you see the meaning of your own limitations until you have received mercy from God, by which you know yourself and Him? It is

not sufficient to forgive others: we must forgive them with humility and compassion. If we forgive them without humility, our forgiveness is a mockery: it presupposes that we are better than they. Jesus descended into the abyss of our degradation in order to forgive us after He had, in a sense, become lower than us all. It is not for us to forgive others from lofty thrones, as if we were gods looking down on them from Heaven. We must forgive them in the flames of their own hell, for Christ, by means of our forgiveness, once again descends to extinguish the avenging flame. He cannot do this if we do not forgive others with His own compassion. Christ cannot love without feeling and without heart. His love is human as well as divine, and our charity will be a caricature of His love if it pretends to be divine only, and does not consent to be human.

When we love others with His love, we no longer know good and evil (which was what the serpent promised) but only good. We overcome the evil in the world by the charity and compassion of God, and in so doing we drive all evil out of our own hearts. The evil that is in us is more than moral. There is a psychological evil, the distortion caused by selfishness and sin. Good moral intentions are enough to correct what is formally bad in our moral acts. But in order that our charity may heal the wounds of sin in our whole soul it must reach down into the furthest depths of our humanity, cleaning out all the infection of anxiety and false guilt that spring from pride and fear, releasing the good that has been held back by suspicion and prejudice and self-conceit. Everything in our nature must find its right place in the life of charity, so that the whole man may be lifted up to God, that the entire person may be sanctified and not only the intentions of his will.

13. God Who is infinitely rich became man in order to experience the poverty and misery of fallen man, not because He needed this experience but because we needed His example. Now that we have seen His love, let us love one another as He has loved us. Thus His love will work in our hearts and transform us into Himself.

12. Recollection

1. Recollection is a change of spiritual focus and an attuning of our whole soul to what is beyond and above ourselves. It is a "conversion" or a "turning" of our being to spiritual things and to God. And because spiritual things are simple, recollection is also at the same time a simplification of our state of mind and of our spiritual activity. This simplification gives us the kind of peace and vision of which Jesus speaks when He says: "If thine eye be single thy whole body will be lightsome" (Matthew 6:22). Since this text refers principally to purity of intention, it reminds us that recollection does this also: it purifies our intention. It gathers up all the love of our soul, raises it above created and temporal things, and directs it all to God in Himself and in His will.

2. True recollection is known by its effects: peace, interior silence, tranquillity of heart. The spirit that is recollected is quiet and detached, at least in its depths. It is undisturbed because the passions are momentarily at rest. At most, they are allowed to trouble only the surface of the recollected soul. But since the fruits of recollection are produced by humility and charity and by most of the other fundamental Christian virtues, it is clear that true recollection cannot exist except when these virtues concur to give it substance and actuality.

3. Concentration is not recollection. The two can exist together, but ordinarily recollection means so much more

than the focusing of thought upon a single clear point that it tends to diffuse thought by simplification, thus raising it above the level of tension and self-direction.

4. Recollection is more than a mere turning inward upon ourselves, and it does not necessarily mean the denial or exclusion of exterior things. Sometimes we are more recollected, quieter, simple and pure, when we see *through* exterior things and see God in them than when we turn away from them to shut them out of our minds. Recollection does not deny sensible things, it sets them in order. Either they are significant to it, and it sees their significance, or else they have no special meaning, and their meaninglessness remains innocent and neutral. For recollection brings the soul into contact with God, and His invisible presence is a light which at once gives peace to the eye that sees by it, and makes it see all things in peace.

5. Recollection should be seen not as an absence, but as a presence. It makes us, first of all, present to ourselves. It makes us present to whatever reality is most significant in the moment of time in which we are living. And it makes us present to God, present to ourselves in Him, present to everything else in Him. Above all, it brings His presence to us. And this is what gives meaning to all the other "presences" of which we have spoken.

6. First of all, we must be present to ourselves.

The cares and preoccupations of life draw us away from ourselves. As long as we give ourselves to these things, our minds are not at home. They are drawn out of their own reality into the illusion to which they tend. They let go of the actuality which they have and which they are, in order to follow a flock of possibilities. But possibilities have wings, and our minds must take flight from themselves in order to follow them into the sky. If we live with possibilities we are exiles from the present which is given us by God to be our own, homeless and displaced in a future or a past which are not ours because they are always beyond our reach. The present is our right place, and we can lay hands on whatever it offers us. Recollection is the only thing that can give us the power to do so. But before we explain that, let us return to the idea that recollection makes us present to ourselves.

As long as we are in this life, we both are and are not. We are constantly changing, and yet the person who changes is always the same person. Even his changes express his personality, and develop it, and confirm him for what he is.

A man is a free being who is always changing into himself. This changing is never merely indifferent. We are always getting either better or worse. Our development is measured by our acts of free choice, and we make ourselves according to the pattern of our desires.

If our desires reach out for the things that we were created to have and to make and to become, then we will develop into what we were truly meant to be.

But if our desires reach out for things that have no meaning for the growth of our spirit, if they lose themselves in dreams or passions or illusions, we will be false to ourselves and in the end our lives will proclaim that we have lied to ourselves and to other men and to God. We will judge ourselves as aliens and exiles from ourselves and from God.

In hell, there is no recollection. The damned are exiled not only from God and from other men, but even from themselves.

7. Recollection makes me present to myself by bringing together two aspects, or activities, of my being as if they were two lenses in a telescope. One lens is the basic substance of my spiritual being: the inward soul, the deep will, the spiritual intelligence. The other is my outward soul, the practical intelligence, the will engaged in the activities of life.*

When my practical and outward self is submissive and ordered to the deepest needs implanted in my inward being by nature and by grace, then my whole soul is in harmony with itself, with the realities around it, and with God. It is able to see things as they are, and it enables

* I do not mean that there are two souls in man with two sets of faculties. Man's one soul acts in two different ways, when dealing with the outward works and inward contemplation. Cf. St. Augustine, *De Trinitate, Lib.* XII.

me to be aware of God. This makes me "present" to myself. That is to say that my outward self is alive to its true function as a servant of the spirit and of grace. It is aware of the mastery of grace, aware of the inward self, aware of its submission to the spirit and to grace, and aware of its power to work among outward things, and by this work to help the inward transformation of the spirit by grace.

But when the outward self knows only itself, then it is absent from my true self. It does not know its own inward spirit. It never acts according to the need and measure of my own true personality, which exists where my spirit is wedded with the silent presence of the Lord's Spirit, and where my deep will responds to His gravitation toward the secrecy of the Godhead.

When I am not present to myself, then I am only aware of that half of me, that mode of my being which turns outward to created things. And then it is possible for me to lose myself among them. Then I no longer feel the deep secret pull of the gravitation of love which draws my inward self toward God. My will and my intelligence lose their command of the other faculties. My senses, my imagination, my emotions, scatter to pursue their various quarries all over the face of the earth. Recollection brings them home. It brings the outward self into line with the inward spirit, and makes my whole being answer the deep pull of love that reaches down into the mystery of God.

8. Recollection, then, makes me present to whatever is significantly real at each moment of my existence. The depths of my soul should always be recollected in God. When they are so, they do not necessarily prevent me from engaging in practical, outward activity. True, there are certain modes of union with God which interfere with exterior action. But recollection as such is compatible with physical and mental activity, and with any ordinate kind of work.

In order to be recollected in action I must not lose myself in action. And in order to keep acting, I must not lose myself in recollection. Hence recollected activity, in carrying out the will of God in the duties of my state of life, means a balance between interior purity and exterior attention. Both these are required. It is a shocking thing to see a monk do his work carelessly because he is trying to work and pray at the same time in such a way that he neither works nor prays properly.

We fail to balance interior purity and exterior attention when, in one way or another, we seek ourselves instead of God. If we seek only our own interests in our work, we will not be able to keep our hearts pure and recollected in an atmosphere of prayer. If we seek ourselves in prayer, we will not give the proper attention to our work.

The secret of recollected action is, first of all, detachment from ourselves and from the results either of our action or of our prayer. We must be detached from the results of our work, in order to deliver ourselves from the anxiety that makes us plunge into action without restraint. We must also be detached from the desire to see ourselves always recollected in God and to feel his presence in our hearts. That is to say, we must go to work for God, trusting that if we seek only to do His will, He will take care of our interior recollection, and make up for the distractions and failings that may creep into our activity.

If we begin our work with peace and recollection and with our hearts directed to God by prayer and a pure intention, we will avoid many baneful concerns and useless preoccupations as we proceed with our work. Scattered powers are easily fatigued. Spiritual fatigue proceeds from wasted and ill-applied effort. The disgust it generates slackens the powers of our soul, so that we waste even more effort and end in even greater fatigue.

9. Thought that does not proceed from recollection tends by its very nature to disperse our powers of thought and will. It may seem to seek recollection, but it cannot be helped by what it can never find. And if it is not strengthened by interior recollection, such thought must seek its strength elsewhere—in the vain power of excitement and interior tension. This tension is a form of unconscious idolatry, centered upon the illusion of a fixed idea, in which we place our trust. We impose this idea upon ourselves by violence, concentrate our thoughts upon it, and hug it to our hearts. This idea may be true in itself, but the violence of our own will gives it a disproportionate place in our own interior life. So it becomes an idol,

drawing to itself the worship and attention and trust that we owe to God alone.

10. Anxiety is fatal to recollection because recollection depends ultimately on faith, and anxiety eats into the heart of faith. Anxiety usually comes from strain, and strain is caused by too complete a dependence on ourselves, on our own devices, our own plans, our own idea of what we are able to do. If we rely exclusively on our own efforts to keep ourselves recollected at work, our recollection will be forced and artificial. It will inevitably come in conflict with our work itself. When the Lord gives us work to do for Him, He does not demand that we work like angels, with our minds at the same time totally engrossed in Him and efficiently given to the work commanded. It is much simpler to use a little common sense, to set about working for the love of God, to keep ourselves detached from the anxieties and cares aroused by the work itself, and not to worry too much about our spiritual state while we are working. It is enough to think of one thing at a time, and the spiritual life is never helped by constant and exaggerated reflection upon ourselves.

At the same time it is not hard to work in a recollected way if our intention is constantly purified by faith in the God for whom we are working, and by trust in His love, which keeps our souls united to Him even though we may not always be conscious of the union. We must remember that our experience of union with God, our feeling of His presence, is altogether accidental and secondary. It is only a side effect of His actual presence in our souls, and gives no sure indication of that presence in any case. For God Himself is above all apprehensions and ideas and sensations, however spiritual, that can ever be experienced by the spirit of man in this life.

11. Recollection also makes us present to God, and to ourselves in Him. The desire to preserve the deepest movements of our soul for God alone, to direct them away from ourselves and from His creatures, and concentrate them entirely on the fulfillment of His will, makes us in a special way present to God. True, we are always present to Him Who sees all and keeps all things in existence by

the very act that knows their existence. But we are more present to Him when we are aware of His nearness to us than when we ignore it. For then the presence is conscious and mutual: it is the presence of a person to a person. And it is only when we are thus present to Him that we truly discover ourselves as we really are. For when we are in the presence of God, seeing Him in His own light, which comes to us in the obscurity of faith, we also see, in this same light, that we are far different from what we thought ourselves to be in the light of our own ambition and self-complacency.

Here recollection becomes tinged with compunction and what the Fathers called "holy fear." Fear is the knowledge of ourselves in the presence of God's holiness. It is the knowledge of ourselves in His love, and it sees how far we are from being what His love would have us be. It knows Who He is and who we are!

But fear that is holy cannot fear love. It fears the discrepancy between itself and love, and flies to hide itself in the abyss of light which is God's love and His perfection.

This fear is sometimes absolutely necessary to keep our recollection from becoming perverted with a false sweetness and from the presumptuous self-assurance which takes the grace of God for granted, which ceases to fear delusion, and which becomes complacent in the thought of our own virtue and our own lofty degree of prayer. Such complacency falls imperceptibly, like an impenetrable curtain, between ourselves and God. He departs from us, leaving us with a terrible illusion.

The more intense, strained, and prolonged our recollection, the greater the danger that we may fall into this illusion. It becomes easy enough, after a time, to recollect ourselves without actually entering into any real contact with God at all. Such recollection is nothing but a psychological trick. It is an act of introversion which can be learned with a little effort. It opens the door to a dark, silent, comfortable interior room in which nothing ever happens and in which there are no more troubles because we have managed to find the switch that turns off all our intellectual activity at its source. This is not prayer, and although it may be restful and even beneficial to us for a little while, if we become attached to it and carry it too far it can lead to very serious harm.

Recollection without faith confines the spirit in a prison without light or air. Interior asceticism should not end by locking us in such a prison. It would only defeat all the purposes of God's grace by doing so. Faith establishes us in recollection not by setting limits to the activity of the soul, but by removing all the limitations of our natural intelligence and will, freeing the mind from doubt and the will from hesitation, so that the spirit is let loose by God and plunges into the depths of His invisible freedom.

12. Recollection is almost the same thing as interior solitude. It is in recollection that we discover the finite solitude of our own heart, and the infinite solitude of God dwelling within us. Unless these vast horizons have opened out in the center of our lives, we can hardly see things in perspective. Our judgments are not in proportion with things as they are. But the spiritual man, says St. Paul, judges all things. He does so because he is isolated from them by his detachment, by his poverty, by his humility, by his nothingness. Therefore, he sees them only in God. To see them thus is to judge them as God Himself judges them.

Recollection brings us, then, to an interior solitude which is something more than either the desire or the fact of being alone. We become solitaries not when we realize how alone we are, but when we sense something of the solitude of God. His solitude isolates us from everything around us, and yet makes us all the more truly the brothers of all things.

We cannot live for others until we have entered this solitude. If we try to live for them without first living entirely for God, we risk plunging with them all into the abyss.

13. How many there are who have solitude and do not love it, because their solitude is without recollection! It is only loneliness. It does nothing to bring them to themselves. They are alone because in their solitude they are separated from God, and from other men, and even from themselves. They are like souls wandering out of hell and finding their way by mistake into Heaven, only to discover

that Heaven is more of a hell to them than hell itself. So it is with those who are forced into the heaven of solitude and cannot taste its joy because they know no recollection.

The man who fears to be alone will never be anything but lonely, no matter how much he may surround himself with people. But the man who learns, in solitude and recollection, to be at peace with his own loneliness, and to prefer its reality to the illusion of merely natural companionship, comes to know the invisible companionship of God. Such a one is alone with God in all places, and he alone truly enjoys the companionship of other men, because he loves them in God in Whom their presence is not tiresome, and because of Whom his own love for them can never know satiety.

14. False recollection occurs when we try by our own efforts to block out all material things, to isolate ourselves from people and nature by main force, hoping that there will be nothing left in our soul but God. When we attempt this, we usually divide our being against itself, call one half (the one we like) God, and call the other our "nature" or our "self." What madness, what a waste of effort, to try to rest in one half of our being, calling it "God," and lock the other out of doors! Our being resists this division, and engages in what we think is a war between light and darkness. But this struggle is only the battle of an illusion against an illusion. Such battles are too often waged in monasteries, where God calls men not to embrace illusion but to abandon it, that they may discover what is real.

False recollection is inevitable without humility. For humility teaches us to accept ourselves as we are, restrains our pride from forcing ourselves to be what we are not. It is better to be content with what is low and unassuming in the spiritual life, for in this life all voluntary poverty is a spiritual enrichment. To be content with a low degree of prayer is to be enriched in prayer. Such contentment is better than the pride that insists on striving for the intellectual purity of the angels before it has even learned to be maturely human.

13. *"My soul remembered God"*

1. The "remembering" of God, of which we sing in the Psalms, is simply the rediscovery, in deep compunction of heart, that God remembers us. In a sense, God cannot be remembered. He can only be discovered.*

We know Him because He knows us. We know Him when we discover that He knows us. Our knowledge of Him is the effect of His knowledge of us. The experience is always one of new wonder that He is mindful of us. "What is man that Thou art mindful of him? Or the son of man that Thou visitest him?" (Psalm 8:5).

"In the day of my trouble I sought God with my hands lifted up to Him in the night, and I was not deceived. My soul remembered God, and was delighted, and was exercised, and my spirit swooned away. . . . And I said, Now

---

* "God cannot be remembered." If taken completely literally, just as it stands, without qualification, this statement would be false. We can have a valid conceptual knowledge of God. This knowledge can be stored in the memory and called back to mind. But the aphorism derives its point from the fact that there is another knowledge of God which goes beyond concepts, which passes through concepts to attain Him in the mysterious actuality of His presence, grasped in some sort, in an "experience." Even these experiences of God remain deeply engraved in the memory: but when we remember them, their actuality is no longer present, but past. This actuality of God's presence is something that does not belong to the past or to the future but only to the present. It cannot be brought back by an effort of memory, any more than it can be elicited by the work of imagination. It is a "discovery," and each time the discovery is new.

173

I have begun: this is the change of the right hand of the Most High" (Psalm 76:3, 4, 11).

We could not seek God unless He were seeking us. We may begin to seek Him in desolation, feeling nothing but His absence. But the mere fact that we seek Him proves that we have already found Him. For if we continue in our prayer, we "remember" Him, that is to say, we become conscious, once again, of Who He really is. And we see that He has found us. When this consciousness is the work of grace, it is always fresh and new. It is more than the recovery of a past experience. It is a new experience, and it makes us new men.

This newness is the "delight" and the "exercise" which are the living evidence of contact with the Spirit of the Lord. It makes us "swoon" in our spirit in a passage from death to life. Thus our eyes are opened. We see all things in a new light. And we realize that this is a new beginning, a change that could only be brought about by the intervention of His Spirit in our lives—the "change of the right hand of the Most High."

2. My Lord, You have heard the cry of my heart because it was You Who cried out within my heart.

Forgive me for having tried to evoke Your presence in my own silence: it is You Who must create me within Your own silence! Only this newness can save me from idolatry!

You are not found in the Temple merely by the expulsion of the money changers.

You are not found on the mountain every time there is a cloud. The earth swallowed those who offered incense without having been found, and called, and known by You.

3. If I find Him with great ease, perhaps He is not my God.

If I cannot hope to find Him at all, is He my God?

If I find Him wherever I wish, have I found Him?

If He can find me whenever He wishes, and tells me Who He is and who I am, and if I then know that He Whom I could not find has found me: then I know He is the Lord, my God: He has touched me with the finger that made me out of nothing.

4. A current of useless interior activity constantly surrounds and defends an illusion.

I cannot find God unless I renounce this useless activity, and I cannot renounce this activity unless I let go of the illusion it defends. And I cannot get rid of an illusion unless I recognize it for an illusion.

Interior silence is, therefore, not so much a negation, an absence of noise and of movement, as the positive rest of the mind in truth.

Man's intelligence, however we may misuse it, is far too keen and too sure to rest for long in error. It may embrace a lie and cling to it stubbornly, believing it to be true: but it cannot find true rest in falsehood. The mind that is in love with error wears itself out with anxiety, lest its error be discovered for what it is. But the man who loves truth can already find rest in the acknowledgment of his mistakes, for that is the beginning of truth.

The first step toward finding God, Who is Truth, is to discover the truth about myself: and if I have been in error, this first step to truth is the discovery of my error. A false and illusory "experience" of what appears to be God's action in the soul may bring with it, for a moment, a kind of interior silence: the silence of a soul that rests in an illusion. But this silence is quickly disturbed by a deep undercurrent of unrest and noise. The tension of a soul trying to hold itself in silence, when it has no truth to appease it with a superior silence, is louder than the noise of big cities and more disturbing than the movement of an army.

5. The god of the philosophers lives in the mind that knows him, receives life by the fact that he is known, lives as long as he is known, and dies when he is denied. But the True God (whom the philosophers can truly find through their abstractions if they remember their vocation to pass beyond abstractions) gives life to the mind that is known by Him. The Living God, by the touch of His mercy in the depths of the soul that is "known" to His mercy, awakens the knowledge of His presence in that soul so that it not only knows Him but, at the same time, loves Him, seeing that it lives in Him. Therefore Jesus said: "The God of Abraham, the God of Isaac and the God of Jacob is not the God of the dead but of the living"

(Matthew 22:32). So true is it that the Lord is the "Living God" that all those whose God He is will live forever, because He is their God. Such was the argument that Jesus gave to the Sadducees, who did not believe in the resurrection of the dead. If God was the "God of Abraham" then Abraham must rise from the dead: no one who has the Living God for his Lord can stay dead. He is our God only if we belong entirely to Him. To belong entirely to life is to have passed from death to life.

"For by a man death, and by a man the resurrection of the dead. As in Adam all die, so in Christ all shall be made alive. . . . And the dead shall rise again incorruptible: and we shall be changed. . . . And when this mortal hath put on immortality, then shall come to pass the saying that is written: 'death is swallowed up in victory'" (I Corinthians 15:21–22, 52, 54).

We cannot find Him Who is Almighty unless we are taken entirely out of our own weakness. But we must first find out our own nothingness before we can pass beyond it: and this is impossible as long as we believe in the illusion of our own power.

6. The monastery is the House of God and all who live there are close to Him. Yet it is possible to live close to Him and in His own house without ever finding Him. Why is this? Because we continue to seek ourselves rather than God, to live for ourselves rather than for Him. Then the monastery becomes our house rather than His, and He hides Himself from us. Standing in the way of His light, we gaze in perplexity upon our own shadow. "Surely," we say, "this has nothing of God in it, for it is a shadow." True! And yet the shadow is cast by His light, and bears witness indirectly to His presence. It is there to remind us that we can turn to Him whenever we cease to love darkness rather than the light.

Yet we fail to turn to Him because we forget that He must come to us as a savior, without Whom we are helpless. We seek Him as if He could not do without our sacrifices, as if He needed to be entertained by our affection and flattered by our praise.

We cannot find Him unless we know we need Him. We forget this need when we take a self-sufficient pleasure in our own good works. The poor and helpless are the first to find Him, Who came to seek and to save that which was lost.

7. The Lord is my rock and my fortress and He dwells in the midst of His people.

Come, let us enter the House of the Almighty and stand to praise Him.

Let us sleep like eagles in the cliff, let us rest in the power of the Lord our God!

Let us hide ourselves in the great mountain of His might, Who dwells concealed in the midst of a forsaken people.

Even His thunder is the refuge of the poor!

14. The wind blows where it pleases

1. God, Who is everywhere, never leaves us. Yet He seems sometimes to be present, sometimes absent. If we do not know Him well, we do not realize that He may be more present to us when He is absent than when He is present.

There are two absences of God. One is an absence that condemns us, the other an absence that sanctifies us.

In the absence that is condemnation, God "knows us not" because we have put some other god in His place, and refuse to be known by Him. In the absence that sanctifies, God empties the soul of every image that might become an idol and of every concern that might stand between our face and His Face.

In the first absence, He is present, but His presence is denied by the presence of an idol. God is present to the enemy we have placed between ourselves and Him in mortal sin.

In the second absence He is present, and His presence is affirmed and adored by the absence of everything else. He is closer to us than we are to ourselves, although we do not see him.

Whoever seeks to catch Him and hold Him loses Him. He is like the wind that blows where it pleases. You who love Him must love Him as arriving from where you do not know and as going where you do not know. Your spirit must seek to be as clean and as free as His own Spirit, in order to follow Him wherever He goes. Who are we to call ourselves either clean or free, unless He makes us so?

If He should teach us how to follow Him into the wilderness of His own freedom, we will no longer know where we are, because we are with Him Who is everywhere and nowhere at the same time.

Those who love only His apparent presence cannot follow the Lord wherever He goes. They do not love Him perfectly if they do not allow Him to be absent. They do not respect His liberty to do as He pleases. They think their prayers have made them able to command Him, and to subject His will to their own. They live on the level of magic rather than on the level of religion.

Only those men are never separated from the Lord who never question His right to separate Himself from them. They never lose Him because they always realize they never deserve to find Him, and that in spite of their unworthiness they have already found Him.

For He has first found them, and will not let them go.

2. God approaches our minds by receding from them.

We can never fully know Him if we think of Him as an object of capture, to be fenced in by the enclosure of our own ideas.

We know Him better after our minds have let Him go.

The Lord travels in all directions at once.

The Lord arrives from all directions at once.

Wherever we are, we find that He has just departed.

Wherever we go, we discover that He has just arrived before us.

Our rest can be neither in the beginning of this pursuit, nor in the pursuit itself, nor in its apparent end. For the true end, which is Heaven, is an end without end. It is a totally new dimension, in which we come to rest in the secret that He must arrive at the moment of His departure; His arrival is at every moment and His departure is not fixed in time.

3. Every man becomes the image of the God he adores.

He whose worship is directed to a dead thing becomes a dead thing.

He who loves corruption rots.

He who loves a shadow becomes, himself, a shadow.

179

He who loves things that must perish lives in dread of their perishing.

The contemplative also, who seeks to keep God prisoner in his heart, becomes a prisoner within the narrow limits of his own heart, so that the Lord evades him and leaves him in his imprisonment, his confinement, and his dead recollection.

The man who leaves the Lord the freedom of the Lord adores the Lord in His freedom and receives the liberty of the sons of God.

This man loves like God and is carried away, the captive of the Lord's invisible freedom.

A god who remains immobile within the focus of my own vision is hardly even a trace of the True God's passing.

4. What does it mean to know You, o my God?

There are souls who grow sick and tremble at the thought of giving You some insufficient name!

I wake up in the night and sweat with dread at the thought that I have dared to speak of You as "pure Being."

When Moses saw the bush in flames, burning in the desert but not consumed, You did not answer his question with a definition. You said, "I am." What could be the effect of such an answer? It made the very dust of the earth instantly holy, so that Moses threw away his shoes (symbols of his senses and of his body) lest there remain any image in the way between Your sanctity and his adoration.

You are the strong God, the Holy, the Just One, strong and shy in Your vast mercy, hidden from us in Your freedom, giving us Your love without restraint, in order that, receiving all from You we may know that You alone are holy.

How shall we begin to know You Who are if we do not begin ourselves to be something of what You are?

How can we begin to know You Who are good unless we let You do us good?

How can we escape the knowledge of You Who are good since no one can prevent You from doing good to us?

To "be" and to "be good" are things familiar to us. For we are made in Your image, with a being that is good because it is Your gift. But the being and the goodness we know fall so far short of You that they deceive us if we apply them to You as we know them in ourselves.

Therefore, they do not tell us, as they should, that You are holy.

5. The wise man has struggled to find You in his wisdom, and he has failed. The just man has striven to grasp You in his own justice, and he has gone astray.

But the sinner, suddenly struck by the lightning of mercy that ought to have been justice, falls down in adoration of Your holiness: for he has seen what kings desired to see and never saw, what prophets foretold and never gazed upon, what the men of ancient times grew weary of expecting when they died. He has seen that Your love is so infinitely good that it cannot be the object of a human bargain. True, there are two testaments, two bargains. But both of them are only promises that You would freely give us what we could never deserve: that You would manifest Your holiness to us by showing us Your mercy and Your liberality and Your infinite freedom.

"Is it not lawful to me," says the Lord, "to do what I will?" (Matthew 20:15). The supreme characteristic of His love is its infinite freedom. It cannot be compelled to respond to the laws of any desire, that is of any necessity. It is without limitation because it is without need. Being without need, His love seeks out the needy, not in order to give them a little but in order to give them all.

His love cannot be at peace in a soul that is content with a little. For to be content with a little is to will to continue in need.

It is not God's will that we should remain in need. He would fulfill all our needs by delivering us from all possessions and giving us Himself in exchange.

If we would belong to His love, we must remain always empty of everything else, not in order to be in need, but precisely because possessions make us needy.

6. Each true child of God is mild, perfect, docile, and alone. His consciousness springs up, in the Spirit of the Lord, at the precise point where he feels himself to be held in being by a pure gift, an act of love, a divine command. The freedom of God's gift of life calls for the response of our own freedom—an act of obedience, hidden

in the secrecy of our deepest being. We find the Lord when we find His gift of life in the depths of ourselves. We are fully alive in Him when the deepest roots of life become conscious that they live in Him. From this consent to exist in dependence upon His gift and upon His freedom springs the interior life.

7. Let the command of His love be felt at the roots of my existence.

Then let me understand that I do not consent in order to exist, but that I exist in order to consent.

This is the living source of virtuous action: for all our good acts are acts of consent to the indications of His mercy and the movements of His grace.

From this we can come to perfection: to the love which consents in all things, seeks nothing but to respond, by goodness, to Goodness, and by love, to Love. Such love suffers all things and is equally happy in action and inaction, in existence and in dissolution.

Let us not only exist, but *obey* in our existing.

From this fundamental obedience, which is a fundamental gift, and the fit return of His gift, all other acts of obedience spring up into life everlasting.

For the full fruitfulness of spiritual life begins in gratitude for life, in the consent to live, and in the greater gratitude that seeks to be dissolved and to be with Christ.

15. The inward solitude

1. Charity is a love for God which respects the need that other men have for Him. Therefore, charity alone can give us the power and the delicacy to love others without defiling their loneliness which is their need and their salvation.

2. Do not stress too much the fact that love seeks to penetrate the intimate secrets of the beloved. Those who are too fond of this idea fall short of true love, because they violate the solitude of those they love, instead of respecting it.

True love penetrates the secrets and the solitude of the beloved by allowing him to keep his secrets to himself and to remain in his own solitude.

3. Secrecy and solitude are values that belong to the very essence of personality.

A person is a person insofar as he has a secret and is a solitude of his own that cannot be communicated to anyone else. If I love a person, I will love that which most makes him a person: the secrecy, the hiddenness, the solitude of his own individual being, which God alone can penetrate and understand.

A love that breaks into the spiritual privacy of another in order to lay open all his secrets and besiege his solitude with importunity does not love him: it seeks to destroy what is best in him, and what is most intimately his.

4. Compassion and respect enable us to know the solitude

of another by finding him in the intimacy of our own interior solitude. It discovers his secrets in our own secrets. Instead of consuming him with indiscretion, and thus frustrating all our own desires to show our love for him, if we respect the secrecy of his own interior loneliness, we are united with him in a friendship that makes us both grow in likeness to one another and to God. If I respect my brother's solitude, I will know his solitude by the reflection that it casts, through charity, upon the solitude of my own soul.

This respect for the deepest values hidden in another's personality is more than an obligation of charity. It is a debt we owe in justice to every being, but especially to those who, like ourselves, are created in the image of God.

Our failure to respect the intimate spiritual privacy of other persons reflects a secret contempt for God Himself. It springs from the crass pride of fallen man, who wants to prove himself a god by prying into everything that is not his own business. The tree of the knowledge of good and evil gave our first parents a taste for knowing things outside of God, in a way in which they are not known truly, instead of knowing them in Him, in Whom alone we are able to find them and know them and love them as they are. Original justice gave our souls the power to love well: to increase our own heritage of life by loving others for their own good. Original sin gave our souls the power to love destructively: to ruin the object of our love by consuming it, with no other profit to ourselves than the increase of our own interior famine.

We ruin others and ourselves together not by entering into the sanctuary of their inner being—for no one can enter there except their Creator—but by drawing out of that sanctuary and teaching them to live as we live: centered upon themselves.

5. If a man does not know the value of his own loneliness, how can he respect another's solitude?

It is at once our loneliness and our dignity to have an incommunicable personality that is ours, ours alone and no one else's, and will be so forever.

When human society fulfills its true function the persons who form it grow more and more in their individual freedom and personal integrity. And the more each individual develops and discovers the secret resources of his own incommunicable personality, the more he can contribute to the life and the weal of the whole. Solitude is as necessary for society as silence is for language and air for the lungs and food for the body.

A community that seeks to invade or destroy the spiritual solitude of the individuals who compose it is condemning itself to death by spiritual asphyxiation.

6. If I cannot distinguish myself from the mass of other men, I will never be able to love and respect other men as I ought. If I do not separate myself from them enough to know what is mine and what is theirs, I will never discover what I have to give them, and never allow them the opportunity to give me what they ought. Only a *person* can pay debts and fulfill obligations, and if I am less than a person I will never give others what they have a right to expect from me. If they are less than persons, they will not know what to expect from me. Nor will they ever discover that they have anything to give. We ought normally to educate one another by fulfilling one another's just needs. But in a society where personality is obscured and dissolved, men never learn to find themselves and, therefore, never learn how to love one another.

7. Solitude is so necessary both for society and for the individual that when society fails to provide sufficient solitude to develop the inner life of the persons who compose it, they rebel and seek false solitudes.

A false solitude is a point of vantage from which an individual, who has been denied the right to become a person, takes revenge on society by turning his individuality into a destructive weapon. True solitude is found in humility, which is infinitely rich. False solitude is the refuge of pride, and it is infinitely poor. The poverty of false solitude comes from an illusion which pretends, by adorning itself in things it can never possess, to distinguish one individual self from the mass of other men. True solitude is selfless. Therefore, it is rich in silence and charity and peace. It finds in itself seemingly inexhaustible resources of good to bestow on other people. False solitude is self-centered. And because it finds nothing in its own center, it seeks to draw all things into itself. But everything it touches becomes infected with its own nothingness, and falls apart. True solitude cleans the soul, lays it wide open to the four winds of generosity. False solitude locks the door against all men and pores over its own private accumulation of rubbish.

Both solitudes seek to distinguish the individual from the crowd. True solitude succeeds in this, false solitude fails. True solitude separates one man from the rest in order that he may freely develop the good that is his own, and then fulfill his true destiny by putting himself at the service of everyone else. False solitude separates a man from his brothers in such a way that he can no longer effectively give them anything or receive anything from them in his own spirit. It establishes him in a state of indigence, misery, blindness, torment, and despair. Maddened by his own insufficiency, the proud man shamelessly seizes upon satisfactions and possessions that are not due to him, that can never satisfy him, and that he will never really need. Because he has never learned to distinguish what is really his, he desperately seeks to possess what can never belong to him.

In reality the proud man has no respect for himself because he has never had an opportunity to find out if there is anything in him worthy of respect. Convinced that he is despicable, and desperately hoping to keep other men from finding it out, he seizes upon everything that belongs to them and hides himself behind it. The mere fact that a thing belongs to someone else makes it seem worthy of desire. But because he secretly hates everything that is his own, as soon as each new thing becomes his own it loses its value and becomes hateful to him. He must fill his solitude with more and more loot, more and more rapine, seizing things not because he wants them, but because he cannot stand the sight of what he has already obtained.

These, then, are the ones who isolate themselves above the mass of other men because they have never learned to love either themselves or other men. They hate others because they hate themselves, and their love of others is merely an expression of this solitary hatred.

The proud solitary is never more dangerous than when he appears to be social. Having no true solitude and, therefore, no spiritual energy of his own, he desperately needs other men. But he needs them in order to consume them, as if in consuming them he could fill the void in his own spirit and make himself the person he feels he ought to be.

When the Lord, in His justice, wills to manifest and punish the sins of a society that ignores the natural law, He allows it to fall into the hands of men like this. The proud solitary is the ideal dictator, turning the whole world from peace to war, carrying out the work of destruction, opening the mouths of ruin from city to city, that these may declare the emptiness and degradation of men without God.

The perfect expression of a society that has lost all sense of the value of personal solitude is a state forced to live as a refugee in its own ruins, a mob without roofs to cover it, a herd without a barn.

8. True solitude is the solitude of charity, which "seeketh not her own."* It is ashamed to have anything that is not due to it. It seeks poverty, and desires to give away all that it does not need. It seems to feel distaste for created things: but its distaste is not for them. It cannot hate them, for it cannot even hate itself. Because it loves them, it knows it cannot own them, since they belong to God. Charity desires that He alone should possess them and receive from them the glory which is His due.

Our solitude may be fundamentally true, but still imperfect. In that event, it is mixed with pride. It is a disturbing mixture of hatred with love. One of the secrets of spiritual perfection is to realize that we have this mixture in ourselves, and to be able to distinguish one from the other. For the temptation of those who seek perfection is to mistake hatred for love, and to place their perfection in the solitude which distinguishes itself from other men by hating them and which at the same time loves and hates the good things that are theirs.

The asceticism of the false solitary is always double-dealing. It pretends to love others, but it hates them. It pretends to hate created things, and it loves them. And

* *"Caritas . . . non quaerit quae sua sunt"* (I Corinthians 13:5).

by loving them in the wrong way, it only succeeds in hating them.

Therefore, as long as our solitude is imperfect it will be tainted with bitterness and disgust, because it will exhaust us in continual conflict. The disgust is unavoidable. The bitterness, which should not be, is, nevertheless, there. Both must be used for our purification. They must teach us to distinguish what is truly bitter from what is truly sweet, and not permit us to find a poisoned sweetness in self-hatred and a poisoned bitterness in the love of others.

The true solitary must recognize that he is obliged to love other men and even all things created by God: that this obligation is not a painful and unpleasant duty, and that it was never supposed to be bitter. He must accept the sweetness of love without complaint, and not hate himself because his love may be, at first, a little inordinate. He must suffer without bitterness in order to learn to love as he ought. He must not fear that love will destroy his solitude. Love *is* his solitude.

9. Our solitude will be imperfect as long as it is tainted with restlessness and *accedia*. For the vice of *accedia* makes us hate what is good and shrink from the only virtues that can save us. Pure interior solitude does not shrink from the good things of life or from the company of other men, because it no longer seeks to possess them for their own sake. No longer desiring them, it no longer fears to love them. Free from fear, it is free of bitterness. Purified of bitterness, the soul can safely remain alone.

Indeed, the soul that does not seek to dress itself in possessions and to revel in purchased or stolen satisfactions will often be left completely alone by other men. The true solitary does not have to run away from others: they cease to notice him, because he does not share their love for an illusion. The soul that is truly solitary becomes perfectly colorless and ceases to excite either the love or the hatred of others by reason of its solitude. The true solitary can, no doubt, become a hated and a hunted person: but not by reason of anything that is in himself. He will only be hated if he has a divine work to do in the world. For his work will bring him into conflict with the world. His solitude, as such, creates no such conflict. Solitude brings persecution only when it takes the form of a "mission," and then there is something much more in it than solitude. For when the solitary finds that his solitude has taken on the character of a mission, he discovers that he has become a force that reacts on the very heart of the society in which he lives, a power that disturbs and impedes and accuses the forces of selfishness and pride, reminding others of their own need for solitude and for charity and for peace with God.

10. Pure interior solitude is found in the virtue of hope. Hope takes us entirely out of this world while we remain bodily in the midst of it. Our minds retain their clear view of what is good in creatures. Our wills remain chaste and solitary in the midst of all created beauty, not wounded in an isolation that is prudish and ashamed, but lifted up to Heaven by a humility that hope has divested of all bitterness, all consolation, and all fear.

Thus we are both in time and out of it. We are poor, possessing all things. Having nothing of our own left to rely on, we have nothing to lose and nothing to fear. Everything is locked away for our sure possession, beyond our reach, in Heaven. We live where our souls desire to be, and our bodies no longer matter very much. We are buried in Christ, our life is hidden with Christ in God and we know the meaning of His freedom.

This is true solitude, about which there are no disputes and no questions. The soul that has thus found itself gravitates toward the desert but does not object to remaining in the city, because it is everywhere alone.

16. Silence

1. The rain ceases, and a bird's clear song suddenly announces the difference between Heaven and hell.

2. God our Creator and Savior has given us a language in which He can be talked about, since faith cometh by hearing and our tongues are the keys that open Heaven to others.

But when the Lord comes as a Bridegroom there remains nothing to be said except that He is coming, and that we must go out to meet Him. *Ecce Sponsus venit! Exite obviam ei!**

After that we go forth to find Him in solitude. There we communicate with Him alone, without words, without discursive thoughts, in the silence of our whole being.

When what we say is meant for no one else but Him, it can hardly be said in language. What is not meant to be related is not even experienced on a level that can be clearly analyzed. We know that it must not be told, because it cannot.

But before we come to that which is unspeakable and unthinkable, the spirit hovers on the frontiers of language, wondering whether or not to stay on its own side of the border, in order to have something to bring back to other men. This is the test of those who wish to cross the frontier. If they are not ready to leave their own ideas and

* "Behold the Bridegroom cometh, go ye forth to meet Him" (Matthew 25:6).

their own words behind them, they cannot travel further.

3. Do not desire chiefly to be cherished and consoled by God; desire above all to love Him.

Do not anxiously desire to have others find consolation in God, but rather help them to love God.

Do not seek consolation in talking about God, but speak of Him in order that He may be glorified.

If you truly love Him, nothing can console you but His glory. And if you seek His glory before everything else, then you will also be humble enough to receive consolation from His hand: accepting it chiefly because, in showing His mercy to us, He is glorified in our souls.

If you seek His glory before everything else, you will know that the best way to console another man is to show him how to love God. There is no true peace in anything else.

If you wish your words about Him to mean something, they must be charged with zeal for His glory. For if your hearers realize that you are speaking only to please yourself, they will accuse your God of being nothing more than a shadow. If you love His glory, you will seek this transcendence—and this is sought in silence.

Let us, then, not seek comfort in the assurance that we are good, but only in the certainty that He alone is holy, He alone is good.

It is not seldom that our silence and our prayers do more to bring people to the knowledge of God than all our words about Him. The mere fact that you wish to give God glory by talking about Him is no proof that your speech will give Him glory. What if He should prefer you to be silent? Have you never heard that silence gives Him glory?

4. If you go into solitude with a silent tongue, the silence of mute beings will share with you their rest.

But if you go into solitude with a silent heart, the silence of creation will speak louder than the tongues of men or angels.

5. The silence of the tongue and of the imagination dissolves the barrier between ourselves and the peace of

things that exist only for God and not for themselves. But the silence of all inordinate desire dissolves the barrier between ourselves and God. Then we come to live in Him alone.

Then mute beings no longer speak to us merely with their own silence. It is the Lord Who speaks to us, with a far deeper silence, hidden in the midst of our own selves.

6. Those who love their own noise are impatient of everything else. They constantly defile the silence of the forests and the mountains and the sea. They bore through silent nature in every direction with their machines, for fear that the calm world might accuse them of their own emptiness. The urgency of their swift movement seems to ignore the tranquillity of nature by pretending to have a purpose. The loud plane seems for a moment to deny the reality of the clouds and of the sky, by its direction, its noise, and its pretended strength. The silence of the sky remains when the plane has gone. The tranquillity of the clouds will remain when the plane has fallen apart. It is the silence of the world that is real. Our noise, our business, our purposes, and all our fatuous statements about our purposes, our business, and our noise: these are the illusion.

God is present, and His thought is alive and awake in the fullness and depth and breadth of all the silences of the world. The Lord is watching in the almond trees, over the fulfillment of His words (Jeremias 1:11).

Whether the plane pass by tonight or tomorrow, whether there be cars on the winding road or no cars, whether men speak in the field, whether there be a radio in the house or not, the tree brings forth her blossoms in silence.

Whether the house be empty or full of children, whether the men go off to town or work with tractors in the fields, whether the liner enters the harbor full of tourists or full of soldiers, the almond tree brings forth her fruit in silence.

7. There are some men for whom a tree has no reality until they think of cutting it down, for whom an animal has no value until it enters the slaughterhouse, men who never look at anything until they decide to abuse it and

who never even notice what they do not want to destroy. These men can hardly know the silence of love: for their love is the absorption of another person's silence into their own noise. And because they do not know the silence of love, they cannot know the silence of God, Who is Charity, Who cannot destroy what He loves, Who is bound, by His own law of Charity, to give life to all those whom He draws into His own silence.

8. Silence does not exist in our lives merely for its own sake. It is ordered to something else. Silence is the mother of speech. A lifetime of silence is ordered to an ultimate declaration, which can be put into words, a declaration of all we have lived for.

Life and death, words and silence, are given us because of Christ. In Christ we die to the flesh and live to the spirit. In Him we die to illusion and live to truth. We speak to confess Him, and we are silent in order to meditate on Him and enter deeper into His silence, which is at once the silence of death and of eternal life—the silence of Good Friday night and the peace of Easter morning.

9. We receive Christ's silence into our hearts when first we speak from our heart the word of faith. We work out our salvation in silence and in hope. Silence is the strength of our interior life. Silence enters into the very core of our moral being, so that if we have no silence we have no morality. Silence enters mysteriously into the composition of all the virtues, and silence preserves them from corruption.

By the "silence" of virtue I mean the charity which must give each virtue a supernatural life and which is "silent" because it is rooted in God. Without this silence, our virtues are sound only, only an outward noise, a manifestation of nothing: the thing that virtues manifest is their own interior charity, which has a "silence" of its own. And in this silence hides a Person: Christ, Himself hidden, as He is spoken, in the silence of the Father.

10. If we fill our lives with silence, then we live in hope, and Christ lives in us and gives our virtues much substance. Then, when the time comes, we confess Him

openly before men, and our confession has much meaning because it is rooted in deep silence. It awakens the silence of Christ in the hearts of those who hear us, so that they themselves fall silent and begin to wonder and to listen. For they have begun to discover their true selves.

If our life is poured out in useless words we will never hear anything in the depths of our hearts, where Christ lives and speaks in silence. We will never be anything, and in the end, when the time comes for us to declare who and what we are, we shall be found speechless at the moment of the crucial decision: for we shall have said everything and exhausted ourselves in speech before we had anything to say.

11. There must be a time of day when the man who makes plans forgets his plans, and acts as if he had no plans at all.

There must be a time of day when the man who has to speak falls very silent. And his mind forms no more propositions, and he asks himself: Did they have a meaning?

There must be a time when the man of prayer goes to pray as if it were the first time in his life he had ever prayed; when the man of resolutions puts his resolutions aside as if they had all been broken, and he learns a different wisdom: distinguishing the sun from the moon, the stars from the darkness, the sea from the dry land, and the night sky from the shoulder of a hill.

12. In silence, we learn to make distinctions. Those who fly silence, fly also from distinctions. They do not want to see too clearly. They prefer confusion.

A man who loves God necessarily loves silence also, because he fears to lose his sense of discernment. He fears the noise that takes the sharp edge off every experience of reality. He avoids the unending movement that blurs all beings together into a crowd of undistinguishable things.

The saint is indifferent in his desires, but by no means indifferent in his attitudes toward different aspects of reality.

13. Here lies a dead man who made an idol of indifference.

His prayer did not enkindle, it extinguished his flame.

His silence listened to nothing and, therefore, heard nothing, and had nothing to say.

Let the swallows come and build their nests in his history and teach their young to fly about in the desert which he made of his soul, and thus he will not remain unprofitable forever.

14. Life is not to be regarded as an uninterrupted flow of words which is finally silenced by death. Its rhythm develops in silence, comes to the surface in moments of necessary expression, returns to deeper silence, culminates in a final declaration, then ascends quietly into the silence of Heaven which resounds with unending praise.

Those who do not know there is another life after this one, or who cannot bring themselves to live in time as if they were meant to spend their eternity in God, resist the fruitful silence of their own being by continual noise. Even when their own tongues are still, their minds chatter without end and without meaning, or they plunge themselves into the protective noise of machines, traffic, or radios. When their own noise is momentarily exhausted, they rest in the noise of other men.

How tragic it is that they who have nothing to express are continually expressing themselves, like nervous gunners, firing burst after burst of ammunition into the dark, where there is no enemy. The reason for their talk is: death. Death is the enemy who seems to confront them at every moment in the deep darkness and silence of their own being. So they keep shouting at death. They confound their lives with noise. They stun their own ears with meaningless words, never discovering that their hearts are rooted in a silence that is not death but life. They chatter themselves to death, fearing life as if it were death.

15. Our whole life should be a meditation of our last and most important decision: the choice between life and death.

We must all die. But the dispositions with which we face death make of our death a choice either of death or of life.

If, during our life we have chosen life, then in death we will pass from death to life. Life is a spiritual thing, and spiritual things are silent. If the spirit that kept the flame of physical life burning in our bodies took care to nourish itself with the oil that is found only in the silence of God's charity, then when the body dies, the spirit itself goes on burning the same oil, with its own flame. But if the spirit has burned all along with the base oils of passion or egoism or pride, then when death comes the flame of the spirit goes out with the light of the body because there is no more oil in the lamp.

We must learn during our lifetime to trim our lamps and fill them with charity in silence, sometimes speaking and confessing the glory of God in order to increase our charity by increasing the charity of others, and teaching them also the ways of peace and of silence.

16. If, at the moment of our death, death comes to us as an unwelcome stranger, it will be because Christ also has always been to us an unwelcome stranger. For when death comes, Christ comes also, bringing us the everlasting life which He has bought for us by His own death. Those who love true life, therefore, frequently think about their death. Their life is full of a silence that is an anticipated victory over death. Silence, indeed, makes death our servant and even our friend. Thoughts and prayers that grow up out of the silent thought of death are like trees growing where there is water. They are strong thoughts, that overcome the fear of misfortune because they have overcome passion and desire. They turn the face of our soul, in constant desire, toward the face of Christ.

17. If I say that a whole lifetime of silence is ordered to a final utterance, I do not mean that we must all contrive to die with pious speeches on our lips. It is not necessary that our last words should have some special or dramatic significance worthy of being written down. Every good death, every death that hands us over from the uncertainties of this world to the unfailing peace and silence of the love of Christ, is itself an utterance and a conclusion. It says, either in words or without them, that it is good for life to come to its appointed end, for the body to return to dust and for the spirit to ascend to the Father, through the mercy of Our Lord Jesus Christ.

A silent death may speak with more eloquent peace

than a death punctuated by vivid expressions. A lonely death, a tragic death, may yet have more to say of the peace and mercy of Christ than many another comfortable death.

For the eloquence of death is the eloquence of human poverty coming face to face with the riches of divine mercy. The more we are aware that our poverty is supremely great, the greater will be the meaning of our death: and the greater its poverty. For the saints are those who wanted to be poorest in life, and who, above all else, exulted in the supreme poverty of death.

OTHER IMAGE BOOKS

OTHER IMAGE BOOKS

OTHER IMAGE BOOKS

Slats,

We hope to get as much enjoyment from this book as we did buying it for you.

Merry Christmas

Love
Edye, Fred, Peter, Guy

1978

ADVENTURES
IN RESTORING
ANTIQUE
CARS

ADVENTURES IN RESTORING ANTIQUE CARS

by Burt Mills

Illustrated with photographs

DODD, MEAD & COMPANY
New York

1 2 3 4 5 6 7 8 9 10

Library of Congress Cataloging in Publication Data

Mills, Burt.
Adventures in restoring antique cars.

Bibliography: p.
Includes index.
1. Automobiles—Restoration.   I. Title.
TL152.2.M54   629.28'7'22   78-17186
ISBN 0-396-07585-1

*This book
is fondly dedicated to
my cousin
Betty,
who suggested
the theme*

Acknowledgment is gratefully made to the following, who either furnished some of the pictures used in this book or allowed photographs of their cars to be taken:

M. N. Estridge, San Bernardino, California
Jim Simmons, Denver, Colorado
Gary Geivett, Littleton, Colorado
F & R Imports, Ltd., Englewood, Colorado
Harold Dawe, Lakewood, Colorado
J. A. Reed, Denver, Colorado

Preface

This book recounts some of the more memorable experiences I've had over the past twenty-five years on trips to buy old cars or to locate parts for them.

What had to be done to restore these cars, and how I made the restorations, is covered in some detail. The search for the correct part, and what was done when it could not be located, is an important facet of the story.

Some of the photographs show cars before and after restoration. Some show the work in progress. Others show the elusive parts, or the solution when parts could not be found.

The book was written for the person who has an interest in old cars, whether or not he owns one. It is for anyone inclined to start the hobby but hesitant because it seems too complex, difficult and expensive. It is also for the man or woman interested in the old car hobby as a sound investment.

Good luck!

Contents

ADVENTURES
IN RESTORING
ANTIQUE
CARS

1

Find the Man
Who Owned One

"You might find some Packard wheel covers in that red shed behind the school bus. I've got a lot of hubcaps in there," Jake said, without moving from under a 1958 Chevy. He added that no Packards had been brought in for a couple of years.

Threading my way through engines, transmissions and other car parts strewn between the Chevy and the school bus, I reached the red shed. It had once been a chicken coop, and I could imagine rats scurrying when the door was opened. I don't think it had been cleaned out before being put to its present use. Opening the low door, I saw literally hundreds of hubcaps and wheel covers. They were piled on the floor, stacked in nests, tossed in the area below the roosts, even hanging on the walls and rafters! If they had ever been in any order, it was not evident now. There was nothing to do but start sorting through the piles, looking for Packard's familiar red hexagon.

Four Stutz hubcaps (year unknown) came as a surprise, and I set them aside for a friend. I saw hubcaps for Marmons, Flints, Gardners and other makes long gone. Half an hour later, grimy from the dirt and dust, I located one Packard wheel cover. I measured it and found it to be the correct size, then dug on with renewed vigor. Shortly after, I found three more. Since all four were in good condition, except for being dirty, I gathered my prizes, fled the hot, smelly coop, and looked for Jake.

No nicely boxed or stacked hubcaps or wheel covers, as at this flea market, when I searched for Packard wheel covers in an abandoned chicken coop.

He had left the Chevy and was nearly headfirst into the engine compartment of a Lincoln Zephyr. When I told him I had found what I needed, he said he'd have to have $20 for the Packard discs, and $10 for the Stutz caps. I thought he meant these amounts for each, which would have been well in line, and got out my wallet to pay. Jake extricated himself from the maw of the Zephyr, wiped his oil-covered hands on the front of his shirt and looked at the money in my hand. He had meant $20 for the Packard set and $10 for the four Stutz caps. He said no one ever asked for Stutz parts, and he had broken up the car several years back. He took my $30 saying, "I don't give no receipts. Don't keep no record on these small parts."

Finding the proper Packard wheel discs and the rare Stutz hubcaps at such a low price really made my day. I'd been searching for over three months for the Packard parts.

This episode came about while I was visiting my wife's home in southern Minnesota. I had some time on my hands and decided to try the local wrecking yards for a list of parts I needed to complete the Packard restoration. The local phone book indicated several yards within a thirty-mile radius. I tried phoning, but experience has taught me that since the phones are usually in the shacks or trailers used as offices, and the men are out among the cars, phoning is not very satisfactory.

"No Packards," I was told at one yard. At another I was told there were a couple of Packards on the lot but the years were unknown. I decided to give up on the phone and drive to the yards to see for myself.

The two Packards turned out to be a badly wrecked 1937 and a nearly stripped 1950. There was a 1956 in another yard, but the wheel covers would have been wrong for my 1953.

In one very small town I could not locate the wrecking yard listed in the phone book. A used-car salesman gave me some directions: "Go back the same road you're on for about four miles. You'll come to a rise with a gravel pit on the right. Turn left and follow that road a couple of miles and you'll reach a church. Take the right by the church and you'll come to the wrecking yard directly."

These instructions were accurate as far as turning right or left, but the distances were way off, and of course the conditions of the roads were not mentioned. I found the gravel pit just over six miles down the road, and made the left turn as directed. The church was nearly five miles, and it was almost another mile before there was even a path to the right. This was a deeply rutted

Nearly complete 1953 Packard Mayfair Convertible as it stood on a Nebraska farm. Wheel covers and rear fender trim parts were all that were needed.

Elusive 1953 Packard wheel covers after cleaning with household detergent and polishing with jeweler's rouge and the buffing wheel of an electric hand drill. Lettering and hexagon were painted after polishing was completed.

dirt road that followed the rolling countryside of southern Minnesota. I was driving a Mercedes and feared I would knock off the vulnerable crankcase drain plug, which would be real trouble in the middle of nowhere. Frankly, I was hoping for a spot to turn around when I spied a field full of cars probably a quarter of a mile ahead.

Aside from a small girl playing with some kittens and a yard full of chickens, there was no one in sight as I parked in the farmyard. The little girl told me Jake was in charge, and he was "out there." I walked toward the cars and finally located Jake when I heard a loud "Goddam" and some banging. The noise led me to him and the start of my successful search.

That evening at a cocktail party I told friends about my lucky finds. Some were as excited as I and wanted to see the by-then-scoured wheel covers and hubcaps. Others were polite but not impressed, not even interested. One couple looked at me as if I were some kind of nut to have spent so much time and trouble locating old car parts when new cars were so readily available.

I brought the parts home, buffed the wheel discs "like new" with jeweler's rouge, repainted the red hexagons and filled in the black lettering. My friend with the Stutz could not believe his luck—a set of hubcaps for $10!

2

It Takes All Kinds

You will meet a grand variety of people if you take up auto restoration. In over twenty-five years with this fascinating hobby, I believe I have met all kinds. I've also seen old-car prices skyrocket to unbelievable heights. Who would ever believe that Model A Fords, which sold for about $500 when new, would be grabbed up at ten times that figure? Classic-era Packards, Pierce Arrows and Lincolns, which I once bought for $350 to $500, now sell for $20,000 and more! Fortunately the prices on old car parts have not kept pace with the prices of cars. Although prices have increased along with demand, usually they are within reason, considering that the supply is constantly diminishing.

Fortunately most of the buffs who restore old cars are delightful people, straightforward and honest. They have a genuine interest in old cars and in seeing that correct parts are found and fairly priced. Most in the business of selling cars or parts are anxious to find a good home for their cars or to help someone locate a needed part. They are like someone giving away a litter of puppies, trying to make sure their pets will not be abused.

Unfortunately, there are others who just want to make a sale, regardless of the consequences. They are sorely lacking in knowledge of cars and the parts they are selling, trying to cover their ignorance with a veneer of bluff and fast talk. Like a woman I met at a recent flea market who was presiding over a fairly large selection of Ford parts. When I asked if a water pump was for a 1937, she snapped back, "If that's the year you're looking for, that's the pump." A closer examination showed it was not a 1937 Ford water pump, and when I called this to her attention, she merely shrugged.

I always attend flea markets put on by the various car clubs, and usually have a list of a dozen or so parts I need. I enjoy talking with the vendors, even if they do not have what I need. They are an excellent source of information and help. Some have offered to try to locate certain parts for me, and have been very helpful.

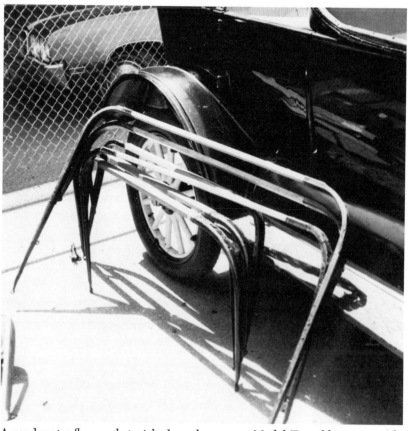

A vendor at a flea market picked up these 1923 Model T roof bows at a sale in a distant city and saved them for me. He refused an offer of $20 more than the price he had quoted to me.

Car club flea markets are an excellent source for parts. Most vendors are honest. Parts usually go for about 20 percent less than the asking price, unless the part is very scarce and in like-new condition.

The top bows for a 1923 Ford touring car I was restoring were so shot they were not worth repairing. I scanned the ads in various car magazines without luck. I mentioned this to a fellow who had some Model T parts. He said he had not seen any roof bows recently but would be on the lookout for them at other flea markets he would be attending. We exchanged addresses, and about three months later I got a letter saying he had located a set that looked as if they had never been used. He bought the set and said he would save them until I could take a look. At the next flea market in the area I located him and could not have been happier with the roof bows. They were indeed just like new! He had received several offers for the bows but had told people he thought they were sold, asking them to check back later in case I turned them down. While I was talking with him, someone offered him $20 more than the price he had quoted me, but he refused the offer. Naturally I bought them, and he refused to let me meet the other offer or even split the difference.

Lately a growing number of fast-buck artists have discovered the market that exists for old car parts and have elbowed their way into the hobby. These people buy parts as cheaply as possible, then sell them for high prices. They could not care less for authenticity, and have no real interest in cars or parts. They just

Wrecking yards are a good source for parts. Usually you have to look on your own, for yard operators do not want to take the time. In many yards you can save money by removing the part with your own tools.

want a sale, and will make any claim to accomplish this. They hurt the hobby and undoubtedly take advantage of many people.

While looking through some ads for Franklin parts, I came across a list that contained some of what I needed. I wrote, asking for accurate descriptions, prices and pictures. The answer to my letter was disappointing. Either the parts were marked "sold" or prices were beyond reason. A snapshot of what was claimed to be a Franklin hood would have been funny if it had not had a $100 price tag attached. As far as I could tell, none of the parts pictured were from a Franklin. I suppose the seller could have made an honest mistake, but from the prices quoted, along with the statement that all sales were cash in advance, and nonrefundable, I think the guy knew what he was doing.

Of course the sellers are not entirely to blame for higher prices and the make-do attitude that is growing in the hobby. Some hobbyists are not too concerned about authenticity, or even about making correct and necessary repairs. They just want to "get her running." They will use any part that works, and will even bypass some parts if locating proper replacements or making repairs is difficult. I do not criticize these people, for they get enjoyment out of cars that might otherwise have been junked. It does hurt, though, to see this kind of person luck on to a rare or wanted model, then treat it in this manner. It is a sad waste.

The restorer who really annoys me is the person with more
money than sense or taste. Not only do they drive prices up, but
they do not really appreciate the cars they have. You know the
type. They will grab a car and with no regard for proper details
start getting it fixed up. Usually they do little if any of the
restoration work themselves. Almost any part that can be removed
they will have chrome-plated, and will add all sorts of accessories.
As a group they are to be pitied, for they do not realize what
they have done to their cars. Neither do they realize what they
have missed by not doing some of the restoration work themselves.

I hate to see someone latch on to a classic car of the 1920s or
1930s and lavish money on it without knowing what he is doing.
These people apparently do not know—or care—that chrome-
plating instead of the original nickel detracts from the car's
authenticity and value. These are the ones who install tape decks
and stereo systems, screwing plastic speakers into fine hardwood
trim parts so the back seat passengers can have the full effect of
stereophonic sound. Spotlights, trumpet horns and bumper guards
are irresistible to them. Their cars will be loaded with more lights
than the electrical system can handle. These are the people who
install musical horns on a staid Pierce Arrow limousine and play
"Colonel Bogy's March" as they tool around town, oblivious to
the fact the horn does not have A-flat.

Of course there are the purists who have both the money and
interest to have a perfect restoration. These few deserve a vote
of thanks from all of us. Their cars are thrilling to see and have
given thousands of people pleasure.

There are also the purists who do not have money to burn but
still want perfection. These people contribute most to the hobby.
It may take them months or years to complete a certain car, but
when it is done they have a perfect specimen. They must also
have a tremendous feeling of satisfaction and pride in their accomplishment. Of course, there are certain jobs these hobbyists cannot
do themselves. After all, few have access to a welding outfit,
machine shop or plating equipment. But these people know what
they want done. Their insistence on perfection benefits the whole
hobby. I admire them tremendously. They take hours sanding or
filing a part before painting. They refurbish every component to
perfection. They are the ones who spend months in search of the
proper part.

3

One of About
Seven Hundred

The Packard V-12s of the mid to late 1930s were big, beautiful cars, the epitome of luxurious transportation and true classics in every sense of the word. Although many were offered with custom and coach-built bodies, the standard factory-fitted bodies were beautifully styled, carefully built and impeccably finished. Each car was road tested on the famous Packard Proving Ground, now owned by Ford Motor Company.

When a 1935 Packard V-12 Club Sedan was offered along with other items in an estate sale, I thought my chance had come. Just over 700 V-12s were manufactured in 1935, so they have become scarce.

Normally one thinks of cars in an estate sale as having been babied, chauffer-driven, kept in meticulous condition in a heated garage. Such was not the case with this car. The odometer showed slightly over 70,000 miles, and everything indicated that at least the last 20,000 had been very hard miles. Little or no care had been given to the car's appearance. The fenders were nicked and dented and the running boards were scuffed through. The tires were badly worn, and the front ones indicated that the front end was out of alignment. Surprisingly, the upholstery was good, although very dirty. The car seemed to be complete. The engine missed occasionally and was hard to start. The oil pressure was good and the engine did not knock, a testament to the quality built into the car.

One glance at the understated elegance of the 1935 Packard V-12 explains why the car has remained a favorite for over forty years. Just over 700 were produced, and the remaining examples are now in great demand.

Before worrying about water-stained upholstery, locate and correct the source of the leaks. Scrubbing with a soapy solution, or with white vinegar and water, will often remove mold and mildew. The panel should be replaced if water spots remain.

The "estate" in this case was that of a small business owner who liked to drive big cars. He would buy these at a low price and drive them to death. He had owned the Packard several years and had driven it daily, with next to no maintenance. He also had a late-model Dodge pickup, but that did not interest me.

To arrive at a bidding price, I made a careful appraisal of the car's condition and what it would take to restore it. I knew others had looked at the car too, and thought they might not realize what repairs cost and thus make higher bids.

A phone call from the attorney notified me that mine was the high bid. He would not tell me the others, and I have no idea how much higher I may have been. A properly endorsed title and bill of sale would be ready when cash or a certified check was presented.

My wife accompanied me on the short drive to pick up the car. With a little priming, and a battery jump from my car, the Packard started, but it did not run very smoothly. I wanted to make some tests, so I drove it slowly and chose a route that had little traffic. I was not sure the tires would make it. The brakes were very hard to apply; it took practically stand-up pressure on the pedal to stop the car. I knew the front end was out of alignment, and found the car hard to steer.

The car smelled absolutely terrible. I had noticed an odor when looking it over a few weeks before, but it was not nearly as strong. To keep from gagging and suffocating, I lowered all the windows and adjusted the front vent planes to direct air into the car.

With my wife following closely behind so no one could crowd in between, I made a careful but quite thorough test drive on the way home. The car was so dirty that I had to hose it down and clean the inside before putting it in my garage.

To really clean the inside properly, and in hope of getting rid of the odor, it was necessary to remove the bottom seat cushions. It was then I discovered the source of the odor: The partly decomposed remains of a cat lay under the front seat. I presume it got trapped inside the car and starved. Once the cat was removed, I pulled the carpets out and scrubbed them with a strong disinfectant. They were worn, but I wanted them as patterns. Although there was no rust on the floor under the carpet pads, I cleaned it thoroughly so it could be coated later with a rust-inhibiting primer.

Starting at the driver's door, I made a complete tour of the car, noting every defect in the body and fenders, making a list of what would be necessary to put it in first-class shape.

Next came the mechanical examination. All of the spark plugs were worn, but none had a gummy deposit that would indicate worn piston rings. The oil dipstick had shown no water droplets on my first check, so I concluded from the test drive that the cylinder block and heads were in good shape. The ammeter gauge had a good charging rate on the drive, and since the horn and lights all worked, I felt no major repairs would be necessary on the main portion of the electrical system. The car had not over-heated, and the radiator showed no sign of leaking. The cooling system was basically sound.

On my drive home I had taken the car through the gears, accelerating and decelerating in each gear, and could find no fault with the clutch or transmission. The universal joints did not make the chucking noise typical of worn joints. There was no whine or hum in the differential, so I knew the drive train was okay.

Remove fenders to sandblast the frame and to clean the engine block and firewall. Shock absorbers are bolted to the frame and can be rebuilt once removed. Jack up the frame to spread spring leaves for cleaning, repainting and lubrication.

No doubt the brakes were bad, but I did not know how bad until the brake drums were removed. The car had the original brake linings, worn to the point where the rivets had scored the drums. This would necessitate turning them down on a lathe before they could be used. The brake cables seemed frozen in the outer, protecting cable. This was part of the reason I had to push the pedal so hard. Evidently the inner cables had not been lubricated in a long time. They would have to be removed from the outer cables, cleaned thoroughly with solvent, and lubricated before they would work correctly. I planned on equalizing the length of both front and rear cables when I did this job.

The examination of the front end showed more work needed than I could do myself. New bushings in the steering system were no problem for me, but I could not do the realigning. This was later completed at a shop specializing in frame and front-end work.

The exhaust system was solid and looked entirely original. There were no leaks in the pipe leading to the muffler. The muffler was intact, and the tail pipe required no attention. Even the attachments on the various exhaust components were solid, another indication of the quality built into the car.

All in all, my examination of the body and mechanism of the car indicated it would be well worth the restoration effort, and that a lot of expensive mechanical work and parts would not be necessary. To do the sort of restoration job the car deserved, I felt it should be disassembled and that I should go all out for perfection.

After removing the door panels and windows, a careful search of each door bottom showed only minimal rust spots. Only one door needed leading. The insides of the doors were cleaned with a wire-bristled brush, then sprayed with a rust inhibitor. New fiberglass insulation pads were fitted to each door.

When the trunk lid and door to the spare-tire compartment were removed, the trunk lining and shelf could be taken out and the entire luggage compartment thoroughly cleaned and primed. The trunk latches and plated parts of the luggage carrier were all cleaned and taken to the plater's. The plated wheel rings were removed for replating at the same time. The bumpers were de-

Remove "bolt-on" parts before repainting the engine. Use high-temperature engine enamel in correct color. Head nuts can be scrubbed clean or replated. Air cleaner, harnesses, horns, filters and other parts should be sanded, primed and painted.

Brackets, spare wheel holders, bumper arms, etc., should be removed, cleaned, sanded, primed and finished separately for best results. Store them out of the way until needed.

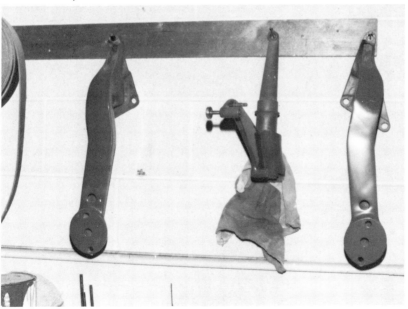

greased and the surface prepared for plating, although these were in surprisingly good condition. The bumper arms and braces were sanded, primed and painted.

All fenders were removed and sandblasted before the few dents were repaired and one torn area was welded. The running boards were removed and new metal welded in to replace a worn spot. After sanding and priming, the replacement metal did not show. Since new padding was needed along with the plated molding pieces, I began to search for these parts. New old-stock matting was located in Maine. Some of the molding could be reused and was replated. The replacement pieces came from a supplier of Packard parts in New Jersey.

While the fenders were off the car, the rear wheel arches were buffed down to bare metal. No replacement metal was needed, and the area was coated with a rust-inhibiting primer plus a thick coat of asphalt undercoating. There were no rust-out spots along the area where the body and fenders joined. New fender welting

Repairs to running boards can be better accomplished when they are removed from the car. Be as concerned with rustproofing the underside as the top.

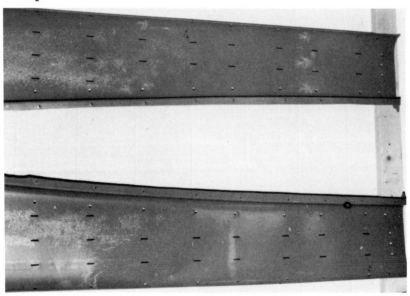

Trunk lid removed from body to repair small dent. Hinges and clasps were removed for plating. After repairs, filling, sanding and priming, lid received four coats of lacquer, lightly sanded between coats.

was made, allowing more material for securing the welting between the body and fenders.

Everything from the fire wall forward was steam-cleaned. Bolt-on accessories on the motor were removed for finishing, and the parts that had originally been plated were replated. Packard, like many other builders of high-quality cars, still used nickel plating on some parts. To keep things authentic, each part was done as it had been originally.

New gaskets were available, so the car got a top-engine overhaul, carbon cleaned, and the valves ground and adjusted. While the cylinder heads were off, the entire engine was repainted with the original green engine enamel. New points, distributor rotor, twin coils, and new wires completed the electrical overhaul. With new spark plugs and the carburetor cleaned and adjusted, the motor purred like a kitten. For a motor that had been driven over 70,000 miles, there was very little to do.

The only way to restore the cosmetics of the engine compartment is to re-move all engine accessories and steam-clean the fire wall before priming and painting. Accessories should be cleaned and painted. Tubing, control cables and linkages should be refurbished.

Nickel and chromium parts of the engine should be degreased and replated if necessary. Usually this does not change the way they work, but it does make the engine compartment look better. Avoid plating anything that was not originally plated.

After reassembling a top-engine overhaul, check cylinder-head nuts, water-hose connections and water pump to be sure there are no leaks. New hoses and fan belts should be installed.

Be sure gas lines and oil lines are tight and no leaks show up at any connection. Packard, like others with large-displacement engines, employed an oil cooler to reduce oil temperature and prolong engine life. Make certain the unit is clean.

It took a geat deal of sanding, filling, priming and resanding to get the surface ready for the lacquer paint job. I chose an original Packard color, and gave the car at least eight coats, carefully applied. Some parts—the trunk lid, for instance—probably got ten coats before it was perfect. Then the car was rubbed down with pumice stone and a coat of clear lacquer applied. The finish acquired a deep luster, which was nicely accented by the replated trim parts. Striping came later, applied with a dagger-pointed camel's hair brush. Fortunately there were raised moldings to use as a guide for the striping.

The wheels were sent to a "stripper," where they were dipped in a chemical solution to remove the old finish. This was the first time I had used this service; I had always had wire wheels sandblasted. I like the stripping method better and feel it is easier on the metal, for there is a risk that sandblasting can remove too much metal. After a complete rinsing, the wheels were primed and given four coats of black enamel. New white sidewalls cost a bundle, but new tires were needed and the whitewalls added to the car's appearance. Some Packard V-12s had wheel discs to cover the wire wheels, but none were with this car. Because I liked the appearance the wire wheels gave the car, I did not attempt to locate discs.

To keep spray from the paint job from getting on the upholstery, I delayed installing the upholstery panels until all painting had been done. The cushions and door panels cleaned up nicely with a readily available foam upholstery cleaner. I used a small, soft-bristled brush to clean the upholstery, for that does a better job than a sponge or a cloth. I mix the soapy solution thicker than the directions indicate so it will not run or evaporate as quickly. The upholstery should always be rinsed after cleaning to get the soap residue from the cloth.

Headliners are hard to clean, for the soapy solution always runs down the cleaner's arms. I tried a spray-on cleaner but was not satisfied with the results. So wet arms and all, I used the thick, soapy cleaner with good results. Before applying anything wet on any upholstery, always sweep and vacuum to remove as much dirt as possible.

Replated bumpers and other trim items gleam against glossy lacquer finish, making all the hours of sanding, priming, painting and rubbing down worthwhile. Replating is not overly expensive and is worth the time and money on a restored car.

Not all cars used white sidewall tires originally. Those that did not look strange with whitewalls. Wide whites, an option on Packards, add to the beauty of Packard wheel trim and hubcaps. A soapy solution on the rim makes mounting tires easy.

Remove instrument cluster bolted on the dashboard. Clean instrument faces with care so numerals are not damaged. Satin finish on the cluster panel can be cleaned with a mild detergent solution. Do not use abrasives to remove dirt or film.

There was no trouble locating replacement carpeting identical in quality and color to the original. The only trouble was the new high price! Using the old front and rear carpets for patterns, new ones were cut. I could not sew the binding on the carpet with my sewing machine because the carpeting was too thick and the backing too heavy, so this job had to be done for me. At the same time, new kick panels to fit under the cowl were made and bound.

The dashboard responded to rubbing compound, and the finish looked fine. A coat of wax was added to keep it that way. The dials were basically clean, but I felt the ivory-colored faces needed a little attention. One by one I removed each instrument and swabbed the finish with a Q-tip dipped in solvent. Each face was wiped dry almost immediately so there would be no damage to the figures or lettering.

The wooden window trim required very careful refinishing. The trim had a delicate inlay that I believe was pewter. Not wanting to use a liquid finish remover, I hand sanded each frame, then wiped on a neutral color filler to build up the surface. Next

Use great care when removing window trim to avoid breaking the wood. Usually a careful but thorough sanding is better than paint remover on old finish. Use filler if necessary, and light coats of stain to build up the surface. Sand carefully.

Courtesy light on the running board goes on when the door is opened. There are refinements to provide passenger comfort throughout the car. New welting was installed between running board, fender and body after painting was completed.

The length of the car was emphasized by sweeping front fender line, horizontal plated trim on hood louvers and raised belt line. Body, hood and doors all fit evenly, showing the care taken in design and assembly of the Packard V-12.

To maintain the value of a car, look for authenticity when buying accessories. Ads in national car magazines, conversations with other hobbyists, and flea markets are sources for parts. Do not add accessories that were not originally offered.

Packard cormorant sits proudly atop radiator cap. It not only adds to the distinction of the car but acts as a guide to determine the center of the car when driving in traffic.

a light color stain matching the original was wiped on, then wiped off to get the shading necessary. Satin gloss lacquer—three coats —carefully rubbed between coats, finished the job. The trim looked wonderful.

The reassembled interior also looked great. I had no trouble understanding why those who could afford a car like this chose it originally. It was big, beautiful, luxurious and very easy to drive despite the 139-inch wheelbase.

Buyers in the luxury market had other cars from which to choose: Auburn, Cadillac, Lincoln, Packard and Pierce Arrow all offered V-12s. But V-12s were fast disappearing. The Auburn did not compare in quality with the other marques and lasted

From the front, Packard's famous radiator shape adapted easily to the "V" shape popular in the 1930s as car designers became conscious of streamlining. Restrained use of chrome-plating adds to the massive appearance of the car.

From the rear, Packard's radiator shape was used at top of the folding trunk rack. Heavy bumpers with overriders protected the body, fenders and taillights. Insignia on the hubcaps was repeated at top center of trunk rack.

only until 1936. Pierce Arrow made it only into 1937. Production of a Franklin V-12 ceased in 1934, when the company folded. Stutz, designating their cars as SV-16 and DV-32, was out of the picture by 1933; these nomenclatures pertained to the number of valves, not cylinders. Marmon made a V-12 prototype but never got it into production. Their V-16 competed with Cadillac's V-16, but Marmon gave up the ghost in 1934. A few custom-built bodies were mounted on Duesenberg chassis and called 1936 models, but the engines and running gear had already been produced in previous years and were held over for sale.

The restoration of my 1935 Packard V-12 took over a year of off-and-on work, but the finished results proved the time and effort were worth every minute. The value of the restored car made it worthwhile. The powerful V-12 engine was whisper-quiet and very responsive; the car could be driven upwards of 70 miles per hour all day, with no mechanical distress and no strain on the driver or passengers.

4

From Deep in Dixie

It is too bad that Kaiser-Frazer was not able to continue in business. Although their cars were not standouts from a mechanical point of view, they were capable machines. The corportion made several worthwhile contributions to the industry. Their Traveler and Vagabond models were the first hatchback sedans. Their stylish four-door convertibles were the only ones on the market at the time, and were very attractive. The Darrin-bodied sports models with the sliding doors, unique front-end styling and rakish windshield were ahead of their time. The perky little Henry-J was one of the first compacts in the 1950s. The sleek, lower, redesigned bodies that appeared in 1951 were offered when Chrysler, Ford and General Motors were still using bodies that had been in production since 1949.

A 1951 Kaiser four-door sedan that had not been driven for a few years was advertised. It was described as a low-mileage car that would take very little to put in tip-top shape. Because the car had been tied up in an estate argument it had not been offered for sale previously. With permission to examine the car, I went to southern Alabama. True, it was a low-mileage car—slightly over 22,000 miles and looked sound. But it had been stored in a corrugated shed for several years, then in an outside storage yard for another year. For want of a better description, the car had suffered a heat stroke.

Suffering from too much sun in a damp climate, the Kaiser needed minor floor repair and body work to the left rear fender panel. A low-mileage car, mechanically it required only attention to the cooling system and starter and a brake system overhaul.

Most of the plated trim parts were in good condition despite sun and weather damage to the paint job. Silicone spray gave new resiliency to weather stripping around the windshield, vent windows and rear window.

The sun had caused problems inside and out. The paint had deteriorated badly. Inside the heat had caused mold and mildew to form on the seats, side panels and carpets. But there was no rust, and there was only one small dent, behind the left rear wheel.

I made as accurate an appraisal as I could since I was not able to get the motor started. With jumper cables attached and the carburetor primed, the starter motor would only whir. It did not engage the flywheel as it should, but this did not concern me too much, because starter drives are easy to repair. Even if a new starter was necessary, it would not be expensive. My offer was accepted. The car was mine.

Because of the distance involved, no one accompanied me on the trip. I took along a tow bar, a set of tools and flasher lights to use as turn signals. The car could not be started and I decided to wait until I was home before working on it. I towed the car out of the storage yard rear end first and pushed it around so the tow bar could be attached. This was hard work, and I was awash in perspiration when the car was finally in the right position. I had a devil of a time with the tow bar. The front bumper guards on the Kaiser had to be removed—no easy job—so the tow bar could be solidly clamped.

Fortunately I had a tire pump and could pump enough air in the tires to get the car to a service station. Finally, with everything tight and the safety chain in place for added protection, I began the trip home.

The station wagon seemed to be laboring more than it should, and the temperature gauge showed higher than usual. When downshifting became necessary on a hill that should have been crested in high, I knew something was wrong. The rear wheels on the Kaiser were very hot, indicating that the brakes were dragging. Crawling under the car, I backed the brake adjusting nuts off as far as possible. I could not turn the bleeder nuts so had to disconnect the brake lines to release the pressure and fluid. This showed some evidence of brake fluid on the brake backing plates, a sign the brakes should now release. Fortunately they did, and there was no more trouble with dragging.

A flat tire on the Kaiser caused the car to swerve a bit before I could stop but did not create any problem. It did slow the trip by several hours, however. The spare tire I had inflated at the beginning of the trip was flat too. This meant unhitching the tow bar from the station wagon, leaving the car by the side of the road, one axle supported by the jack, locating a service station, and having both tires repaired. From that time on, I have always made sure the spare would hold air.

I could not remember passing any service station for several miles before the flat occurred, so with the two tires in the wagon I drove ahead probably five miles to locate a station. It took nearly an hour for the attendant to repair both tires, since he was the only one there and was interrupted by customers wanting gasoline. With the tires finally repaired, I headed back to the Kaiser.

Maybe a mile or two from the gas station, I saw a pickup truck coming toward me towing a car. My Kaiser! Turning the wagon at the first opportunity, I lit out after the truck. It did not take too long to pull up behind. I tooted the horn steadily. The driver made no effort to stop, so I pulled alongside, shouting, leaning on the horn and motioning the driver to pull over. Fortunately I had sense enough not to try to force the truck off the road. My wagon had no difficulty pulling ahead of the truck, and once there, I kept in the middle of the two lanes and slowed to twenty miles per hour, with every intention of slowing to a complete stop. It had not entered my mind what I would do when I stopped. Certainly I would be against two people, and there was no telling if they were armed. I never carry a gun.

For some reason the CB in my wagon had been removed and had not been put back before I left. However, the aerial and call numbers were in place. Trying to make my eyeglass case look like a mike, I pretended I was calling for help. The ruse worked; since the pickup truck did not have a CB, they thought I was summoning the state police, or asking anyone who heard me to send help.

Fortunately for the few miles that I was ahead of the truck there were no side roads onto which the driver could turn. The wagon was probably down to ten miles per hour. It was good that we were going slowly, for I was keeping a close lookout in the mirror to anticipate the truck trying to pass on the left or right. As the driver turned his wheel, so did I, and he could not get by me with the load he was pulling. The driver pulled the truck off the road. Both men jumped out, ran past some trees that bordered a fence and disappeared.

I have seen too many chase scenes on TV to bother going after them. I had also seen enough crime programs on TV to realize I had better not try unhooking the tow bar from their truck and hitching it back to my wagon. I could just see them sneaking up on me as I was squatting down to work. I did, however, leave the station wagon long enough to remove the ignition key from the truck. There was no sign of the men as I sat in my locked station wagon, with the flasher lights blinking. A trucker going in the opposite direction stopped to offer help. I asked him to notify the highway patrol on his CB, which he did, and drove on. Several cars passed but none stopped. In fifteen or twenty minutes a highway patrol car arrived. Identifying myself, and showing papers on my station wagon and on the Kaiser, I explained what had happened.

The officers were very helpful but did not seem to accept my story completely. A second patrol car arrived, and I explained the situation again. While one officer checked headquarters on his radio, two others helped me detach the tow bar from the truck and hitch it to the station wagon. The report came over the radio that the truck had been stolen. They had used the truck's spare to replace the missing wheel on the Kaiser. Luckily I had come across them, and luckily they did not hit my wagon as I tried to stop them. I gave as complete a description of the two as possible, and gave the key to the officer. I completely forgot about the truck's wheel till I was home. I wrote the patrol about it but got no reply.

With the car at home, the first job was to get the motor running. This meant disconnecting the starter housing from the flywheel. Normally this would present no problem, but the unit did not want to come out. A bolt holding the spring in the starter drive had somehow worked loose and wedged against the housing, making it impossible to free the assembly. It took some careful handling to extract the bolt. Had it dropped into the flywheel housing, there would have been a lot of dismantling to retrieve it. With the starter unit out, there was no trouble replacing the bolt holding the spring on the starter drive. When

The starter motor needed repair only to the drive unit, but was thoroughly cleaned with air under pressure while it was out of the car.

the unit was cleaned and lubricated with powdered graphite, it worked fine on the next try. The motor started okay but did not run as it should; there seemed to be an electrical short that I could not locate. I waited until after dark, started the motor and could see several places where the current was arcing. This showed me where to look, and as a temporary repair these spots were taped. Later I replaced the wires.

The cooling system seemed to be clogged. I put in a good radiator flush, but this did not help because the core was too badly clogged to let the flushing agent work. It spilled out the overflow pipe as the coolant circulated, which meant the radiator had to be thoroughly cleaned. I bought a back flush unit, which is simply a threaded pipe that screws into the bottom drain plug, with a coupling to accommodate a garden hose. The theory is to force water up through the radiator core, just the opposite of the direction it usually moves. This will free rust and scale, cleaning the system.

With the radiator cap removed so the pressure would not rupture the radiator core, a light stream of water was forced into the bottom of the radiator. This released rust and scale into the header tank. With the pressure increased a bit, all the junk flushed out of the system.

Along with the rust and scale came some stringy substance I could not identify. It looked like some sort of vegetation, but I could not imagine it growing in a car's radiator. A friend said it looked like Spanish moss, and it certainly did. If that is what it was, I have no idea how it got there.

After testing for leaks, I put in a 50/50 solution of permanent antifreeze and water, plus a can of lubricant for the water pump. Permanent antifreeze and water in a 50/50 mixture is a better coolant than plain water, so I keep that in all my cars.

The motor required very little attention other than a general cleaning, which was later done at a coin-operated car wash. New, properly gapped spark plugs, and a carburetor adjustment were all that was needed, other than some general tightening and lubrication. Of course, the oil was drained, the system flushed, and new oil and filter added. The motor ran well.

The brake system presented the biggest problem. The car had sat unused for a long time in excessive heat, and the brake fluid had all but solidified in the lines and wheel cylinders. The master cylinder had to be removed, cleaned and thoroughly rebuilt. Each brake line had to be removed and a wire run through it to clean out the granulated brake fluid. Then the line was flushed with solvent. Some of the wheel cylinders were beyond repair, so solidly set up by the solidified brake fluid that they had to be replaced. Fortunately there was no trouble finding new parts.

The brake linings were good and needed no work. To inspect and replace the wheel cylinders, each hub had to be removed. While these were off, the inside of the backing plates were cleaned, and the adjusting ratchet and springs were cleaned and lubricated. The wheel bearings were cleaned and repacked at the same time. When these parts were reassembled and the hydraulic system was filled and bled, the brakes worked fine.

Time and heat had taken their toll on the tires. I bought a new set of wide white sidewalls but did not mount them until the paint job was completed later.

Inside the car, the hot damp climate of southern Alabama had caused some problems. The vinyl upholstery was mildewed and the carpets were rotted from the moisture. A friend markets

Wheel cylinders in each brake were "set up" by brake fluid that had solidified, making it impossible for the fluid in the lines to operate the plungers in each cylinder. New wheel cylinders were installed.

an excellent vinyl cleaner that I had used for cleaning upholstery but never for removing mildew or mold. After washing the door panels and cushions with a solution of white vinegar and water, I applied the vinyl cleaner. When it dried, I wiped the areas clean of mildew and found there was a nice shine.

When the old carpets were removed the floor showed some weakness from rust, but not enough to warrant cutting out old metal and welding new in place. Reinforcing plates were cut from eighteen-gauge sheet steel. The old floor was cleaned, using a wire-bristled brush in an electric hand drill. After removing the rust, the entire floor was sprayed with zinc-chromate. Holes were drilled around the perimeter of the new pieces. When these were properly placed, I used a pencil to indicate where tiny holes had to be punched in the floor. After coating the floor area and the bottom of the patches, self-tapping screws were put in to attach the patches. With everything in place, the entire floor was painted with asphalt roof coating, making an excellent and durable repair.

New carpets were no problem, for material like the original was easy to locate. It was light enough so the binding could be attached on my home sewing machine. When these were in place, the inside looked fine.

A two-tone blue paint job seemed appropriate. The car was originally blue and the upholstery was keyed to this. It took a lot of hand sanding to get the finish ready for priming. I used the "wet" type emery paper, No. 400 grit, in a rubber sanding block, then finished with No. 600 grit. Between the two coats of primer the car was rubbed lightly with 0000 steel wool.

Plated trim parts were removed and a minor dent in the left rear fender panel pounded out, filled, sanded and primed before the new paint job. Because of poor surface, three coats of primer were applied, with light sanding between coats.

Top portion of the car was painted first to prevent marking the lower portion of the body with the air hose or other equipment. Bottom portion was masked off during top painting operation.

Two-tone blue finish really sparkled. Because plated parts were removed before painting, the new paint covers the entire surface, preventing later peeling around plated parts.

Most of the trim pieces were removed. I left the plated molding on the windshield and rear window, and the broad spear-shaped trim pieces below the windows. I rented a one-horsepower paint compressor that would maintain a steady 40 pounds pressure and gave the car four coats of acrylic enamel. The masking operation, which covered everything but the top, allowed me to paint the top first. When this was completed and had dried overnight, the masking was removed and the top part was masked to prevent any spray from settling on the newly painted top. Before the last coat to the bottom portion of the car, I used 0000 steel wool to make it smooth as glass. A tack cloth removed all grit, so the final coat really glistened.

The bumpers had to be replated, as did some of the grille parts. The other parts could be cleaned up sufficiently without plating being required. With a set of wide white sidewall tires the Kaiser took on new life, a far cry from the rusty car I had towed home from Alabama.

5

Like Blondes, Convertibles Are More Fun

Possibly because I grew up in Syracuse where Franklin cars were manufactured, and because my parents and many of my friends' parents drove Franklins, I have always been interested in these cars. I had been following ads for Series 11 and 12 Franklins for some time but had not been able to locate a body style I wanted at a reasonable price. A Series 12-A Coupe was for sale in a small town in Tennessee. After some correspondence and phone calls, I decided to look at the car. The owner told me the wooden frame was rotted out and broken at the cowl, but the car was complete and the motor ran well.

I borrowed a car-hauling trailer, had a trailer hitch installed on my Chevy station wagon, and left southern Ohio to see the car. The empty trailer jolted behind the car, and somehow one of the nuts holding the hitch jarred off. I did not realize this until the trailer started to swerve as the tongue dropped, leaving the trailer attached only by the safety chain. The chain kept it from breaking away, but allowed it to swerve violently, especially as I braked the station wagon to a stop. There was no point trying to locate the missing nut, so I made a hasty repair by wrapping the chain around the bumper and hitch to hold the tongue in place. I hoped it would hold until I could get to a service station and have it fixed. Fortunately I did not have to drive very far. A mechanic on duty not only rebolted the hitch but put on additional bracing.

When I mentioned why I was towing an empty car-hauling trailer, he said, "There's one of those Franklins about two miles up the next road. You can't miss the place—there are twin red silos, and the house is on the left side of the road." He added that an old man owned it, had not driven it for years and might sell it. He did not know anything about the car's condition, for he had not seen it in ten years. Since I was not very far away, I decided I should at least look.

The road was quite narrow. I did not want the station wagon and trailer to block any cars that might come by, so I turned into the drive, stopped the car and went to the door. When I mentioned that I had heard he had a Franklin he might sell, the owner looked at my station wagon and trailer and said, "You're pretty sure you'll get her, aren't you son, bringing that trailer all the way here from Ohio." I explained to him that I was on my way to buy another Franklin, and that I had heard about his. He said he might sell it if anyone really wanted to fix it up.

The car was in a lean-to shed beside the barn, a 1923 Series 10 two-door sedan, one of Franklin's most distinctive—and homely—models. Tall and narrow, it featured a sharply pointed windshield and sloping horsecollar hood. The car had not been moved in years. All the tires were flat, and a couple of the rims had settled into the ground and rusted away. Years of dirt and dust, bird droppings, and neglect made it a sorry looking mess. One door had stood open for years after some sort of damage, and the weight of the door had torn the aluminum cowl panel, as the supporting wooden framework had rotted. The body was aluminum so had not rusted, but the wooden upright supports were splintered and decayed. There was almost nothing holding the body together. The shed roof had leaked, and in time the car roof had also leaked. As a result the upholstery was badly mildewed and shredded. The entire car looked beyond repair to me.

I decided I really did not want to tackle a car that badly decomposed so I did not make an offer. The owner said it used to run "real good," and if he were feeling better he would put a battery from his truck in it and "fire her up." I did not want to hurt his feelings, and wondered how I was going to get out of there. It was obvious he was not aware of the miserable condition of the car, nor what it would take to fix it. Looking at the instrument panel, I saw the odometer only registered a little over 15,000 miles. I asked how long he had owned the car—since 1925. He said he had not driven it since he put it up in World War II because of the gas shortage. His eyes welled with tears as he said, "Me and the wife had a lot of good rides in this car, and I hate to see her go. But if you want her, you can have her for $50." I did not know what I would do with it but felt I could sell at least $50 worth of parts, so I paid him. He wrote a receipt, saying he would "have her ready, young fellow" when I came to pick it up. (See Chapter 6 for the story of this car.)

As is often the case when dealing with people who are selling old cars, I met a most interesting man. He was running a local factory making spring washers. He had retired some years ago from one of the car companies in Detroit, moved to the town in a kinder climate, and set up the small factory. There was a small college nearby, and he was using college students on a part-time basis to make the washers. He said the factory just about broke even, but he felt any minor loss he sustained was offset by the knowledge that he was helping kids get a college education in an area where there were few part-time jobs.

The Series 12-A Coupe looked pretty sad. The wooden chassis frame had rotted through at the cowl, so the car sagged badly. He had removed both front fenders in an attempt to repair the frame, and they were piled to one side. The fabric-covered top had rotted away, allowing rain into the car; the upholstery was shot. All of the glass had been broken, and the driver's door sagged so badly it could not be closed.

As with the other Franklin, I was not sure I wanted to attempt such a complete restoration. I told the owner it might be too much of a job for me. He said it was not as hopeless as it might appear, that he had a replacement wooden frame that he would give with the car, along with some additional parts he had bought when he was considering restoring it himself.

I decided I would chance it and paid for the car. The only title he could find was dated 1937, although he thought the car had been driven since then. To straighten the frame so we could

Several years outdoors reduced this Franklin Coupe to a near basket case. The broken wooden chassis at cowl is propped up by a cinder block. Cowl was made of sheet steel but the remainder of the body was aluminum. All the parts were there.

at least load it on the trailer, we jacked up the middle of each side and bolted some pieces of steel to the original chassis. This helped somewhat, and we eventually got the old car on the trailer.

I had not realized that the trailer I had borrowed was made to haul Model A Fords. These had only a 103-inch wheelbase and next to no overhang front or rear. The Franklin was on a 119-inch wheelbase and did have overhang both front and rear. When the car was loaded on the trailer the back wheels were an inch or two from the end of the trailer. We had to chain the front and rear axles to the cross members of the trailer so the car would stay in place. This put the center of gravity too far back, and the trailer was actually lifting up on the back of the station wagon rather than pressing down. I gathered all the loose parts and extra pieces, covered the Franklin with a big tarpaulin I had brought along, and started home.

The road that led back to the highway was highly crowned and uneven. I had to fairly creep along. When I got on the main highway I started to pick up some speed, and at about forty I felt the trailer whipping quite violently. I could just picture the trailer causing me to lose control of the car, and car and trailer diving into the ditch. When I slowed to about twenty-five the swerving lessened enough so I could control it, and I had to keep at that speed. Figuring that I had about four hundred miles to drive, if I could average twenty-five miles per hour it would take me sixteen hours! That was much longer than I'd allowed, but I did not have any choice. It would be monotonous but, I hoped, safe.

My route took me through Knoxville. I reached there about 5 P.M., rush hour. I had to go to the center of town on one main thoroughfare, make a left turn onto the main north-south street for about half a mile, then turn right onto the main thoroughfare leading east, and out of town. It was not easy driving through rush-hour traffic, having to change lanes for a left turn, then change again for a right turn. I had to drive very slowly, trying to anticipate the traffic lights since the trailer had no brakes. One light turned from green to red in a couple of seconds, just as I was at the crosswalk. I stopped, but my station wagon was a good six feet into the cross lane, blocking traffic. I could not see behind me to back up so had to wait there, much to the annoyance of the people in the blocked lane. There was nothing I could do but shrug and smile as several people shouted directions. Fortunately no traffic cop appeared, and when the light changed to green I pulled on, taking a whole block to get into the left lane for the turn I knew I'd have to make.

I stopped for another traffic light near the center of Knoxville, but the car behind my trailer did not stop as quickly. I heard a crash and felt the trailer nudge the station wagon. Setting the hand brake and putting the transmission in "park," I got out. A nice shiny Oldsmobile had hit the rear of the trailer. The channel steel pieces in which the Franklin's wheels set had broken a headlight on the Oldsmobile and punched a hole in its radiator. There was glass on the pavement, and liquid pouring from the front of the Oldsmobile. Knowing an officer would soon appear, I got my license and registration ready to show.

When the driver of the Oldsmobile did not get out, I hoped there was not an injury. I doubted if there was, since only the car's front was damaged. An officer appeared, but the driver of the other car still did not get out. I showed my license to the officer, explaining that I had stopped for a traffic light and was hit in the rear. When the officer went back to the Oldsmobile, he found the driver incoherent and so drunk he could not get out of the car.

The officer filled out a report while another policeman directed traffic around us. I imagined I would have to drive to the police station and explain it all again. Instead, when the officer found I was not hurt, he told me to drive on because he did not want to tie up traffic any longer. I meant to pick up a Knoxville paper for the next few days to read about the accident but did not get around to doing so. I never heard another word about the accident.

The rest of the trip home was simply boring because of the slow pace. I arrived home after dark and backed the trailer into my driveway, wanting to get the car in the garage before my neighbors saw it. I discovered, however, that I needed help unloading the Franklin, so it was there for all to see the next morning. One neighbor asked on what river bank I'd found the car. Another merely shook his head and muttered that I must have taken leave of my senses. A friend helped me unload it and volunteered that I certainly was a glutton for punishment to tackle such a heap.

Restoration was slow but interesting. The top was so badly rotted I decided to make the car into a convertible coupe. I needed all the material and pictures I could find on Series 12

Badly rusted hood side panel was repaired by welding a new piece behind the rotted metal. Epoxy filler provided a smooth surface. Cowl rings and hood latches were cleaned, then nickel-plated.

New chassis frame rails came with the car. With these in place, mechanical and body restoration could begin. Large sheet-metal fan housing at the front of the engine was sanded and primed, then given two coats of black engine enamel.

Coupe body was removed and placed on blocks. Doors were tied closed so patterns could be made for new wood. Later, after rebuilding, top and rear portions above the window line were cut from each door. The coupe top was removed.

Franklin Convertible Coupes. I studied everything carefully, for I wanted to make this as near to factory specifications as possible.

The body had to be removed from the rotted and broken wooden chassis. This was not hard, for the wood in both the body sills and chassis rails was almost pulverized in spots, and nothing held. On Franklin cars with the wooden chassis the body was only attached at the cowl and at a point over the rear axle. Three bolts per side were all that had to come off. I did not need any help to raise the body enough to slide it onto blocks.

The Series 12 Franklins had a steel cowl, but from there back the rest of the body was aluminum. There was some rust-out at the bottom of the cowl, and the wooden upright cowl supports were weak. The wooden framework along the bottom of both doors was rotted. The wooden framework in the rumble seat area had decayed and splintered, leaving the aluminum body skin unsupported. This caused cracks at each lower corner of the rumble seat opening. The hinges had rusted and would not function, and the screws had pulled out of the spongy wood.

I discarded the decayed wood, after making patterns from the more recognizable pieces. The seat frames were stored but all the rotted top material and upholstery were thrown out. I knew the body would have to wait until the chassis was completed and all the mechanical problems were solved.

Replacement wooden chassis rails had been included with the car. To install these, the car had to be safely blocked. Then I removed the old rail from one side and attached the new one. This meant disconnecting everything bolted to that side of the chassis, which included the channel steel front frame extension, the front spring holders, the motor supports, the cross brace at the cowl section, the running board supports, the rear spring holder and body support, and the channel steel rear frame extension. Nuts that would not budge after soaking with solvent were sawed or cut with a nut-splitter. When the old frame rail was out, the new one was set in place, and everything that had been disconnected had to be attached to the replacement.

One side was replaced at a time, which was a mistake. It would have been much easier to have blocked the motor and transmission in place and worked both sides of each component from front to back. I did this later on the Series 10.

With the replacement frame in place, the car could be moved. The next step in the restoration process was to push the car out of the garage and clean the motor and running gear. A rented kerosene-burning steam cleaner did the job, to the amusement of some neighbors who wondered why I was using that strange-looking contraption in the rain. Because it was raining, the dirt and accumulated grease flowed down the drive, into the gutter and drain. With this job finished and the car back in the garage, the next step was to get the motor running.

One should always drain the oil from an engine that has been idle a long time. On this car, after draining the oil, the base of the oil pan was removed so the sludge could be inspected for metal shavings, which would indicate worn bearings. An inspection of the main and rod bearings showed no scorched metal, so the motor seemed sound. The oil pump and oil lines were removed, and I ran a thin copper wire through the oil lines before they were cleaned with solvent. With the oil pan cleaned and back in place, a completely cleaned filter and new oil, the motor was ready to run once the cooling fins were cleaned and the carburetor and electrical systems checked.

Series 12 Franklins had a down-draft forced-air cooling system (the cross-draft engine was not introduced until 1930). To

The largely aluminum engine cleaned up easily. The intake and part of the exhaust manifolds were painted with aluminum paint as on the original. Vacuum tank, horn, wire harness covers and cooling shrouds all took two coats of black enamel.

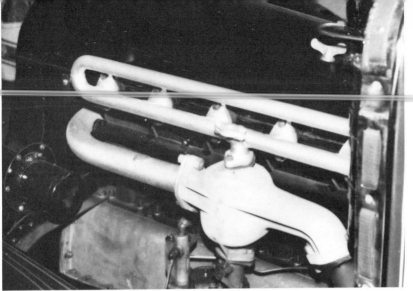

Left side view of Franklin engine shows attention given to details. New welting was installed at cowl and front hood, the former to stop squeaks and rattles. Double striping seen on cowl was applied with a striping wheel.

clean dirt, grime and mud daubers' nests out of the vertical cooling fins I had to borrow an air compressor, for the job required more pressure than the exhaust cycle of a vacuum cleaner could produce. After running a thin wire down each fin, a strong blast of air cleaned these spaces, littering the floor with dirt and bugs.

Rather than tape the bare spots on the spark plug wires, I cut and installed new wires, then put in new spark plugs. The points were not pitted, so after checking the dwell and cleaning the distributor cap. I had only the carburetion to check before trying to start the engine.

Like most cars of this period, Franklin used a vacuum tank mounted on the fire wall. This syphoned gasoline from the rear tank and stored it in a reservoir. From there it was gravity fed to the carburetor. In vacuum tanks that are not used for long periods the gasoline evaporates, residue forms in the float chamber and the tank will not operate. This one had to be completely disassembled. The rust was removed and every part was thoroughly cleaned. To start the motor, I simply primed the vacuum tank; I did not try to clean out the gas line to the gas tank or the gas tank itself.

With the cylinders primed, I was surprised at how quickly the motor caught. It did not run smoothly or evenly, but there were no knocks as I revved it briefly. Afterward, to free a sticky valve, I cleaned the push rod, valve guide and spring. Later I ground and adjusted the valves, and the motor ran smoothly.

Before road testing the chassis, I flushed and refilled the transmission and differential. The brakes required a complete overhaul—new seals and plungers for each wheel cylinder and a rebuild kit for the master cylinder. There was no problem cutting and fitting new steel tubing to the front brakes. The brake linings were good enough for a test drive, but I knew they would have to be replaced as part of the restoration.

I took a short test drive, using a soda-pop case for a seat. Because the body had been removed, there were no gauges to monitor. The car ran well enough, so I went back to the body work, knowing there would be plenty of time for adjustments and fine tuning.

The body was rough looking. The paint was mostly gone, and there was rust in the cowl section. I had removed the rotted sections of the roof but did not want to tear out any upright supports until the doors were rebuilt. The uprights had to be tied in place so patterns could be made for new wood for doors and upright door supports.

The Walker-built body used wooden body sills with steel supports. The first job in body rebuilding was to cut and fit new body rails, which ran from the cowl to the rear of the body.

A local lumberyard still had some air-dried oak, which they cut and planed to my basic measurements. The final fitting required use of a plane and a draw shave. Before installation, the new wood was coated with a mixture of turpentine and linseed oil.

Dovetailed joints that had to be glued together required several hours under tight clamp pressure before they could be released. The original corner braces needed only sanding and painting to make them usable again.

When the upright door supports were installed at the front and back of each door opening, the doors could be fitted and hung. At this time the doors were still full-height coupe doors. When changing a body from a fixed-top coupe to a convertible, it is necessary to provide extra bracing for the upright supports, which have to be cut off at window level. A good way to provide this needed support is to cut a piece of plywood to the exact

Doors were rebuilt and new glass with nickel frames installed before the doors were remounted on the car. New wood framework for other body supports were cut and fitted. Aluminum skin was attached by short serrated nails, as in the original.

measurements of the braces for the seat back. I used ⅝-inch plywood, treated it to prevent rot, then screwed it to the seat back supports. L-shape braces were made from strap iron and were attached to the upright supports just below the belt line. These extended along the area from the door post to the seat back support, and about six inches on the plywood-reinforced seat back support. This gave added strength to the upright, against which the door had to close and the main folding roof bow was hinged.

Sometimes a rebuilt door requires shims under the hinges to get a correct fit. In this case no shims were needed; the doors fitted fine with no gaps. The top portion of each door was cut off at windshield level. This left the door with all three original hinges for support and also kept the window channel to the top of the door frame. It was very close to the method the original body builder had used in making convertible coupes. The rear of the door was cut off at sill level and a cap plate made to cover the cut off portion. The doors looked good.

Liquid paint remover took the body down to bare metal. Tears at each lower end of rumble seat opening were heliarc welded and filed. When painted, the welds did not show. The car took over a year to restore on a part-time basis.

A new header bar was made to fit across the front, over the winshield frame. This had to be thick enough to hold one part of the latching device. I used angle iron on the outside and a piece of varnished oak on the inside. This was the part to which the folding-top front roof bow would attach.

New oak roof bows were cut and fitted. As with the factory-produced model, landau bars were attached for support. I had been able to locate both the landau bars and the convertible-coupe rear window frame. When the webbing was attached to the bows, the roof had the same conformation as the original convertibles. Later I cut and sewed an inside lining for the top, and after that was attached I cut and fitted the outer top covering. Shatter-proof glass was used in the windshield and in the side and rear curtain windows.

Instead of using new metal at the bottom of the cowl, I used fiberglass to repair the rust-out. This went in place easily. When the edges were feathered and the area was sanded and primed, the repairs were invisible and permanent.

The steel cowl section required a tremendous amount of sanding to remove the old finish and rust. Then several coats of primer, sanded in between, were needed to build the surface as smooth as I wanted it. A welder came to my garage and welded the torn aluminum skin at the lower edges of the rumble-seat opening. Then, using paint remover, all the paint was scraped off the aluminum doors and body. With paint remover the metal always has to be scrubbed with a strong detergent and rinsed with clear water to remove all traces of the caustic material. This is always a job I do outdoors because of the fumes from the paint remover.

With the body down to bare metal, minor dings and dents were hammered out. Then, to build up the surface for the color coats, the body was given several coats of primer. I chose a green lacquer as near to an original factory color as possible. I gave it six light coats of paint, sanding lightly between coats. When the final striping was applied, the body looked as good as any the factory had turned out. This was the first time I had used a striping wheel; it worked well, saving a lot of money over professional striping.

These cars originally had leather upholstery, so leather was used in the restoration. I chose a saddle tan that looked great against the green body. The pattern for the seat was made from measurements of the cushion frameworks. After spraying the springs and attaching webbing side to side and front to back, I added a one-inch layer of foam padding instead of the fiber used in the original. Cutting and fitting a muslin cover first allowed me to make a perfect-fit leather cover, which I sewed on a home sewing machine using a leather-work needle. I cut the pieces for the padded fascia over the dash, which was made of heavier leather, and had the one seam in the middle sewed at a shoe repair shop.

The front grille and headlights had been nickel-plated, and to save money I did the first steps in the replating process. I thoroughly degreased them and prepared the surface for plating. Using a brush and solvent, I scrubbed the headlights and grille, then soaked and scrubbed them in a strong solution of washing soda and hot water, rinsed in clear water. When the parts were thoroughly clean, I used a sanding block with 220-grit paper on the flat parts, followed with 600-grit paper. To avoid sanding marks, I cross-sanded and finally used 0000 steel wool. On the curved surfaces of the headlights I used 400-grit paper and 0000 steel wool, finishing the job with rubbing compound and a buffing

Finished car looks very much like the factory-produced convertible. Dimensions of folding top were taken from duplicate of the original factory drawings. The handsome car drew crowds every place it was parked. Interior was upholstered in tan leather.

wheel in my electric hand drill. All the plater had to do was the actual plating. My initial work saved about 60 percent of the final cost.

The fenders took a good deal of sanding and priming to build a satisfactory undercoat. These I finished black for that was the way the factory usually turned out these cars. When I mounted them and the splash aprons, I used new fender welting I had made. It is less expensive to buy plastic clothesline rope, cut strips of black vinyl, and make your own cording using the cording foot on a sewing machine. This will be wider than ready-made welting, and when fit between body and fenders will help prevent squeaking.

The Franklin had painted wheels. Although most of the paint was gone, I did not dare use paint remover because it would be next to impossible to rinse off all traces, especially where the spokes joined at the hub and where they met the rim. Using pieces of glass, I scraped away as much as possible of the old paint, then sanded and filled the spokes. The wheels were sprayed green to match the body.

It was a smart-looking car and handled well. I never entered it in any shows, but usually several people clustered around when I parked it anywhere. Later, when I had a Phantom III Rolls Royce coming from England and needed the room the Franklin occupied, I sold the car.

6

Out of the Tennessee Hills

As promised, I returned to Tennessee in a few weeks to pick up the Series 10 Franklin I had bought for $50. This was a car I really did not intend to restore, intending to get my investment out of it by selling the salvageable parts. I knew there were some people needing these parts.

It was rather poignant to see what the old gentleman had done to spruce up the Franklin. After pushing it out of the lean-to, he had washed it and even cleaned the glass. He had pumped up the one tire that still held a little air. He had cleaned it inside, and although there was still mold and mildew, the dirt and mess that had accumulated over the years was gone. He had wired shut the sagging door and had the car ready for me to load.

The Series 10 Franklin was smaller than the Series 12 I had brought home a short time before, but I rented a larger trailer, complete with brakes and a winch on the front to help load the car. The car set forward in the trailer, and I was able to drive at fifty with no trouble. Since I did not want to drive through Knoxville again, the bypass route through Maryville looked good.

Because my garage was filled with old cars, I took this latest prize to a storage garage I rented. My neighbors did not see it until much later.

As I suspected, the Series 10 was beyond any restoration efforts I wanted to make in its original body style. There was next to nothing holding the body panels together. The jarring and jolting

Moisture from a dirt floor caused the rims to rust through. There was no choice but to replace the wheels. A new chassis frame had to be installed. Only the cowl could be used.

Not much left to work with. Rotted wood on the cowl allowed the weight of the door to tear the aluminum skin. Cowl metal was cut at an angle from the centerpoint of the windshield to the sill line. New wood was fitted to shape of redesigned cowl.

the car took while on the trailer must have caused bits of wood to drop off from time to time, for quite a bit was missing.

Because I planned to sell the salvageable parts, I made a tentative list of those I thought someone might want. The more I examined the old car, the more I realized that from a mechanical standpoint it showed little wear. It was the body that was so decrepit. The fact that the engine had only a little over 15,000 miles intrigued me. I should be able to make the little car into a speedster . . . it should be an interesting project. I sketched how I envisioned it, with the cowl trimmed away to remove the torn metal, bucket seats added, an oval gas tank and a toolbox mounted on the rear. I would make it into a smaller version of a Stutz Bearcat, and have fun doing it.

Many old cars with uninteresting bodies, or cars like my Series 10 whose body was beyond repair, can be made usable again as speedsters. Several companies make bucket seat frames and gas tanks in a variety of sizes and shapes, as well as toolboxes, step plates, monacle windshields, and other replica parts. Of course, when you are done with this type of conversion you do not have an authentic speedster, but you do have a usable and interesting car.

With this thought in mind I sold the body, except the cowl section, to a person who had a Series 10 and wanted the panels in case his car was damaged. At the low price I got for the panels, I had the buyer remove the body. I did not intend to work on the car until after the Series 12 was well along, but I did start looking for a replacement frame, better front fenders, wheels and rims.

No replacement frame was available, so I had a lumberyard secure the wood and cut new chassis rails to factory specifications. A man near Binghamton, New York, had a pair of new, unused front fenders he had bought when a long-time auto dealer sold out. Headlights turned up in Bangor, Maine; two wheels from Cazenovia, New York; another wheel from Lima, Ohio. For nearly a year I kept locating and buying parts, storing them as they arrived.

During this time I was restoring the Series 12 and making it into a convertible coupe. When the time came that I could finally start working on the Series 10, I kept in mind what I had learned replacing the Series 12 chassis. This time I blocked the engine,

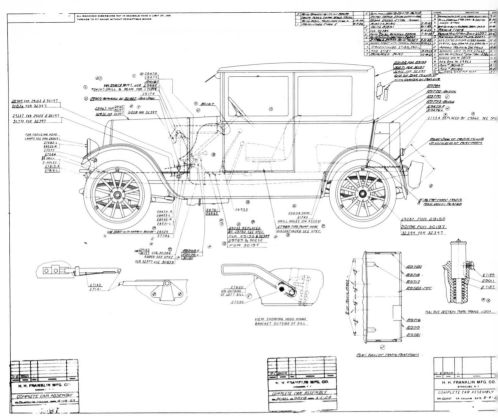

Factory blueprint for Series 10 Franklin taken from H. H. Franklin Club's *Air Cooled News* furnished measurements and dimensions used in making the replacement body.

Simple straight top of chassis frame rails made cutting easy. Dimensions from factory drawing were easy to scribe on the four pieces of ash. The two pieces for each side were glued, then screwed and bolted.

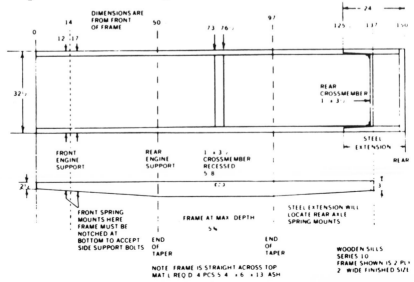

transmission and running gear, removed both sides of the old chassis, set both rails in place and bolted each component on each side rail as I went along. It was a much easier method.

The motor cleaned up very well. The Series 10 had a cast-aluminum fan shroud and air duct, so there was no rust to contend with and no repainting was necessary. The insulation looked good on the wires until I tried to move one—it cracked and crumbled. New wires were the answer. The carburetor and gas line required soaking in gasoline and solvent to clean out the gum. The vacuum tank had atrophied, so this took some patience. With a friend helping, we primed the engine, hooked up a good battery and tried to start the motor. The starter would not make a sound. We took turns hand cranking the engine. We tried putting the car in high gear and turning a jacked-up rear wheel. Finally we replaced the coil and got some spark to the cylinders. With my friend manipulating the hand throttle and clutch pedal, we pushed the car and got the motor running, not well but at least running.

Back in the garage, with the car's rear wheels on jack stands, I was able to hand crank the car. With the top air duct off, I tested the spark at each cylinder. The motor was running on gasoline dumped into the vacuum tank and would not run too

The engine was cleaned and put in running condition before new chassis rails were installed and rebuilding into a speedster was started. Air ducts on Series 10 Franklins were aluminum. Later models used sheet steel.

long at a time. By priming the vacuum tank and running a rubber hose into a gas can, we could keep the engine going long enough to adjust the valve clearance and fiddle with the carburetor.

I thought that once the car was put in running condition, a drive of 100 miles would probably loosen things up a bit. I had drained the base, cleaned the oil pan and oil lines, and lubricated and cleaned every moving part and control, yet the controls worked hard and the motor was not as smooth as it should have been. The exhaust pipe and muffler had long since rusted through, so the engine sounded like a truck during these adjustments. To quiet it down a bit, I clamped some flexible tubing over the end of the broken exhaust pipe, which took the exhaust gases and some of the noise out of the garage. I practically flooded the valve lifters and guides with transmission fluid, then added a quart to the oil in the base to free the sluggish valves. Finally the valve mechanism loosened up and the engine ran much smoother. In time it ran well.

Since the cowl section had been torn, I had designed the speedster body so the cowl would be longer from front to back at the bottom than on the top. I drew the line on the cowl with a sharpened nail so I could see where to cut. Before I cut the heavy aluminum skin, I cut a piece of heavy plywood to fit inside the

Famous horse-collar hood on Series 10 was hinged at front. The mesh grille, curved at the bottom and surrounded by an aluminum apron, was cleaned with compressed air. Notice the broken wood at the front of the chassis frame rails.

cowl so the metal would not bend as I tried to cut it. This brace worked so well that I later stained and varnished it for the inside fire wall, on which I mounted the small instrument cluster from the original dashboard. I cut the aluminum cowl skin with a saber saw, which made a clean cut that took only a minimum of filing to make perfectly smooth.

Again using heavy plywood, I made new floorboards to conform to the simple body. There was no side metal on the new body except for a piece about four inches high that ran from the lower edge of the cowl to the base for the seats. I bought two metal bucket seats, and altered the springs from the original seat cushions to fit. I probably should have reupholstered them in leather, but instead I used Naugahyde. To cover the smooth but exposed edge of the trimmed cowl, as well as the pieces I had added on each side, I split half-inch plastic garden hose, covered it with Naugahyde to match the seats, and forced it over the raw edges. It looked fine in its new job.

I bought a round gas tank, made wooden holders for it and mounted it behind the bucket seats. But I left the original gas tank at the rear of the car, because it looked a little strange with

Metal frames for bucket seats were located through an ad in a national car magazine. Upholstery was stripped off and the cushion framework and springs were repaired and painted. Sawed-through bottom frame on one seat was welded.

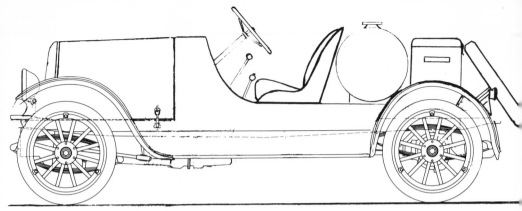

Old, beyond-repair sedan body was removed and simple speedster body, as in drawing, was constructed as a replacement. Original cowl section was trimmed to the new shape because of irreparable damage. Seats, large gas tank and toolbox were added.

nothing back there. I considered fashioning some sort of apron to go between the fenders and to cover the area where the gas tank would be removed, but I never got around to it.

After building up the surface of the metal with prime coats and careful sanding, I painted the car light yellow, with the fenders and aprons black. It was a nifty little car. The wheels were yellow with black striping. I did not locate a monacle windshield at what I considered a reasonable price so I went without one.

Actually the car was not too good as a speedster. The Series 10 Franklin's foot brake worked on the transmission and was somewhat lacking in stopping power. With the lightweight body the car would get up to fifty but could not be stopped in a safe distance at that speed.

After a rather close call when I had to drive on someone's lawn because I could not stop in time, I decided to sell the car. I sold it with the warning to the buyer to drive it slowly, and not to count on stopping as quickly as with other cars. Whether he heeded my advice and tired of driving under twenty-five, or whether he didn't intend to drive it, I don't know. A friend of mine said he saw it on display in an old-car museum in Kentucky, and when he stopped at the same museum a few months later the car was gone. I never heard what happened to it.

I sent a picture of the rebuilt car to the old gentleman in Tennessee but never heard from him. I hope he was not too disappointed with what I did to the car.

7

A Tiger by the Tail

"Surely you can't be serious—you don't want a heap like that," was my wife's first comment when she saw the car. "I sure am serious. I know it looks rough and will take a lot of work, but this is a highly desirable model," was my reply. The car was a 1935 Auburn Convertible Coupe.

There is nothing wrong with getting out of a mistake the best way you can. In such an instance, the reason for the mistake becomes secondary. In this case I found myself with a car that needed far more repairs than I had bargained for, and it would not have been worth the restoration costs.

The Auburn attracted my attention when I saw it alongside a fence with a for-sale sign. It was in rough shape and apparently had been used very hard. The fenders were all dented, there was considerable rust-through on parts of the body and several body parts were missing. I glossed over these obvious faults, figuring those parts could all be repaired or replaced without much difficulty.

The car seemed complete mechanically. It was not in operating condition so I really could not make much of a test. I could push the brake pedal to the floor, so I knew the hydraulic brake system would have to be overhauled. I made my first mistake not pouring some brake fluid into the master cylinder reservoir so I could at least drive the car a short distance if the motor started.

Although the front bumper, headlights, windshield frame and other trim parts were missing, the basic appeal of this 1935 Model 851 Auburn Convertible Coupe was overwhelming. Failure to hear the motor run before purchase was a mistake.

The large amount of play in the steering system indicated the front bushings needed replacement. The car sagged a bit to the left, but I rationalized that this could be caused by a lot of things, and did not check as I should have.

Auburns used Lycoming motors, so I thought any parts required to put the engine into condition would be readily available. There were no visible cracks in the cylinder head or block, and no water showed on the oil dipstick. The motor was complete, so I did not bother to get a battery and start the engine. That was my second mistake.

In fairness to the seller, I have to say that he did not misrepresent the car when he said it would take total restoration. My trouble was not realizing just how truthful he was. His asking price was reasonable, and he quite readily accepted something less. I was really pleased with the deal and made immediate plans

The 1935 Auburn's sporty lines show through despite much hard use and neglect. The only body rust-out was in molding above the running board, just behind the door. The fenders could have been straightened satisfactorily.

to tow the car home. There was no front bumper, so I bolted an old bumper in place and attached the tow bar. In doing this I noticed that the front frame ends showed evidence of a front-end collision and incomplete repair. This should have alerted me to look for more damage, but at this point I wasn't looking for trouble. Besides, I had already bought the car.

A thorough clean-up in a coin-operated car wash was my first step. It did not take many quarters to clean the engine block, firewall and visible parts of the chassis and suspension system. Then, with the car in my garage on jack stands, I started a careful examination to discover what needed repair or replacement.

The dented fenders did not really bother me; I had fixed worse. The rust-through spots on the body were not too serious, and I made notes for both fiberglass and new metal repairs. I assumed I would have some difficulty obtaining new windshield posts and frame, as well as the missing interior trim parts. The seats were missing, but I did not think it would be difficult finding replacement seat springs, or rebuilding seats from another car. All in all, the work to restore the body was not going to be too bad.

The mechanical appraisal was something else. With a new battery and carburetor priming, I got the motor running after a few tries. My first shock. To keep the motor running, I had to set the carburetor so the motor was turning over at probably 1000 rpm. I did not dare rev it up any higher, for a terrific knocking indicated the connecting-rod bearings were in bad shape. The engine would stall when I slowed it to what should have been a fast idling speed. There was a persistent loud clunking deep in the guts of the engine that could mean the main bearings on the crankshaft needed replacing too. Without tearing it apart, I knew it would take a complete engine rebuild, starting with a reground and balanced crankshaft. This would be very expensive. If the cylinders needed reboring, as they probably did, this could mean well over $1000 to get the engine into shape.

I thought I had better make some temporary repairs on the brake system so I could at least make a short test drive to determine the condition of the transmission, differential and other mechanical components. It took a master-cylinder rebuild kit to fix that part of the system. When I pressed the brake pedal, brake fluid squirted around a front brake backing plate. I removed the hub and found there were no brake shoes on that wheel, and that the plungers on the wheel cylinder were also missing. The other front brake was complete, but the linings were shot and the rivets had scored the drum. The rear brakes had slightly better linings, but the drums showed scoring and would need turning down on a lathe. The brake system would need complete rebuilding.

To make my test drive, I disconnected the front brake lines and capped the connections at the master cylinder. This meant I would be driving with only rear wheel brakes. At about this point I discovered there was no linkage for the hand brake.

With the engine knocking badly and smoking to beat the devil, and with only two wheel brakes, I started on a short test drive. Naturally I picked a route with little traffic. It did not take long to realize the clutch slipped, and a clutch-release problem indicated a worn throw-out bearing. On acceleration the transmission seemed fairly good, but on deceleration a growling noise indicated extreme wear. The dual ratio lever on the steering column was not operating. I assumed the vacuum hoses had rotted and were leaking air. The differential howled, even at fifteen to twenty miles per hour. The familiar "tumbrils over cobblestones" sound meant worn universal joints. The steering was terrible. I had to fight to keep the wheels pointed straight ahead. All in all, the test drive was a disaster. The car was a bucket of bolts. Had I gotten the motor started before I bought the car, I am sure I never would have paid my money. Very disappointed, I brought it back to the garage.

With the car back on jack stands, I examined the steering linkage and found that every bushing had to be replaced. Examination of the springs showed badly worn shackles and probably some broken leaves; I could not be sure about the leaves until the springs were dismantled, but that would explain the list to the left I had originally noticed. The vacuum unit on the rear axle was missing, explaining why I had no reaction to moving the steering column lever.

The car was a mess. Totaling my estimated repair and replacement costs, I realized I would have far more in the car than I could ever expect to get out of it. Since I did not want to keep

The car sagged to the left and lacked a rear bumper and taillights, as well as seats and other interior parts. When finally made to run, mechanical condition was so poor the restoration costs would have exceeded the car's worth.

the car ten years or so until it might appreciate in value and bail me out, I decided to admit my mistake and get out of the situation any way I could.

I ran an ad in a large newspaper that circulated in several contiguous states. I simply stated: "1935 Auburn Convertible Coupe, needs complete restoration, or use as a parts car." I gave my address and phone number but did not quote a price. I had in mind pricing the car for exactly what I had in it, the original price and the cost of my efforts to get it home and running. I got loads of phone calls, and described the car honestly. Several people came to look. I got the usual number of letters wanting pictures, and a few offering a really low price for a car they had not even seen.

One fellow was genuinely interested in the car as a basis for building a stock-car racer. He had a souped-up Buick V-8 engine that would furnish the power he needed. He realized he would have to rebuild and change the steering and suspension but he did not seem concerned. I hated to see the car "ruined" in this manner, but it seemed the best way to get my money out of it, and so I sold it. I guess the new owner did just what he planned; I never saw him or the car again.

I really did not like taking a classic car out of existence, but I had made a mistake in buying it. Occasionally a car will be used or abused to the point where it is beyond reasonable repairs. Such was the case with the Auburn. I swore to myself that I would never buy another car without hearing the engine run and making a test drive. I have kept this pledge.

At least my conscience was clear. I had not misrepresented the car. But then neither had the person who sold it to me.

8

It's Not the Principle,
It's the Money

The "Spirit of Ecstasy," the flying lady radiator ornament on Rolls Royces, is in such demand that they are often stolen from unattended cars. For this reason, when I purchased a used Rolls Royce in England and had it shipped via the St. Lawrence Seaway to the Port of Cleveland, I asked the seller to box the mascot and mail it to me. This he did, and the car arrived with a small black rubber cap on the radiator. When I paid the customs fee on the car, I paid it on the total price of the car.

A week or so after the car arrived, I got a notice from the Post Office that there was a package for me and that they would hold it for only a certain number of days. The notice indicated that payment of customs charges was required before the package could be released.

The postal authorities insisted that I pay the customs fee, based upon a value of $200, which was the declared value of the article. I explained that I had already paid the customs charges on the total price of the car when I picked it up in Cleveland. Since the radiator ornament was part of the car, and had been included in the selling price of the car, there should be no extra charge for it now.

This seemed perfectly simple and logical to me, but no matter how many times I explained this, I could not seem to make any-one understand my point. They insisted on the money, saying

Photo of Rolls taken in England before shipment clearly shows the famous "Flying Lady" mascot in place atop the radiator. The price of the car included the mascot, of course, but this photo and the bill of sale did not convince U.S. Customs.

they would mark it "refused" and send it to the place where unclaimed and refused articles go if I did not pay the charge.

Another alternative was to fill in an Importers Objections form and return the form and the package to the Collector of Customs, in hopes the matter would be adjudicated and the item someday returned to me. A Post Office form in duplicate was to accompany the customs office form. I could check my objection to the assessed value, rate or amount. There was not a column for my objection, but the form was printed on only one side, with the notation "Further Advice Is Requested on the Above Items," so I could write my objection on the back.

It all sounded too complicated, and I had a premonition that I would never see the Flying Lady again if I did either of the above. So I paid the charges, deciding I would write to the Collector of Customs and send the Post Office forms along with my letter. I was warned that I must make my initial complaint within ninety days in order for it to be considered.

Within a couple of days I wrote a long and complete letter, and with the letter I enclosed copies of my customs payments when I picked up the car, the bill of sale and any other paper that seemed appropriate. This made a nice fat letter, which I sent by registered mail in a nine by twelve envelope.

The mascot, obviously a part of the car but shipped separately to prevent theft, arrived in excellent condition in a cardboard box. U.S. Customs demanded duty to be paid on it.

The receipt for my registered letter returned promptly with some unintelligible scrawling on it. I relaxed knowing that the documents had arrived at the proper office and that in time I would be told I was right and a check would be sent to me. I guess it was a month before I received a form letter from the Customs Department in Washington, requesting that I fill out the enclosed form and send the required documents with it. The form was the same one I had sent in originally. I filled it out, made additional copies of all the documents, plus copies of my original letter, the receipt for registered mail, and copies of the original forms I had submitted. These I mailed by registered mail, return receipt requested.

Several weeks elapsed before I received a second form letter from the Customs Department, but the letter contained a different form. Again I filled out and made copies of everything that had been previously submitted. This time I added that I should also be reimbursed for the cost of three registered letters.

Time passed. I received a third form letter, identical to the first, asking for supporting information, etc. It was past the point of being funny; it was downright annoying. I was determined to get my money back, so I wrote a long letter, making all the details so lucid that even a slow learner should have understood it. It was a sizable sheaf of papers that I mailed this time, again registered with return receipt requested. I was so certain that I was right in my contention that the radiator ornament was included in the price of the car, and that my customs payment on the car included all the car's parts, that I could not understand anyone questioning it, nor the delay. It was not a large sum of money, and I was fast approaching that amount in copying charges and postage.

Over a month elapsed and I heard nothing on my last letter, except for the receipt from it. I wrote President Johnson, asking what the Customs Department was doing with my money and what sort of personnel he had there who could not understand a simple problem. I sent along a copy of everything to date. Now I thought I would get some action. This time I received another form letter from an administrative aid in the White House saying my letter had been received and was being sent to the proper department, and that it would be given proper attention at the earliest time.

Upon receipt of the letter from the White House I composed a long letter to Ladybird Johnson, stating all the trouble I was having over a simple matter. I added that I was with her in efforts to Keep America Beautiful, and felt that driving a Rolls Royce was a step in the right direction, even if it was a thirty-year-old car. One of her secretaires sent an acknowledgment, hinting that Mrs. Johnson was concerned and would do what she could to help.

Feeling that at least my complaint had been heard, I took the letters from President and Mrs. Johnson to the Post Office and showed them to the person who had started all my problems. I pointed to the large picture of President Johnson on the wall and warned that the President was looking into this, and told him not to be surprised if he was called on the carpet for not handling such a simple and just problem on the spot.

I have no idea whether there was any correspondence between the White House and the Customs Department concerning my letters. I expect they went in the wastebasket as soon as the form letter reply was sent. One day I received a check in the amount of $2.41. This was not the correct amount, and there was no decipherable code on the check to explain it. I made a copy of the check, cashed it and wrote again, this time subtracting $2.41 from the amount due, but adding the cost of postage and making so many copies of everything. I even sent copies of this correspondence to President and Mrs. Johnson.

No acknowledgments came from the White House. After a long lapse a form letter came from the Customs Department explaining how I should go about making a claim for an improper payment. With it was a punched computer card. I was to return the card with my answer. I took a razor blade and cut a whole series of little rectangles on the card, thinking that when it went through the computer it would be kicked out and get some per- ersonal attention. Possibly my rectangles indicated that the matter was settled to my satisfaction, for I never heard another word.

I fully intended to follow up but had other matters on my mind so did not get around to it. In the meantime we moved and everything was packed away in boxes, so the matter is still un- resolved. I am still annoyed and may pursue the matter further when time allows. It's not the principle, it's the money.

9

Doctor to the Rescue

The gas-line connection was tight enough, and I should have left it at that. But that urge for one final quarter turn of the wrench brought a sickening crunch. I had broken the carburetor bowl on my Phantom III Rolls. I felt sick as I looked at the shattered parts. I also felt thoroughly disgusted for having given that last stupid and unnecessary twist of the wrench. I had put myself in the position of having to locate a replacement carburetor.

The center portion of the Phantom III carburetor contains the bowl and the throat in which the twin venturi and jets are located. It is a complicated and highly refined piece of equipment. Only 715 Phantom III Rolls Royces were built from 1936 to 1939, and although a large number of them are still in operation, I knew I would have a helluva time locating a replacement carburetor.

The first step was to phone the places that advertise parts in *The Flying Lady,* the publication of the Rolls Royce Owner's Club. None had a P III carburetor, nor did they know of any available. I wrote to owners of P III's listed in the club directory asking for help. I got plenty of replies, but not one had a carburetor to sell.

A letter to the Rolls Royce factory in England brought the distressing news that they "no longer supply direct spare parts for pre-war chassis," and gave the name of a firm from whom requirements should be ordered. They very nicely passed my

Adams & Oliver Ltd.,

Spares Department,

Ramsey Road Garage,

Warboys, Hunts.

England.

JBMA/EC/Spares Export   20th April, 1970.

B.B. Mills, Esq.,
45, South Street,
Jackson,
Ohio 45640,
U.S.A.

Dear Sir,

Thank you for your letter of 11th April.

I am sorry to say that we have no chance whatever of
supplying the carburettor bowl. Many people are seeking this
part. No new ones are available and we see no hope of ever
finding a good secondhand one.

Regarding the wiper parts. If you can send the old parts
giving the exact distance between the boxes and the length of
cable from the motor to the drive box, we can help you. There
are too many variations for us to be able to supply "blind".

Yours very truly,

J.B.M. Adams
Director

Disappointing news from one of the largest suppliers of Rolls Royce parts, after failure to locate a replacement in the United States. Over a dozen friends were assisting me in the search for a new carburetor.

The Rolls Royce factory advised that they no longer supplied direct spare parts for prewar cars, but helpfully passed my letter along to Rippon Bros., who did have a "rebuild kit."

HER MAJESTY THE QUEEN
MOTOR CAR MANUFACTURERS

ROLLS-ROYCE LIMITED

IN YOUR REPLY
PLEASE QUOTE
CHASSIS NUMBER
J.S/RH/6/MC

HYTHE ROAD. SCRUBS LANE
WILLESDEN
LONDON N·W·10
ENGLAND
LONDON REPAIR DEPOT

TELEPHONE
LADBROKE 2444
TELEGRAMS
"SILVAGOST LONDON N·W·10"
TELEX 25133

B. B. Mills, Esq.,
45 South Street,
Jackson,
Ohio, 45640,
U.S.A.

16th June, 1970.

ROLLS ROYCE PHANTOM III   CHASSIS NO. 3.CP.58

Dear Sir,

We thank you for your letter of the 5th June.

We have to advise you that we no longer supply direct spare
parts for pre-war chassis, and requirements should be ordered
from Rippon Bros. Limited, Viaduct Street, Huddersfield,
Yorkshire, England. We are today passing your letter to
Rippon Bros. and asking them to deal with your requirements
and you will doubtless be hearing from them in the very near
future.

Yours faithfully,

R. Haynes,
For Technical Manager.

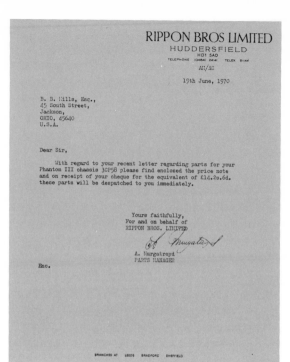

Rippon Bros. supplied parts necessary for rebuilding the inside of the carburetor if and when the center portion, which included the bowl, was found.

letter along to this company, but unfortunately the company could not supply the carburetor. Another firm that supplied parts for prewar Rolls Royces answered my letter promptly: ". . . We have no chance whatever of supplying the carburetor bowl. Many people are seeking this part. No new ones are available, and we see no hope of ever finding a good secondhand one."

I was referred to a carburetor specialist in Rochester, New York, who seemed to know a lot about P III carburetors. He thought I might locate a Duesenberg carburetor, and with some modifications he thought it might work. This would have to be a last resort, for I did not want parts from another car if it could be avoided. And locating a Duesenberg carburetor would be about as difficult as finding one for the Rolls.

An Owner's Club member in Michigan wrote that he had an extra P III engine he had rescued from a car that burned. He wanted to keep the engine for parts, but very kindly offered to lend that carburetor to me while I was trying to locate a replace-

```
                        2 Macclesfield Road,
                        Leek, Staffs.

                        8th July 1970

B B .Mills Esq.,
45 South St.,
Jackson, Ohio.


Dear Burt,

        Apologies for not answering your letter earlier, but
I have been driving my 3½ litre OPen Vanden Plas Bentley
in a number of Continental rallys and I have only just
got back after being out of England some six weeks.

        I have good news for you about your carburettor.
As you probably know, the factory at Crewe have no
carburettor bowls, not have they any intention of
having any made.  Ned Estridge is taking this very
seriously indeed and when he was over here about ten
weeks ago staying with me, he went to see a good friend of
mine called Stan Brunt who does most of the pre-war
Rolls work for the factory.  Stanley has found an equiv-
alent carburettor which, it seems, will adapt realive-
ly easily.  The big difficulty is that the fitting
flange on a Rolls commercial engine is different.  These
carburettors are in relatively good supply.  Ned has
taken one back to the States with him, to work out what
is necessary to adapt the carburettor.  I don't know
how far he has got with thi,s but it does seem to be a
pretty sure fire answer to your problem.

        Perhaps you would like to get in touch with him
direct, his address is 365 E. 21st St. San Bernardino,
California.

        All the best, keep in touch with me and if there is
anything I can do to help about anything, all you have to
do is ask.

                    Yours,

                    Bunty
```

A friend in England offered some hope by referring me to the person who made a new center portion of the carburetor, using the broken pieces to make a mold.

ment. This was most generous but I hesitated to accept his offer, fearing I might not locate a replacement in a year, if at all.

A Rolls enthusiast in England from whom I had bought a car referred me to a club member in the United States who was a technical expert on the Phantom III. Somehow I had missed his name in the club directory. My British friend wrote that this gentleman had looked into adapting another type of Rolls carburetor to the P III, and had taken one of these carburetors home to the States with him. I wrote, stating my problem and asking for any suggestions or help.

A prompt reply was encouraging. He was planning a trip to London in a couple of weeks and would stop by the Zenith factory to see if some new ones could be made. He thought that perhaps he could get the dies for it, adding that the machining should not be too much of a problem. It seems my problem was not so unusual after all; others must have had the urge to give that last quarter turn of the wrench.

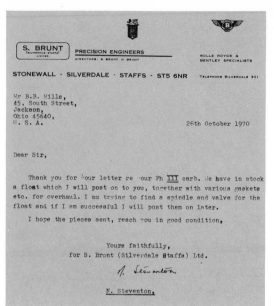

More carburetor parts from another British source made it possible to renew all the interior parts once the outer casting was made.

S. BRUNT (SILVERDALE, STAFFS) LIMITED · PRECISION ENGINEERS
DIRECTORS: S. BRUNT, H BRUNT

ROLLS ROYCE &
BENTLEY SPECIALISTS

STONEWALL · SILVERDALE · STAFFS · ST5 6NR   TELEPHONE SILVERDALE 301

Mr B.B. Mills,
45, South Street,
Jackson,
Ohio 45640,
U. S. A.   26th October 1970

Dear Sir,

Thank you for your letter re your Ph III carb. We have in stock a float which I will post on to you, together with various gaskets etc. for overhaul. I am trying to find a spindle and valve for the float and if I am successful I will post them on later.

I hope the pieces sent, reach you in good condition,

Yours faithfully,
for S. Brunt (Silverdale Staffs) Ltd.

N. Steventon,

Upon his return from London he wrote that Zenith had destroyed the molds and no more could be made there. He said there was a slight possibility that some may have been sold when Zenith closed out their excess stock. He had located a person who thought he might have one but could not get at it in a garage packed with parts. The man would let us know if and when he could get to the parts in his garage. Meanwhile he said that if I still had all the pieces, he might be able to epoxy them together, make a mold and use the lost wax process to fashion a bronze casting. It would be difficult but interesting, he added.

Of course I had all the parts. I had picked up every tiny shard and sliver I could find and had them all in a box. These I sent promptly, along with a carburetor rebuild set that I had ordered from England, containing new filters, gaskets, needle valves and other replacement parts for the carburetor. Elated at this help, I phoned to convey my thanks and to assure the man everything was on its way. It was then I learned that he was a doctor, and technical challenges like this were his hobby. The reassuring tone of his voice made me feel a lot better; he did not think the job was impossible. He said he would keep in touch as he worked on the mold.

Cementing the broken parts together, the doctor made a mold. He used the "lost wax" process to make this pattern for the bottom portion of the carburetor bowl and throat.

With the hope in mind that I might have a repaired carburetor for my car, I contacted the gentleman in Michigan who had offered to loan one. I told him what steps were being taken to repair mine, and he said, "Come on up and get it."

We drove from southern Ohio to the apple country of Michigan, and enjoyed the trip. The gentleman had several fine cars he had collected over the years, all of them perfectly restored. I particularly admired his Phantom III Rolls with a Windovers body, his 1953 Mercedes 300 convertible sedan, and a Milford electric coupe. He gave me several good tips on maintaining my Phantom III as I removed the carburetor from the extra engine.

With the borrowed carburetor on my car I was able to enjoy it during a time when it would otherwise have been unusable. I shall always be grateful for the man's generosity.

The first letter from the doctor was encouraging. Everything had arrived, and he had been successful in piecing the carburetor parts together, using epoxy to hold things in place. He planned to made a mold of the original in wax, encase it in plaster, then melt the wax out of the plaster mold. This would leave a mold he could use for casting the new part. I was not familiar with the lost wax process, so I went to our library to read about it. To my surprise, I found it was commonly used by dentists to make inlays. Of course, making a replacement section for a carburetor was a bit more complicated than making an inlay. A bit larger, too!

Positioning the carburetor jets and drilling the holes in the new casting was very exacting, required tremendous skill and

Wax pattern, from the top, shows the complicated job of casting and machining involved in making the new carburetor section for Phantom III Rolls.

patience. Figuring what the shrinkage would be in the bronze called for mathematical knowledge too. And cutting the correct threads demanded expertise in handling a milling machine.

From time to time a letter would arrive with a picture enclosed, telling and showing me what stage the project had reached. One letter told of a problem that had arisen in securing the right paint for the part. The doctor was taking great pains to finish the outside of the new part so it would match the high standards Rolls Royce used originally. Rolls engines are finished in very glossy black enamel, a specially formulated paint that will withstand the heat generated by the engine. The doctor finally finished the new part in a glossy black epoxy paint that has not deteriorated a bit in the seven years it has been in use. In fact, I believe the finish on the replacement part is even better than the original factory finish.

One Saturday afternoon I received a phone call from the doctor asking if I could hear anything. I could hear a motor running in the background but did not really get the connection. He said, "That's your carburetor installed on my motor. It seems to be running great." To test the newly rebuilt carburetor, he had installed it on his own car and had made all the little adjustments that are necessary in rebuilding a carburetor. "I've opened a bottle of champagne to celebrate," he said. I replied that I would raise a glass from my end too, and thanked him for all his efforts. I really do not know what I would have done without his help!

The dies partially assembled give some idea of the thought and study that went into making a new throat and bowl section for the carburetor. The "shrinkage" of the brass had to be estimated. Threads had to be cut after holes were drilled.

He said he would send it to me in a few days. Soon a plywood box arrived, and carefully packed inside was the sparkling new carburetor, with some adjustment instructions from the doctor.

I could hardly wait to get the new carburetor on my car. Yes, I was very careful in tightening the gas line. You can imagine my elation and relief when it worked perfectly. I noticed a little gasoline trickled out of the spillover pipe from time to time. The doctor had warned that I might have to adjust the float level, and jokingly (I hope) added that I should take care when tightening all connections. With a minor adjustment to the float level, the carburetor has worked perfectly ever since. The big 7338 cc engine delivers thirteen miles per gallon on the open road in top gear, about ten in town. This is better mileage than I know of on any other twelve-cylinder car. Of course, the four-speed transmission helps.

I cannot begin to estimate what this would have cost had I found a machine shop competent and willing to tackle the job. The doctor's charges were so small, I had good reason to open another bottle of champagne. He wanted the box sent on to

The replacement piece in position with top and bottom sections of original carburetor back on the Phantom III engine. Once the float was adjusted, the carburetor performed perfectly. Careful finishing of the new part exceeds that of originals.

another Phantom III owner in Pennsylvania who also needed a replacement carburetor.

No doubt there are wonderful people in every hobby, but I will never find two finer men than the one who so generously loaned me a carburetor and the one who built a new one. They are the greatest.

10

The Standard from Morningside Heights

Combining attendance at an American Press Institute Seminar on Newspaper Management at Columbia University with the purchase of a 1948 Standard convertible left me with a drive from New York City to Bristol, Tennessee. I wanted the car for my older daughter, who was just about to get her driver's license. The car seemed to be in fine condition except for the left front door, which did not close quite as it should and rattled badly.

The day before I was to leave, New York City had one of its famous snowstorms with snow piled high along the curbs. The car had a heater, but I knew that drafts would come in around the ill-fitting left door and over the windshield and the right door window. So I knew driving the car could become quite uncomfortable. I had nearly frozen on a winter trip bringing a Jaguar from New England to Ohio, so I prepared myself for this one with some thermal underwear, a slip-on sweater and fur-lined gloves. I knew these would keep me warm and would not be too bulky.

The car had been serviced. I got an early start on Saturday morning from the Morningside Heights section of New York. My trip across the George Washington Bridge to New Jersey's Garden State Parkway was not bad at all. The little car ran well, my only concern being that whenever the choke knob was pushed all the

Solid little car had oversize grille guards in front to protect against additional damage. Left door did not close quite right and flew open after a short distance on my first trip, necessitating emergency repairs with my belt.

way in, the motor would miss. I decided to drive with the choke partially out and not worry about repairing it until I was home.

The Standard (which later became the Triumph) had what are commonly known as "suicide" doors, the type hinged at the back. Some icy ruts just as I was entering the Jersey Turnpike jarred the left door open, and it swung out with some force. Luckily it did not hit or catch on anything. I was able to pull out of traffic, reach over from the right side and pull it closed. Perhaps the force of the door swinging open sprung the hinges, for it would not close as well as before, and I feared it would swing open every time I hit a bump in the road.

There were no stores on this particular stretch of road and I had nothing with me to secure the door. So I removed my belt and looped it around the door handle and through the grab handle on the fascia above the dashboard. This kept the door from opening, but I could not make the belt tight enough to actually close the door completely, which left a nice space for the wind to whip in. Since I was driving on the right side of the car, I was thankful it was not the right door. I was left without support for my trousers, which now seemed quite loose at the waist. I figured this arrangement would suffice until I could locate a hardware store to buy rope. I did not realize I would have to drive beyond Baltimore before I would be off limited access highways. I stopped for gas just before leaving New Jersey, and grabbed my trousers just in time as I got out to pay. Driving in the tunnel under Delaware Bay, I guess the noise of a truck keeping too close behind me rattled me to the point where I pushed in the choke knob; the motor began to miss and the car slowed down. The truck driver raced his motor and down-shifted, and that roar in the tunnel was really frightening. Fortunately I pulled out the choke a bit, the motor caught and I was able to keep ahead of the truck the rest of the way through the tunnel. He roared past me as soon as he could get out of his lane.

Finally beyond Baltimore I found a supermarket and bought some clothesline rope, allowing me to secure the loose door and my trousers.

Having had trouble at toll booths while driving cars with the steering wheel on the right side, I was prepared with half a glass full of change: quarters, dimes and nickles. I could pick out the change I needed before reaching the booth, put the car in neutral and reach over to lower the window as I approached the booth, then toss the coins into the receptacle. This worked well, but since I had to drive out of the toll booth before I could wind up the window, I got a complete change of air for probably a quarter of a mile. This was exhilarating to say the least, for the inside of the car was below the freezing point.

I made good time. It was just 3 P.M. when I passed the White House. The traffic pattern that took me over to Virginia was a little confusing. I went around the traffic interchange three times before I could get into the correct lane. The other drivers seemed to know where they were going and would not give an inch as I tried to squeeze to the right. Finally, by anticipating a green light by a few seconds, and with the good luck of the driver of the car to my right looking at the gal beside him, I got into the right lane and could cross the bridge. I stopped for the night at Charlottesville.

The drive the next morning across the highlands of Virginia was pleasant but chilly. Lunch in Roanoke helped warm me up, and I arrived in Bristol around five. To my surprise no one was home. A little later my fourteen-year-old daughter drove in the driveway in our Edsel station wagon. My wife was kneeling on the middle seat, facing the tailgate. I could not imagine why my younger daughter, who did not have a license, was driving, nor why my wife would be kneeling facing the rear of the car.

The answer was soon forthcoming. We had been planning a trip to Florida, and my wife was trying to get a head start on a nice tan by using our sunlamp. She had gone to sleep accidentally with the lamp focused on the back of her thighs, and awakened an hour or more later to find herself with second degree burns. She was in such pain that she could not sit to drive to the doctor's office. My daughter sympathized with her mother's pain and was glad to do the driving, even if illegally.

A blacksmith repaired the sprung hinges on the left door of the Standard. With some shims behind the latch and a turnbuckle inside the door, I was able to make it close perfectly. The choke trouble was in the cable, and was no problem. I painted the car silver-gray. I removed an oversize grille guard and installed two driving lights to cover a damaged place in the grille. It was an attractive little car.

I had taken out the left front bucket seat to repair the leather and so had to sit in the back seat while my older daughter was learning to handle a clutch-type car and gearshift. We were on a seldom traveled road, approaching a dead end. She was bare-

Body and fenders were carefully sanded and the car was primed before being sprayed with gray metallic lacquer. The plating cleaned up easily. The leather interior required some stitching and cleaning with saddle soap.

Missing part at bottom of grille was camouflaged by a pair of driving lights. Smaller bumper guards were installed, improving the appearance of the front end.

footed and put her left foot on the brake, as one used to a car with automatic transmission is apt to do. Of course the car was still in gear, and as she approached the end of the road she said, "It's not stopping, what do I do?"

"Put your right foot on the brake too, and push like hell," I answered, envisioning crashing into the trees at the end of the road.

She took her right foot off the accelerator and pushed as hard as she could, bringing the car to a screeching halt. The sudden stop threw me forward where the left front seat had been, and I saw my daughter had her left foot on the brake and her right foot on the clutch. She thought this cross-legged way of stopping was confusing and difficult. She added that she thought automatic transmissions were nicer than four-on-the-floor. The car's ribbed-metal clutch and brake pedals were uncomfortable on bare feet.

Both my daughters learned to drive the car and handle the clutch and gearshift, as well as the problems of parking a right-hand-drive car. My older daughter got her driver's license and

That is not a dummy spare. The nut in the center holds a cover over the spare wheel. The luggage-compartment lid folds flat to give tremendous carrying space for so small a car. The rear bumper later cleaned up nicely.

used the car during the summer. I was quite annoyed when some boy pried off the little enameled British flag that was part of the radiator ornament, and even more annoyed when I saw the same lad with a car full of fellows driving the car without my daughter being along. He was revving up the motor and going through the gears and around corners as if he was driving in the Grand Prix at Watkins Glen. Something went wrong with either the car or driver; the transmission locked and the car had to be towed home. A replacement transmission could not be found, and there was a long delay in getting repair parts. Meanwhile my daughter used the Edsel station wagon.

The repairs to the transmission were never quite right; the shifting was not as smooth as before. I sold the car to a young reporter who fancied things British. He wore tweeds, even in hot weather, smoked a pipe with a curved stem and worked "old chap" and "I say!" into almost every sentence. I feared for my life when he took a test drive. He had absolutely no comprehension of the car's capabilities and put it into curves at well above prudent driving speeds.

Evidently he never learned how to corner properly, or mistakenly thought he was driving a Bentley. After owning the car about three months, he underestimated his speed on a corner and crashed into a tree. Fortunately he was not injured, but there was too much damage to the car for it to be worth repairing.

11

Those Big Franklin Lights

You can imagine how difficult it is to locate certain parts used over fifty years ago on limited-production cars. I wanted a set of headlights to replace some badly rusted lights on a Series 11A Franklin. The Series 11A was made only in 1925 and 1926, and probably not over 10,000 were produced. These cars differed from the Series 11B and Series 12 cars in having a thin round bar at the inside middle attaching the headlights. Later models had the bar attached to the headlight stanchions, following the curve of the headlight rim to about midpoint and then crossing over to the other side. This bar held the front license plate.

No Series 11A lights were advertised in *Aircooled News*, the publication of the H. H. Franklin Club, and none were in any of the parts-for-sale ads in the national car magazines. I ran an ad seeking these lights but got no response. I also checked with various car club members, to no avail. Nor did I have any luck at the flea markets I attended. I had about decided to have the lights patched with new metal and to paint the body of the lights and have only the headlight rims replated. After all, there was some precedent for doing this, for Franklins could be ordered to suit customers' tastes. I had a picture of a Series 11A with a painted grille instead of plated one. I knew I would not be too happy with this compromise but was willing to make it necessary to get the car in operation.

I took the lights to a welding shop and they were willing to try to patch them, but they were wary that the thin, brittle metal would disintegrate when the welding torch was applied. I agreed to leave them at my own risk.

Not long afterward I visited a friend of mine who restores horse-drawn carriages. These require a lot of expertise in working with wood, and he showed me how to make spokes for wooden wheels. He was working on a beautiful open carriage he had promised to a museum, and was so close to his deadline he could not take time to help me with the spokes. The carriage had a very ornate pair of lamps that he wanted plated, and he asked if I would take them by the platers for him.

Walking into the plating shop with the two carriage lamps, I spotted a cardboard box on the floor with what looked at first glimpse like Franklin headlights. I left the carriage lamps on the counter and took one headlight out of the box. To my surprise these were not only Series 11A Franklin headlights, but printed on a piece of masking tape stuck to one of the lenses was: "Ser. 11A Franklin, 1925 $75." I asked the proprietor about the lights, and he gave me the name and address of the owner. The lights had been converted to hold regular house lamp sockets, but this change affected only the reflectors. Nothing had been done to the outside of the lights. I explained why I wanted the lights, and asked the plater not to start on them until I could contact the owner. He agreed, saying he did not think the owner was in any hurry since he was planning to use them on an outdoor terrace that was not completed.

Not wanting to take the chance of being turned down on the phone, I drove my Franklin, minus headlights, over to the house of the owner of the lights. I explained my problem, showed the restored car and asked to buy the lights. The owner said he liked the big Franklin lights and liked the idea of the old car lights on his terrace. He told me about the trouble he had gone to having an electrician install the sockets for 110-volt lamps, and that he had paid $75 for the lights. I felt I was not going to get the lights, but had to try anyway.

I told him about the lights I had left in the welding shop. We could switch reflectors from his lights to mine. He admitted the painted lights would not really make too much difference, in fact might even look better. Since I would be paying the repair

These big nickel-plated Franklin headlights turned up at a plater's shop when I delivered a friend's coach lamps for plating. The owner planned to use them on a patio and had rewired them for household current.

and plating costs on both pairs, plus switching reflectors and paying him $75, he would only have the original payment to the electrician as his cost.

I had a sinking feeling: What if the welding shop ruins my lights? What will I have to swap for these? I thought I had better get to the welding shop and caution the welder once again to be extremely careful with the torch. When I explained the dilemma to the welder, he suggested that since the headlights would be painted, he could use silver solder on the cracked areas. This would not require as much heat, and there was less chance of damage to the lamps.

The lamps turned out very nice, and I had them painted to the new owner's color choice. There was no trouble swapping the converted reflectors with my original pair. When my newly acquired lights were nickel-plated they looked just great, allowing me to authentically complete the work on the 1925 Series 11A Franklin.

The man told me he had picked up the lights at a general flea market in Binghamton, New York, and had stored them for several years. At that time he had not even thought of a terrace. He just wanted those nice big lights.

12

Half a Car
from Muscatine

The load seemed to be riding well on the trailer. Every time I glanced in the mirror I saw the imposing shape of the Franklin grille and marveled that the little four-cylinder Toyota was hauling such a load—the front half of a Franklin, including the engine. We had left Muscatine, Iowa, around noon and were already beyond Lincoln, Nebraska. We had reservations at a nice motel, with an indoor pool, not too far ahead, and were looking forward to a relaxing swim, a pleasant dinner and a good rest.

Then a noise developed, which I thought was in the Toyota's engine. It sounded as if the fan belt had split and was hitting something in the engine compartment as it turned. When I could find nothing wrong under the hood, I walked around the car and trailer, checking the hitch and the tie-down ropes on the tarpaulin. On the right side of the trailer I found the cause of the noise: The tires were retreads, and most of the tread on the right tire had separated. It would not last much longer.

I was relieved to see a gas station in the distance. Perhaps at ten miles an hour, or less, the tire would last to the service station. It did not! It blew out a few hundred feet down the road, and the trailer did not have a spare. I was willing to buy a replacement tire if the station had one, and because the wheel jack with the Toyota was not strong enough to lift the trailer, I hoped the station would install it. Leaving my wife in the car with instruc-

The front half of the Franklin just fit in the trailer, and our Toyota had no trouble pulling it. The engine had been completely overhauled and used less than two weeks. The shell had rusted through in spots but was solid otherwise.

tions not to open the doors or lower the windows for anyone, and lifting the hood in the traditional distress signal, I started walking toward the station. The sky had been menacing for the past hour and the radio had warned of coming thunderstorms, so I walked briskly, hoping to have the tire changed before the rain came.

Nearing the station I saw a trailer-rental sign from the same company from which I had rented the trailer. This seemed lucky; I presumed they would be able to furnish another wheel and tire. The attendant was sympathetic and helpful. The only trouble was that their serviceman had just taken the truck and driven home for supper. They thought it would be about an hour; they would send him out with a wheel and a tire as soon as he returned.

Not wanting to leave my wife sitting in the car alongside the highway for an hour, I gave the attendant explicit directions on where the car was located. Walking back, I could feel the wind increasing. The sky was black to the west. A storm was not far away. When I reached the car I noticed the hood was closed, and wondered why my wife had closed it. She explained that it had slammed shut with a terrifying bang when the first semitrailer sped by.

While we were waiting we listened to news of the approaching storm on the car radio. As dusk approached I turned on the car's flashers. We had waited about half an hour when one of the

After starting life as a 1928 Series 12B Franklin Sedan, the front half was converted to a stationary power plant following a rear-end accident. The wooden chassis was cut at the cowl and the fan housing had rusted through at the bottom.

Nebraska Highway Patrol trucks stopped to see what was our trouble. The driver said he knew where the service man lived and would drive by his home and tell him to hurry. We were very grateful for this assistance, and even more grateful when we saw the approaching service truck cut across the median and pull up ahead of us. The driver had a wheel and tire, but it was a different size and would not fit our trailer. After he examined the trailer and our rental papers, he said the rental people should never have let that trailer leave town because it had a wheel size no longer in use. He added that they did not have anything to fit. Before I could complain, or even ask his advice, he said they would switch trailers with me. I was to drive very slowly behind him to the station.

We fairly crept along. Meanwhile the wind was increasing, and we could see flashes of lightning in the distance. With a hoist on the wrecker, the half-Franklin was lifted out of one trailer and deposited in a larger one, the only trailer they had for over-the-road use. It had a portion of the floor missing at the back, which meant the engine had to sit well forward in the trailer, shifting the balance of weight considerably. I did not realize how difficult this would make the next hour's driving.

It started to rain lightly as the engine was placed in the trailer, so the tarpaulin was hurriedly secured. By the time I pulled back on the highway it was raining quite hard and was already dark. It started to pour so hard that it was difficult to see the road ahead. The weight of the engine sitting farther forward in the trailer, plus the extra weight of the larger trailer, pushed down harder on the back of the Toyota, lifting the front end somewhat. This caused the headlights to dazzle oncoming cars without helping me much in seeing the road ahead. I did not want to drive as fast as the cars and trucks that sped by me, so I could not follow their taillights. It just was not safe driving with such poor visibility. I was really glad when lightning would flash, giving me a good view of the road.

We drove probably thirty nerve-racking miles to the exit for our motel. What a relief to turn into the motel entrance! I dashed through the rain to register and get the key, then drove to the entrance near our room. By the time our luggage was in the room I was soaked. My wife phoned the desk to ask about dining-room reservations and was told they were sorry, but the electrical storm had knocked out the current to the kitchen, and they could neither cook nor wash dishes. In addition, there would not be hot water for the bath because the water heater was on the same circuit. A truck stop across the road that had not suffered any damage was recommended.

We were getting pretty hungry. The rain had not stopped by the time we hurried to the car (trailer still attached) and drove to the diner. The parking lot was full of cars and trucks, so it was necessary to park some distance away because of the extra room we needed to maneuver. We were a disreputable-looking couple when we got stools at the counter. The truck stop had fed so many people from the motel that there was not much on hand by the time we ordered. We settled for hamburgers and French fries, and were glad to get them.

Not wanting to eat at the truck stop the next morning, and fearing the electrical problems to the motel's kitchen might not be repaired, we drove after dinner to a combination grocery store and filling station a short way down the road. There we got a package of sweet rolls, some canned orange juice and milk. We

It took a hoist to unload the engine. Pipes at the front supporting the engine used the same holes as the original front springs. The hood was removed for this operation to prevent damage from the chain hoist.

had brought along a percolator and coffee so there would be an early morning cup of coffee.

The rain still had not stopped, but the thunder and lightning had ceased. We got another dousing from the car to the motel.

We were so bushed, we watched the news on TV and turned in, planning an early start the next morning. The light had not been out two minutes before something dropped on my face and crawled down my neck. It felt huge, and I could not imagine what it was. I turned on the light and jumped out of bed trying to swat or brush off the intruder. It was a huge cockroach, the type called a water bug. It had been crawling on the ceiling with several others, lost its footing and fell on me. When I brushed it to the floor, it disappeared immediately into the heavy shag carpeting. I rolled up a magazine and tried to swat it, but it was gone. Two of those on the ceiling fell to the floor and disappeared as I tried to hit them. Some others I swatted. All that night I imagined they were crawling on me, and my wife said she was thinking the same thing.

The next morning was clear but soggy. We washed in cold water, ate our breakfast in the room and got on our way as quickly as possible. In the daytime the peculiar angle of the car because of the heavier trailer did not make much difference. We made good time and got home on schedule.

As usual, neighbors flocked around to see what treasure I had brought home. They seemed to like seeing the wrecking truck lift the Franklin engine out of the trailer and deposit it on the dolly I had made for it. There were only a few snide remarks about a mechanic who would bring home only half a car.

13

Just Something
I Wanted to Do

When I explained to other hobbyists why I drove from Denver to Muscatine, Iowa, and back to pick up only the front end of a car, they did not seem surprised. Several said they would really like to build their own car but had not yet gotten around to it. To them it did not seem unusual. Only those who thought the job impossible for an amateur, or those who had little interest in cars, thought I might be nuts. When I told them I planned to build the body too, they really thought I was off my rocker.

My plan was to build a Franklin Sports Tourer. As a lad of twelve I had sat in such a car in the display room of the Franklin factory in Syracuse, waiting to see Mr. H. H. Franklin about what I called "my invention." This was a simple plan for moving the front seat forward on two-door cars, making it easier to get in and out of the rear seat. The idea had come to me after hearing my grandfather complain about the difficulty of crawling over someone every time he rode in the back seat of my mother's car. My father had arranged for me to see Mr. Franklin, who treated me very nicely and took me to the design department. I was offered a job when I got out of college, but of course by that time the Franklin Company was long gone.

I have been unable to find out anything about the Sports Tourer body, although I've checked with the few remaining custom body designers. They do not recall any such body being

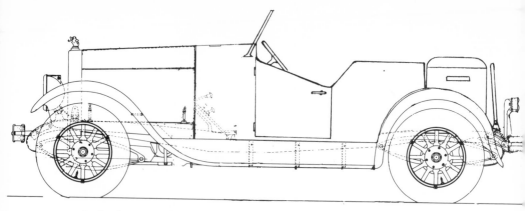

Scale drawing of Sports Tourer body superimposed on factory drawing of chassis and running gear. Original cowl extended four inches, necessitating lowering the steering column. The body ends just ahead of the rear axle.

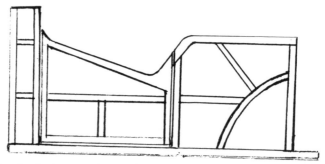

Framing for the body is made of kiln-dried oak. The front piece bolts to the existing rear cowl bracing. The door is hinged at the front for easy entry. Iron braces for the upright pieces were forged at a blacksmith shop for strength. Aluminum body skin covers the frame.

offered by American custom body builders. No picture of this car has ever shown up in any of the custom body books.

Several years ago I saw such a body on a 1929 Peerless chassis at an old-car show. At another time I saw a picture of a DuPont with a similar body. Unforuntately the Peerless had no nameplate attached to the body.

These attractive bodies may have been built by a foreign body builder on special order. They had an extended cowl, cut-down front doors, sharply raked windshield and a folding top that was

Although on a shorter wheelbase than Franklin's 119 inches, this sports body is similar to the replacement body. Top bows and roof can be removed when not in use, giving a clean, unobstructed line to the rear quarter panel.

usually removed when not in use. They were short, ending at about the rear-axle line. Bucket seats were fitted in front and a narrow bench seat in the rear. If the spare wheel was carried in the front fender, as it was on the Peerless and the Franklin, there was a trunk rack at the back; otherwise the spare was rear-mounted. The bodies resembled those seen on SS Jaguars, Bentleys and some other foreign sports cars.

The biggest problem would be to get the remaining chassis parts. I would need everything from the transmission back, plus both axles, all four springs, the steering system, rear frame cross member, gas tank, bumpers and miscellaneous chassis and drive-train parts. I would need the front and rear fenders, plus splash aprons. The rest of the body would be handmade.

When searching for old car parts, it is often necessary to buy parts you do not need or want in order to get those you do need. Usually this is not the result of an effort by parts sellers to take advantage of someone's needs. More often it is because the seller no longer needs the parts himself and sees no reason to keep them. Occasionally it will be for the money the parts can bring. Nevertheless, sellers usually are interested in helping another hobbyist.

Because the Series 12 Franklins had a wooden chassis frame, new side rails were needed. The dimensions were in a copy of

Grease and caked dirt on this universal joint typifies the condition in which many parts were received. Each had to be thoroughly cleaned and inspected, and repairs made before the part was installed on the chassis.

Rust inside the vacuum tank had to be removed. The entire unit was reconditioned and repainted before it was remounted on the firewall. The float chamber must be free of anything that can obstruct free movement of the float.

Since the engine had been operated by hand when it was used as a stationary power plant, the foot-throttle linkage had to be located and mounted on the fire wall.

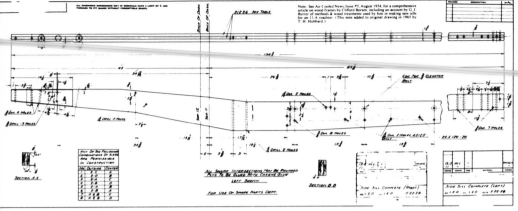

Factory drawing of Series 12 chassis was used when making new chassis rails. Ash boards were 12 inches wide to allow for drop frame without any splicing being necessary. After being glued, the rails were drilled for all brackets and attachments.

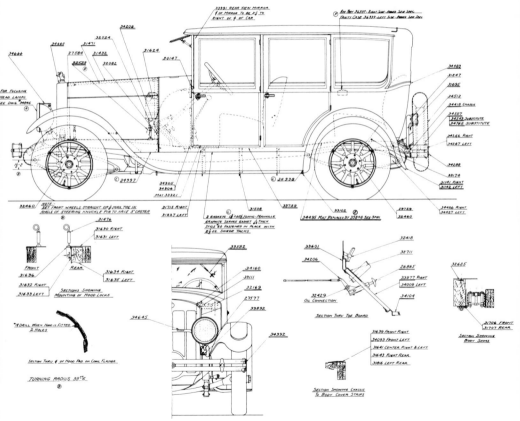

Dimensions for location of certain mechanical components were taken from H. H. Franklin Club magazine. Although this is a Series 11 car, the basic overall dimensions are the same, and necessary changes were made for Series 12 components.

Air Cooled News, the publication of the H. H. Franklin Club. I had some difficulty locating the kiln-dried ash and having the boards planed, glued together and readied for sawing. This required six ash boards twelve feet long, twelve inches wide, and one inch thick. Each board had to be planed to 37/64th in thickness, and the average lumberyard is not able to trim wood to tolerances so exacting. When three boards were glued together, the overall thickness of each side rail was 1¾ inches.

The planks were under terrific pressure for twenty-four hours as the glue dried. The measurements were then drawn on each rail, and the rails cut at the lumberyard. The next job was to locate and drill the necessary holes for spring holders, braces, brackets, screws, etc. Each rail was then given several coats of linseed oil thinned with turpentine.

The first source for parts was to try to locate a parts car. If I had been so lucky, I could have removed the needed parts and sold the remainder to someone else. In several months of searching, no parts car could be found. During this time I was also looking through ads in national car magazines for Franklin parts, and writing each advertiser. I also wrote members of the H. H. Franklin Club seeking their help, as well as running ads in Parts Wanted sections of car publications.

Cut frame rails were coated with a mixture of linseed oil and turpentine. Several coats were given to protect wooden chassis against future deterioration.

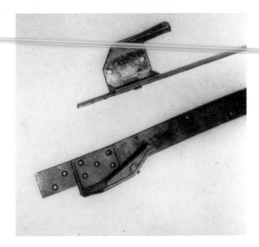

Since new body rails could not be located, steel extensions cut to correct measurements were welded to what was left of the original front body supports, which had been cut at the cowl when the engine was used as a stationary power plant.

As parts arrived from all over the United States, they were stored in the service area beside the garage. As time permitted, each part was examined, cleaned and refurbished before being crossed off the "want" list.

When it was obvious that no parts car would turn up, it was necessary to start ordering parts from the various letters I had received. From one person I was able to buy the front and rear axles and the drive shaft. From another came a steering column. The rear frame brace and gas tank came from Pennsylvania, a fine taillight from Utah, the hand brake assembly from Georgia. Rear fenders and a trunk rack came from Oregon, front fenders and the front apron from Washington.

Drum and brake band for hand brake. Brake band and actuating mechanism were removed, and a new lining riveted to the brake band. The actuating mechanism was cleaned and lubricated with graphite. The unit was painted before being installed at the rear of the transmission.

After reconditioning, the springs were attached to the already reworked rear axle. Franklin used lots of aluminum to keep weight down; the differential case is aluminum. New hydraulic brake lines were also installed.

Several sellers had written of odds and ends of spring parts, rear spring hangers, shackle bolts, extra leaves, etc. One person wrote that he had some springs in a shed, but would have to wait until the spring thaw to find out what he had. I bought a good-size box of nuts and bolts from Franklin cars from a man in Ohio, the best $15 investment I ever made.

Boxes and crates started arriving from all over the United States. They came by parcel post, UPS, motor freight, and on bus lines. As each package arrived I examined the parts. If they were satisfactory, I crossed those parts off my want list. I had to order springs from several sources, and these heavy crates caused some complaints from motor-freight drivers whose job was simply to bring the truck to my house. I was supposed to do the unloading, but often had to ask the driver's help. One driver tried to charge me a figure well above the correct one on the invoice. He thought he was smart enough to get away with the overcharge. He muttered something unintelligible when I showed him that the typed figures on the second copy of the invoice did not match the penciled-in figures he had written on the face of his copy.

Before the parts could be assembled and installed on the chassis, each had to be thoroughly cleaned. And if any repair was

The hand-brake lever, mounting bracket and linkage came as a unit. A release rod actuated by a thumb button was set up in the brake lever. It took a lot of solvent and elbow grease to get the unit working properly.

necessary, the repair had to be made. The parts were then sprayed with at least two coats of black enamel, as had been done originally. It took many hours of scrubbing and grinding to get up to fifty years of accumulated dirt and grease from the parts. Some had to be soaked for days in either a detergent solution or a solvent to soften and remove the solidified grease and tar. Some sheet metal parts had to be sandblasted before priming. It was a slow but satisfying period, as I visualized the assembled chassis.

Franklin featured full-elliptic springs on both axles. The same spring would fit several model years, but the number of leaves

Grease, grime and surface rust had to be cleaned from the U-bolts that hold springs to axles. On some bolts there was damage to threads. After thorough cleaning, bolts and nuts were painted with rust-resisting black enamel. Threads were protected.

With surface rust, but otherwise solid, the top air duct had to be sand-blasted and given several coats of primer to build up the surface for satisfactory finish coats.

varied by car weight and chassis length. In order to assemble four complete and correct springs, I had to buy fourteen springs. They came from several sources. Some had broken leaves, others had badly worn spring eyes where the top and bottom springs are connected. All had years of grease, dirt and rust, so complete cleaning was necessary before assembly. Using the best parts on hand, I found I was short two of the bolts that connect the springs through the spring eyes. A frantic plea failed to locate the bolts.

A machinist had to make them for me from larger bolts. Using bolts from a truck-spring shackle, he machined them to the correct diameter, cut them to the right length and threaded them so the Franklin washer and castellated nut would fit. When this was completed, the spring could be assembled and attached to the axles and the axles could be attached to the chassis, giving some semblance of automobile for the first time.

A tire company in California advertised tires made from the original molds for cars of the 1920s. The correct tread and side-wall design are important, so I ordered five tires and tubes. These were mounted after the rims had been sandblasted, primed and painted.

I had the most difficulty locating the hydraulic master cylinder. This was a Lockheed unit that bolted to the chassis and

Although I bought fourteen springs, I could not locate two bolts that connect the upper and lower springs. A machinist turned down two bolts from a truck spring shackle to the correct diameter, then cut threads to accept the Franklin washer, retainer and nut.

Three master cylinders had to be purchased before one complete cylinder could be assembled. Replacement parts, made by Lockheed, are still available. Inside of the reservoir and cylinder must be thoroughly clean for proper brake operation.

combined the reservoir with the master plunger. No one answering the first inquiries listed the part. An ad in two national car magazines plus one in *Air Cooled News* brought some replies. Two people listed incomplete cylinders that could be had if I would buy the rest of the parts on their lists. Since I could use most of the other parts, I bought from both sellers, hoping the two cylinders would make one. Unfortunately, the same parts were missing from both. Later a letter offered a complete cylinder, which I snapped up. As it turned out, this one was not complete either, but it did contain the parts missing from the other two. New seals and plungers are still available to rebuild Lockheed systems, for they are the same size as some currently in use. The completely rebuilt master cylinder should give years of service.

Assembling the components to build the chassis and running gear took some time and thought. The front frame extensions were set in place and bolted to the chassis. A blacksmith made new bolts to attach the front springs to the chassis from drawings I furnished. With the front axle in place, the next job was to bolt the motor mounts to the chassis. On wooden-frame cars the motor is attached front and rear to two lengths of angle iron, which are bolted to the chassis on each side. The holes were already drilled in the frame, their position being determined by the blueprint.

Front frame rails and steel ends were positioned. Spring hanger bolts made by a local blacksmith hold the spring to the frame. Bolts through the chassis are not too long, for the front fender braces are not yet bolted in place.

Even though the engine was used only two weeks after a major overhaul, it needed thorough cleaning before mounting in the new chassis. The vertical fins on the cylinders were cleaned by compressed air. Most of the wiring had to be replaced.

The engine and transmission were blocked to support their weight while the hand-brake drum was installed. The aluminum transmission case cleaned up easily. The clutch inspection plate was later painted. The drive shaft fits in the splined hub on the front universal joint.

The steel rear frame member containing the gas-tank apron and hangers bolts to the end of the wooden chassis rails. Lack of cross braces allowed the frame to flex over the bad roads of the 1920s. Full elliptic springs at each wheel gave a soft ride.

While the motor was being installed, it was held in place by planks running under the base and supported by blocks.

Franklin used a steel rear frame extension that combined a rear cross member with the apron over the gas tank. This had been sandblasted and painted, and was bolted in place next. The rear spring hangers are combined with the rear body rail supports. Once these were in place the rear springs were attached, having already been attached to the rear axle. To complete the running gear, the drum for the hand brake was attached, the front universal bolted in place and the drive shaft installed. At this point the connecting linkage for the hand brake would have been the next logical component to be installed. However, because of the extended cowl on the new body, the possibility that the hand-brake lever might have to be repositioned made it wiser to leave it until later.

The steering column was not installed at this point either, because some minor alterations might be necessary. The longer cowl on the new body could change the seating position some-

Rear springs are mounted outside chassis rails. Spring hanger bracket also contains rear body mounts. To conserve weight, many of the braces and brackets on Franklin chassis served more than one use.

Rear fenders required an additional piece welded to the inner apron to fit the new, shorter body. The last three bolt holes had to be filled in, since that area was exposed in the replacement body.

what, which could necessitate moving the steering column. For this reason the holes through the frame for the steering column were not drilled along with the other holes. The steering column might have to be mounted two or three inches to the rear of the normal position, and if this were the case, the arm connecting the steering column to the left front wheel would have to be lengthened by a like amount.

One of the running-board supports crosses the frame to give added stiffness, but since running-board supports cause skinned shins, these were left off to be installed later. Bumper arms also cause scrapes and bruises if they are in place before the bumpers, so when the arms were sandblasted, primed and painted, they were put aside. The bumpers had to be disassembled and sandblasted, the pitted surfaces ground smooth, before they were sent to the platers. By doing this work myself I saved well over half the plating cost.

The gas tank is held in place by two straps. I used a piece of rope to hold the tank in place as I installed these straps. To clean rust and scale out of the tank, I put in some crushed stones and water and sloshed this mixture around vigorously. Two small but obvious holes were sealed with self-tapping screws, and liquid sealer was poured into the tank in case there were pinpoint leaks. The float and sending unit were cleaned, and a coat of clear lacquer was sprayed on the float to help it maintain buoyancy. To prevent possible vapor lock, the gas line was rerouted outside the left chassis rail instead of inside it, to keep it away from the exhaust system.

To test the motor, transmission and rear end, the engine was run without being connected to the gas tank. Gasoline was fed to the carburetor by gravity through a rubber tube as the engine was fine-tuned. Although there was no load, the clutch, transmission and differential sounded fine. Both transmission and differential had been thoroughly inspected, cleaned and refilled before the car was assembled. New felt grease retainers had been ordered from a factory in Texas that made them to specifications I had received from the H. H. Franklin Club librarian.

If room had permitted, the chassis would have been put together on one side of the garage and the body built on the other side. This would have made comparing measurements easier, simplifying a myriad of details. But space did not permit this, so the chassis was finished only in the details already listed. The steering column, hand brake, fuel system and exhaust system were not completed at this point. The vacuum tank and oil filter were to be mounted on the firewall, so these had to wait. Because of the different seating position for the new body, the underseat battery case was not installed at this point.

All in all, gathering the parts, refurbishing them and assembling them into a workable chassis was a challenging, interesting job. I am sure building and mounting the new body will also be a challenge, and hopefully a rewarding one.

Two small leaks in the gas tank were repaired by covering the area with sealant and inserting a self-tapping screw and washer into each hole. Later a filler was spread over screw heads, sanded and painted. Liquid sealer was poured inside the tank.

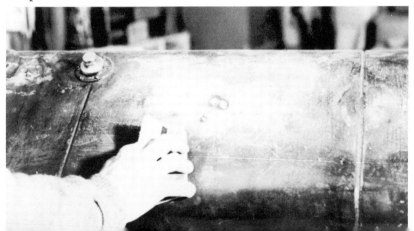

14

Blood, Sweat and Tears

There was a time a few years ago when it was difficult to obtain certain parts for some foreign cars. Replacement parts for the major components could be had in a few weeks, but what the manufacturers considered minor parts could take months to get to dealers and repair shops, if they ever arrived at all.

I had a delightful Austin that had a tachometer and speedometer in twin dials on the dashboard. Without warning the speedometer decided to quit. I thought that the cable probably had worked loose either where it attaches to the instrument head at the dashboard or where it attaches to the transmission, or that at worst the cable had broken. When I found that both attachments were secure and the cable was intact, I knew the malfunction was in the instrument itself.

I took the speedometer out of the car and back to the dealer, where I learned they had no facilities for repairing it, but would send it to a major supply depot in New York to be repaired and returned. The shop foreman guessed it might take a month, certainly no longer. This did not seem unreasonable, so instead of trying to repair it myself, I left it with the dealer.

About a week later I was stopped for speeding. I told the officer that it was highly unlikely that I was speeding since I was watching the tachometer from time to time and it had not been above 2500 rpm. When he looked inside the car and saw the gaping hole where the speedometer should have been, he would not listen to my claim that gauging speed by the tachometer was valid. I got a ticket.

Shortly after that I was stopped again, fortunately by a different officer. He was more reasonable and did not issue a ticket, but strongly advised that I "get that spedometer back in and fill up that hole."

The dealer could give me no idea as to when the repaired part would arrive. After a month he sent a tracer to the supply depot. Apparently this got lost too, for he received no answer. I tried to buy a replacement speedometer but was told it would take a month or so to get one, and the cost would be about $90. I decided to wait for the repaired speedometer, but to at least fill up the hole in the dashboard.

I had seen a nice colored head-and-shoulders picture of Winston Churchill a week or so before in a magazine. It seemed about the right size, so I cut it out and pasted it on the glass where the speedometer had been. It looked as though it belonged there, and gave the dashboard a nice finished appearance. With Mr. Churchill's pensive smile in view as I glanced at the instruments, I must have driven slower, for I was not stopped again. This allowed me to relax somewhat, and I forgot about the missing speedometer. A few months later I inquired again at the dealer's and was told "nothing yet, we're having a bit of time getting parts, you know." After several more inquiries I forgot about the missing instrument; the dashboard looked complete anyway.

While visiting a city about 150 miles from home, I spotted a Mark V Jaguar Drophead Coupe in a used-car lot. It appeared in good condition, and when a test drive confirmed this, I made a deal and swapped cars. I forgot to mention the substitution on the dashboard, and the salesman did not notice it either, so the Austin was traded in with Winnie's picture replacing the speedometer.

Well over a year later I drove into a parking garage and parked next to an Austin that looked just like the one I had owned. I glanced inside, and sure enough it was the same car, with Winston Churchill still looking through the hole in the wooden dash that should have contained the speedometer. The new

Winston Churhill's picture fitted nicely into the speedometer frame to cover the hole in the dashboard. When the car was traded in on a Jaguar, the picture was left in place. Apparently the new owner did not realize the former prime minister was hiding something.

owner may have thought that was standard equipment on British-built cars, but he must have wondered how the driver kept track of speed and miles traveled. I left a note on the windshield explaining how Churchill's picture happened to be in his car, and I gave the dealer's name and address so the repaired speedometer could be recovered. Unless the new owner acted promptly he never retrieved the speedometer, for within a few weeks I noticed the dealer was out of business.

The Mark V Jaguar was an excellent car and I enjoyed driving it, especially when I could get out on the open road and give it its head. I quite often drove it on out-of-town trips where I could enjoy its performance. On one trip I noticed the heat gauge climbing rapidly to the boiling point. When I opened the hood, I could see a split radiator hose. After the motor cooled down I tried driving very slowly, hoping to find a service station. The heat gauge got to boiling again and I stopped. Several short runs and stops later, I saw a service station at an intersection some distance ahead. I drove on to it despite the boiling engine. Just before I arrived at the station the engine started to miss very badly. Fortunately the station carried a good assortment of radiator hoses, and we found one the right diameter and cut it to the proper length. This at least would keep the engine from overheating. But the damage was done: I had blown the cylinder-head gasket. There was nothing I could do but limp along, keeping the car below twenty-five miles per hour and hoping the blown gasket would not let the coolant down into the oil pan, and make me locate a tow truck.

In a fair-size city an hour or two after the hose had been replaced, I drove into a garage featuring repairs on foreign cars. They listed Jaguar on their sign as one of the makes they could repair. The shop foreman came up to the car, put his hand on

Stylish Mark V Jaguar Drophead Coupe that could not be identified by a so-called specialist in foreign cars. Badge on front of the radiator shell clearly spelled out the make of the car. Fortunately an East Coast distributor rapidly furnished parts by mail.

the radiator shell, not two inches from the Jaguar badge, and asked, "What in the world kind of car is this?" Somehow his question did not inspire confidence in me. When I said that the badge next to his hand spelled J A G U A R, he said he had never seen one like this and what was the matter with it. When I told him the head gasket had blown and needed to be replaced, he asked if I had the new gasket. I replied that I did not have a spare gasket with me, and was told that when I got it, bring the car back and he would have it put on for me. I asked if they could obtain the part, and when he shrugged and mumbled something about not wanting to store the car for a couple of months until the gasket came in, I told him to forget it. I drove out, after commenting that they really should not advertise foreign car service until they learned to identify the cars and had some parts available.

Fortunately I made it home, a slow and tedious drive, but with no additional damage to the engine. I had seen a Jaguar distributor's ad in a national magazine and wrote about the needed gasket. I got an immeditae reply saying the set of gaskets necessary for the repair were being sent airmail, and they would bill me for them. That immediate response restored my fatih in the efforts British car manufacturers were making to service their products. When the gaskets arrived I made the repairs myself, and when the suprisingly small bill for the parts arrived, I paid it promptly and enclosed a note of appreciation for their efforts. I drove and enjoyed that car for several years with no further problems.

15

The Missing Screw

Trying to locate the proper screw can be prettty frustrating. I had just finished a complete restoration on an MG-TD and was taking my first real drive in the car. I heard something hit the running board but did not notice anything as I glanced in the rear-view mirror. When I got out of the car, I saw that the right door handle was missing. The screw must have worked loose and let the handle jar out of place. I decided to retrace my steps and try to locate the handle. Fortunately I remembered where I had heard the noise, for I recalled seeing a church in the mirror.

Driving back to the area, I parked on a side street so I could walk along the curb to look for the handle. I walked back and forth in the area but without seeing the handle. Thinking it might have hit the running board and not fallen to the street immediately, I walked along the curb for about a quarter of a mile before I saw it, near the center of the inside lane. This was a busy street with a lot of traffic in each lane and no signal lights to cause open spaces between cars. I pictured myself getting the handle, and getting a free ride on someone's front bumper. After a few minutes I noticed more than the usual space between two approaching cars. As soon as the first car passed I darted out and grabbed the door handle. Fortunately I did not try to get back to the curb at that time, for the second car had speeded up some-what and there would not have been time. So I stood, clutching

A complete restoration, with the mechanical components rebuilt like new. There had been no problem securing mechanical replacements, so it did not seem that locating a screw for a door handle would require maximum effort.

The body had been hoisted off the chassis to make it easier to complete the mechanical work. The frame was sandblasted and repainted. The running gear was completely checked and needed repairs were made.

The dashboard was disassembled while the body was off the car. At this time the instruments were reworked and the instrument panel was refinished. Seat cushions were reupholstered and new carpets were fitted.

the door handle, with traffic whizzing by in both directions. I did not dare try to run to the curb, but apparently some drivers thought I might make the attempt—many honked horns as a warning that they were not about to slow or stop for me.

After what seemed like an eternity I saw a slight break in traffic and dashed to the curb. When I got back to my car I found the meter-maid writing up a parking ticket. I had not even noticed the parking meters when I stopped. I tried to talk her out of it, but I have never been successful in these attempts. I was glad to have the handle, and decided a parking ticket was much less than the cost of a replacement.

The problem arose when I tried to find the proper screw to attach the handle. The screw in the left door was chrome-plated, with a slightly convex top. In addition, it was quite thick at the shank, tapered sharply, and was less than an inch long. A screw I had on hand attached the handle but did not match the screw

Doors were removed and weak wood was replaced. Before newly reupholstered panels were put on the doors, the inner skin was coated with a rust-inhibiting primer.

on the left door. There was no reason to believe there would be any difficulty locating a similar screw.

My first attempt was at an MG dealer's parts department. They did not stock the part and said they could not order one. The parts man suggested a wrecking yard, so I tried those that bought wrecked foreign cars. There were no MGs in these yards. I looked at other makes but could not locate what I needed. It did not seem like a big thing, so I removed the screw from the left handle to carry with me, planning on checking at hardware stores and other car parts stores.

I had done so much work on the car, with such good results, that I did not want my restoration spoiled by incorrect screws. Probably no one else would notice, but I would know and it would bother me.

For nearly a year I carried the chrome-plated screw along with my pocket change. I remember stopping at one big family-owned hardware store that claimed to have about everything anyone could want in hardware. I showed the clerk the screw and said I would like to buy two like it. He took it from my hand, looked at it critically and said, "What's it from?" I made the mistake of saying it was from an MG. "What's that?" was his reply. I said it was from the door handle of a sports car. "Don't carry no car parts," he said, handing it back to me. I asked if it mattered that it was from a car. Surely similar screws were used in other products. He shook his head and left to wait on another customer.

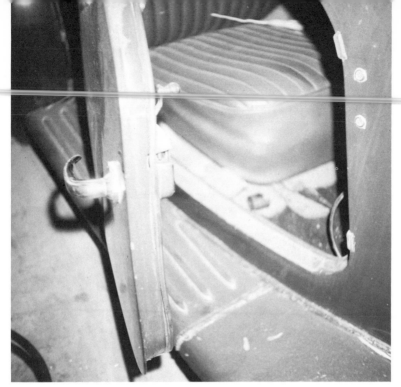

MG door handle protrudes through wooden door frame and attaches to latch mechanism inside the door. Doors close solidly, preventing accidental opening from a jar or bounce.

Reworked interior of MG. Under-dash radio was added, but no holes were drilled in the dash to accommodate it. The little car ran beautifully after complete mechanical and body restoration.

I had experienced no trouble locating mechanical parts as I worked on the MG restoration. Everything I needed, including dashboard trim parts, had been available without trouble. I had removed the body from the chassis during the work and had been able to get every part I needed. This simple screw really stumped me.

I tried auto dealers and auto supply houses in other towns with no success. I was sorely tempted to swipe some from a parked MG, but thought how embarrassed I would be if caught. It was becoming a real challenge to find the proper screw.

In the course of business over the next several months I must have stopped in at least fifty places. None had the correct screw, nor could they give me any idea where I might locate one. None of the ads for parts for sale in the national car magazines carried anything like this, and letters to MG owners who advertised other parts did not help.

Tidy rear-end treatment on MG included external gas tank with rear-mounted spare and an apron between the body and the rear bumper. The aerial was added to get good radio reception.

Elusive screw in the MG door handle. No replacement could be found in wrecking yards, at dealers, through ads in national car magazines, in car-parts stores or hardware stores.

I had some business in Minneapolis and parked my car in front of a place that made custom-built kitchen cabinets. Some sample cabinets were displayed in the front window, and I saw what seemed to be identical screws in one of the cabinet hinges. The salesperson looked at the screw I handed him, and said he thought he could help. From a drawer of hinges he pulled out a pair in a plastic bag. The screws were the same! I could hardly believe it. No, they did not have any loose ones lying about, not even a box of similar screws in the stockroom. I had to buy a set of hinges to get the screws, and ended up with twelve. I would be glad to help other MG owners looking for the proper screw.

16

You Never Know
Where You'll Find 'em

While on a trip to buy a 1926 Marmon I came across a 1930 Chevrolet that the owner wanted to sell so badly he offered it to me for $100. I did not really have room for the Chevy, but at that price I decided to make room. It looked pretty decrepit but was a low-mileage car and was missing only the radiator and radiator shell. The owner said he had taken the radiator off to have it repaired, subsequently got sick and left it at the repair shop for over a year. He added he thought it was still there, and I could pick it up if I bought the car.

The radiator was at the repair shop and had long since been repaired. I paid a reasonable amount for it, but the shop owner said the radiator shell had not been brought in with the radiator. So I made a trip back to the farm, where the car's owner insisted he took them both in, and if it was not in the shop he thought the shop owner had sold it. He added that he had never trusted the man anyway. A thorough search of the shed in which the car had set for some years did not turn up any parts, so I left, assuming I could get a replacement radiator shell without much difficulty.

Offhand, I do not know how many Chevrolets were produced in 1930, but at the time I assumed enough were sold so there would be no real trouble locating a radiator shell. I thought that the 1929 was the same, which would add to the supply available.

I had to store the Chevy while I worked on the Marmon, but I started searching for the 1930 radiator shell. None of the wrecking yards I checked had any 1930 Chevrolets. I did not see any radiator shells listed in the parts ads in the national car magazines, and I got no response to an ad I ran listing the radiator shell among other parts I needed. I had enough work to do on the Marmon, so I did not panic over the hard-to-find shell.

My real problem was finding a replacement steering wheel for the 1926 Marmon. I tried every possible source: the Marmon Owner's Club, the Classic Car Club, ads in national car magazines. I even tried to identify the manufacturer, hoping to learn if a steering wheel from another make would be interchangeable.

Restoration on the Marmon was finally completed except for the missing steering wheel. While I marked time with the Marmon, I decided to work on the Chevrolet.

I soon had the Chevrolet in order. A carbon and valve job along with ignition points and new spark plugs had the motor running fine. I made and fitted a new convertible top, and had the landau bars and some other parts plated. I repainted the fenders, splash aprons and wheels, and mounted a new set of tires. The car was complete except for the radiator shell.

With two cars restored except for one part each, I was getting quite concerned wondering what I would do to complete each job. I even tried to locate a parts car for the Chevy, planning on keeping only the radiator shell and selling the remainder. I could not even find that; I must have had a dozen friends in on the search.

The missing steering wheel was really bothering me, for I had a lot of money tied up in the Marmon and of course I could not drive it. I wanted to take it to a Classic Car Club show but realized I would have to tow it and display it minus the steering wheel. Since our club's remuneration for car shows was based upon the number of cars displayed, I did tow the car for display without the steering wheel.

One fairly elderly gentleman showed continuing interest in the Marmon. Ordinarily cars are roped off at shows to keep people from climbing over them and causing damage. This man told me he had owned a Marmon quite like mine years ago and would really appreciate having a closer look. I took him inside the

Beautiful walnut wood, carefully fitted, made the Marmon steering wheel almost a work of art. This elusive wheel was given to me by an elderly gentleman who liked the marque. It is a very scarce item, and I was indeed lucky to locate an authentic wheel.

roped-off area and explained what I could about the car as he studied it. The car had never been his, but it was the same year and model. He told me of a friend who owned several Marmons and might either have a steering wheel or possibly could help me locate one. He gave me the address of his friend in a small town outside Birmingham. I wrote him and I got a fairly prompt reply that amazed me. He did indeed have a steering wheel, and since he was now too old to work on his cars, he had sold all but one Marmon and a few parts. He wrote that if I would pay the freight charges, he would be glad to give me the wheel.

I felt I was taking advantage of him. I asked that he send the wheel as soon as possible, and enclosed a check for $50, which would have been a most reasonable price for the wheel. The steering wheel arrived shortly, and a few days later I received a letter with my check enclosed, stating that he was glad to help me and could not accept any payment. One does not often find people like him.

The replacement steering wheel allowed me to complete the Marmon restoration, and I enjoyed the car for some time before selling it to a person who just had to have it.

The missing radiator shell for the Chevrolet still haunted me, but not for much longer. Walking into a flea market at a local shopping center, I spotted a 1930 Chevrolet radiator shell in perfect condition. It fairly jumped at me. I was surprised at the low price of $45, and bought it immediately. The seller seemed surprised that I did not dicker for a lower price.

After a long search, the Chevy radiator shell fairly jumped at me in a flea market. It was in perfect condition and even included the badge. Evidently the seller would have taken less than his $45 asking price, but I was too delighted to bargain.

17

The Jag That Got Around

One car-buying trip I will certainly never forget. For some time I had wanted a Mark VII Jaguar. The few I had seen for sale had seen far better days, so I was still looking when I answered an ad in a national car magazine. The car was in New Hampshire and I lived in Ohio, so it meant a flying trip to New England and the long drive home. The owner did not have a phone, which struck me as odd, but answered my letter in great detail, including pictures of the car. It looked great, and his description of the engine, transmission, body, etc., were in such detail I decided to buy it sight unseen, and sent him a certified check. I asked that he have it greased, have the oil changed, and top up the gas tank, and I would reimburse him when I arrived on a given date.

It was a warm October day when my wife dropped me off at the Columbus airport. I had only an overnight case with a change of underwear, shirt and socks, and carried a topcoat without lining. After all, it would only be a weekend trip, and I saw no need for anything else.

The flight was delayed a short time because the plane's elevators were not working correctly. They wheeled out a large scaffold and several men worked on the plane's tail section. I decided to sit in the bar until the flight was called. A couple of Scotches later, announcement was made that our flight was ready for loading. Once in the plane we sat for ten or fifteen minutes; this delay was

Clean, sleek styling of Mark VII Jaguar has timeless appeal. Smoothly contoured front fenders incorporate the front door and blend with the rear fender at the rear door. Sliding metal panel in roof was optional at added cost.

Traditional Jaguar grille blends into streamlined front end, giving a smooth continuity of design. Headlights and driving lights are nearly flush-mounted. Turn signals are combined with parking lights on the front fenders.

not explained. We had to sit at the end of the runway several minutes before the plane was cleared for takeoff. I was glad to get going, for I had a rather tight connection at New York's LaGuardia. Evidently they had fixed the elevators properly, for we made the hour-and-fifteen-minute flight in less than an hour, giving me just minutes to make connections.

It was wet and cold in New York, but since I was out of the plane only for a few minutes I did not mind. Our flight was to land at Hartford, but a wet snowstorm diverted it to Boston. I had hotel reservations in Hartford and had reserved a rental car for the drive to New Hampshire. The airline furnished a room in Boston, but I swear it must have been on the runway. It was so noisy I thought some of the planes taking off were headed straight for my bed. A neon sign outside the motel kept the room as bright as Broadway and 42nd Street.

There was no trouble arranging for a rental car for the drive to New Hampshire, but there was some question concerning the drop-off spot for the car, since I would be driving back in the Jaguar. With that detail finally arranged, I lit out as fast as possible. It was cold and snowy, but the car's heater soon warmed things up. The exact date slips my mind, but it was the opening of deer season in New Hampshire and there was quite a lot of traffic. When I stopped along the route for coffee, the hunters who had stopped there too were glad for the snow, which made tracking easier. The snow did not please me at all because the roads were not cleared. There was also a brisk, bone-chilling wind that kept the snow swirling.

I got to town without any problems but did not have complete directions to the man's farm. All I had was a P.O. Box number. I learned from the Post Office that he lived on County Road 232; nothing more. I had some difficulty getting directions, for the people I asked seemed suspicious and did not want to indicate the way. Finally a gas station attendant said, "If that's the old man with the old cars, that's on County Road 232, about a mile ahead and off to the right about a mile or so."

Finally locating what I presumed to be the right farmhouse, I stopped on the road to make sure. When I found I was right, and wanted to turn into the driveway, the car would not move.

I was stuck in the snow on an unplowed road. Before I could ask for help, a large woman came out of the house with a bucket of ashes, which she poured ahead of each rear wheel. She pushed as I inched ahead to her home.

By this time I was cold. I had stepped in snow way over my shoe tops and my feet were wet, so I was glad to get into the warm kitchen. She and her husband explained that in cold weather they heated only the one room. An old white iron bedstead was in one corner, and everything indicated this was their entire living space for cold months. I do not know whether there was an indoor bathroom, but a chamber pot under the bed indicated that if there was one inside the house, they did not use it. They left water trickling from the one faucet in the sink so the pipes would not freeze. There were at least half a dozen cats and two dogs crowded around a large cast-iron cookstove.

They offered me a cup of coffee, and I was glad to get it until I looked at the cup. It was a cracked mug, badly stained and dirty around the edge. But I was cold, and figured the coffee was hot enough to kill some of the germs. I was offered what I thought were raisin cookies until the plate was passed, and I saw some cockroaches scurry off, leaving plain sugar cookies. I declined, claiming I was not hungry.

Although I was anxious to see the car, I could not seem to hurry anyone. The man complained about the worthless people on welfare. When he learned I was a newspaper publisher, he gave me his views on how newspapers were to blame for much of the mess he thought the country was in. The woman spoke of her unusual collection of wall and mantle clocks, and took me from one icy room to another showing me. She had been collecting them for years and would not sell me one.

Finally I was escorted across to the barns where his cars were stored. He must have had thirty, all either on wooden blocks or on planks to keep them off the dirt floor. He had five or six Stutz cars, complete down to the Stutz insignia on the little padlocks for the side-mounted spares. He had two Stanley Steamers, including a 1923 closed model that was new to me. He had two Silver Ghost Rolls Royces, a Rolls Picadilly Roadster, he had bought for $225 at an estate sale, and other expensive, hard-to-find cars. It was a really fabulous group of cars, all dirty and dusty, but complete. These were his pets, and he cranked each one over every month or so to keep the motors from seizing. He would not sell any of them, although I am sure he realized they were worth perhaps a quarter of a million dollars. It was hard for me to understand these people living in such primitive conditions when the sale of a few of these cars would have changed things completely.

We finally got to the Jaguar, which was parked behind the other door to the barn. It appeared to be all he had said, although lack of electricity in the barn made it hard to see. His only reason for selling was that he had bought a new Jaguar and needed space for it.

I was left to look at the car while the man and his wife went to the house for the battery and a bucket of hot water. He had not had the oil changed or the car lubriated as I had asked because he had not wanted to go into town. With the hot water in the radiator (it took two trips) and the battery installed, the car started easily. It sounded fine. Time was flying. I suggested we drive into town and get the title notarized. I would turn in the rental car and drive them back so I could start the trip home. This was fine with them. They drove the Jaguar and I followed in the rental. What they did not mention was that since they were going to town, they would do some grocery shopping too. While they were doing this, I had antifreeze added to the radiator of the Jaguar, the oil checked and the gas tanks filled. I decided the oil change and grease job would have to wait until I was home.

After leaving the couple at their farmhouse, I followed the man's directions to the highway so I did not have to backtrack into town. It was a few miles shorter but probably took me longer, for there were several quite steep hills. There were deer hunters everywhere, and I hoped they would not shoot at the car simply because it was moving. One deer bounded across the road right in front of me. He looked scared, and I hoped he found a secure place to hide for the next few days.

The car worked fine. It warmed up inside, and I was pleased with the way it drove. About an hour out, the engine began to heat up rapidly. After my previous experience with a split radiator hose on a Jaguar, I wondered if this was the problem. When I

As beautiful as it is competent, the Mark VII Jaguar double overhead cam engine uses many cast-aluminum parts, which clean up easily. A high-performance engine, also used in Jaguar sports models, it was docile enough for city driving.

When the small molded fitting on the heater broke, the car lost its coolant. It was temporarily clamped shut for the trip home, but that left the car without heater or defroster. Failure of the starter solenoid on the fire wall made manual starting necessary.

opened the hood, I discovered the trouble was in a small L-shape molded hose that led into the heater. I guess it had rotted through as the car stood without any coolant in it. Luckily I found a piece of bailing wire in the luggage compartment and was able to crimp the hose back against itself and hold it pinched together with the wire. When the engine cooled down a bit, I removed the radiator cap and stuffed snow into the radiator. It was a slow process but I had no choice, for I was in the middle of nowhere. When water showed on top of the radiator core, I decided I could go on until I found a gas station. In about five miles I did find a station and got some water, but no help on the hose.

In Bennington, Vermont, I located a garage, where the attendant was able to clamp both hoses so I would not lose any more coolant. I had more antifreeze added, and started on my way. I did not realize that I would be driving the rest of the way without a heater or a defroster. It was snowing lightly and there was quite a brisk wind.

By late afternoon I reached Troy, New York, and stopped for dinner. I was cold enough to think I had better buy a thermos bottle and a bottle of Scotch. I did not think about trying to buy a sweater or gloves.

After dinner I discovered that the starter solenoid would not work and I could not start the car in the normal way. This meant I had to start the engine by raising the hood and shorting the solenoid connections on the fire wall with a screwdriver, which I luckily had along. This process was no big thing, but it took some time and turned out to be a nuisance.

There was a toll both as I entered an approach to the New York State Thruway. The Jaguar was a right-hand drive, so to reach over, lower the left window and pop the money into the slot meant a lot of stretching. I should have put the gearshift into neutral, but I did not. My foot slipped off the clutch but not the brake, and the car stalled. The only way I could start it was to get out, open the hood, short the starter solenoid and get back in the car. This took more time than people in the cars behind me wanted to allow, so horns started tooting. This only confused me and made me try to hurry a job on which there are no shortcuts. In fact, it unnerved me to the point where I stalled the car after moving about three feet into the toll both lane in high gear. I had to get out and do it all over again, much to the annoyance of the horn-tooting drivers behind me. To make sure I would not make the same mistake again and stall, I raced the motor and slipped the clutch as I shifted through the gears. The racing motor made the rear wheels spin in the snow, and I got off to a slower than normal start. It was not long before the cars that had queued up behind me at the toll booth raced past. Some tooted their horns long and loud on their way by; I believe a couple may have shouted obscenities. I was relieved to be out of the situation, and promised myself I would not stall at any more toll booths or stop signs.

It was snowing much harder, and soon I was miserably cold. The car was drafty, and with neither heater nor defroster, driving was difficult and uncomfortable. I stopped at a Thruway station near Syracuse to gas the car, use the facilities and get some warm food. My hands were so cold I could hardly move them. I was actually shaking when I ordered my food. After filling the gas tanks (there's one in each rear fender panel on the Mark VII) and going through the starting ritual in the blowing snowstorm, I decided to try to reach Buffalo. As I neared Batavia and the storm worsened, it was just too cold and miserable to drive any further. Passing vehicles made the snow swirl around my car, and I was almost blinded by the glare of my own lights against the snow. I could hardly see the road because the windshield and side windows were frosted over. The small patch of windshield I kept clear in front of me was not adequate, and when I found myself perilously close to a road marker on the right side, I figured I had pushed my luck far enough.

Fortunately there was a vacancy at the first motel I tried. My hands were so numb I could hardly write my name on the sign-in card. I took as hot a bath as I could stand, piled blankets on the bed and finally thawed out. Since I knew I could not buy any long underwear or other clothes on Sunday, I stole two of the hotel's towels to wrap around each of my legs as I drove toward home. This helped somewhat, but I was still cold.

When I reached Pennsylvaina the snow stopped, although it was cold that close to Lake Erie. There was snow on the ground, but the sun broke through and the car become more tolerable. In the first city in Ohio, I came across a large discount store that was open. I bought a sweater, gloves and a pair of heavy socks. This made the rest of the trip bearable, and I got home with only the inconvenience of having to start the car by shorting the solenoid switch.

A new starter solenoid, replacement heater hoses and some general cleaning put the Jaguar in good shape. Later I painted it. I enjoyed the car for a few years before deciding to sell it.

This was at a time when college students were protesting the "Establishment" and the Vietnam War, and tearing up the college campuses. Our son was a freshman at the time, and we thought it might be better to send him someplace for the spring break than to have him stay on campus. We had bought property on Great Exuma Island in the Bahamas but had never seen it. So we arranged for him and a roommate to fly to Miami, spend the night, then go to Nassau for another night before spending a week at a beach club on Great Exuma. Our only condition was that he take a picture of our lot from each of the four corners.

I had advertised the Jaguar for sale, and someone from Michigan was interested and bought it. We combined picking up our son on his return to the Cincinnati airport with delivering the Jaguar to Cincinnati, where the buyer would fly in and drive it back. This meant we had to drive two cars to Cincinnati, so we started out one afternoon. We had not bothered to make motel reservations for the first night. Around five we drove into a large motel where there were not a dozen cars on hand. I drove up to the office, and my wife followed in the other car. I went back to her car to see if the place looked satisfactory. When she nodded "yes," I went to the office. Evidently the room clerk thought that driving up in two cars with Ohio tags and getting a nod of approval from the blonde in the Cadillac indicated we were not married and were having an affair. She very tersely said they had no vacancies, and her disgust and displeasure were evident in her look and speech. Although the incident was annoying at the time, my wife and I laughed about it when we checked into another motel a short distance away.

We met the buyer the next morning as planned. He tested the car, then headed home to Michigan. We met our suntanned son

Plated body trim and window frames cleaned up easily, making replating unnecessary. Body integrity was very high on Mark VIIs; all panels fitted properly. Heavy doors opened and closed easily on concealed hinges.

Wood on dashboard, fascia and windows can easily be removed if refinishing is necessary. Once refinished, waxing will keep it beautiful. Mark VIIs with four-speed manual shift used front bucket seats. Automatics normally used a bench-type seat.

Often mistaken for a Rolls Royce, the Mark VII Sedan has classic proportions, long hood, close-coupled passenger compartment and large sloping luggage boot. Although an outdated design, the car has remained popular with restorers.

and roommate at the airport. They had enjoyed their stay, helped some girl get her VW started in Nassau and loved Great Exuma. My son had snorkled and played on the beach, and taken some good underwater shots of reefs. He forgot to take pictures of our lot. His best memories of Great Exuma were trying to dodge land crabs while riding a Honda, and buying Beefeater martinis for forty cents each and not being asked for an ID.

A few years ago I spotted the same Jaguar parked in Georgetown, Colorado, but did not stop. Another time, again in Georgetown, I saw the car, and left a note under the windshield wiper. The car had California tags on it, but the original British tags were still in place. I never heard from the new owner, so I do not know how the Jaguar I bought in New Hampshire, used in Ohio and sold to a person in Michigan ended up with California plates, parked on a street in Georgetown, Colorado.

18

It's Nice to Have Friends

"That picture gives me a good enough idea of what you want. I can measure the bumper support and gauge the rest of the measurements from that," said a friend, looking at a picture of the front end of a Mercedes 290 that showed the plated spacing blocks that attached the front bumper to the frame ends. These were missing on the Mercedes I was restoring, and I had not been able to locate any. I hoped he would be able to make replacement parts.

The person to whom I was talking was the manager of a large blue-jean factory. An M.I.T. graduate, he had set up a small but quite complete machine shop in his basement. He was a good friend and had helped me on previous occasions by making parts I could not find. Usually it was only necessary to show him a picture or a rough sketch and he could fashion just about anything.

The spacing blocks I needed fitted the front end of the Mercedes frame. They were tapered slightly to follow the curve of the lower edge of the front fender where it attached to the front end of the frame. Each spacer consisted of two pieces, cut out to accept the bumper brace and drilled so two bolts could attach the spacer to the frame end. These were plated and gave a nice finished appearance to the area where the bumper attached.

To make these, my friend would have to get some bar steel, cut it to correct overall dimensions, then drill the holes for the

The extension to hold the front bumper the correct distance from the frame end had to be fabricated for my Series 290 Mercedes. The steel block is tapered slightly to follow the fender line. The piece is shown here before completion which allowed a tight fit.

attaching bolts. He would have to measure and cut the slot through which the bumper brace fitted so that when the bolts were tightened, only a slight mark would indicate that the spacer was two pieces instead of one.

It was not a difficult job as far as figuring how to go about it, nor would it be difficult to do the cutting or drilling. But it would take patience to cut and grind to such close tolerances that the bumper brace would not slip sideways. Of course the attaching bolts would have to be threaded to fit the metric threads in the frame ends.

I sat and watched as my friend drew an exact-size drawing of what he needed to make. He even included the slight curve in the top and bottom thickness of the bumber brace so there would not be a square edge on the slot. I was amazed at the care and detail he was taking on the drawing.

During the next week he located and bought the steel bar stock he needed, and the following weekend I assisted as he cut the steel to the overall dimensions. There was a taper of about one-eighth inch from front to rear, and about the same taper on the bottom edge from the frame end to the end of the spacer. These he scribed on the metal, then cut and ground the pieces to exact measurements.

The next step was to drill the holes into the spacers so they would line up perfectly with the threads in the frame ends. This called for extremely accurate center-to-center measurements of the holes in the frame. For some reason the left was slightly different than the right, and luckily he discovered this before the holes were drilled.

With the holes in place, my friend cut the slot on one of the thinner outside pieces. He ground the top and bottom edges so they were identical to the rounded top and bottom edges of the bumper brace. I would not have taken these pains, but he is a perfectionist and would not have done it any other way. It took many tries—fitting the piece over the bumper brace, filing a bit and trying again—before he had one side that suited him. He repeated this careful and time-consuming operation on the other side until both outer clamps on the spacers were perfect fits.

The same procedures were followed fitting the bumper brace to the larger section of the spacer that attached to the frame. Fitting and filing, he worked hours until each clamp and brace fitted so closely to the rounded top and bottom of the bumper brace that the joint looked like a single line. He even figured the thickness of the plating that would be applied, then allowed for that. I have never seen such care and precision with parts that were not being made on a lathe or a milling machine. When the spacers were attached to the frame, the fit was perfect. They followed the subtle curve of the fender line and front apron and looked great. Although the bumper arms had been painted before this job started, the many fittings it took to gain perfection scarred them, so they needed refinishing before final assembly.

My friend did let me pay for the steel bar stock he had bought, and of course I paid for the plating. But he would not accept a dime for the hours he spent on the spacers, simply saying, "I'd like to drive that car someday."

Replacement parts for old foreign cars really can cause some headaches. I needed two hood latches, landau bars, trunk-rack braces and other minor trim parts for a 1933 Mercedes 290 Cabriolet D. This is the four-door Convertible Sedan, a very able and attractive automobile. The restoration was extensive as well as expensive, so I did not want it ruined by either substitute or less than perfect parts.

I contacted Mercedes Benz Owner's Club members, ran ads in national car magazines and wrote the factory in Stuttgart to try to locate a source for parts. The people at the factory expressed regret that they could no longer supply parts for these cars, but did send a list of parts suppliers. It was hardly likely that over forty years and a war later I would have any luck with these suppliers. However, I wrote several of the firms that had made some of the parts.

About a month later a handwritten letter came from Germany. A friend read it for me, since it was in German. The writer stated that the company was long out of business but he was operating a business at the same address. He said if I would send a picture of the needed parts, he would look for these for me! Can you imagine that sort of offer?

I sent a picture of hood latches. I did not have any landau bars to photograph and could only send a sketch, with the measurements between the mounting holes. One broken trunk-rack brace was photographed and the measurements written in. Since I did not think there was much hope of his finding any of these parts, I kept looking.

Hood latches located in Germany and bought for me by a friend, who had located them on a wrecked car. Once cleaned and plated, they matched the other two originals perfectly.

A few weeks passed and a second letter arrived, this one in English. Believe it or not, he had located hood latches and trunk-rack braces! The cost would be $25 plus air freight, which he estimated at another $25. I was so pleased at this news that I sent a money order with a thank-you letter immediately.

Soon the post office notified me there was a package too large to leave in my mailbox. Packed in a cardboard carton about the size of a shoebox, and heavily wrapped, were the hood latches and trunk-rack braces. They were in average condition, but complete.

The parts needed replating. This meant taking apart the hood latches, and cleaning them with solvent to remove the oil from the latch and spring, as well as degreasing the outside. Light rust was removed by scrubbing with fine steel wool and detergent. They cleaned up nicely and took plating beautifully. After scrubbing the trunk-rack braces, there were two rust spots that had to be ground off with a grinding wheel in my electric hand drill. The spots were small, and by tapering the grinding in each direction from the spot, there was no need to have new metal welded in. With these parts finished and crossed off my list, I felt very

Trunk-rack braces also hold the rear bumper in place. These were located by a friend in Germany and sent to me. I could never have found replacements in the United States.

grateful to my German friend. He had found a wrecked Mercedes 290 Sedan and bought the parts. There were no landau bars on the car.

A former Mercedes dealer in California located a pair of landau bars for me and offered them "as is" for $150. Although this seemed expensive, I was glad to get them. One was slightly bent, and since these are a casting, I was afraid to straighten it myself. At a garage the bar was heated and, while nearly red-hot, put in a hydraulic press and straightened. Both had peeling chrome, so after degreasing them, I used number 600 emery cloth to remove all the old plating and give them a satisfactory base for new. They turned out perfectly. I still needed the inside top braces, but I could go ahead with the framework.

Occasionally, no matter how long and hard you search for a part, there just is not one to be found. This is true for low-production models, custom-bodied cars and old foreign makes. I was in desperate need of a folding center pillar for the left side of the Mercedes Convertible Sedan. The bottom part of the pillar contained half of the hinge on which it pivoted, as well as the latching mechanism that held it in the upright position.

The car had set out in the weather for some time. The hinge and latch mechanism on the left pillar had rusted so they would not move. Someone had forced the pillar down, and it broke just above the hinge. The broken part must have been thrown away, for I could not locate it. Even if it had been found, it would not have helped much because the casting was of pot metal and could not have been welded.

After a long soaking in solvent, the latch portion would work properly. When this was installed on the center post between the front and rear doors, measurements for the replacement pillar could be made.

A retired machinist had set up a small but quite complete machine shop in his garage. He did excellent work, and he liked to work on something that required some thinking. Taking the right side pillar, the bottom part of the left one and a drawing with dimensions for the left pillar, I asked if he would make one for me. He discovered the dimensions on my drawing were different from the measurements he made of the right side pillar, so he could not use it as an exact pattern.

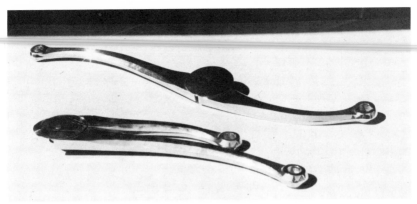

One of a set of "as-is" landau bars was dented and both had surface rust and peeling chrome. But even at $150 I was glad to get them so that the roof mechanism would work.

A machinist friend made a folding center pillar and attached it to a portion of the original hinge. It was made to dimensions I furnished, which were slightly different from those for the other side. The fit was perfect.

Had I rebuilt the doors wrong, making the difference between the size of left and right pillars to compensate for error? This was not the case, and any error or difference between the left and right sides of the car was not mine. That is often true on bodies where a lot of hand work was used in original construction; although the right and left sides look alike, there may be small differences in several parts. I first discovered this when having some parts plated for a 1936 Rolls Royce with a Sedance de Ville body by Windovers. There was as much as an eighth of an inch difference between some of the left and right side parts.

This was true on the Mercedes body. The distances between the front and rear windows in the raised position were slightly different. Mass-produced cars would use a rubber gasket to fill the gap. But since the Mercedes body builder wanted the windows to fit snugly to prevent drafts as well as rattles, the pillars were made to fit exactly.

"Guess we can do it," the machinist said, and asked how soon I needed the part. "Whenever you can make it," I replied, knowing he would get at it in a day or two.

The uneven edges where the casting had broken had to be filed even so a part could be attached to the remaining stub. Because there was not much room for fitting the upright to the stub, thin pieces of steel had to be cut and machined for each side. These fitted inside the hinge portion, in place of metal that had to be removed to allow room for them. Holes had to be drilled in the new metal to line up with holes in the original piece so the hinge pin would fit. With these two pieces in place, a third piece was cut and machined to fit between them. Holes, with the tops reamed to allow countersunk bolt heads, were drilled and threaded. Slot-headed bolts held the pieces together. Additional holes for the steel channel that holds the weather stripping were drilled and threaded.

When the pieces were assembled and ground smooth, the pillar was plated. It looked fine and fit perfectly. The new one is stronger than the original, and if kept properly lubricated it will last for years.

The machinist made the job look far easier than I had envisioned, and his solution to the problem was ingenious. Like so many other artisans, he enjoyed the work, and his charge was very low. Over the years he has come to my rescue by making other parts I could not locate.

"Yes, I think I can make one. Biggest problem is going to be finding the stock. Sure you can't find one like it somewhere?" This is what a machinist friend said when I showed him a brace for a convertible top, on a car long out of production. This was the brace that fitted on the wooden upright behind the door window, with a curved portion that followed the curve of the window frame.

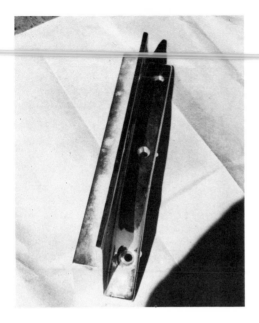

This is the original top brace, which was used as a pattern to make one for the other side. I thought it might have been a casting, but a knowledgeable friend made it from bar steel. When plated, these completed the top framework.

The body was decrepit when I came across it, after someone had aborted a restoration. I am sure I got every piece of the body, for there was nothing else in the place. Frankly, I did not realize I was missing one important piece until later. I had a left piece but also needed the right one.

For several months I tried without success to locate another roof brace. I decided to try to have one made. My machinist friend thought the piece was a casting, but I have never agreed; I do not feel that the low production of this body style would have warranted the expense of making a mold for this piece. I felt it must have been machined from a piece of bar stock. There were no seams to indicate pieces being welded together, nor were there the usual signs of a casting.

The bar stock was located at a welding shop, and I cut it to the correct overall length. The trimming to width and depth would have to be done at the machine shop. Cutting the large notch so the piece would fit against the wooden upright was no problem. The real problem was cutting and shaping the curved portion, yet not cutting so deeply that there would be any weakening of the metal.

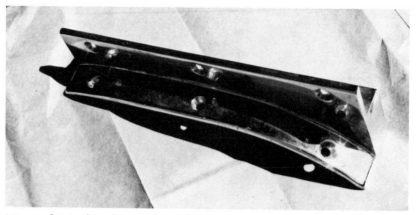

My machinist friend used the left piece to get measurements to make a similar piece for the right side. It was made out of bar steel to exact measurements. When plated, it looked just like the original, and it fitted perfectly.

The solution was to cut as much of the stock as possible along a straight line, then grind the excess metal to form the curve. This took many hours, but the piece was finally shaped, then ground smooth. Drilling the necessary holes and reaming a space so the screw-heads could be countersunk was not a big problem, except that it was hard to hold the curved portion of the metal at the correct angle so the drill bit was perpendicular to it. With all the holes drilled, the piece was given a final grinding, eliminating any rough edges and readying the surface for plating. When completed, the only way to tell the new one from the original (other than being a right-hand piece) was a tiny mark purposely put in the bottom.

Because of the hours that went into fabricating this top brace, and the plating cost, it was a fairly expensive piece of metal. I could not have assembled the top without it, so whatever the cost I had no alternative.

19

All Help
Gratefully Accepted

It's great to have friends to help you solve problems. Friends with similar interests can often offer advice and assistance. Sometimes they are a godsend!

Engine repairs on a 1948 Packard required cleaning carbon and grinding and adjusting valves. The replacement cylinder-head gasket, two valve-cover gaskets and valve-grinding compound were on hand. With the oil-filter bracket, power-steering unit and carburetor removed, access to the cylinder head was easy. To avoid continual head bumping, the hood was also removed.

Loosening each head nut half a turn, alternating left to right, front to back, before completely loosening each nut lessened the chance of the head cracking under uneven pressure. Knowing the head would be tight, I left the spark plugs in place and pressed the starter so engine compression would force the head free. It did, but only enough to let compression escape around the head gasket. Nothing came loose.

With spark plugs removed, solvent was squirted around each stud. Some disappeared down the stud while some remained on the head, not soaking in at all. The engine had sat for years without any coolant, and rust had formed around the studs, holding the head so tight it could not be budged. I did not want to force anything between the head and block, for the force could crack the head. Squirting more solvent around the studs, I tried tapping against a solid oak block. This did jar some of the rust loose so the solvent could soak down a few more studs. The biggest problem was at the back of the engine where it sat in a recess in the fire wall, making it very difficult to get a good swing with the hammer.

In desperation I ran a screwdriver blade between the block and head gasket, but could not do this on the side where the intake and exhaust manifolds did not allow room. More solvent and tapping did not seem to be accomplishing anything. I left the job, and told a friend about my troubles. He came over and tried the solvent and tapping, but found I had loosened about all that would budge. He asked if I had a couple of extra spark plugs. I was planning on new plugs after the carbon and valve job and had eight extra plugs.

His idea was to break out the porcelain in a couple of plugs and weld in a piece of steel rod. When these were screwed into the head, they would give something to lift with. Taking the plugs to his workshop, he chipped out the porcelain and welded rods into place. He heated the top of the rods and bent them to form a hook. With these screwed into number-two and number-seven spark plug holes, and a piece of welded chain slipped over the hooks, we tried lifting the head. He squirted more solvent and tapped around the studs while I lifted, which seemed to do some

Reinforcing rods for concrete work were welded into the bottom part of the spark plug and bent at right angles at the top. When these were screwed into the spark plug holes and a welded chain was slipped over each end, pressure from a hydraulic jack lifted the head.

good but not enough. We needed more leverage, and more lift than I could apply.

The studs extended about three-fourths of an inch above the cylinder head to allow room for the washer and nut. With these removed I had room enough to place the base of a small hydraulic jack on the centermost studs. Extending the shaft on the jack until the chain between the hooks in the plug holes was tight, I tried applying some hydraulic force. Very carefully I pumped the jack handle a time or two until the chain was tight. I was afraid that the chain might break, so I slipped a piece of pipe over the jack handle, which allowed me to stand well outside the engine compartment; if the chain did break, I would not be hit by anything.

Before applying more pressure, I squirted solvent around each stud and tapped each area with the hammer. Then I gave the handle about half a stroke and squirted and tapped again. Nothing seemed to be happening, so I left everything in place, with the head under this tension overnight.

The next morning, before applying any more tension, I doused the studs and tapped all over the head. I pumped the handle, and was surprised that it moved as easily as it did. Looking in the engine compartment, I saw that I had raised the head as far as possible by this method. The head had been pulled up to where it was flat against the base of the jack. Removing the jack and chain, I tapped the head back in place and squirted more fluid around each stud. This time the head raised easily to the base of the jack. I could not pull it any higher by hand.

Another friend had a frame he had built for lifting engines out of cars. It was solid and heavy. He let me use it with his chainfall. With this straddling the car, and the hook from his chainfall attached to the chain on the spark plug hooks, I was able to lift the head from the block. Examination of the holes through which the studs passed showed considerable surface rust. There had been enough of this on the studs, so the head could not have been removed without this force. The holding power of a little rust is amazing!

Removing a rear brake drum can sometimes make you feel there is a sinister force trying to ruin your life. In theory, once the wheel is removed, the cotter pin, nut and washer and a felt seal are all that have to be removed to pull the brake drum. The

Imagine the tremendous pressure exerted from a hydraulic jack against the brake drum to cause it to warp in this manner. The drum cracked when put in a press to force it back in shape. The correct wheel puller would have prevented this trouble and expense.

key on the axle shaft will allow the wheel to be pulled off, or the key can usually be removed. These procedures are theory only, for the drum is sometimes so solidly in place you would swear it had been welded.

I had to remove the rear brake drums on a 1947 Cadillac so I could rebuild the wheel cylinders. My own wheel puller would not fit and I could not locate one from any of my friends or at any tool-rental store.

One friend said he had never seen a brake drum he could not remove. I replied that I thought he might meet his match, as I had been working on two for several hours without any luck at all. In fact, I had applied so much force to the left drum that I had actually warped the metal. You can imagine the force needed to do this! Once this drum was off, I knew I would have to find a replacement, for I doubted it could be pressed back in position.

My friend volunteered to help. We got three pieces of welded chain, each about 18 inches long. We bolted the ends of the chains to the drum, using the regular wheel studs. Fortunately the car was solidly placed on jack stands, so we could apply plenty of force without worrying about the car dropping on us.

We squirted solvent on the axle shaft, then positioned my hydraulic jack against the axle nut we had threaded back on the shaft. The jack was pumped until it was tight against the chains. My friend hit the brake drum a few raps, shook his head and

With a replacement brake drum installed and the brake system rebuilt, there was no trouble stopping my heavy 1947 Cadillac 75 sedan. The replacement drum was turned down on a lathe before installation.

said, "Doesn't have the right ring, needs to be tighter." I forced the jack handle an inch or so, which was as far as I could move it. We put more solvent on the shaft, and the added pressure on the jack handle made the chains so tight that when my friend hit the drum again, it rang loud and clear. A few more raps and the drum popped loose.

I am sure it would have been easier with a correctly fitting wheel puller. Since this could not be found, my friend's idea of the chain and jack, along with his sledgehammer, did the trick.

I took the warped brake drum to a machine shop to find out whether it could be pressed back into shape. The operator said he doubted it but would put it on the press and try. With the drum solidly seated, and the correct collar fitted to the ram on the press, he connected the air hose and pressed the foot pedal. The drum started to straighten, but the metal cracked before the bent portion was back in place. It was a good try, but I had to locate a replacement drum to finish the brake job.

20

Just Keep Looking

Normally parts for cars manufactured in the 1950s are readily available. The exceptions are parts for orphaned makes and low-production models. My 1953 Packard Mayfair Convertible falls into both categories, so finding certain trim parts has been difficult. Many times convertible cars used slightly different interior hardware, and this was my problem. The window winding cranks on the front doors were in rough shape. They are made of pot metal and cannot easily be replated, so replacements were on my want list.

At a flea market there was a huge pile of interior fittings. The vendor had no idea what was in the pile; potential buyers simply had to look through it. I had one of the original cranks with me to be certain I got a perfect match. Starting at one end of the pile, I worked my way around, delving about halfway in as I searched. Of course, I was not the only one searching through the thousands of pieces, but I was the only one looking for Packard parts.

There was about every imaginable piece of interior hardware. Door handles, window cranks, windshield-adjustment handles, glove-box knobs, grab handles—you name it, one was probably in the pile. Although I was not looking for other than Packard window cranks, I did come across a pair of interior door handles decorated with the familiar acacia leaf pattern used on the Series 11 and 12 Franklins, so I put them to one side.

After much searching I was rewarded by finding one of the cranks, complete with escutcheon plate and filler. This raised my hopes, and I spent another hour sifting through the piles of hardware. But no luck. If there was a second Packard window crank in there, I never found it. I'm still looking for a second.

Taillights for a 1934 Hupmobile were on my list of wanted parts. The rear fenders of the car I was restoring had been dented, smashing beyond repair the fender-mounted taillights. Constant scanning of car parts ads did not help, nor did I come across any

Literally thousands of door handles, window cranks and other pieces of interior hardware all in a confusing jumble of patterns and shapes. You have to sort through the pile to find what you need. Take along one of your own to get a perfect match.

Window crank with ring and escutcheon plate for a 1953 Packard Convertible was found in a huge pile of interior hardware at a flea market. I needed two but found only one. A soap pad with detergent and water cleaned the window crank like new.

in flea market sales. I do not like to use other than authentic parts on my restorations, even though very few people, if any, would notice the difference. I was about ready to give up on this car and substitute some Chrysler taillights that looked similar. In fact, I had bought a set of Chrysler lights for this purpose and planned to install them in another week.

A friend asked me to drive him to a nearby town where he had bought a Graham Paige. He wanted someone to follow him home in case he had car trouble. We put in a tow chain just in case, along with a set of tools, including a tire iron and a wheel jack. We did not need any of these, for the car started easily and ran fine all the way back.

In talking with the car's previous owner before leaving, we had learned that a fellow a short distance out of town had loads of old car parts in a former gas station. He thought we might like to see what he had. We located the place without trouble, but no one was around and we could not find anyone to ask. A guard dog inside the place went into a frenzy as we tried to make someone hear us. We peeked into windows and could see hundreds of parts piled around, but the windows were so dirty we could not identify much. We decided to find a hamburger stand and have lunch, then return, hoping the owner would be back. We were in luck, for the door was open when we drove back.

There were loads of parts for cars from the 1920s, 1930s and 1940s, most of which were unidentified. There were a couple of large boxes full of taillights. We sorted through one box and came across a pair that looked right. The owner did not know what they were from; he said he had lists somewhere but had only been in the place a few years and had not found time to sort and tag parts. "Parts move out so fast, I can hardly keep track of what I've got and what I've sold," he said. He added, "Them lights is $5 each." They were good solid lights, needing only plating, so I bought them. I wasn't convinced they were from a 1934 Hupmobile but decided they would have to do, for they looked like the right lights.

After having them plated, and before installing them, I had a chance to see a 1934 Hupmobile at an old-car meet. I rushed home to get my lights to compare with those on the car, and to my delight I found I had located the correct ones.

Normally I buy only parts I need for my own cars and parts I know friends need. But once I spent $125 for a set of headlights I've never used, and so far no one else has wanted them either.

I heard of a 1933 Chrysler Roadster that was for sale. I was told the car looked pretty rough but was in good mechanical condition. So I drove to the place where the Chrysler was sitting in a garage. It looked pretty sad—it had not been run in several years. The tires were flat and the sidewalls were cracked, indicating they had been flat for a long time. The top was missing, but the roof bows were in place. The upholstery was shot and the windshield was broken. There were several dents in the fenders, but the body was sound and I could not locate any rust-outs. When I opened the hood I found it packed with shredded paper and rags. It also smelled pretty foul. It had been a rat's nest, and there may still have been some rats in residence. I did not wait to find out; I closed the hood fast. The headlights were missing, as was the front bumper. All in all, it was a good example of a desirable car in rough shape.

The owner told me all the good points about the car and glossed over the defects. He had put a high price on the car and did not want to come down any. I try not to find so much fault

It took a lot of searching to locate these fine taillights for my 1934 Hupmobile. To save money, they were degreased, scrubbed lightly with steel wool and thoroughly washed before being taken to the plating shop.

with any car that the seller would be tempted to ask why I would want it in such rough condition. I did point out that although the body was sound, it would need reupholstering, a new top, considerable fender work and plating and a paint job. "Yep," he agreed, "and she'll need a front bumper and headlights too." I assumed those might be in the garage someplace. I had not mentioned new tires or mechanical work.

He did not think it would take much to make the car run, and discounted the work and money involved in making the repairs. He said there was a place in town that would paint any car for $39.95, and every once in a while they would throw in $10 worth of body or fender work free.

The car did have attractive lines, and I felt I would enjoy restoring and driving it, but I just did not want to pay his price. I made an offer, as a beginning for bargaining. He refused, but made no counteroffer. I do not think anyone else had showed interest in the car, at least not recently, for the dust on it was thick and undisturbed. We just were not getting anywhere. I raised my offer a bit and suggested he consider it. I told him I would be back in a week to talk with him again.

A few days later, with the picture of the Chrysler Roadster in my mind, I saw a pair of 1933 Chrysler headlights in a shop that specialized in restoring Model A Fords. I asked how they happened to have Chrysler lights and was told the owner had bought all the car parts one man had. They were mostly Model

Anticipating the purchase of a 1933 Chrysler Roadster, I bought these correct headlights. The deal fell through on the car, leaving me with the lights. Unless you are sure you will get a car, do not buy too many parts in advance. It can be expensive!

A parts, but these lights and a couple of other parts were included in the deal.

The Chrysler headlights were large bullet-shaped lights with pointed, sloping lenses. The Chrysler wings were on the top of the headlight rim, and I thought I might as well buy them before someone else did, for I knew they would be scarce. I paid $125 for the lights, and considered this quite a bargain. Of course, I thought I would get the Chrysler Roadster to put them on.

The next week I returned to look at the Chrysler, fully expecting we would make a deal this time. When I drove up the owner greeted me and said; "I see you've come about the car."

"Yes," I replied, "I hope you've decided to accept my offer."

"Didn't have to," he said, smiling. "Sold her a couple of days ago. Got my price too."

That was disappointing, and it was surprising that someone would pay the price he wanted for that car. Either I had underestimated the value of the car, overestimated the necessary repairs, or the buyer was the one who had made the mistakes. Of course, the seller could be misleading me. In any case, I did not get it. I asked for the buyer's name and address, mentioning that I knew where there was a set of headlights he might like to buy. "Where they at? Are they at that Model A Ford place in town?" he asked. "If those are the ones you know of, they're the ones I sold him. Figured I'd get just as much for the car without the lights, and that Ford man give me $75 for them. Sold him some other parts too, front bumper among 'em." He seemed pleased at his business acumen, and I have to admit I learned a lesson from him on selling at a profit.

It was really annoying to find the car sold, although I would not have paid his asking price. I have no way of knowing what he actually got for the car. I wrote a letter to the buyer saying I had a set of headlights that had originally been on his car, and recounted the conversation. I added that I had not seen the front bumper at the restoration shop but was told it was there.

Evidently the owner was not interested. I never got an answer, and my letter was not returned. I kept the lights and offered them at a few flea markets, but no one was in the market. Later I advertised them in one of the national car magazines but got no response. So I still have the lights, and may have to buy a 1933 Chrysler on which to mount them.

Attracted by a beautifully restored 1920 Model T Ford Roadster, I examined it closely. I was restoring a 1923 Model T Touring car and wanted to see how the restorer had handled certain details. The perky little roadster had about every accessory made for cars of the time—more, no doubt, than the original owner would have bothered with. I made some notes on things that interested me, and thought it would be quite appropriate if I could find the combination spot-trouble light that was clamped to the windshield post. The trade name was "Auto Reelite," and patent dates from 1916 through 1919 indicated it would be an authentic accessory for my car.

Of course this was not a necessity. It would have nothing to do with the operation of the car and would not really add anything to the car's value. But it seemed so right for the car that I decided to try to find one. At flea markets I would look at groups of Model T parts and other parts of the period. Some of the people I asked had heard of Auto Reelites, but had not seen one lately. Others knew nothing of the light. I did come across a similar one, but it had "Dodge Brothers, U.S.A." stamped on it, and the attaching plug was different. Later I saw a couple of nickel-plated trouble lights, but although no trade names were stamped on them, they were obviously for larger, more expensive cars.

Once while advertising for some other parts I included the light but got no response on that item. I wanted one but it was not critical, so I put it on the back burner while I worked on more important things.

I had a friend who was nuts about Plymouths. What he did not know about Plymouths was not worth bothering with. He had heard of a man in Colorado who had just about every Plymouth part one could imagine, plus a large assortment of Plymouth cars in every state of repair. We drove to the place so my friend could look over the cars and parts, and possibly find some needed items. The place was not easy to find, but in time we did locate it. The stories we had heard were true. In a fenced-in area on a farm there must have been one hundred Plymouths, all models and body styles. I had forgotten that in 1932 Plymouth

Authentic spot-trouble light was located with many other parts at a Plymouth fancier's place. The light was completely original and needed merely a thorough cleaning and minor repair to the wires and cable. It cost only ten dollars.

offered a seven-passenger sedan; it must have been quite a load for the four-cylinder engine. A 1939 four-door Convertible Sedan attracted my attention, and I made a mental note of what it would take to restore the body alone.

The owner walked with us among the cars and answered our questions on parts interchangeability, etc. In his barn he showed us some completely restored cars, which were just like new. He was planning on entering a red 1932 Convertible Coupe in a coming show. He showed us a 1951 sedan that had been driven less than 5000 miles; I have never seen a "newer" old car.

My friend bought the parts he needed, and some for another person who had not come along. The owner took us into a small building where he was working on two other cars. Here he had shelves with parts stacked high, and boxes of parts around the sides of the building. I noticed some parts that were not for Plymouths, and he stated that from time to time he had to pick up parts for other makes in order to get the Plymouth parts he wanted. Some were new, original stock, but not for any car I was working on. While the owner and my friend were talking about Plymouths, I continued to look through the boxes. In one box I came across the spot-trouble light I needed. It appeared

You seldom find a forty-five-year-old car this solid and complete. This 1933 Plymouth Coupe even has the original ship radiator ornament. The side-mount aerial is not original. The owner tired of preparing car for a paint job, so it sat like this for two years.

Restorable 1948 Plymouth Convertible sitting in a field with other Plymouths. Little needs to be done to restore this snappy car. The owner had the spot-trouble light I was looking for, and was glad to sell it to me.

in original condition; it had never been repainted. The reflector would need polishing, as would the small nickeled adjusting nut. The wires were in excellent condition, and the protecting cable could easily be fixed. The end plug was missing, but otherwise it was complete. The light bulb even looked okay.

The light cost only $10, and I considered it a bargain at the price. I knew that with a minimum of work I would have an authentic trouble light for my Model T. The owner did not remember when or where he had acquired it but assumed he had it for some years, for he had moved all of the boxes and parts into the building when he built it about ten years ago and had not added any parts since.

The trip was interesting and worthwhile for my friend and me, and I enjoyed meeting the Plymouth expert.

21

New Faces for an Old Girl

The easiest way to renew the appearance of instruments on the dashboard would be to find replacements in excellent condition and install them. But this usually cannot be done on cars long out of production. In these cases it is necessary to repair the existing instruments and refurbish the dials. Removing instruments from the dashboard or instrument cluster is not the easiest task. The space is cramped and there is a maze of wires and cables, and sometimes a lever for opening a cowl ventilator. It takes a lot of patience, a fairly supple body and common sense. In many cases the insulation on the wires is very brittle because of age and heat. The nuts holding the instruments in place may be rusted, making them hard to turn. Space is a factor, for often little room is left for turning a wrench. But the instruments can be removed if you work hard enough. Tag the wires, of course, so installation can be done without difficulty.

"Be sure the center hole in the dial face lines up perfectly with the center mark on the plate holder, or we'll have a distortion," said Tom, who was operating the camera for me. We were photographing the speedometer face of a 1933 Mercedes, the first step in reworking the instrument faces that had become scarred and scratched as the car sat unused and unprotected outdoors for a few years.

Our plan was to photograph the original dial faces to show the marks and scratches. We intended to blow up the negatives

200 percent so even the smallest blemishes would be easy to spot. We would then opaque these marks on the negative and rephotograph the enlarged negative. With the retouched face photographed, we would reduce the photo to its regular size and make a Velox. With the back of the Velox sprayed with mastic, it could be applied over the old face, giving a "like-new" face on each dial. The speedometer was the first to be attempted. This was the only way I could think of to get new dial faces.

The original faces were metal, with the figures and trade name applied as decals. The solvent used to loosen the holding nuts dissolved some of the figures, but not enough to cause a problem. After the faces were photographed they could be scrubbed clean so the mastik would adhere properly.

The large camera we were using normally photographed offset-produced newspaper pages. The page holder had an exact center mark that lined up with the center on the lense. It was this

Broken glass allowed dial faces to deteriorate, necessitating new faces. The best way seemed to be the offset photographic process. Faces were damaged even more in removing them from the instruments.

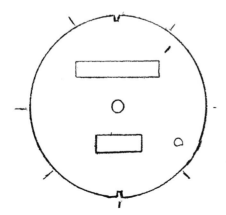

Speedometer face was enlarged 200 percent in first step, so concentric circles could be drawn in. Lower rectangle that exposes trip mileage was originally cut wrong, but the error did not show up before the enlargement.

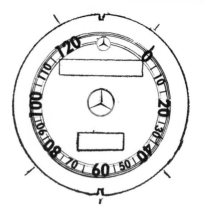

Offset numerals were run through wax-applying machine so they would adhere to the photographic paper.

center mark that Tom referred to when he cautioned me on the exact position of the dial face.

Once the exact position was accomplished, the face was photographed. The original face was black with white numerals. We reversed the negative, making the print white with black numerals. With the 200 percent enlargement, the smallest imperfections could be seen. These were opaqued over a light table. Some of the numerals had come off as the instrument was removed from the dash, or when the face was removed from the instrument. Rather than try to match the type, new numerals were typeset. To remake the two concentric circles that contained tiny cross marks to indicate kilometers between numerals, a compass was used and the cross lines drawn in. This was photographed, trimmed and pasted over the enlarged dial. After the new numerals were pasted in place, the remade dial face was photographed. White-out was used to hide any marks that would show up because of the layers pasted in place. The enlarged face looked good, so it was then reduced. The rectangular openings for the odometer and trip miles were cut out, as well as the hole through which the trip set lever extended. The center hole for the shaft that held the needle was punched, and the tiny hole for the pin that kept the needle from being pulled back below the zero mark was punched with a needle.

Mastic was applied to the old face, after the numerals on the revolving odometer wheels were cleaned. With the new face in place, the instrument looked fine. The same procedure was used on the ammeter, fuel, temperature and oil gauges.

166 •

The instrument rims were cleaned and replated. New glass had to be cut, and then the instruments were reassembled. They looked fine, and when in place gave the dash a like-new look. It was a slow job, but well worth the effort since replacement dials were not available on this car.

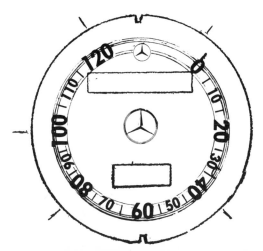

Finished dial face in white with black numerals. The new face was photographed in a 100 percent reduction and compared with the original for size and numeral spacing before being reversed.

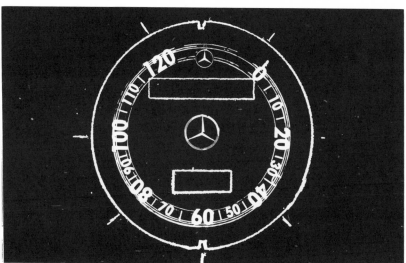

Reversed photo of dial face shows black face with white numerals as on the original. After the mileage and trip odometer rectangles were cut out with a sharp blade, the back of the face was sprayed with mastic and the photo was applied to the instrument.

22

There'll Always Be
an England

I had heard from several people that the best way to buy a used British car was to fly over to England, see for yourself and have the car shipped over. The next best way was to follow the ads in the two major British car magazines circulated in this country. I knew some people who had bought their cars through ads and were completely satisfied. There was an element of excitement and surprise involved, like receiving a package ordered through the mail.

I wanted what the British referred to as a "pre-owned" Rolls. The prices for used Rolls Royces in the United States seemed too high. I corresponded with some dealers and received lists and pictures of the cars. One "Purveyor of Horseless Carriages to the Gentry and Nobility" sent some pictures and completely frank descriptions of several cars. A 1932 Rolls with an H. J. Mulliner Sports Saloon body interested me. It was built for the "owner-driver," had good lines and was described as in top condition. My bank quoted the current exchange rate, so I had a bank draft made in the necessary amount and ordered the car.

A day or so later I got a call at about two in the morning. Between the crackling on the overseas line and the British accent, I gathered that the car I wanted had been sold just before my check arrived. "I'll either return your draft or let you have the 1936 Rolls with the Windovers Sedanca de Ville body for the

The 1936 20/25 Rolls Royce as it looked in England before shipment to the Port of Cleveland. The Flying Lady mascot shows in the picture. Wire wheels are covered by a set of Ace wheel discs.

same amount. You'll see it's on the list I sent you, and it's priced at 200 pounds more. You can have it for the amount you sent me. What say?"

I was disappointed at not getting the particular model I wanted but told the fellow I would take the other car. With a "very good" and "cheerio" he was off the line. I spent the rest of the night wondering what sort of fool I was, and thought perhaps I had better wire the man that the deal was off. But as I studied the picture of the car and read the description over and over, I liked the idea of the 1936 car, and convinced myself I had made a pretty sharp deal.

It was not long before I received a batch of papers. One was the title for the car, complete with a wax imprint of the Queen's ring. (At least that's what I thought it was.) I also found the shipping papers, and saw that the car would arrive on the S.S. *Herman Schulte* in Cleveland on a certain date. The bill of lading simply referred to my prize as "one used Rolls Royce, dented and scratched." The description did not really send me, until my wife recalled that each time we had moved, the movers had listed even brand-new pieces as "marred, scratched, dented, etc." So I

Although properly authenticated in England, this bill of sale was not acceptable in my county until it was signed by a notary public, because the rule book called for a notarized signature. My signature does not appear on this document.

thought probably the steamship company did this to protect itself.

We planned a vacation that would bring us back through Cleveland on the date the car was to arrive.

The clerk at our county courthouse read the instruction book on what was required to register a foreign car in the country. The instructions clearly called for a notarized bill of sale. I had the bill of sale, all right, but the British call their notary public something else. Even though the papers were signed, witnessed and affixed with the impressive wax seal, the clerk refused to issue a title. When I saw that I could not get the point across that the signatures, seal, etc., were the required authentication, I presumed I would have to go to the head of the department. But that was as frustrating as the first encounter. Apparently the department head had reached that esteemed position by following an exact interpretation of the rules. I pointed out a typographical error in the rules book and asked how that was interpreted. "Oh, that's a mistake, and it doesn't matter. Unless your papers are notarized, we can't issue a title."

Damning bureaucrats all the way back to my office, I decided to play their own game. I asked my bookkeeper, who was also a notary public, to stamp, sign and affix her seal. This she did, and a little later the same day I took the now notarized papers back to the same clerk. "You were right," I said, and handed over the papers. "You can see where this is now notarized, and the seal affixed."

"That's more like it," I was told, and the title was issued on the spot. How the clerk rationalized that a notary public in this country could witness and notarize a signature from England was beyond me. Since the clerk did not question the matter, I forgot about it and accepted the title.

With the bill of lading, car title and license tags, I arrived at the downtown office of the shipping company and paid their charges so the car could be released to me. Then I headed for the motel to pick up my wife, and we went to get the car.

On this particular vacation we had taken my niece, who was ten days younger than my son. The children were restless in the car and had been at each other's throats the entire trip. Finally we separated them by keeping one in the middle seat of the station wagon and the other in the third seat. Because the seats were not the same width, and to overcome the plaintive argument that "he's got a bigger seat than me," we made them switch seats twice a day.

Although it was July, Cleveland was cold and wet when we arrived. We had planned for the kids to play around the swimming pool at the motel, but it was too cold. No matter what was on television, the two could not agree on any one program. My wife had been climbing the walls while I was attending to the paperwork. When I arrived at the motel to report on my progress, I was told to take the kids with me; she had had it.

Since I thought I would be driving back from the wharf in the Rolls, and my wife had had such a rough afternoon with the

It took plenty of scrubbing to remove the protective film sprayed on the car for her sea voyage. At first I thought the finish was ruined. A dock worker suggested lacquer thinner for the plated parts to remove the coating.

kids, I said the children and I would take a cab to the wharf. The children thought that would be neat. They were just fine in the cab, and stayed right with me when I walked into the dim warehouse to look at the car.

The Rolls was a tall, stately car. It must have sat a good eighteen inches higher than the shipment of new Jaguars that surrounded it. At first glance I was very disappointed, for the finish on the car looked awful and the radiator, headlights and other plated parts looked terrible. I gave the release papers, etc., to the warehouse attendant, who said he would "get her out for me."

For shipment the oil had been drained from the engine, the battery removed and the gasoline drained from the tank. The car was pushed out on the dock, and I was distressed about the appearance of the finish. Presently a dock worker appeared with a hose and a sponge and started washing the car. Most of the grime and dirt washed off easily, leaving the body looking quite presentable. But the plated parts still were very bad. I guess my disappointment must have showed, for the worker said, "That's just a protective coating put on to protect the chrome from the salt air. Use some lacquer thinner and it'll shine right up." That was a relief, and I could hardly wait to get the plated parts cleaned. But first, gasoline was needed, and oil for the engine. Neither was available on the dock.

The children and I walked a few blocks to a gas station, where I borrowed a gas can and bought the gasoline and oil. I guess the radiator had not been drained, for it was full when I got back, and no one admitted to having filled it. After the battery was installed I pressed the starter button, and a few turns later the engine started. The children piled in. I thought we could leave as soon as I picked up some papers I had presented to the attendant.

"She can't leave the dock until the customs man has okayed the papers, and he won't do that until the underside has been steam-cleaned," was the reply when I asked for the papers. It seems the Agriculture Department was concerned that there might be come kind of larvae in any mud or dirt that was caked to the underside of the car. This delay was annoying, of course, but I did not think it would take long. After looking through the papers, I showed the customs official the certificate stating the car had been steam-cleaned in Liverpool before loading it on the ship. That made no difference. I was told the car had to be steam-cleaned here, which would cost $25. That did not really upset me, and I still did not think it would take long. The children liked the inside of the car, especially the folding occasional seats, the intercom for the chauffeur, and all the little doors and knobs on the back of the front seat. They amused themselves quietly, and I could not see that they were doing any harm to the car. My son twisted one of the bone knobs off the handle that controlled the window to the chauffeur's compartment, claiming "it just came off." I told them sharply to leave things alone and sit still until we could leave.

The operator of the steam-cleaning machine was at another dock. I was told that as soon as he finished the job there he would come over to clean my car. There was nothing to do but wait. The children were getting restless, so we walked along the dock watching the gulls and the boats in the lake. After an hour that seemed more like three, the man arrived with the steam-cleaning machine. He explained that they would have to hoist one end of the car so he could spray underneath it, then raise the other end so he could complete the job. This would not have taken long, except the mobile hoist was not working and they had to use another one, but it was in use at the moment helping unload some cargo. Obviously we had to wait, so the children and I walked around some more to kill time.

Eventually the hoist was freed from the other job and the cleaning operation could begin on my car. With the front end raised for or five feet, the operator sprayed jets of steam along the axle, springs and engine base. There was not much dirt to remove, as that had all been done in Liverpool. When the rear of the car had been given the same treatment, I paid the operator, and he signed the papers that had to be given to the representative of the Agriculture Department. The only trouble was that by then it was after four o'clock, and the government servant had gone home for the day. There was no one else who could sign; I could not get the car until morning. With this disappointing news, I took the children, called a cab and headed for the motel. The Rolls was driven back into the warehouse.

My wife was a good sport about the delay, and when we found that the motel furnished bonded baby-sitters, we decided we had earned a little time to ourselves. We hired the sitter to take care of the children after their evening meal, and we went to dinner. We found a nice restaurant with a piano bar, and enjoyed the evening. When we returned to the motel, the children were fine and about ready for bed.

The next morning we checked out of the motel and drove to the dock, thinking that in a few minutes we could get the car and head for home. What a surprise we had in store.

There was some delay locating the agriculture representative, then some delay in locating the customs official. It was about eleven before I got clearance to leave.

The children wanted to ride with me, so my wife went ahead in the station wagon. The street by the docks carried heavy traffic, but I was not concerned about that. The car worked fine for about two blocks; then the motor quit. Fortunately I was in the curb lane, and although no parking was allowed along the street, people could get around me. When my wife found I was not behind her, she pulled onto the first side street and waited. When I did not show after about ten minutes, she drove back and saw the car sitting along the curb. The car acted as though it was out of gas. What was more, after a few minutes of operation the starter would just hum.

I had to walk back to the dock office and ask for help. I knew the car was not out of gas, for I had put in five gallons the afternoon before, and the gauge showed just under a quarter full. I thought perhaps the battery was now so low that it would not turn the motor over. No one at the dock could offer any help, so I walked to the gas station. I had forgotten to return the borrowed gas can from the day before and the attendant was sore at me. I explained the delay and said I would gladly pay for the can, but right now I needed help to get the car out of traffic and started again. Almost grudgingly he agreed to push me to the station with his Jeep. I thought I would take advantage of the push and slip the car in gear, and maybe it would start with the push. It did not, and the Jeep bumper overrode mine, causing a small dent in the trunk lid.

No matter how we tried, we could not get the car started. My wife took the kids to find a place for lunch. There was a mechanic of sorts at the station, and he tapped first this, then that, and fiddled around with the wiring. He finally admitted he did not know what the matter was. I located a Rolls Royce dealer and asked that he come pick up the car and see if one of his mechanics could locate the trouble. Meanwhile the afternoon was slipping by, and it was probably around four o'clock when the tow truck arrived. The Rolls Royce garage was across town, and it took nearly an hour to tow the car there. I could not expect everyone to stop what they were doing and concentrate on my car, but it was quite annoying to see everyone going on about their business, paying no attention to my car.

Finally the shop foreman said he would have his best mechanic take a look, but since it was now nearly quitting time, I would have to pay the overtime rate for the mechanic. I agreed, of course. He was indeed an excellent mechanic, and diagnosed the trouble in only a few minutes.

My Rolls had a vacuum tank on the fire wall to furnish gas to the engine, and when the tank was drained in Liverpool before shipment, the vacuum in the gas line was broken. The motor had been operating only on the gas in the carburetor bowl and the little in the gas line between the vacuum tank and the carburetor.

He thought when the tank was primed and the vacuum restored to the system it would run. He primed the tank and the car did start up quickly, but it ran only until the gas put in to prime the system was used up. An additional diagnosis was made that sounded quite farfetched to me. Showing me tiny hammer marks on the fitting in which a tiny steel ball about the size of a BB shot moves back and forth by engine suction, he said he thought the opening had been restricted, preventing the BB from doing its job.

He removed the fitting and very carefully reamed out the hole, removing the flat spot on the top caused by the hammer. He had to be extremely careful not to remove any metal from the other sides of the hole or the vacuum would be lost. When he finished the job, reassembled the fitting and connected the gas line, he primed the system again. This time the car continued to run. We could hear the tiny BB rolling back and forth as the engine vacuum drew it forward, allowing more gas to be sucked into the vacuum tank.

I asked about the odd noise the starter had made before but did not make now. He said the car had small corks on the starter clutch, and if they were worn, the clutch would slip when the motor was hot. He did not have replacement corks but said I could get them from a supply house, for some Diesel trucks used the same thing. He added that if I shut off the motor I would have to wait about half an hour until it cooled before the starter would work. I decided as long as I knew about the problem I could live with it until I got the car home and replaced the corks.

It was too late to start home that night, so we went back to the motel. Fortunately they had room for us. We all went to an Italian restaurant, and my son caused some amazement when he ordered plain spaghetti, adding that he meant "without sauce." The waiter seemed surprised, and I guess the kitchen help must have been too, for we saw the cook follow the waiter out of the kitchen door and peer at our table as the waiter pointed out my son to the cook.

The next morning we started for home, one child in each car. Things went fine. My wife said for me to lead the way, since I knew the route, and she would not have to worry as long as she could see the Rolls above the other cars. Remembering the faulty starter, I left the motor running at the first gas stop. However, at

All fenders were removed for the best paint job, and new welting was installed when fenders were remounted. Bumpers, headlights, fender lights, driving light, windshield frame, door knobs and other plated parts were removed and replated.

a rest stop demanded by one of the children I forgot and shut the motor off. Sure enough, we had to wait until the motor cooled before I could start it. I made sure I did not let that happen again.

The car ran well. It was a little sluggish on hills, but I imagined that was a matter of carburetor adjustment, worn plugs or timing. Because the tires were not anything to rave about, I kept the car under fifty. People whizzed by me, and I really feared for one woman who turned and stared so long as she passed me that she just missed a bridge abutment. My son got a big kick out of sitting on the left side pretending he was driving. We stopped at a wrecking yard and I bought an old steering wheel. As people would look at the boy driving he would move the steering wheel up and down, giving some a scare.

Fully assembled after the paint job, the Rolls presents a dignified yet rakish appearance. I preferred the looks of the wire wheels, so the wheel discs were used only on the spares.

The Rolls was an excellent automobile. My first job at home was to buy some paint thinner and clean off the coating put on the plated parts. Over the next year or two I restored the car to its original splendor. Some plating, a new front carpet, refinished interior wood and a beautiful green-and-black lacquer paint job, plus a little mechanical work, and the car ran beautifully. I found the starter corks and had them installed, and also received a set from England. The seller had discovered the problem and secured a new set of corks, sending them to me with his apology for not having noticed the problem and repairing it before shipment.

The Rolls Royce Company looked back in their records and told me that the body builder had produced the lovely Sedanca de Ville body for a member of the Spanish nobility. They shipped the car to Calais in 1936, then lost track of the car after that. The

Unusual feature of Windovers Sedanca de Ville body was the pillarless construction between rear door and quarter window. Sliding walnut panel could cover quarter window, giving extra privacy to rear-seat passengers.

Unique raised molding allowed this beautiful two-tone paint job. To comply with Ohio regulations, license plate with light was mounted on the trunk lid. A pair of metal spare-tire covers purchased in England had not arrived when this picture was taken.

Spanish Civil War was raging in 1937, and I do not know anything of the car's use during those years. In 1939, when World War II started, the car was somehow back in England, and how it was used during the war years is also unknown to me.

After enjoying the car for several years I sold it. The car is still around and is registered in the Rolls Royce Owner's Club Directory. It was advertised for sale recently at about four times what I paid for it.

23

Once Is Not Enough

The Silver Wraith is one of the most desirable of the post-World War II Rolls Royces. Although basically the same from a mechanical standpoint as the Silver Dawn, these cars carried custom coachwork by the world's finest body builders. The Silver Wraith was introduced in 1946, when there were about twenty coachbuilders producing bodies for Rolls Royce cars. The Wraith saw the demise of all but H. J. Mulliner, Park Ward, before production ceased in 1959. The introduction of the high-styled Silver Cloud, a factory-produced car, is credited with hastening the end of the custom-bodied car. In all, 1780 chassis were produced during the fourteen-year production span. It is not hard to understand why I, like so many other collectors, wanted a Silver Wraith.

My chance came late in December 1972, when a Sports Saloon with a James Young body was offered for sale in Chicago. I phoned the owner and got a complete description of the car. I told him I would ask a friend in Chicago to drop by to examine and drive the car, and if he gave a satisfactory report, I would take it if we could negotiate a price. My friend drove the car and examined it thoroughly before phoning me to say the car was really such a good buy that he would take it if I decided against the purchase. With this glowing recommendation, I phoned the owner. When he found that I had no car to trade in and would pick it up myself, saving him delivery costs, he accepted my cash offer.

Stately and traditional Rolls Royce radiator shell graces the front end of streamlined body and fenders. Headlights are flared into the fenders. Twin driving lights perch in front of horn grilles. Parking lights and turn signals are in each front fender.

A convention in Minneapolis the first week in January gave me an excuse to pick up the car. My wife decided she would go along, visit her mother while I was attending the meetings, then fly on to Chicago with me. We would drive back together.

While we were at my mother-in-law's the day before the convention, we received a phone call from our son-in-law that our daughter had been rushed to the hospital, where she delivered a premature baby girl. The child weighed slightly over three pounds and was being moved to a high-risk hospital in Peoria, Illinois. My wife left immediately so she could take care of our other granddaughter; my daughter was fine but had caught the flu and would need help. It seems she experienced some contractions

The long sweeping fender line, large doors and curved luggage space made the Silver Wraith Sports Saloon with a James Young body a most attractive car. Wheel discs cover bolt-on steel disc wheels. Fender mirrors help on right-hand-drive cars.

and her doctor told her to drink nearly a bottle of bourbon to calm the spasms. The spasms were not calmed and the baby was born, so our daughter had the pains normally associated with birth, plus the flu and a horrible hangover.

I kept in touch with the situation while at the convention, then flew to Chicago as planned. The seller met me at the airport in his own car, for he did not want to drive the Rolls in the snow. The car was ready and waiting for me in his garage. It was a two-tone gray and black with one minor dent in a rear fender. It was so outstanding I decided I would take it even though I had not driven it.

While talking with the owner I commented on a beautiful copper and brass samovar on a coffee table. He said it was probably at least seventy-five years old. When I examined it more closely and admired the craftsmanship, he offered to sell it. I did not know where I would put it but bought it anyway, knowing that if my wife did not want a samovar, one of our children would be happy to have it.

This particular Rolls had a complete set of fitted luggage that completely filled the luggage compartment. My own two bags and the samovar had to be placed on the rear seat for the trip home.

Graceful rear-end design is devoid of extra ornamentation. British license plate and stop/backup lights were built into the trunk lid. I repositioned the Colorado plate so it did not scrape on low curbs. Gas-filler door is opened from inside the car.

My wife had decided to stay on a week or two to help my daughter, and we agreed to meet at the hospital in Peoria so I could see the baby. I stopped at Marshall Field's and bought a huge stuffed animal for my five-year-old granddaughter and a fancy little dress for the baby.

When I saw the tiny girl in the incubator, I did not think she'd make it. We watched the nurse try to feed her, then put her back in the incubator. Wanting to cheer up my daughter and son-in-law, I took them to dinner before driving on. When we parted, I thought I would be seeing them soon at a memorial service.

My wife had loaned our daughter one of those large dress-making forms, and it was brought to Peoria so I could take it home. This also had to go in the back seat of the Rolls, plus a large box of things our daughter wanted us to pass along to our son. So the back end of the car was loaded when I headed west after dinner.

With no reservations for the night, I decided to drive until I found a nice place to stop. An hour or so out of Peoria, I noticed the ammeter gauge was showing a discharge. To cut this loss of current I shut off the radio, and later the heater. This did not help much. It appeared to be about fifty miles to the next town, so that was the place I would stop for the night. It was clear and cold, and bright moonlight reflecting on the snow made it possible to drive with only parking lights. This brought the ammeter gauge back to just below the even mark. Fortunately there was very little traffic, so the headlights had to be turned on only as a car approached. I was glad there were no state police on that road, for they would have taken a dim view of my dim lights.

The next morning I tried to locate a service station and have the voltage regulator checked. No luck, so I kept driving. The car worked fine except for the generator. In an effort to conserve current for future stops, the radio and heater were not used.

At each gas station I tried to find someone who might be able to cure the low generator output, but no one seemed to have any ideas. At one station a hitchhiker asked for a ride. I told him to hop in, but did not mention the lack of heat and music. A few miles down the road he remarked that it sure was cold, didn't the car have a heater? I told him it did but something was wrong with the generator, and to save current I had to drive without the heater and the radio. He shivered for a few miles, then asked to be let out at the next crossroad, where he would try his luck for a car with heat. He did not have to wait long; he soon passed me riding in a Buick. He must have mentioned the incident to a gas station attendant, for when I stopped for gas I was asked if this was the cold Rolls without a heater.

After a rather sluggish start, I got the distinct feeling I had better find a motel with a good service station nearby, or find one on a hill where I could coast the car to start if necessary. The car was using more current than the generator was producing, and this could not keep up indefinitely.

Luckily a motel advertised that it was located on an access road above the noise of the highway, and that is where I stopped. Explaining to the desk clerk that the car might have to be coasted to start, I parked it headed downhill. In the morning I did not try the starter. After scraping ice from the windshield, I pumped the gas pedal a few times, set the starting carburetor lever and coasted downhill. When the speed seemed sufficient, I let out the clutch. There was enough ice and snow so the wheels slid rather than turning over the motor. Pressing the clutch and coasting again, I tried to start the car, but with no luck. Again the wheels slid. The bottom of the access road was closer, and I could picture myself on the highway with a dead motor. Cursing the highway department for not having scraped or put chemicals on the road, I tried the starter. The motor caught easily, and I drove onto the highway with no trouble.

At a truck stop a mechanic volunteered to take a look. He said he did not know anything about gasoline engines, that he worked only on diesels. I suggested the electrical systems were somewhat similar, for it does not make any difference in the operation of the generator whether there is gasoline or diesel fuel turning the fan belt.

It turned out the mechanic was not only truthful when he said he did not know anything about gasoline engines, but he could have included a lot of other subjects in that claim. He was one of the sorriest excuses for a mechanic I have ever come across. To make matters worse, he would not stop fiddling with things that had nothing to do with the problem. Along with that, he kept admitting he did not know what he was doing. I told him he was really screwing things up and to get his head out from under the hood, then shut the hood with a real authoritative slam. He walked away muttering something, and I drove away muttering something else.

Fortunately he had not made things any worse, but neither had he improved anything. A garage was advertised on a roadside sign, and it seemed the place to stop. The foreman said they had never worked on a Rolls but had a sharp mechanic who might help. This time I at least found an interested and intelligent person. At my suggestion he removed the old voltage regulator and put on a temporary twelve-volt replacement. This helped some, but the brushes in the old generator appeared worn, and those he could not replace. He gave the battery a quick charge, which would help. In working on the generator he inadvertently broke the fan belt. The only replacement anywhere near the necessary size was much thicker and would not ride down in the pulleys as it should. It might work, but there was a possibility the thicker belt riding near the top of the pulleys might jump out.

The original carpets had worn thin in spots and were used as a pattern for new ones. Leather on the bottom front cushions needed only cleaning with leather rejuvenator. Door panels, containing storage compartments, were of leather in good condition.

But it was a chance I had to take. He adjusted the generator brackets out as far as possible to keep the belt tight.

Although concerned that the new belt would let fly, I moved right along. I was still without heater and radio, but the ammeter gauge was nearly breaking even. There was no real trouble the rest of the way, and I reached home tired, cold and a little disgusted. When asked why I bought the car, my reply was that I wanted to be the first on the block with two Rolls Royces.

By mail I was able to get a new voltage regulator and brushes for the generator. These I installed, along with the correct fan belt. A new battery completed the repairs to the electrical system, and there was no more trouble.

A close inspection of the front carpet and kick pads showed they had taken quite a lot of wear, which had been hidden by a spray coat of paint. Using the old ones as patterns, I cut and fitted replacements. The leather welting around the doors was scuffed through, so new welting was made. The leather on the back of

Quick-action window control on driver's door required new metal welded on teeth and careful filing to make it work properly. Woodwork on doors, dash panel and folding trays in the rear compartment required only waxing.

the front seats was so brittle it needed replacement. There was no problem getting the correct shade, and I cut and sewed new leather coverings for the cushions, using old pieces as patterns. To make sure the threads would not pull through on the seams, each seam was triple stitched (these reinforcing seams did not show).

The door window on the driver's side had a quick-control lever instead of the regular window crank. A ninety-degree movement of the large lever completely raised or lowered the window. The teeth on the small gear attached to the shaft were worn. New metal had to be welded in place and the teeth filed to fit. I did not do the welding but did spend several hours painstakingly filing the teeth. When the mechanism was cleaned and lubricated with graphite, it worked fine. In removing the door panel on the driver's side I noticed that the plywood backing for the door upholstery was warped and split at the bottom. So new plywood was cut as a replacement, and treated with a preservative before the leather was put back on. These were all things I had not noticed until after the car had been purchased, and they

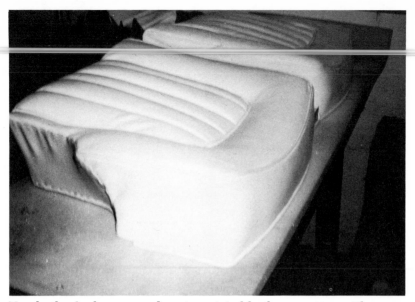

New leather backs were made, using original leather as patterns. The material was stitched on a home sewing machine, then hand stitched to framework around the back of the cushions.

were not serious. Replacement leather and carpeting had cost a pretty penny, but by doing the work myself I saved about two-thirds of the cost of having it done. And I probably did a better job.

The trunk lid did not work right. The car had not been damaged in that area, but for some reason the screws holding the prop-up arm had pulled loose, and someone had forced the lid closed. This split a piece of wood and bent the prop-up arm. The carpeted lining for the trunk lid was removed and a piece of strap iron bent to fit the curve of the lid. With six holes drilled in the brace, it was screwed over the split wood to hold it securely. The prop-up arm was straightened and replated. The latch on the body against which the hook on the handle fit was shimmed out to make a tighter closure. The lid fit fine. The interior of the luggage compartment showed no water stains, a testament to careful construction by the body builders, James Young, Ltd.

The set of matched luggage that came with the car needed a thorough cleaning. It was rawhide, so saddle soap did the job beautifully. The lining in the cases was somewhat stained, but

Having only one ignition key, I wrote Rolls Royce asking where I could obtain a blank so an additional key could be cut. The company very generously sent me a key at no cost.

In its new two-tone blue paint job, with the lighter shade on top, Wraith Sports Saloon looks longer and lower. The plated parts required only cleaning and polishing.

there was not much I could do about that. I removed the lining from one case and replaced it with leather, making it into a bar case with places for bottles, glasses and other equipment.

Several keys came with the car, but only one fitted the ignition. No local key shop could locate the proper blank so a new key could be cut. Fearing I would either lose the key or break it, I

wrote Rolls Royce, and they very kindly sent me a duplicate. In
the same letter I asked about a blank key for my Phantom III, and
they advised me where such a blank could be ordered.

Fortunately the dent in the rear fender panel had not torn
the metal or chipped the paint. By removing the rear wheel, I
was able to push the aluminum skin back in shape without even
using a bumping hammer.

The paint on the car was original and, though shiny, had worn
thin in spots, so I decided to repaint. This meant removing the
plated molding strip along the bottom of the car, the fender mirrors, trunk handle and bumpers. I masked the plated window
frames, keyholes, etc. After a thorough cleaning and sanding,
and two carefully applied coats of primer, the car was ready for
the new paint. I chose dark blue for the bottom and a much
lighter shade of blue for the area above the belt line. I felt the
lighter shade on top would make the car appear lower.

It took six coats of lacquer for each color. The top was painted
first so there would be no chance of damaging the new paint
while the bottom was being painted. The area was very carefully
sanded between coats, then masked off to protect the newly
painted surface from spray while the bottom part was painted.
Although the seat cushions had been removed, the interior was
carefully protected against spray by plastic drop cloths held in
place with masking tape. This allowed me to paint the door jambs
and frames without injuring the upholstery.

The bottom portion was treated in the same manner as the
top. Between coats the paint was lightly sanded, allowing a good
thick body of paint to be built up with six light coats. When the
paint had dried, I ran a sharp blade along the masking tape to cut
through paint that stuck to the tape so it would not peel off
as the tape was removed.

The plated parts needed only cleaning and polishing, so they
were ready to install after the car had been thoroughly rubbed
down with a diluted rubbing compound. The lacquer took on a
fine gloss, and with the trim items back in place, the car was
really beautiful. The wheel discs had been painted the same color
as the bottom portion of the car.

We enjoyed the stately Wraith, as did our friends. One ride
was particularly memorable. Friends of ours are naturalized

Americans, having come from England in the early 1950s. The woman had been seriously ill, and although physically recovered, she was in the dumps emotionally. To cheer her, we bought a bottle of her favorite sherry and took the couple for a ride. The car was full of sliding panels, a space for flasks in the armrests and other convenient cubbyholes.

We were driving along, enjoying the sherry and each other's company. At a crossroads a highway patrol car was sitting awaiting speeders. We were not speeding, so I gave it no thought. A moment or two later the car sped up behind us, lights blazing and siren wailing. I pulled over, suggesting everyone hide glasses and the bottle. This was easily done in the various compartments. When the patrolman walked up, there was no sign of any liquid refreshments.

He wanted the registration and my license, at which he only glanced, and mentioned that the car lacked a current state inspection sticker. Indeed it did; somehow the windshield sticker had come off. Fortunately I had the written copy of the inspection report in the glove compartment. I pointed to the outline of the sticker on the windshield and said truthfully it had somehow come loose and fallen off. He suggested I get another sticker as soon as possible, and gave me a warning ticket. He then started asking questions about the car. He had never been this close to a Rolls and wanted to look it over. I raised the hood so he could see the engine, and he marveled at the shiny black engine with nickel-plated accessories. He liked the luggage compartment, with its fitted luggage, and asked about the obviously missing bag. I did not say it was on the floor beneath my wife's feet. He was impressed by the lack of external gutters over the doors, and when he saw that rain troughs were actually formed in the metal roof pan as styling creases, he was amazed at the care taken in building the body. After admiring the car, he thanked me, and cautioned me again about getting a replacement sticker.

After he had gone we got out the sherry and continued our relaxing drive, relieved that he had not discovered the open bottle or smelled the sherry.

Needing cash, I sold the car after enjoying it a year. I liked the car so much I have promised myself another Silver Wraith someday.

24

Back Out,
and Point Her Right

While living in Bristol, Tennessee, I often read the Sunday Washington *Post*. Along with the news and features it carried, I also enjoyed the used-car ads, especially the private-party ones. I had no particular car in mind but wanted something that would be interesting to restore. The following ad caught my eye: "Must sell '48 Hillman Conv. Cpe. Good condition, phone. . . ." I had a friend who had owned one of these cars, and I remembered it as a stylish little number that was fun to drive. It was by no means a sports car, yet because of its light weight would move right along. The car had only one window on each side, with a large cloth-covered quarter panel and a bustle-type trunk. It looked sort of like a miniature Lincoln Continental. I thought it might be fun to own one.

The owner was a dental student at Georgetown University. He told me all about the car, and from his description of what he had done to the car already, it was obvious he really liked it. When I asked why he was selling it, he replied that he needed the money. We talked some more about the car's condition, and he kept mentioning that he had to sell it. His price seemed high to me, and when I asked how he had arrived at it, he replied, "That's what I have to have, and I need it soon." More questions from me about the car satisfied me that it was probably a car I'd like, but the price was still out of line. I told him I thought the price high, and offered what I thought the car was worth. I do not know whether he cringed at my offer, but his voice indicated disappointment. He said, "I've got to have the money, and the car is the only way I know to get it. We're going to have a baby any day now, and I don't have medical insurance that will pay for it, and I've got to sell the car." I congratulated him on the coming baby but said I could not offer a higher price, and that the offer was contingent on the car being in the condition he described. I added that if he had not sold it by the time he had to have the money, and would accept my offer, to phone me collect and we could make a deal.

In a few days I got a collect call from Washington. The fellow said the baby was on its way, that he had just rushed the soon-to-be mother to the hospital, and he guessed he would have to accept my offer as he had not had any others. I told him I could be in Washington the next afternoon, and would have the money with me. He seemed relieved, saying that he would meet me at the airport with the car.

The car worked fine. I filled the gas tank and started into Virginia. I was sort of tired, for I had rushed to get things together so I could leave. Knowing there would be plenty of motels along the way, I had not made a reservation. About 190 miles out of Washington I noticed the gas gauge had hardly dropped from full, and wondered if the gauge was faulty or if the car was getting over 50 miles per gallon, which did not seem likely. The map indicated the next town was about twenty miles ahead, so I was not worried. There had been signs along the road indicating a restaurant ahead that specialized in Virginia ham. The signs made it sound so good that I stopped for a leisurely dinner, planning on spending the night in the next town.

A short distance after the restaurant I had to take a detour. I must have missed a sign, or some practical joker had removed it, for I found myself on a high-crowned country road. I could see no glow in the sky indicating a city ahead, and only occasionally did a car come from the other direction. This is a hell of a detour, I thought, and wondered if I should turn around and retrace my route. There really was not any convenient place to make a U-turn, but I decided that at the next driveway or crossroad I

With the three-position top in the de Ville position, the little car had style not usually associated with an economy car. Semaphore turn signals located below the belt line had to be removed and cleaned with air pressure to make them work.

would turn around and head back to the main road. I did not remember going through any intersection where I could have missed a sign. Of course it was dark by now, and with all the growth along the fences that lined the road I felt I could easily miss a sign. I probably drove only a mile more when I saw a small sign indicating the detour turned left. The only problem was that there was not any road or even a cow path to turn on, left or right.

I had no choice but to drive ahead, hoping I would either find the real detour road or at least a place to turn around. Stopping the car, I tried to read the map to see where I was. The car had no dome light, and the dash lights were too dim to illuminate the map. I wished I had a flashlight with me, but had not bothered to bring one. Finally I tried to read the map in front of the head-lights, but the print on the map was pretty small and I could not be sure of what I read. If I was on the road I thought, it appeared there should be a small town along the way where my route inter-cepted another road. Perhaps there would be a gas station there.

I started out, hoping to find a gas station before I ran out of gas. Sometime later, when I glanced at the odometer, I found I had driven 220 miles since filling the tank. I wondered what size tank the car had, and came to the sickening realization that it was probably ten gallons, a standard size for small British cars. I reassured myself that this would mean ten Imperial gallons, so I probably still had a few miles left. The gas gauge was not even down to the three-fourths mark, and I concluded the gauge was not accurate.

There appeared to be a farmhouse ahead, and when I reached the driveway I turned in. I planned to ask directions, and possibly buy some gas. Not over 100 feet into the drive that led the house a bright spotlight blinded me. The light had been aimed directly at my windshield, and I could not see a thing. I stopped the car and blinked my headlights, thinking the light would be turned off. It was not. I realized there were people who did not want trespassers, and that people living in a really remote area such as this might not want uninvited cars in their driveway. I knew I had better back out, for I could not see to drive ahead. The light was so bright the shadow of my car obscured some of the driveway behind me, but I could see enough to allow me to maneuver out. As I slipped the car into reverse, the motor coughed and quit. I restarted it. After a few turns it quit again. I'm out of gas, I thought. What the hell do I do now? It seemed I had better get out of the car and walk toward the house, if I could find my way in the blinding light. As I started, I could hear dogs barking, and I realized that the dogs had been turned loose. I do not know what I thought. I guess I was too scared to run for the car, and probably would not have beaten the dogs there. In a moment two large, menacing dogs were within a foot of me, barking viciously. I tried to calm them with, "Hi fella, nice dog, etc.," but they did not respond and were not going to let me move one way or the other. I guess I shouted, "Call off your dogs," or something to that effect, but for what seemed an eternity, nothing happened. I was frozen in the glare of what appeared to be the world's most powerful spotlight, and two misearble big dogs would not let me move. Fortunately neither dog snapped or tried to bite me. I'd have been a gonner if one had.

A voice nearby called off the dogs, but the light continued to blind me. I thanked whomever it was for calling off the dogs, and asked if the light could be turned off. I said I had gotten lost off the detour and needed directions, and now my car had run out of gas. There was no answer, and I could not see the person to whom I was talking. I repeated that I just needed some gasoline and directions on how to get back on the highway, and asked that the light be turned off. A powerful hand flashlight lit up, motioned the house, and the searchlight was shut off. Now I was as blind as before, for my car's lights were off, and aside from the flashlight it was dark as pitch. I again said that I had turned in the driveway for directions after getting lost on the detour, and now my car had run out of gas.

"Come on up to the barn," ordered the voice behind the flashlight, pointing the way along the drive. I walked along, closely followed by the now silent but still unfriendly dogs. At the barn a door opened, and the light inside revealed a couple of men in blue jeans. I walked in the barn, telling my story of becoming lost and running out of gas. The men who had met me at the car with the flashlight turned out to be a good-size guy who, along with his flashlight, had a rifle. He put the rifle down, saying, "Can't be too careful out here, never know who's coming up the drive." The dogs were still sniffing around my feet and knees but were no longer growling. I put my hand down toward one and he backed off, so I made no further attempt to be friendly with the dogs.

Since no one said anything, I gave my name, told how I had just bought the little car in Washington and was heading for Bristol, Virginia, but had gotten lost on the detour, and now had run out of gas. I asked if they could sell me some gas and point me back toward the highway. About that time a fourth man walked in, saying there was nothing in the car, as far as he could see, but that he had not looked in the trunk. "Well, go look in the trunk," the large man said, and the newcomer disappeared.

"What do you want to look in the trunk for?" I asked, "As far as I know it's empty. I haven't even looked."

"Just checking," was the answer.

I saw a couple of trucks in the barn and asked if they could sell me a gallon or two of gas so I could get on my way.

"Nothing but the spare wheel," the man reported when he returned to the barn.

With this assurance that there was nothing in the car, they

relaxed. They got me some gas and gave me directions as well. They gave me their first names, and I shook hands with each. This seemed a little strange, but I did not question it then. I was beginning to feel a little more comfortable, but not in really friendly surroundings. One man filled a large can with gasoline from a big drum, while another got a funnel. I moved to get the gas and take it to the car, but the large man said, "They'll fill her for you."

I asked where I was, and how I got so far from my detour.

"Don't matter where you are, we'll head you in the right direction," was the answer.

Trying to make conversation, I asked what kind of a searchlight they had, said I had never seen one so bright. Seems it was off a Coast Guard boat, and they had it rigged up to a special generator driven by a Model A motor.

"We got a second one bigger'n that," one man volunteered, pointing toward an area to the side of the barn door. There on a pipe pedestal was a huge searchlight, placed squarely behind a window in the barn, and I presumed it was also pointed down the driveway.

While the two men were putting the gas in the car, the large man asked if I had any identification.

"Sure," I replied, "I've got my driver's license, credit cards and other identification. Why?"

"Let's see the driver's license," he said.

I thought this a little out of line, but did not think I was being too meek when I drew it out of my wallet and showed it to him. He read off the Bristol street address and asked if I knew someone whose name I no longer recall. I admitted I did not know him. He handed the license back to me, and I asked what I owed them for the gas.

"We'll give you the gas, then you get the hell out of here," was his reply."

"Okay, thanks, I appreciate the gas, but I want to pay you for it."

"Nope, just head on out. Back out of the driveway, point her right and you will come to a crossroad about a mile ahead. Turn left and keep on it. You'll hit a town down the line."

I was wondering why it was taking so long to dump a little gas into the tank, when the two men walked back in. "She's ready," they said. I thanked them again and again offered to pay, but was answered by shaking heads. The man with the flashlight walked back to the car with me. Meanwhile the searchlight had been turned on, and I realized I would be in the same blinded position I was in before. I asked the man to have them turn off the light so I could see to back out. He motioned with his light and the searchlight was turned off.

Once in the car I started the motor, backed out the drive and followed the simple direction given me. I was glad to be out of that peculiar situation, glad to have the gas and glad to have some general directions. My watch indicated it was 10:30. I found the

With a new black top and British racing green body and fenders, the Hillman Convertible was a stylish little car. It ran exceptionally well and was quite peppy despite the small four-cylinder engine. The oversize grille guard was later removed.

crossroad and turned left. I came to a tiny settlement after a while, but there was no gas station. I continued on the same route and eventually came to a grubby little town where I could get some gas. At a diner I ordered coffee and studied the map to see where I was, and where I had been.

It appeared I would have a drive of at least two hours until I was back on the main road and would be likely to find some decent motels. The car worked fine and I did not really mind the drive, except for being very tired. To help keep alert, I turned the radio volume up, but was not receiving very good reception in the hilly country. Once I felt the right wheels bounce off the side of the road, which awaked me with a jolt. I must have dozed off for a few seconds. I had heard that driving in stocking feet helps keep a driver awake, so I took off my shoes. That did not seem to make much difference. I lowered the windows to blast cold night air in on me. That helped somewhat, and by concentrating on deep breaths I managed to shake off the drowsiness.

When I hit the main highway I found I was not over thirty miles down the road from where I had begun the detour. To this day I do not know where I had been, nor why I was treated in such an unusual manner when I turned into a driveway in search of help. Some friends believe I probably happened on a moonshine operation and the operators were suspicious of anyone and everyone.

When I located a motel for the remainder of the night and took my overnight bag into the room, I found the bag had been pawed through. Everything must have been taken out and just crammed back in. Nothing was missing, but there was not anything of any real interest or value in it.

The rest of the trip was uneventful. When examining the car at home I found that the bottom of the gas tank had been bumped upward, and while the tank was not cracked or leaking, the dent severely restricted the amount of gas the tank would hold. Once removed, the tank was easily straightened and the sending unit to the gauge was checked. From then on it seemed to work fine. I made a new roof for the car, painted it British racing green and enjoyed it.

I had the little car a few months when I received a letter from the medical student in Georgetown. He said that a steering column he had ordered a long time ago had finally arrived, and if I would pay him what it cost along with freight charges, he would send it on to me. I do not know why he ordered it, for there was no play in the wheel, but decided it would be good to have. I never installed it, but sold it with the car sometime later.

25

You Might Get Taken

The law of averages is bound to make one out of every so many deals turn out badly. I have been lucky in my dealings with other restorers and people interested in the hobby. Most of the cars and parts I have bought have been more or less as they were represented. I would like to think any variation from this was accidental, but being realistic, I know that is too much to expect.

My most common method of searching for parts is to read the ads in the national car magazines and the publications of various car clubs. In most cases either the parts I need turn up or I get information on how I can obtain them.

I had bought a Locomobile Junior Eight. The car had been pulled out of a burning barn, and in the process a beam had fallen across the hood and dented it badly. This, in addition to considerable rust damage to the hood, made me think I should at least try to locate a replacement. I knew the chances were slim, for few of these cars were produced in their short lifespan.

Other hobbyists have told me that their best results in advertising come from ads for parts for one make at a time. I have not found this to be true, but thought maybe I would get better results if I listed only Locomobile parts. My ad carried a list of what I needed to put the old car into good shape.

One letter in reply contained a list of some mechanical parts, including a complete engine and transmission. I did not need these, but thought that if I got the car restored as I planned, the extra parts might be nice to have around. In writing to the seller, I told of my plans, and of the possibility that I would contact him later.

A second letter came from an owner of a Locomobile Junior Eight advising me that he did not have any parts for sale but if I located any I did not need, to please refer the seller to him.

My third and last letter came from a man in Indiana who said he had a complete hood and trunk from a Locomobile Junior Eight. He said there was slight damage to the left lower panel of the hood, but otherwise it was solid. He said the trunk was in excellent condition. He would only sell them as a "pair," and he wanted $400. My car did not have a trunk, and had no place to put one, so the trunk did not interest me, but I thought that if I had to buy the trunk in order to get a hood, I would be wise to do so, then resell the trunk. I wrote asking for more complete descriptions and pictures, and included a stamped, self-addressed envelope for his convenience. I got a letter saying about what the first letter had said, but including the vital information that the hood was light brown.

Anxious to start work on the car, I phoned the man and asked particularly about the hood. He told me that there was slight damage to the lower left panel of the hood, that it had not been in a wreck but had got creased in storage. He gave some details about the trunk, but since the trunk really did not interest me, I paid little attention. He agreed that he would send me a snapshot, but said he wanted a dollar for each picture. As soon as my money arrived, he would take the photos and send them to me.

I can understand a person charging for a photo. Otherwise photos would go to everyone who asked, many of whom are not interested in buying. I sent the money.

Probably a week later two photographs arrived with a brief note restating the price, plus shipping charges, and the statement that money would not be returned if the buyer was not satisfied with the parts. This did not upset me too much, but what really shook me were the two pictures. The hood was nothing even remotely similar to the hood I needed. I do not know what it was from, but it certainly was not from any Locomobile, the Junior or the Senior series. The trunk appeared to be metal. If it had

Trunk that was not at all like its descriptions, and also in very poor condition. I am glad I paid a dollar for the photo. Otherwise I would have been out quite a bit of money.

been fabric-covered, the covering was long gone. I have no idea what it would fit, and from the apparent condition I was not going to bother to find out.

I phoned the seller asking if he could have made a mistake and sent me the wrong pictures. "Nope, that's the trunk and the Locomobile hood, just as I wrote you," he told me. I told him it could not possibly be a Locomobile hood unless he had come across a factory experimental model. It was no experimental model, he claimed. He said he had known the owner and had seen other Locomobiles. That was the hood all right. I was about to tell him he was nuts when he added, "Why don't you let me send it to you, and if it don't fit, sell it to someone else?" When I said I did not do business that way, knew it would not fit my car and had no idea what it would fit, he took offense.

"That's a Locomobile Junior Eight hood and trunk. Are you calling me a liar?"

"Either you're sadly mistaken as to what the hood is, or perhaps you are a liar," I replied, and hung up.

Probably I was a bit harsh in thinking he was trying to peddle parts under phony descriptions, as I doubt if he would have any luck once prospective buyers saw the photographs. I guess he was mistaken, but I am glad I bought the photos.

One person really took me when I bought a tonneau windshield he claimed was from a 1929 Lincoln with a Locke body.

Supposedly a hood for a Locomobile Junior Eight. It was completely different from what I needed—far too short, big slash louvers, and rusty to boot. The damage to the left side was claimed to have occurred during storage. Luckily I did not buy it.

My car had the metal tonneau panel, but the windshield and posts were missing. I could tell from the holes what width the windshield should be, so I sent the dimensions with my letter. The reply indicated the windshield and posts he had would fit, and the price was $275 plus freight. The price seemed high, except for the fact that only a few were made, and my chances of finding another were slim indeed. The seller added that the glass had been replaced with safety glass and the posts replated. I sent him a check asking that he have it crated and shipped to me freight charges collect.

When the windshield arrived it was in great shape. As promised, the posts had been replated, and safety glass had been installed. There was even a new rubber along the bottom. I could hardly wait to get it on the car.

To my astonishment and disappointment, I found it did not fit. The posts were closer together than the holes in the tonneau panel. This was a measurement I had given him. What was worse, the curvature of the bottom of the windshield frame was completely different. I did not know what it was from, but it was not from a Locke-bodied Lincoln.

Quite a bit of money was involved, so I phoned the seller. I had some difficulty finding him at home, and left my number each time I called. One evening I did reach him, and he expressed amazement that the windshield would not fit. He mentioned the new glass, the replated posts, etc., and I agreed with all this, but insisted that it did not fit, was too narrow, had an entirely different curvature. I asked in detail about his car. At first he claimed it was a 1929. Later he said it could have been a 1926. Then he said the body might have been by Brunn.

He would not agree, though, to return my money if I returned the windshield with freight charges paid. Instead he again insisted it was from a 1929 Lincoln with a Locke body. He suggested that now that I had it, I should sell it to someone else. I told him he would hear from my attorney, and hung up.

My attorney was sorry that I had not kept a copy of my correspondence stating the width between the posts. All the seller's letter stated was that it would fit. The attorney wrote him suggesting he accept the windshield and send me a certified check for my purchase. The letter was pretty strong, hinting at using the mails to defraud, etc. I got a terse phone call advising me to send the goddam windshield back freight paid and I would get my money. This I did, but got a personal check in return. It came back to my bank with the notation that payment on the check had been stopped by the writer. Now he had the windshield and my money as well. My attorney wrote another letter, stating what terrible consequences awaited him if he did not send me a certified check by return mail.

I received a certified check, but for $100 instead of the $275, and no explanation for the difference. I was advised to cash the check, and the attorney wrote a third time. When there was no response in a month, my attorney suggested I forget it and charge my loss up to experience, as any additional effort would cost more than it was worth.

Since I was paying for this advice, I heeded it. I have no idea who may have bought the windshield, as I never saw it advertised, nor did I see anything else advertised at that address.

Fortunately there are not many of this type around. I have come across only two in my experiences with cars. Most of my friends have had good experiences too, proving that though there are a few ignoramuses and crooks taking advantage of car restorers, by far the great majority are honest people.

26

TV Is Very Educational

It is unusual to find a true classic car advertised at a reasonable price in a local newspaper. Most cars of this type are advertised in the national car magazines at much higher prices, or are consigned to auctions. When a 1934 Mercedes four-door Convertible Sedan was offered within fifteen miles of my home and at a really low price, I lost no time phoning the seller and making an appointment to see the car.

It was a rough-looking car. I do not know how many years the car had stood outside, but there was no top left, and leather upholstery was in shambles, the door bottoms had rusted through, there were many tears and dents in the fenders, the grille was dented and most of the chrome was rusted. The body would need a complete rebuild.

Mechnically the car appeared complete—at least all the major components seemed to be in place. But there was no battery, the rear brake shoes were on the floor of the car, the brake pedal was resting on the floorboard, and the ignition key was broken in the switch.

Because of the independent suspension of the wheels, the rear ones were closer together at the bottom than on the top, since the car was empty. This gave it a weird look. There was no crank, so the only way to be sure the motor had not "seized" was to put the car in gear and push it by hand to make the motor turn. This

The sleek, sophisticated styling of the Mercedes Cabriolet D appealed to me. I had been looking for such a car for several years. What a surprise to find one advertised in our local paper.

simple test showed that at least nothing was broken in the engine, and that it had not set up from years of disuse. The radiator had been drained, of course, and it looked pretty rusty when I peered into the filler hole.

The dipstick showed there was oil. It was black as tar, but of the right consistency. The owner said he had never heard the car run. He had bought it along with a group of other cars and had planned to restore it when the others were sold, but now he lacked the time. He had no title to the car but would furnish a notarized bill of sale.

Even though I would have liked to hear the engine run, I knew a test drive was out of the question with no brakes. The more I examined the car, the more intrigued I became. Here was a 1934 automobile with independent suspension on all four wheels, a four-speed transmission, built-in oiling for the front end, a flexible connection on the steering column and other advanced engineering features. To match these, the car had a most attractive fender line, and the body was styled in the true classic idiom. I tended to visualize the car as it could be rather than as

Nearly complete, but in rough shape, the classic proportions of the four-door Convertible Sedan were evident despite several years of neglect outdoors.

Really advanced for its day, Mercedes offered a flexible coupling on the steering column, an oiling system for every joint in the front-end suspension, four-speed transmission and independent suspension on all four wheels.

it was. The owner wanted cash and accepted my offer. He even offered to deliver it to my garage on his trailer for only $15.

Had it been an Essex, Durant or Studebaker that was delivered by trailer to my home, my neighbors would have laughed their heads off, the car was that rough looking. But since it was a Mercedes, they showed more respect. When I mentioned a price, about three times what I had paid for it, they agreed that maybe I had something there.

The car looked sleazy in my garage next to my Phantom III Rolls, and it was dwarfed by the big limousine. Everything had to be removed from the car. Parts were tagged if possible; unknown bits of hardware were put in a box marked simply "Mercedes?" Some just plain junk that would never be used was tossed in the trash. The bumpers were missing, but the bumper braces were on the car; these were the first parts to be removed for storage, for I banged my shins every time I walked around the car.

To some, the task of rebuilding this sporty convertible was beyond comprehension. The top and roof bows had long since deteriorated. The leather interior was beyond use even for patterns. Wooden body supports were badly rotted.

Partially dismantled, sitting on blocks, with newspapers spread underneath to catch excess solvent sprayed on rusted bolts, the old car looked decrepit. Evidence of fine quality materials and workmanship showed up in the dismantling process.

Oddly enough, all the glass was intact, even though the car had sat outside for so long. I planned to change it, however, because it was plate glass, not shatterproof.

Disassembling the car took a good deal of time. It was necessary to make sketches and take measurements of pieces not good enough for reuse. The upholstery on the door panels was largely gone, so what was left was discarded. The door and window hardware was hard to remove, even after dousing with solvent; in time they came off. The windows, which were framed in chrome, were removed so the frames could be replated and the glass could be used as patterns for shatterproof replacements.

Although I did not think it would do any good, I wrote the Mercedes factory in Stuttgart-Unterturkheim, giving the motor number, body number and a general description of the car and asking for any information they could supply. I remembered all those late-night movies on TV, where Van Johnson and other Air Corps officers had flattened the factories in Stuttgart. Surely they could tell me nothing other than that they built cars at that time.

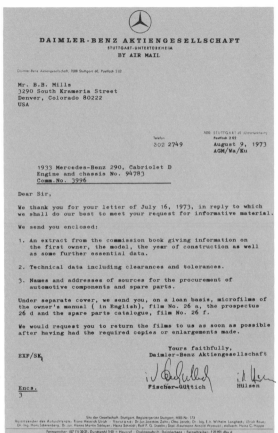

A prompt reply from Mercedes-Benz in Stuttgart indicated the car was a 1933 model. Obviously records were not in the area severely bombed during World War II.

To my surprise a prompt reply stated that my car was a 1933, and they included a copy of the original bill of sale! What was more, under separate cover they were sending me on a "loaner basis" microfilms of the owner's manual and the parts/suppliers catalog! Evidently information of this nature had been well hidden and protected during World War II.

A firm made 8½ x 11-inch prints of each frame of the three microfilms, so I had all the information needed to restore the car, and the owner's manual for operation after restoration.

With this information in hand, I began work in earnest. I had already got the motor running, after draining and flushing the

Verifax copy of the original bill of sale for Mercedes Cabriolet D was an interesting document and helped convince the people at the license bureau that the previous 1934 title was in error.

crankcase and cleaning the oil lines. An examination of the oil showed no bits of metal which could have meant engine damage. The radiator would not hold water but was good enough for a test start. The distributor was cleaned, the plugs were cleaned and gapped, the cylinders and carburetor were primed. When a new battery was connected, the engine started, after some coaxing. A bad exhaust system made so much noise it was hard to listen for any unusual sounds in the engine. But as far as I could tell, there was no burned-out rod or crankshaft bearings. That was a relief, since I bought the car without hearing the motor run.

The car was then blocked so it could be torn down and the wheels, fenders, radiator, grille, running boards, etc., removed. Since new tires would be needed, the old ones were discarded and the wheels taken for sandblasting. Inside, the car was gutted so

The Mercedes factory sent two microfilms, one of the Owner's Manual (in English), and another containing the prospectus and the spare parts catalog. I had copies made for future reference before returning the films.

The radiator was removed, flushed, pressure-tested and found to be without leaks. The water pump was repacked and a new gasket cut. Replacement fan belt and hoses were no problem. Four-blade fan received a coat of black enamel after cleaning.

The hole for the hand crank extends through collecting tank at radiator bottom. Front transverse spring, which forms the bottom of the front suspension system, was disassembled, cleaned and given a coat of rust-resisting paint.

The wheels were sandblasted and stored out of the way. Rear apron and fenders had some nuts and bolts so stubborn they had to be drilled through to be removed.

Much of what was removed was useless, even as patterns for replacement. Rotted wooden supports in the cowl and doors gave partial measurements; others had to be taken from the metal skin these supported.

Because of compound curves in the doors, they were left in place as new wood was measured, cut and fitted. Final installation of the new wood was done at a workbench with the doors off the car. When possible, bolts were used instead of screws.

Final test of correct measurements and fittings on a convertible door is the fit of the window glass in the raised position as compared to what it must fit against. Plated molding with weatherstrip on windshield post makes door glass a perfect fit.

new wood could be measured, cut and fitted. Kiln-dried oak was used for the cowl, door and other support pieces.

When rebuilding doors, it is better not to remove them from the car until the correct measurements have been taken and an initial fitting made. The Mercedes doors were all hinged to a steel center post. This rigid casting gave ample support. The front door closed against the cowl, so the curve of the front door, from top to bottom, had to match that of the cowl support against which it closed. The rear edge of the rear door had to conform to the top-to-bottom curve of the leading edge of the rear quarter section. Cardboard patterns were cut for each piece before the wood was cut. Initial shaping was done with a band saw, final fitting with a plane and draw shave. Once these pieces were made to the correct dimensions, one door at a time was removed, the wood was replaced and that door was rehung and fitted. This was a slow process but it paid off, for the compound curves of the body were maintained and each door closed solidly, with even spacing along the entire closure.

The window-winding mechanisms were cleaned, repainted to prevent rusting, lubricated with powdered graphite and put back in place. The latch mechanisms on each door were also reconditioned. Mercedes used chrome-plated pieces on the opening edge of each door. I had these replated, then used new plated screws to attach them to the newly reframed doors. To give the doors added stability, a sheet of quarter-inch plywood was cut to the exact inside measurements of each door and screwed in place. Before this was done, however, each piece of wood in the door, as well as the plywood, was coated with a wood preservative for added protection. The inside of each door was sanded to remove any rust, then coated first with a rust-inhibiting primer followed by a thick coat of asphalt roofing paint. While this was still wet, pieces of inside/outside carpeting were cut and installed as sound-deadening insulation on the doors; the body did not have this sound deadener before. Although at this point the rusted metal skin on the doors had not been repaired, each door closed solidly and securely.

Each door required repair to the metal skin around the bottom edge. New metal had to be welded in place on two of the doors, and patches were secured in place on the other two. Epoxy filler was used to hide the seams. When this was feathered at the edges, primed and sanded, the replacement metal did not show.

The body sills were solid, but the floorboards were rotted away. There was no problem taking the measurements for replacements, and these were cut from half-inch plywood rather than from solid lumber as in the original. Rebuilding the floor in the rear compartment was more difficult because of the recessed foot wells and the drive-shift tunnel. New metal had to be cut for the bottom of the rear seat support, which also was the rear support for the floor. The drive-shaft tunnel metal only needed sanding and priming to be reused. When the replacement pieces were bolted in place, the rebuilt rear floor was strong and solid. It was coated with a preservative for protection.

Rebuilding the rear quarter section came next. The wood framework around the bottom had rotted away and had to be taken out in small pieces. The rear apron had been removed, but it was necessary also to remove the gas tank so a pattern could be

Window-operating mechanisms were removed, cleaned, adjusted and given a coat of rust-resistant primer. Powdered graphite was used to lubricate springs, cogs and gears. All replacement wood was coated with a preservative before and after installation.

To give added strength to rebuilt doors, a sheet of quarter-inch plywood was installed. This did not interfere with either the fit or the action of the door and window hardware.

The interior of each door was coated with a rust-inhibiting primer, then a thick coat of asphalt roofing paint. This protects the door against further deterioration and adds to the solid "clunk" each door makes when closed.

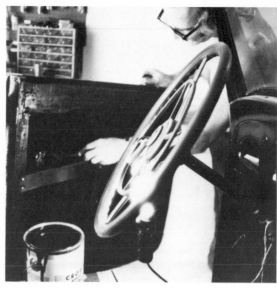

While asphalt coating inside the doors was still wet, pieces of indoor/outdoor carpet were installed to act as insulation on the doors. A sheet steel brace, extending about six inches in height, was installed at the bottom of each door.

Front apron, after straightening, priming and painting. Rear apron that covers the gas tank was given the same treatment. As many parts as possible were repaired, refurbished and repainted off the car, and installed when completed.

traced on cardboard. The pattern for the replacement wood was made in three parts: one for each side, including the curve, and the center portion. These were traced on the hardwood, which was cut in one piece for strength. When the wood was in place, holes were drilled in the metal skin and screws put in to hold the wood solidly. A coat of epoxy filler hid the screws without changing the conformation of the panel.

One of the steel braces that ran from a point on the wheel arch to the upper wooden quarter-panel brace was gone. This piece had a hole for a pin that acted as a pivot for the main folding top bow. Measurements were taken from the one that was still in place, and a new one was cut from heavy sheet steel. When bolted in place, it added support to the quarter panel as well as providing the main support for the rear top bow.

The car had molding that ran completely around at the belt line. This was lead, with plated steel crimped over it. Nails embedded in the lead attached it to the doors and other body panels. Where this molding fitted around the rear quarter section of the body, the wood was rotted beyond repair. New wood was cut, then held in place with screws through the skin in addition to the small serrated nails commonly used by body builders to attach the

Wooden replacement for brace across the rear body panel was fitted by holding wood over the metal panel and tracing the outline. After cutting on a band saw, it took very little shaping and planing to get a snug fit.

skin to the wooden framework. The molding was replated and left off until after the paint job, for it would cover the line where the two tones of paint joined.

On the fenders patches were welded in place under the torn metal. This gave a much more solid repair than butt welding. The fenders were completely repaired, with each rear fender having a reinforcement strip welded in place underneath the area where the fender joined the body. The fenders were primed and filled, then loosely mounted on the car. They would not be solidly bolted in place until the paint job was complete and new fender welting was installed.

With the body work nearly complete, attention was given to the mechanical components of the car. When a new cylinder-head gasket had been secured, the head was removed and the carbon cleaned. The valves were ground and adjusted, and new valve-cover gaskets were cut to fit. The water pump was removed to be repacked and lubricated. The generator was also removed and cleaned, and new brushes were installed. The radiator had to be taken to a radiator shop, where it was boiled out and the leaks were soldered. A new fan belt and new hoses completed the engine work, and the cooling system held a 50/50 solution of permanent antifreeze and water without leaking.

Patches were welded in back of cracks in the fenders for added strength, and edges butt-welded. Fenders were primed, filled and sanded, then left in primer coat. Undersides of fenders were given a thick coat of under-coating for protection.

After repairs, the fenders were loosely bolted to get them out of the way. Care was taken on fender repairs not to lose conformation on compound curves at front and rear.

The hydraulic brake system required complete overhaul. The master cylinder and reservoir were cleaned and new packing was installed on the pedal-operated plunger. Each brake line was traced from the master cylinder to the wheel, making sure there were no breaks or abrasions. New flexible hoses were secured for the front brakes. New brake linings had been installed as part of the previous owner's restoration efforts, and the front linings were in place. The rear brake shoes had to be installed and all four brake cylinders rebuilt.

The rear brake drums are not attached to the hub in the same manner as in most cars. The drums are secured by the bolts that hold the wheel in place. This made installing the rear drums over the newly relined brake shoes quite a problem. High spots on the linings had to be filed off, and even with the adjustment ratchets

The Mercedes begins to take shape. Replated headlights and cross bar are bolted in place, along with the front apron. Grille was not yet repaired. Fender lights are not originals but were installed to conform to the turn-signal laws; I am still looking for the right ones.

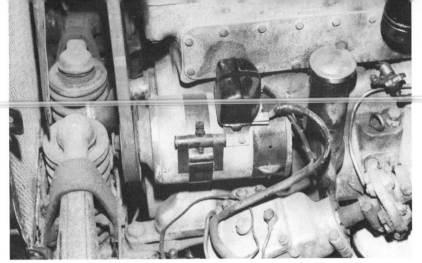

Electrical system was cleaned by using compressed air to blow dirt from the generator and starter motors. The cutout to divert exhaust gases and the coil were checked, then painted. New points, condenser, spark plugs and spark plug wires were installed.

After the carburetor, fuel pump and strainer were cleaned and overhauled, the valves were ground and valve clearances set. New gaskets were cut to fit the newly repainted valve covers.

pulling the shoes together, the drums did not fit easily. Finally, after more lining was filed off the shoes, the drums slid in place, but the rear brakes dragged for some time until the linings wore down.

Removal of the inspection plate on the transmission made it easy to check the gears. No teeth were chipped, and there were no scorch marks on the gears or shafts. Once the transmission was flushed and refilled, it was ready for operation. The gear-shift lever had been removed and replated, as had the hand-brake lever.

Rebuilding the exhaust system required having a new tail pipe fabricated at a muffler shop. The operator took a piece of straight tubing and bent it to the measurements I had provided. The front muffler was reusable, but the rear muffler had to be replaced. The car had a dash-operated cutout that diverted exhaust gases through a damper into a straight pipe under the right running board, which exhausted just ahead of the right rear wheel. This pipe had to be replaced as well as its metal covering plate, which was chrome-plated.

A valve lever on the inside of the fire wall allowed the driver to switch the tank to "reserve," which gave one or two additional gallons of gas. There were two gas lines leading from the tank. The regular pipe extended to about two inches from the bottom of the tank. The reserve pipe was longer, nearly to the bottom. These lines joined just below the fire wall, where a single line fed the carburetor. The valve must have leaked at one time, and someone tried repairing it by clamping off the reserve line. A new pet cock had to be located and attached to the control lever. This came from a later-model Mercedes that used the same system.

The boots that attached to each side of the differential and axle housing were worn and leaked grease. After the differential was checked, flushed and refilled, new boots from a Mercedes dealer in California were installed. With them came some sponge-rubber weather stripping, and instructions to wrap the weather stripping around the axle housing so the new boots could be clamped tight since the original size was no longer available. These worked all right, and no leaks developed.

Refurbishing the interior was slow. With the wooden trim removed from the doors and windshield, a small piece of the

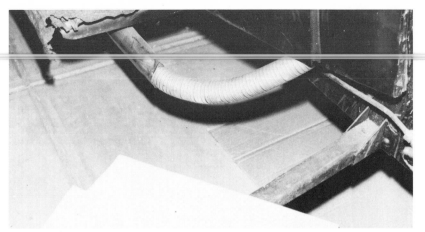

When rebuilding the exhaust system, new flexible tubing was installed to connect to the straight pipe under the right running board, which is put in use by a hand-operated cutout. A new rear muffler and tail pipe completed the exhaust-slystem repairs.

Differential unit is bolted to rear chassis cross member, and independently sprung axles are coil-spring mounted. After cleaning and refilling the differential, new rubber axle boots were installed to prevent leakage.

Leather was supplied to match the original covering on the seats and doors. When I accidentally overpaid the supplier, he wrote me about the overpayment and returned my check.

original leather was located. This was sent to a leather supplier, who buffed it to its original color and sent a sample back for approval. New blue leather was then ordered for the seats and door panels. This soft, supple leather could be sewed on a home sewing machine.

The original upholstery was in such bad condition from years of exposure that I could not be sure of the pattern used in stitching the leather on the seats. Also I had no idea of any pattern or design used on the door panels. None of my literature had pictures of the interior. I wrote the two owners I had heard of who had somewhat similar cars and asked for sketches and photographs of the seats and door panels used in their cars. They both obliged, but added that their leather seats were not original and they could not vouch for authenticity.

With expensive new leather on hand, I certainly wanted the leather cut and stitched as near to the original fashion as possible, so I put off cutting until I could be sure.

There was also a problem with the correct boot for the folding top, once it was in the folded condition. There was no trouble cutting and sewing the top, and fitting it to the new framework. But I did not know what the boot that covered the folded stack looked like from the inside. Consequently this had not yet been made.

Unbelievable luck came on a late-night TV movie featuring a team of British commandos who went to Holland to smuggle diamonds out of the country before the Nazi invasion. The com-

Not much could be determined about the pattern used on the seat cushions, doors, etc. New foam rubber and polyurethane were used instead of cotton padding, as on the original.

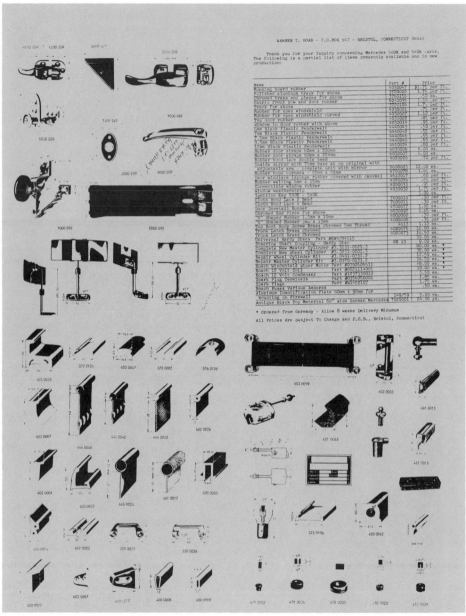

Fortunately new rubber moldings and other trim parts were readily available from a nationally known supplier. Prices were most reasonable, so everything needed was purchased at one time.

mandos were met by a counterspy driving a car identical to mine, and in most of the scenes the top was folded so the viewers could watch the characters. I spent the time making hurried sketches of the doors and seats.

A close-up of some whispered information concerning the diamonds gave me almost as good an idea of the way the front seats were upholstered as I would have gotten sitting in the car. There was no way of measuring the width of each seat panel, but I did get an idea of the correct proportions. Another close-up showed the rear cushion, first with the center armrest down, then folded up to conceal a gun.

A view from the back seat looking forward showed the folding tables on the back of each front seat, and the robe rails too. This was great. As I made sketches my wife estimated measurements.

The design of the door panels was different from those sent by my friends. I would have been way off. The placement of the armrests was much higher than I had imagined. The storage pockets in the front doors were also different.

The pleating for seat cushions and seat backs was sewed on my home sewing machine with no. 16 needle and nylon thread. As a precaution, a second reinforcing seam was used.

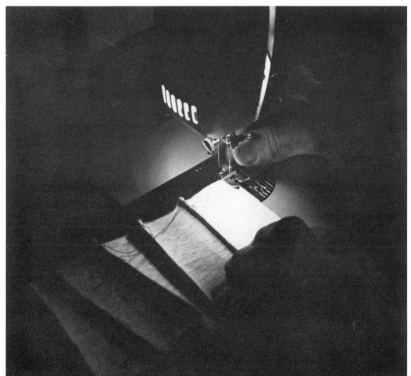

New folding tables for the backs of the front seats were made of plywood. Wood-grained formica was glued to the inside part; the outside was leather-covered, as on the original.

Fortunately the top was in the folded position in so many scenes that I got the information needed to make an authentic top boot. The luck in happening on this old movie on TV was too much. I found valuable information that I never would have known otherwise.

The movie ended on a sad note when the car was driven into the Zuider Zee in a chase scene. I would have liked the hubcaps before it sank below the waves.

Minor parts had to be secured here, there and all over. Some came from Germany. Others came in response to my ads in the *Star*, the publication of the Mercedes-Benz Club of America. For a few years parts arrived. Some could be used "as is" while others needed refurbishing. A few parts had to be specially made by machinists. But the car finally was assembled and could be given careful test drives.

The engine is listed as 68-brake horsepower, and this moves the 3500-pound car very nicely. The four-speed transmission is easy to handle, and the top gear is a vacuum-operated overdrive that cuts down considerably on engine revolutions. Steering is light and precise, and the brakes are more than adequate.

Sitting behind the wheel, peering at the three-pointed star in the center of the radiator and looking over the large chromed headlights, the driver of this luxurious convertible feels sybaritic. This feeling alone makes it worth the time, effort and expense required to rebuild such a car.

27

Queen of the Classics

The car was sitting in front of a lawn-mower repair shop with a for-sale sign on the windshield. From the quick glance I got while driving by, it did not look bad. The car was a 1941 Lincoln Continental Coupe, and the repair shop was in Largo, Florida.

Running late for a business appointment in Dunedin, I could not stop to take a closer look, but I vowed to drive back later to examine the car. Having owned a 1937 Lincoln Zephyr, which was a fine road car, I had long been interested in the beautiful Lincoln Continentals offered from 1940 through 1948.

Of these stylish cars I liked the 1940-41 models best, for they seemed more like the originals built in 1939. The 1942 models, although rarest because of the shutdown for World War II, lacked the clean lines of the earlier models. The fussy front end detracted from the design concept of the original. The postwar cars were beautiful and contained many mechanical improvements, but changes to the front end gave a more massive appearance and different rear fenders detracted from the car's simple, sleek lines. Although I would have preferred the Convertible Coupe, I had not seen one for sale at a reasonable price. The Coupe with its smooth, flat steel roof and plated window frames suited me just fine.

As soon as the business in Dunedin was concluded, I hurried back to Largo to take a closer look at the car. The paint was not

Sleek and sophisticated 1941 Lincoln Continental Coupe has clean lines not found in later Continentals. A solidly built car, mechanically similar to the Lincoln of the same year, it has remained extremely popular.

A large trunk beautifully molded into the body lines, plus an outside rear-mounted spare wheel, was one of the Lincoln Continental's most distinctive style treatments. The body of the Coupe and the Convertible Coupe are identical.

The right rear view during restoration shows sanding and filling necessary to bring body and fenders to the condition shown in the previous photo. Hours of hand sanding after trim items were removed produced a smooth, ready-to-paint finish.

bad, although there was some rust-through just ahead of the rear fenders and at the bottom of the cowl. A small patch of rust had formed at the upper right of the roof where it joined the windshield. There was also a bit of rust where the metal top joined the body across the back, just ahead of the trunk opening. All in all, the car appeared quite sound. It was locked and I could only look inside, but it seemed to need a complete reupholstering job.

A sign in the lawn-mower shop indicated that the owner would be back around 4 P.M., so I spent that time examining the outside of the car very closely. It still had the V-12 engine, which showed no sign of having thrown oil around the breather pipe. These V-12s did not have an oil dipstick. Instead, a small float between the cylinder banks indicated the amount of oil in the base. Each

Rusted-through metal ahead of rear wheel and the panel below the left door were removed. A stiff, thin piece of cardboard was used as a pattern for cutting new metal. When properly finished, the replacement metal and seams did not show.

A saber saw will cut out old, weak metal. To follow the curve of the wheel arch, either use several small pieces or cut narrow wedges out of larger piece. When the weld seam is ground smooth and the area is primed and painted, the repair is permanent.

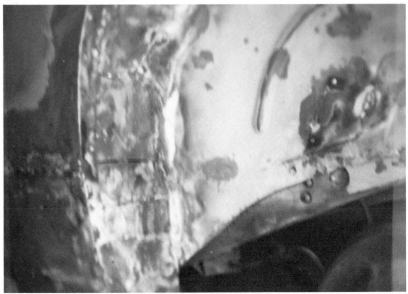

time I pushed the indicator arm down, the float bobbed it back up to the same position, so I knew the car had not run low on oil, at least not since the last fill-up. There was no gummy or sooty deposit on the tail pipe, so I assumed the car was not burning oil to any great extent.

The tires were fair, but that only meant I could probably get it home without a blowout. A set of new tires would be needed in any case. The front ones were worn evenly, which meant there had not been excessive wear on the kingpins and the front end was in line. Pushing down on one corner of the car at a time indicated that the shock absorbers were badly worn, for the car bounced back too quickly. I ran out of things I could check from the outside, so I drove to a small cafe a mile or so away to wait for the four o'clock return of the owner.

It was about 4:30 when he got back, and I was waiting for him. He gave me the keys so I could start the motor and get a good look inside. The engine started quickly but did not run evenly. There seemed to be a lot of valve noise, and possibly one or two sticky valves. To find out more about the car I would need a test drive. The owner said he could not leave his shop, but if I would leave the registration for my car as security, I could make any test I wanted. This was fine; I would much rather test a car without the owner sitting next to me, trying to explain away any problems I discovered.

The car needed gas, so my first stop was at a service station. The operator put the car on his lift so I could take a close look at the underside. Like many cars around salt water, there was some rust-through on the floor pan and along the rocker panels. It did not seem to be a serious problem.

With the weight off the car's wheels, I could carefully check the front end. Grasping each front wheel at the top and bottom, I tested for movement, which would indicate wear to the kingpins. There was no trouble there. To check for worn bearings or worn bushings, I grasped each wheel at front and back to test for movement. They were in good condition.

There was no indication that the frame had ever been straightened, which would have meant a serious collision. Everything under the car seemed solid, even the exhaust pipe and muffler.

A jackstand holds axle in proper position for body or mechanical work. Starting with 1935, Ford moved the rear spring behind the rear axle to lower cars. Double-acting hydraulic shocks can be easily removed for rebuilding with a readily available kit.

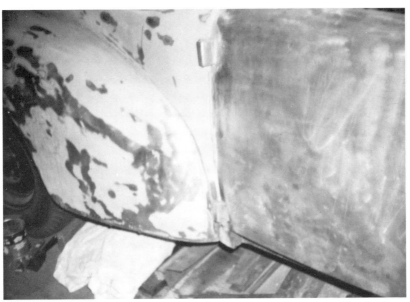

Rust-through at bottom of cowl panel where fender meets the body is common. After cleaning away rust, small holes can be brazed, filed, sanded and primed for permanent repair. Cracks around door hinges would indicate metal fatigue.

Rocker panel along bottom of doors is a two-section box. Often the outer panel needs replacement while the inner panel is sound. If original inner panel is retained, it should be coated with rust-inhibiting primer before installing replacement outer panel.

With upholstery panel removed, any rust damage can be spotted along the bottom of the doors. After cleaning door interior with a wire brush, it was coated with rust-inhibiting primer. Drain holes in the bottom of the door were cleared.

While the car was on the lift I had the oil in the transmission and differential checked, and added some to the differential. The spring shackles were dry but not excessively worn. Since I had about decided to buy the car, I had it greased at this time.

My "test drive" had taken almost an hour, and the seller asked where I had gone. I told him I had put it on a lift at a gas station to check the underside, and had found the car to be in at least average condition. We then got down to some serious price bargaining, which ended when we agreed on $100 off his asking price. He accepted my check, saying he would endorse the title when the check cleared. This was fine with me, for I could not take the car at that time anyway. A week later I flew to Tampa and drove the car home. It was in just about the condition I expected, and the drive went well.

The V-12 engine had some problems. The simple carburetor did not evenly distribute fuel to the end cylinders, making the engine somewhat rough when idling. It had plenty of power, but even with new plugs and points I could not get it to run smoothly. I finally had to tear into the engine and discovered that it had three broken valve springs. With these replaced and the valves ground, the motor was somewhat better but still did not perform as I wanted.

It was popular in the 1950s and 1960s to replace the V-12 engine with various V-8s. I would not do this today, for there is no reason why the V-12 engine with later carburetion cannot be made to run smoothly. At the time, however, the engine-swap idea was so common that adaptors were marketed to mate various engines to the Continental bell housing. It seemed I would be wiser to install a higher powered V-8 rather than worry with the original V-12.

The first engine I chose was from a 1951 Oldsmobile. The car had been smashed in the rear and junked. The odometer showed less than 5000 miles. The engine was taken out of the car and loaded in the back of my station wagon. Since I did not have a hoist or proper facilities for an engine swap, I had the swap done at a local garage. With the newer, more powerful engine in the car I had power to spare, but some problems surfaced.

The 1951 engine pumped water through the radiator at a faster pace than did the original. The result was coolant being

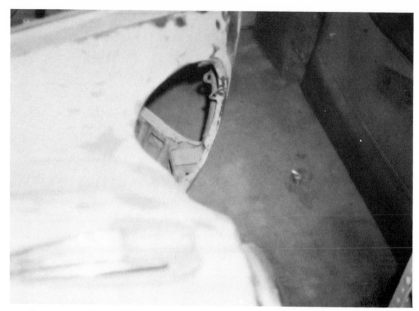

For best results, the plated grille and front trim pieces should be removed so metal surfaces can be thoroughly cleaned and smoothed. New welting should be installed when grille is refitted. Dust from sanding must be removed from the hood latch mechanism.

With V-8 engine replacing original V-12, air intake/silencer is often a problem because of the low hood line. Flexible tubing from carburetor intake to air cleaner mounted below or ahead of the engine solves silencing problem and backfire danger.

forced out the overflow pipe if traveling above fifty for any distance. The radiator core was boiled out and put in perfect condition, but it just could not handle the excess flow, and the car would overheat in no time. Once while the car was overheating a valve head broke. It fell into the cylinder head, cracking the head and breaking a piston.

Rather than repair the engine, I installed a low-mileage 1954 Lincoln overhead-valve V-8. This smaller, lighter engine was equipped with a six-blade fan, and since it sat farther back in the engine compartment, a shroud had to be built to help the fan do its job. Because the coolant capacity in the overhead-valve engine was less than the flat head it replaced, I had no more trouble with overheating.

However, the lighter engine did cause some problems with the front suspension. It was necessary to remove the front spring and

With spare wheel and holder removed, along with rear bumper arms and taillights, it is easier to work on rear section of the body. Drain hole at the bottom of the tire well must be open.

completely rebuild it, using fewer leaves. With the rebuilt front spring and with telescopic shock absorbers in front, the car handled beautifully.

When the mechanical problems were solved, it was time to finish the body work. I had the old metal cut out where there was serious rust-through and new metal welded in place. When the edges of the new metal were properly filled and ground smooth, the area was simply touched up, for a complete paint job would come later.

The plated trim parts were removed and the surfaces built up with several coats of rust-resisting primer. Between coats they were lightly and carefully sanded. Gray metallic lacquer was chosen for the final coats. After careful hand rubbing, the results were outstanding. The grilles and bumpers were replated; nothing else neded replating. I had located new rubber pieces to go around all four vent windows; these were put in place after the lacquer paint job.

The hot, humid weather of Gulf Coast Florida had mildewed and rotted the upholstery, so everything was taken out. New fiberboard panels were cut for the doors and rear quarter panels. Before these were reupholstered and mounted, the inner side of

Window moldings and rear cushion should be removed when replacing the headliner. If new upholstery panels are needed, the old ones can usually be used as a pattern. Inside of panels should be scrubbed with a wire brush and coated with rust-inhibiting primer.

Seat framework and cushions should be removed for repair and reupholstering. Pivoted backs of front seat necessitate careful finishing of lower portion of seat back cushion, as well as top portion of carpet scuff pad along seat framework.

Use of vinyl in reupholstery project was wrong for a car of this caliber. It should have been leather, or cloth and leather. Completely reupholstered and newly carpeted, the interior was attractive and comfortable, and surprisingly roomy.

the body panels was coated with zinc chromate to prevent rusting, then lined with one-inch slabs of fiberglass.

The new headliner was made of black vinyl, and went up easily after a careful fit. I sewed new upholstery for the doors, side panels and seats—black for the door and side panels, and black with white inserts for the seats. When new carpets were cut and fitted, the interior looked great. Were I restoring the car today, I would not use vinyl. The car is too valuable and should be upholstered with leather or a combination of leather and cloth as in the original.

During restoration, a vacuum booster was added to the car, and the brake system was entirely rebuilt, so the car now had power brakes. Because some of the wiring under the dashboard had suffered from the Florida sun, a new wiring harness was installed. This was a knuckle-scraping job, for everything was so close there was little room for either hand or tool.

The restored car turned out to be a beautiful automobile and extremely capable. With the lighter, more powerful overhead-valve engine and front telescopic shock absorbers, it handled superbly. The car drew admiring glances when parked near the ponderous, overtrimmed cars then being produced. I am not a particularly fast driver, but there were several occasions when I had it up to ninety. Not many cars could keep up with it when it came to road handling. I drove the car thousands of miles in my business without any repairs.

Traveling in South Carolina one night, I was stopped by the state police. They were on the lookout for a foreign car that had been stolen, and the officer thought perhaps my 1941 Lincoln Continental was the car. When I showed the registration, the officer was surprised. "Wonder why they stopped making them?" was his question.

The reasons for the car's demise are not hard to understand. The beautiful Lincoln Continentals of 1940–48 were low-production automobiles. They were a "cobbled" car in that they were made of Lincoln body parts. The sheet metal was remade to fit. A longer, lower hood and longer front fenders meant extra labor and extra expense. The trend was toward wider bodies, with fenders actually becoming the front and rear body panels. The

Long and low, 1941 Lincoln Continental Coupe attracted attention when parked near overdecorated cars of the 1950s and 1960s. Gray lacquer finish was highlighted by the replated grille. White sidewalls added to the smart appearance of the car.

basic design was outdated, and in an age when even a few cents per vehicle meant a lot to the maker, the Continental could not be justified.

Since I was driving long distances frequently, I wanted an air-conditioned car. I bought an air-conditioning system from a nearly new, wrecked Cadillac. I mounted most of the parts, but needed to know what size pulleys should be used to keep the compressor working at the right revolutions. The Lincoln dealer was not at all helpful. A letter to the Lincoln Motor Company was forwarded to the local dealer, from whom I had gotten no help, and they still could not help. In a weak moment I advertised the car. It was sold almost before I realized how foolish I had been.

From the time the new owner drove out of my driveway, I have wanted another Lincoln Continental. Preferably a 1940 or 1941 Convertible Coupe, but as scarce as the Mark I Continentals are becoming, I would be glad to get any one of them.

28

Where There's a Will . . .

Almost nothing on an old car looks worse than a dented or rusty radiator grille. If the grille is in good shape, it makes a world of difference. Many times hobbyists have given up on dented or rusted-through grilles and have resorted to painting parts that should have been plated. In desperation others have tried to substitute grilles from other cars or from other model years. These substitutions and changes from original specifications lower the car's value.

A rusted-through grille that has been coated with filler and painted does not affect the way the car runs, but it does lessen its authenticity. Filler materials cannot be plated; hence the painting. If a grille is to be plated, new metal must replace any that has rusted through. Pitted metal must be ground smooth; if the pitting is severe, the low spots must be filled with metal before plating. There are no shortcuts.

After repairing several grilles I have found that unless a grille is dented almost beyond recognition, or is made of nonweldable pot metal, most can be satisfactorily repaired. On certain cars where replacement grilles just cannot be found, there is no alternative to repairing the grille if it is to be plated.

"Do you really believe you can repair that?" a friend asked as he viewed the rusted-through and pitted grille of a Series 12 Franklin I brought home from Iowa.

"Sure I'll fix it, or get it fixed," was my reply. "After all, there aren't many of these around. I've tried for months to locate one. It won't be as rough a job as it looks."

The grille was in bad shape, there was no denying that, but it was made of stout metal and seemed repairable. I felt once it was disassembled I could have new metal welded in place, the pitting ground down, the low spots filled and the whole thing nickel-plated.

Rusted original Franklin radiator shell necessitated cutting out old metal and welding in replacement pieces cut from 20-gauge steel. The ninety-degree angle was shaped in a bench vise. Biggest problem was making an even seam weld.

Since I am not a welder and do not have the equipment, I knew I would have to locate a welding shop that would tackle the job. I have had lots of welding done and I knew just about what to expect. When I showed the grille to one welder, he said he would not touch it with a ten-foot pole. All I could reply was to forget the ten-foot pole and try it with a welding torch.

Another welder said the metal was too thin. He was afraid he would burn it up when he tried attaching new metal, and advised me to find another grille. Evidently he did not know how scarce parts can become. Nor would a third welding shop take the job. Again the comment was fear of the thin metal burning when the welding torch was applied.

"Why don't we try it?" my friend asked. He was a pressman for a local newspaper and had done some welding at work. "We can rent the outfit and do it ourselves." I had little to lose, for the job had been refused by three competent welders, and if worse came to worse I could fill the grille and paint it—just what I did not want to do.

The library had a few books on welding, including one aimed at beginners. I read the book and made some notes, then rented a welding outfit complete with tanks and masks. I had bought some 20-gauge steel and was ready to try my luck.

We followed the directions very carefully, and I have to admit I was more than a little scared when we could not light the torch immediately after turning on the valves. In those few seconds I could see an explosion rivaling that of the Hindenburg in intensity. When the flame started and we adjusted it to the pointed blue flame we needed, my fears subsided. I enjoyed my first experience, cutting out the old rusted metal. I had already cut the replacement piece with tin snips, but found I had under-estimated the amount of metal that would have to be replaced. As I cut with the torch, metal on the side of the grille burned away, as well as the metal I intended to cut out on the front. This meant the piece I had cut was useless, which taught me not to fashion replacement pieces before the old metal has been cut out. A new piece was cut, and the 90-degree angle was crimped in my bench vise.

The directions in my book were right. Vise grips held the piece well enough so we could weld the upper end in place.

On a curved piece at the bottom of the shell, replacement metal was welded over the outside of the original. It was ground so smooth that the edges did not show after plating. The entire shell had to be ground with a grinding wheel in an electric hand drill to remove pitting.

When the metal cooled sufficiently to handle, we put the vise grips on the other end and welded the bottom. The next job was to run a seam weld the length of the new piece, joining the new to the old.

The seam weld was more difficult than we thought. It was hard to keep the seam even. Either too much metal or too little formed along the seam. I could tell we would have a difficult grinding job ahead. "Why not do the seam in the inside of the shell where it won't show?" my friend suggested. That sounded logical, so we tried that, along with trying to make a thinner seam. When it was finished it did not look bad. We tried flowing some metal into the low spots on the outside seam and had good luck. When we finished the first piece, we had a rough but solid job. It appeared that we could grind down the outside seam metal satisfactorily.

The second welding job would be more difficult, for we had to fashion a curved piece and weld it in place. My friend suggested we not try to cut out the old metal, but instead weld the new piece over the old, flowing enough new metal at each end so it could be feathered out and not show. We made a pattern from cardboard, trimmed it and traced around it on the new metal.

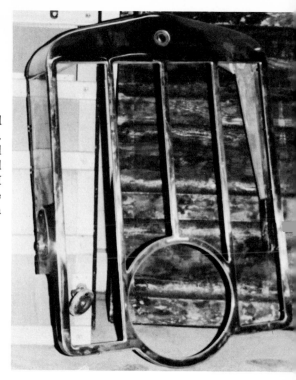

The repaired and replated shell, resplendent in nickel. Mesh grillwork in the shell was cleaned and repainted black as it was originally. I am still looking for the badge that proclaims the car is a Franklin.

We allowed extra metal at each end so the joint would be in the least noticeable place.

Again using vise grips, we spot-welded each end of the new piece. My friend had a steady hand and ran a fairly good seam along the top edge of the new piece. The bottom seam, which really was not necessary and would not show as much, turned out to be much more even.

With the new metal in place we thought of ourselves as expert welders. I did not realize how rough a job we had done until I started grinding the seams. I spent many hours hand filing and grinding the visible ones. Finally I got the surface smooth enough to hide the joints. The entire shell had to be filed and sanded to remove grinding marks, pitting and surface rust. With this done,

Mercedes shell was dented at top, necessitating a section of new metal. Because of thin metal, no welding shop would take on the repairs. Cast grille was straightened and plated.

the grille was thoroughly scoured and rinsed, and was then ready for the plater.

Rebuilding the grille and shell for a 1933 Mercedes was a more difficult job. The car had sustained some damage to the top and front of the shell and grille. It did not look like much of a job, but it turned out to be one of the toughest repairs I have ever made. There was no trouble removing the shell and grille. Being careful not to break the die-cast grille portion, I was able to straighten the upright bars satisfactorily. Once thoroughly cleaned, this portion could be rechromed.

For the top and front of the shell I thought at first the dented metal could be hammered back into place like any other dent. But the metal was brittle and thin, and it cracked in several places as I tried hammering out the dent. My next plan was to straighten as much as I could by hammering, then weld and fill the cracks. With the metal pounded into the approximate position, I asked several welders if they would handle the job. No one wanted to touch it, although I left it with one welder for a few weeks. He never got around to working on it, and seemed quite relieved when I retrieved it.

My friend and I tried welding the broken parts together, but under the torch the metal practically disintegrated. Now I understood why the professional welders did not want the job. It looked as though a new piece would have to be welded in place. As it turned out, two pieces had to be cut, then welded together, then joined to the old shell.

While there was still enough of the old shell from which to get measurements, I made a pattern of the front piece, including the "V"-shape top center portion of the shell. This was more difficult than I thought, for there was a small crimp in the metal all around the edge of the shell that met with the grille. I had this crimp put in the metal at a metal-forming shop before I did anything more with the piece.

Shell was welded at the bottom beneath the crank hole cover and at each side. When these welds were ground smooth, the repairs did not show after replating.

Making the pattern for the top piece was difficult because of the compound curve, which could not be exactly scribed on cardboard. The top piece also had to bend up to meet the metal around the filler hole. After cutting the pattern piece as accurately as I could, I scribed the pattern on the metal. I allowed a little extra on the back of the piece, knowing it could be trimmed off later. The two pieces were welded together, forming the curved and pointed section that makes up the top front of the shell. When the seam was ground smooth, I was really pleased with the results of our second welding experiment.

The next problem was to weld the new front piece to the old shell. This meant cutting out the old metal, which was no easy job. I tried first with tin snips but found I could not follow the line. So we cut it out with the welding torch, cutting about a quarter inch inside the scribed mark, for the torch seemed to cut that wide a swath. With the old metal cut out, I hammered the cut edge as smooth as possible. The new piece was placed over the opening, and from the back side the exact outline of the opening was scribed on the new piece. By trimming and filing, the new piece was made as close to the size of the opening as possible.

After a new piece was welded in the top, extra metal had to be flowed in to fill low spots. Many hours were spent filing and grinding away the excess metal to maintain proper curvature.

Replated shell looks like new! The new metal portion at the top does not show at all. Compound curves on the top portion of the shell were maintained as originally stamped.

Clamping it in position with vise grips, we welded the new piece in place. It made a very rough seam, with quite a buildup of weld to be ground away. There were also some low spots that had to have metal flowed in. With each task I understood better why professional welders would not do it: They have to charge by the hour, and although they would be able to do the job faster than my friend and I, still there would be so many hours devoted to the job the charge would be prohibitive.

Possibly because I did not know any better, or because there was not much choice, work continued on the shell. Excess metal was filed or ground off, and when a low spot appeared new metal was flowed in and then ground smooth. I kept the welding outfit a week, and used it some part of every day as the work was progressing. After at least 150 hours of work, the shell looked good. I still had some extra metal to trim off the top of the filler hole, and the hole to drill for the insignia. With these jobs done, the whole shell was taken to a metal stripper, where it was dipped in a caustic solution to remove any acid remaining from the repair. It took plating beautifully, and allowed me to complete the front-end restoration of the Mercedes.

256 •

29

And in the End . . .

Over the years I have bought cars and parts from all over the country and from England. At times I have flown to distant cities, picked up a car whose true condition was really not known to me, and driven it home. The confusion of strange traffic patterns, routes and distances, combined with the uncertainty of the car's mechanical capabilities, made the trips challenging, interesting and memorable.

Other times I have driven to where the car was located and towed it home. Again the problems of traffic and routes, as well as those that can arise in towing made the trips fascinating if uncertain. Fortunately they have all been safe trips, despite some narrow escapes.

Because of the possibility of mechanical breakdowns that could be a real annoyance to anyone accompanying me, I prefer to make most such trips alone. If I am to be stuck in the middle of nowhere with a broken-down car, I do not want the responsibility and worry for anyone else's comfort or safety.

It is a real challenge to locate a desirable old car and restore it. One must make the necessary deal with the seller, after as thorough an appraisal of mechanical and structural conditions as possible, and then get the car home. Weather has been my biggest opponent. Blizzards, torrential rains and extreme heat have all conspired to make some of the trips near disasters.

In almost every instance the sellers have been honest, and the cars or parts were honestly represented. Sometimes my own enthusiasm for a particular car or part has made me overestimate its true condition, but seldom to the point where money has been lost on the deal. Luckily, perhaps, I have been able to at least get out the dollars I have put into these cars or parts.

The search for parts during the restoration process has been fascinating as well as frustrating. I have met and corresponded with some wonderful people over the years, and have made good friends throughout the country.

When replacement parts could not be located, I have been able to find dedicated people who have made parts for me and have used their expertise and knowledge to solve problems. Their charges have been embarrassingly low. They have come to my rescue with mental and physical help. I do not know how some of the restorations could have been completed without them.

It is a great satisfaction to restore a rusty old heap back to original condition, giving it a new lease on life. The feeling of accomplishment cannot be overemphasized. It is just great! Many times a restoration has been long and slow, and a bruised ego has accompanied bruised knuckles. In the end, it has all been worthwhile.

Bibliography

AIR CONDITIONING REPAIR

Chilton's Auto Air Conditioning Manual. Radnor, Pa.: Chilton, 1976

Automotive Air Conditioning, A. G. Lithgow. San Diego, Calif.: National Automotive Service, Inc., n.d.

AUTOMATIC TRANSMISSION REPAIRS

Automatic Transmissions, Mathias F. Brejcha, Chicago: American Technical Society, 1974

Automatic Transmissions, Walter B. Larew, Radnor, Pa.: Chilton, 1966

CONVERTIBLE RESTORATIONS

Convertible Restorations, From Rags to Riches, Burt Mills. New York, N.Y.: Dodd, Mead & Company, 1977

GENERAL AUTOMOTIVE RESTORATION

Chilton's Auto Restoration Guide, Burt Mills. Radnor, Pa.: Chilton, 1975

LEATHER WORK

Leather Work for the Restorer, Butler. Arcadia, Calif.: Post Motor Books, 1969

MECHANICAL REPAIRS

Chilton's Auto Repair Manual, 1940–1953; 1954–1963; 1964–1971. Radnor, Pa.: Chilton

PAINTING

Car Spraying Made Easy, Jaspar. Birkenhead, England.

PLATING

Electro-plating for the Amateur, L. Warburton. New York, N.Y.: International Publications Service.

SHEET STEEL REPAIR

Automobile Sheet Metal Repair, Robert L. Sargent. Radnor, Pa.: Chilton, 1969

Minor Auto Body Repair, Robert D. Harman, Radnor, Pa.: Chilton, 1975

WELDING

Modern Welding, Andrew D. Althouse. Turnquist and Bowditch. South Holland, Ill.: Goodheart-Wilcox, 1976

WOOD WORK

Antique Auto Body Wood Work for the Restorer, C. W. Terry with Arthur Hall. Arcadia, Calif.: Post Motor Books, 1969

ADDITIONAL INFORMATION

Additional specific information can be found in the catalogs published by the following:

CARBOOKS, INC., 181 Glenn Ave., Sea Cliff, New York 11579

CLASSIC CARBOOKS, P.O. Box 1, Osceola, Wisconsin 54020

CRANK'EN'HOPE PUBLICATIONS, Box 90H, 450 Maple Ave., Blairsville, Pa. 15717

Sales literature on most U.S.-made cars is available from: Tom Bonsall, P.O. Box 7298, Arlington, Va. 22207

Index